Essentials of Accounting for Governmental and Not-for-Profit Organizations

Preface

The preface to the first six editions of this text noted that the text was intended to provide a much more comprehensive coverage of accounting and financial reporting for governmental and not-for-profit accounting than is available in advanced accounting texts but that would be brief enough to allow coverage of the material in less than a three-semester-hour or four-quarter-hour course. The first six editions have been well received by instructors whose objective is to provide less coverage of the material than is available in larger texts, such as *Accounting for Governmental and Nonprofit Entities* by Wilson, Kattelus, and Hay (McGraw-Hill, 13th edition) as well as those whose objective is to stress preparation for the CPA Examination. The text is also used by some who wish to supplement basic accounting and reporting principles with other materials.

This edition and the accompanying *Instructor's Guide* and the *Suggested Quiz and Examination Questions and Problems* have been revised in accord with suggestions of users of the first six editions and to incorporate changes in standards issued by the GASB, FASB, AICPA and Comptroller General.

This text presents materials up to date through GASB Statement 39, *Determining Whether Certain Organizations Are Component Units;* FASB Statement 136, *Transfer of Assets to a Not-for-Profit Organization or Charitable Trust that Raises or Holds Contributions for Others;* the AICPA's revised *Audits of State and Local Governments;* and the exposure draft of the Comptroller General's *Government Auditing Standards.*

This text uses a particular approach to present the governmental reporting model. The assumption is made that fund accounting is the basic model used for internal accounting and for part of the external reporting. Then, worksheet adjustments are made to produce the government-wide statements. After the introductory Chapter 1, Chapter 2 presents an overview of the financial reporting model. Chapter 3 presents budgetary accounting for the General and special revenue funds, leading to the Budgetary Comparison Schedule. Fund accounting and reporting are then presented for governmental (Chapters 4–5), proprietary (Chapter 6), and fiduciary (Chapter 7) funds. Chapter 8 presents a worksheet approach for the preparation of government-wide statements and reconciliation schedules. As has been the case for the first six editions, an integrated example (the Village of Elizabeth) is presented throughout as well as an integrated continuous problem (the City of Everlasting Sunshine). Chapter 9 presents an analysis of governmental financial statements, special-purpose government reporting, and reporting for public colleges and universities in accordance with GASB *Statement 35.*

The not-for-profit chapters for voluntary health and welfare organizations and other not-for-profits (Chapter 10), private sector colleges and universities (Chapter 11), and private sector health care entities (Chapter 12) continue the approach of reflecting assets and liabilities as common to all net asset classes and reflecting revenues, expenses, and net assets by net asset class. Chapter 13 presents the new

Government Auditing Standards, the single audit act and amendments, taxation of exempt organizations, and service efforts and accomplishments.

The authors are indebted to members of the Governmental Accounting Standards Board and to the GASB research staff for access to their ideas, as well as permission to use GASB materials. The authors also wish to express their appreciation to the American Institute of Certified Public Accountants for permission to use their materials.

The authors wish to express thanks to anonymous reviewers of the sixth edition of this text, to Lisa Cole for accuracy checking for the text and *Instructor's Guide,* to G. Robert (Smitty) Smith for accuracy checking of the *Suggested Quiz and Examination Questions,* and especially to Deborah Prasad of Walsh College for her extensive suggestions for the text and solutions materials. The authors also express thanks for the many users of this text for suggestions.

The authors would appreciate suggestions from users of this text for improvements in presentation of this material and suggestions for additional or improved questions and exercises. Please send suggestions to Pcopley@terry.uga.edu or to Jengstrom@niu.edu.

John H. Engstrom

Paul A. Copley

Contents In Brief

Preface v

1 Introduction to Accounting and Financial Reporting for Governmental and Not-For-Profit Organizations 1

2 Overview of Financial Reporting for State and Local Governments 23

3 Budgetary Accounting for the General and Special Revenue Funds 64

4 Accounting for the General and for Special Revenue Funds 90

5 Accounting for Other Governmental Fund Types: Capital Projects, Debt Service, and Permanent 126

6 Proprietary Funds 158

7 Fiduciary Funds; Interfund Transactions 192

8 Government-Wide Statements; Fixed Assets; Long-Term Debt 224

9 Analysis of Governmental Financial Statements; GASB Accounting for Special-Purpose Entities; Accounting for Public Institutions of Higher Education 261

10 Accounting for Not-For-Profit Organizations 300

11 College and University Accounting—Private Institutions 333

12 Accounting for Hospitals and Other Health Care Providers 360

13 Governmental Auditing; The Single Audit Act; Tax Exempt Organizations; Service Efforts and Accomplishments 386

Appendix: Governmental and Not-For-Profit Accounting Terminology 414

Index 435

Contents

Preface v

Chapter 1
Introduction to Accounting and Financial Reporting for Governmental and Not-for-Profit Organizations 1

Objectives of Accounting and Financial Reporting 3
  Objectives of Accounting and Financial Reporting for the Federal Government 3
  Objectives of Financial Reporting by Not-for-Profit Entities 6
  Objectives of Accounting and Financial Reporting for State and Local Governmental Units 6
Outline of the Text 6
State and Local Governmental Financial Reporting 6
  Comprehensive Annual Financial Report 7
  Measurement Focus and Basis of Accounting 7
  Fund Structure for State and Local Government Accounting and Reporting 10
  Number of Funds Required 11
  Budgetary Accounting 12
  Accounting for Capital Assets, Including Infrastructure 12
  Accounting for Long-Term Debt and Other Long-Term Liabilities 14
Additional Resources 14

Chapter 2
Overview of Financial Reporting for State and Local Governments 23

The Governmental Reporting Entity 24
Overview of the Comprehensive Annual Financial Report (CAFR) 25
Introductory Section 26
Financial Section 26
  Auditor's Report 26
  Management's Discussion and Analysis (MD&A) 27
  Government-Wide Financial Statements 27
  Fund Financial Statements 31
  Notes to the Financial Statements 37
  Required Supplementary Information Other than MD&A 41
  Combining and Individual Fund Statements and Schedules 45
Special Purpose Governments 45
Public Colleges and Universities 49
Other Governmental Not-for-Profit Organizations 54

Chapter 3
Budgetary Accounting for the General and Special Revenue Funds 64

Budgets as Legal Documents 65
Balance Sheet and Operating Statement Accounts 65
Budgets and Budgetary Accounts 66
Recording the Budget 68
Accounting for Revenues 69
Accounting for Encumbrances and Expenditures 70
Budget Revisions 75
Budgetary Comparison Schedule 75
Classification of Estimated Revenues and Revenues 75
Ad Valorem Taxes 77
Classification of Appropriations and Expenditures 79

Chapter 4
Accounting for the General and for Special Revenue Funds 90

Accounting for Nonexchange Transactions 90
  Classes of Nonexchange Transactions 91
  Eligibility Requirements 91
  Recognition Requirements for the Four Classes of Nonexchange Transactions 92
  Other Features of GASB Statement 33 92
Modified Accrual Accounting 94
  Revenue Recognition 94
  Expenditure Recognition 94
Interfund Transactions 95
  Interfund Loans 95
  Interfund Services Provided and Used 95
  Interfund Transfers 95
  Interfund Reimbursements 95
General Fund Account Structure 96
Illustrative Case—General Fund 96
  Recording the Budget 97
  Re-establishment of Encumbrances 97
  Recording Prior Year Property Taxes as Revenues 97
  Tax Anticipation Notes Payable 98
  Payment of Liabilities as Recorded 98
  Encumbrance Entry 98
  Recording Property Tax Levy 98
  Collection of Delinquent Taxes 99
  Collection of Current Taxes 99
  Revenue Recognized on Cash Basis 100
  Repayment of Tax Anticipation Notes 100
  Recognition of Expenditures for Encumbered Items 100
  Payrolls and Payroll Taxes 101
  Payment of Vouchers and Other Items 101
  Correction of Errors 102
  Amendment of the Budget 102
  Interfund Transactions 102
  Write-off of Uncollectible Delinquent Taxes 104
  Reclassification of Current Taxes 105
  Accrual of Interest and Penalties 105
  Deferral of Property Tax Revenue 106
  Special Item 106
  Preclosing Trial Balance 106
  Closing Entries 107
  Year-End Financial Statements 107
Illustrative Case—Special Revenue Fund 108
  Motor Fuel Tax Revenues 110
  Expenditures for Road Repairs 110
  Reimbursement to General Fund 110
  Reimbursement Grant Accounting 110
  Closing Entry 111
  Year-End Financial Statements 111
Recognition of Inventories in Governmental Funds 111

Chapter 5
Accounting for Other Governmental Fund Types: Capital Projects, Debt Service, and Permanent 126

Capital Projects Funds 127
  Illustrative Case 128
Acquisition of General Fixed Assets by Lease Agreements 132
Construction of General Fixed Assets Financed by Special Assessment Debt 133
Debt Service Funds 134
  The Modified Accrual Basis—Meaning for Debt Service 135
  Additional Uses of Debt Service Funds 135
  Debt Service Accounting for Serial Bonds 136
  Illustrative Case—Regular Serial Bonds 136
  Debt Service Accounting for Deferred Serial Bonds 139

Debt Service Accounting for Term Bonds 139
Debt Service Accounting for Capital Lease Payments 139
Bond Refundings 140
Permanent Funds 140
Financial Reporting for Governmental Funds 142
Balance Sheet—Governmental Funds 142
Statement of Revenues, Expenditures, and Changes in Fund Balances—Governmental Funds 142

Chapter 6
Proprietary Funds 158

Internal Service Funds 159
Establishment and Operation of Internal Service Funds 159
Illustrative Case—Supplies Fund 160
A Note about Risk Management Activities 164
Enterprise Funds 164
Illustrative Case—Water Utility Fund 165
Accounting for Municipal Solid Waste Landfills 171
Proprietary Fund Financial Statements 172
Statement of Net Assets 172
Statement of Revenues, Expenses, and Changes in Fund Net Assets 172
Statement of Cash Flows 176

Chapter 7
Fiduciary Funds; Interfund Transactions 192

Agency Funds 193
Tax Agency Funds 194
Accounting for Tax Agency Funds 194
Financial Reporting for Agency Funds 196

Private-Purpose Trust Funds 196
Accounting for Investments 196
Illustrative Case—Private-Purpose Trust Funds 198
A Note about Escheat Property 199
Investment Trust Funds 200
Public Employee Retirement Systems (Pension Trust Funds) 201
Accounting and Reporting for Defined Benefit Pension Plans 201
Summary of Employer Reporting 206
A Note about IRS 457 Deferred Compensation Plans 208
A Note about Other Postemployment Benefits 208
Interfund Transactions 208
Reciprocal Interfund Activity—Interfund Loans 209
Reciprocal Interfund Activity—Interfund Services Provided and Used 209
Nonreciprocal Interfund Activity—Interfund Transfers 210
Nonreciprocal Interfund Activity—Interfund Reimbursements 210
A Final Comment on Fund Accounting and Reporting 211

Chapter 8
Government-Wide Statements, Fixed Assets, Long-Term Debt 224

Conversion from Fund Financial Records to Government-Wide Financial Statements 224
Recording Capital Assets, Removing Expenditures for Capital Outlays, and Recording Depreciation 225
Changing "Proceeds of Bonds" to Debt Liabilities, Changing Expenditures for Debt Service Principal to Reduction of Liabilities, and Adjusting for Interest Accruals 227
Adjusting to Convert Revenue Recognition to the Accrual Basis 228

Adjusting to Record Expenses on
Accrual Basis   229
Changing Proceeds on Sale of Fixed
Assets to Gain on Sale of Fixed
Assets   229
Adding Internal Service Funds to
Governmental Activities   229
Eliminating Interfund Activities and
Balances within Governmental
Activities   231
Eliminating Fiduciary Funds   232
Worksheet to Illustrate the
Adjustments   232
Government-Wide Financial
Statements   233
Statement of Net Assets   233
Statement of Activities   236
Required Reconciliation to Government-
Wide Statements   237
Accounting for Fixed Assets, Including
Infrastructure   240
Accounting for General Fixed
Assets   241
Accounting for Infrastructure   242
The Modified Approach for Reporting
Infrastructure   243
Collections   244
Accounting for Long-Term Debt   244
Types of General Long-Term Debt   245
Debt Disclosures and Schedules   245

Chapter 9
Analysis of Governmental Financial Statements, GASB Accounting for Special Purpose Entities, Accounting for Public Institutions of Higher Education   261

Analysis of State and Local
Governmental Financial
Statements   261
Public Finance Market   262
Analysis of the Comprehensive Annual
Financial Report   262

Additional Analysis   266
GASB *Statement 34* Reporting Rules
for Special-Purpose Entities   266
Reporting by Special-Purpose Local
Governments Engaged in Governmental
Activities   267
Reporting by Special-Purpose Local
Governments Engaged Only in
Business-Type Activities   270
Reporting by Special-Purpose Local
Governments Engaged Only in
Fiduciary-Type Activities   270
Accounting and Financial Reporting for
Public Colleges and Universities   271
The Environment of Public Higher
Education   271
Accounting and Financial Reporting
for Public Institutions of Higher
Education   272
Illustrative Case—Northern State
University—Beginning Trial
Balance   274
Illustrative Case—Journal Entries   275
Illustrative Case—Closing Entries   281
Illustrative Case—Financial
Statements   284
Summary   288

Chapter 10
Accounting for Not-For-Profit Organizations   300

Organizations Covered in This
Chapter   302
Overview of Not-for-Profit
Accounting   302
Three Classes of Net Assets   302
Financial Reporting   303
Note Disclosures   303
Accounting, Including Reclassifications
of Net Assets   304
Special Topics: Accounting for
Contributions   305
Illustrative Transactions and Financial
Statements   307

Beginning Trial Balance 307
Transactions 308
Financial Statements 315
Alternative Procedure for Recording Fixed Assets 317
Performance Evaluation 320
Summary of Academic Research 321
Summary of Not-for-Profit Accounting and Reporting 321

Chapter 11
College and University Accounting—Private Institutions 333

Overview of Private College and University Accounting 334
   Net Asset Classification 334
   Financial Statements 335
   Revenue Reduction versus Expenses 335
   Academic Terms Encompassing More than One Fiscal Year 336
   Other Accounting Guidance 336
Illustrative Transactions and Financial Statements 337
   Illustrative Transactions 338
   Illustrative Financial Statements for Private Colleges and Universities 344
Split-Interest Agreements 344
Academic Research 349
Summary of Accounting and Reporting 349

Chapter 12
Accounting for Hospitals and Other Health Care Providers 360

Accounting and Reporting Requirements of the *Health Care Guide* 361
Illustrative Transactions and Financial Statements 636
   Beginning Trial Balance 363
   Illustrative Statements for Private Sector Not-for-Profit Health Care Entities 370
Financial Reporting for Governmental Health Care Entities 374
Financial Reporting for Commercial (For-Profit) Health Care Entities 374
Academic Research 375
Summary and Conclusions regarding Health Care Accounting and Reporting 375

Chapter 13
Governmental Auditing; The Single Audit Act; Tax-Exempt Organizations; Service Efforts and Accomplishments 386

Governmental Auditing 386
The Single Audit Act and Amendments 393
Tax-Exempt Organizations 396
   Applying for Tax-Exempt Status 397
   Federal Filing Requirements 398
   Public Disclosures 402
   State Filing Requirements 402
   Unrelated Business Income Tax (UBIT) 402
   Summary and Some Conclusions Related to Exempt Entities 403
Service Efforts and Accomplishments 404
   Example of SEA Reporting: School Report Cards 405
   Summary 405

Appendix: Governmental and Not-For-Profit Accounting Terminology 414

Index 435

Chapter One

Introduction to Accounting and Financial Reporting for Governmental and Not-For-Profit Organizations

Governments differ from business organizations discussed in other accounting courses in that governments have no stockholders or other owners, they commonly render services with no expectation of earning net income, and they have the power to require taxpayers to support financial operations whether or not the taxpayers receive benefits in proportion to taxes paid. Also, governments are not subject to federal, state, or local income taxes. Further, the form of government in the United States requires interrelationships that have no parallel in business organizations, between a state government and local governments established in compliance with state law and within any one government between the executive and legislative branches. Similarly, nongovernmental not-for-profit organizations exist to render services to constituents with no expectation of earning net income from those services, have no owners, and seek financial resources from persons who do not expect either repayment or economic benefits proportionate to the resources provided.

Accounting and financial reporting standards for the federal government are recommended by the Federal Accounting Standards Advisory Board (FASAB). Recommendations of the FASAB are reviewed and become effective unless objected to by one of the principals, the U.S. General Accounting Office (GAO), the U.S. Department of the Treasury, or the U.S. Office of Management and Budget (OMB). These standards apply to financial reports issued by federal agencies and to the Consolidated Financial Report of the United States Government. Accounting and financial reporting standards for the federal government are beyond the scope of this book and are available at http://www.fasab.gov/.

Accounting and financial reporting standards for state and local governments in the United States are set by the Governmental Accounting Standards Board (GASB). The GASB also sets accounting and financial reporting standards for governmentally related not-for-profit organizations, such as colleges and universities, health care entities, museums, libraries, and performing arts organizations that are owned or controlled by governments. Accounting and financial reporting standards for profit-seeking businesses and for nongovernmental not-for-profit organizations are set by the Financial Accounting Standards Board (FASB). The GASB and the FASB are parallel bodies under the oversight of the Financial Accounting Foundation (FAF). The FAF appoints the members of the two boards and provides financial support to the boards by obtaining contributions from business corporations; professional organizations of accountants, financial analysts, and other groups concerned with financial reporting; CPA firms; debt-rating agencies; and state and local governments (for support of the GASB). Because of the breadth of support and the lack of ties to any single organization or government, the GASB and the FASB are referred to as "independent standards-setting bodies in the private sector." Standards set by the FASAB, GASB, and FASB are the primary sources of **generally accepted accounting principles (GAAP)** as the term is used in accounting and auditing literature.

FASAB, GASB, and FASB standards are set forth primarily in documents called **Statements.** From time to time, the boards find it necessary to expand on standards in documents called **Interpretations.** Boards also issue **Technical Bulletins** to explain the application of standards in certain situations or industries. Independent auditors are engaged to express their opinion that the financial statements of a client present fairly, in all material respects, the client's financial position as of the end of a fiscal year and the results of its operations and its cash flows for the year then ended, in conformity with generally accepted accounting principles (GAAP). Since FASAB, GASB, and FASB Statements, Interpretations, and Technical Bulletins do not cover all possible situations, auditors often have need to refer to other publications. However, these other publications do not take precedence over Statements and Interpretations. Illustration 1–1 presents the hierarchy of GAAP published by the American Institute of Certified Public Accountants for the guidance of independent auditors.

Some organizations possess certain characteristics of both governmental and nongovernmental not-for-profit organizations, and it is necessary to determine whether those organizations are governmental or nongovernmental for purposes of applying GAAP, in accord with the hierarchy shown in Illustration 1–1. Recently, the FASB and GASB agreed upon a definition of a government. As reproduced in the AICPA *Audit and Accounting Guide: Not-for-Profit Organizations,* the definition is as follows:

> Public corporations and bodies corporate and politic are governmental organizations. Other organizations are governmental organizations if they have one or more of the following characteristics:
>
> *a.* Popular election of officers or appointment (or approval) of a controlling majority of the members of the organization's governing body by officials of one or more state or local governments;
> *b.* The potential for unilateral dissolution by a government with the net assets reverting to a government; or
> *c.* The power to enact and enforce a tax levy.

Furthermore, organizations are presumed to be governmental if they have the ability to issue directly (rather than through a state or municipal authority) debt that pays interest exempt from federal taxation. However, organizations possessing only that ability (to issue tax-exempt debt) and none of the other governmental characteristics may rebut the presumption that they are governmental if their determination is supported by compelling, relevant evidence.

OBJECTIVES OF ACCOUNTING AND FINANCIAL REPORTING

All three standards-setting organizations—the Federal Accounting Standards Advisory Board, the Financial Accounting Standards Board, and the Governmental Accounting Standards Board—take the position that the establishment of accounting and financial reporting standards should be guided by conceptual considerations so that the body of standards is internally consistent and the standards address broad issues expected to be of importance for a significant period of time. The cornerstone of a conceptual framework is said to be a statement of the objectives of financial reporting.

Objectives of Accounting and Financial Reporting for the Federal Government

The Federal Accounting Standards Advisory Board (FASAB) was established to recommend accounting and financial reporting standards to the "principals," the U.S. Office of Management and Budget, the U.S. Department of the Treasury, and the U.S. General Accounting Office. The FASAB has passed three Statements of Federal Financial Accounting Concepts (SFFACs). These concepts apply to financial reporting for the federal government as a whole and for individual reporting agencies.

SFFAC 1, *Objectives of Federal Financial Reporting*, outlined four objectives that should be followed in federal financial reporting. The first, **budgetary integrity,** indicates that financial reporting should demonstrate accountability with regard to the raising and expending of moneys in accord with the budgetary process and laws and regulations. The second, **operating performance,** suggests that financial reporting should enable evaluation of the service efforts, costs, and accomplishments of the reporting entity. The third, **stewardship,** reflects the concept that financial reporting should enable an assessment of the impact on the nation of the government's operations and investments. Finally, the fourth, **systems and controls,** indicates that financial reporting should reveal whether financial systems and controls are adequate.

SFFAC 2, *Entity and Display*, defines a reporting entity of the federal government, provides criteria to determine which entities should provide reports, and lists reports that should be provided. These reports are more extensive than required by the FASB or GASB.

SFFAC 3, *Management's Discussion and Analysis*, indicates that "Each general purpose federal financial report (GPFFR) should include a section devoted to management's discussion and analysis (MD&A)," and provides guidance regarding what should be included in that section.

ILLUSTRATION 1-1 GAAP Hierarchy Summary

Established Accounting Principles

Nongovernmental Entities		State and Local Governments		Federal GAAP Hierarchy
.10a FASB Statements and Interpretations, APB Opinions, and AICPA Accounting Research Bulletins	.12a	GASB Statements and Interpretations, plus AICPA and FASB pronouncements if made applicable to state and local governments by a GASB Statement or Interpretation	.14a	FASAB Statements and Interpretations plus AICPA and FASB pronouncements if made applicable to federal governmental entities by a FASAB Statement or Interpretation
.10b FASB Technical Bulletins, AICPA Industry Audit and Accounting Guides, and AICPA Statements of Position	.12b	GASB Technical Bulletins, and the following pronouncements if specifically made applicable to state and local governments by the AICPA: AICPA Industry Audit and Accounting Guides, and AICPA Statements of Position	.14b	FASAB Technical Bulletins and the following pronouncements if specifically made applicable to federal governmental entities by the AICPA and cleared by the FASAB: AICPA Industry Audit and Accounting Guides, and AICPA Statements of Position
.10c Consensus positions of the FASB Emerging Issues Task Force and AICPA Practice Bulletins	.12c	Consensus positions of the GASB Emerging Issues Task Force² and AICPA Practice Bulletins if specifically made applicable to state and local governments by the AICPA	.14c	AICPA AcSEC Practice bulletins if specifically made applicable to federal governmental entities and cleared by the FASAB and Technical Releases of the Accounting and Auditing Policy Committee of the FASAB
.10d AICPA accounting interpretations, "Qs and As" published by the FASB Staff, as well as industry practices widely recognized and prevalent	.12d	"Qs and As" published by the GASB Staff, as well as industry practices widely recognized and prevalent	.14d	Implementation guides published by the FASAB staff and practices that are widely recognized and prevalent in the federal government

.11 Other accounting literature, including FASB Concepts Statements; AICPA Issues Papers; International Accounting Standards Committee Statements; GASB Statements, Interpretations, and Technical Bulletins; FASAB Statements, Interpretations, and Technical Bulletins; pronouncements of other professional associations or regulatory agencies; AICPA *Technical Practice Aids*; and accounting textbooks, handbooks, and articles[1]

.13 Other accounting literature, including GASB Concepts Statements; pronouncements in categories (a) through (d) of the hierarchy for nongovernmental entities when not specifically made applicable to state and local governments; FASB Concepts Statements; FASAB Statements, Interpretations, Technical Bulletins, and Concepts Statements; AICPA Issues Papers; International Accounting Standards Committee Statements; pronouncements of other professional associations or regulatory agencies; AICPA *Technical Practice Aids*; and accounting textbooks, handbooks, and articles[1]

.15 Other accounting literature, including FASB Concepts Statements; pronouncements in categories (a) through (d) of the hierarchy in paragraph .10 when not specifically made applicable to federal governmental entities; FASB Concepts Statements; GASB Statements, Interpretations, Technical Bulletins, and Concepts Statements; AICPA Issues Papers; International Accounting Standards of the International Accounting Standards Committee; pronouncements of other professional associations or regulatory agencies; AICPA Technical Practice Aids; and accounting textbooks, handbooks, and articles[1]

[1] In the absence of established accounting principles, the auditor may consider other accounting literature, depending on its relevance to the circumstances.
[2] As of the date of this edition of this text, the GASB had not organized such a group.

Source: AICPA Professional Standards: AU411, The Meaning of "Present Fairly in Conformity with GAAP." Copyright © 2001 by the American Institute of Certified Public Accountants. Reprinted with permission.

Objectives of Financial Reporting by Not-for-Profit Entities

In its *Statement of Financial Accounting Concepts No. 6*, the FASB emphasized that its concern is with financial reporting to users who lack the authority to prescribe the information they want and who must rely on the information management communicates to them to make economic decisions. Therefore, the FASB stresses that the objective of financial reporting by not-for-profit organizations is to provide information to "present and potential resource providers and others in making rational decisions about allocating resources to not-for-profit organizations."[1]

Objectives of Accounting and Financial Reporting for State and Local Governmental Units

The Governmental Accounting Standards Board was established in 1984 as the successor to the National Council on Governmental Accounting (NCGA). In 1987 the GASB issued its *Concepts Statement No. 1, Objectives of Financial Reporting*, for state and local governments. In that statement the Board noted the following:

> Accountability requires governments to answer to the citizenry—to justify the raising of public resources and the purposes for which they are used. Governmental accountability is based on the belief that the citizenry has a right to know, a right to receive openly declared facts that may lead to public debate by the citizens and their elected representatives. Financial reporting plays a major role in fulfilling government's duty to be publicly accountable in a democratic society.[2]

Financial reports of state and local governments, according to the Governmental Accounting Standards Board, are used primarily to: (1) compare actual financial results with the legally adopted budget; (2) assess financial condition and results of operations; (3) assist in determining compliance with finance-related laws, rules, and regulations; and (4) assist in evaluating efficiency and effectiveness.

In 1994 the GASB issued its *Concepts Statement No. 2, Service Efforts and Accomplishments Reporting*, to encourage state and local governments to experiment with reporting more complete information about a governmental entity's performance than can be displayed in traditional financial statements. Indicators of service efforts include inputs of nonmonetary resources as well as inputs of dollars. Indicators of service accomplishments include both outputs and outcomes.

OUTLINE OF THE TEXT

The remainder of this chapter and Chapters 2 through 9 are concerned with accounting and financial reporting standards—generally accepted accounting principles—applicable to state and local governments in the United States. The remainder of this chapter provides an introduction to state and local governmental

---

[1] Financial Accounting Standards Board, *Statement of Financial Accounting Concepts No. 6* (Norwalk, Conn., 1985), par. 9.
[2] Governmental Accounting Standards Board, *Concepts Statement No. 1, Objectives of Financial Reporting* in GASB *Codification*, Appendix B, par. 56 (Norwalk, Conn., 2001).

accounting. Chapter 2 provides an overview of the Comprehensive Annual Financial Report (CAFR). Chapter 3 discusses and illustrates the role of budgeting in governmental funds. Chapters 4 through 7 describe accounting and financial reporting for governmental, proprietary, and fiduciary funds. Chapter 8 illustrates the worksheet adjusting entries needed to prepare the government-wide financial statements.

Chapter 9 covers three topics: (1) analysis of financial statements of state and local governments, (2) GASB standards for special-purpose governments, and (3) GASB standards for public colleges and universities. Chapters 10 through 12 discuss and illustrate FASB and AICPA standards for nongovernmental not-for-profit organizations including general not-for-profit organizations, private colleges and universities, and health care entities. Chapter 13 is concerned with three topics essential to an overall understanding of governmental and not-for-profit accounting: (1) the unique aspects of auditing for these organizations, (2) taxation of exempt entities, and (3) service efforts and accomplishments.

STATE AND LOCAL GOVERNMENTAL FINANCIAL REPORTING

GASB Concepts Statements stress that accounting and reporting standards for state and local governmental units should meet the financial information needs of many diverse groups: citizen groups, legislative and oversight officials, and investors and creditors. The Concepts Statements also make clear that reporting standards for governments recognize that decisions made by these groups involve political and social decisions as well as economic ones. Accordingly, governmental financial reporting standards are much more inclusive than FASB standards, which consider the needs of only investors and creditors concerned with economic decisions.

Comprehensive Annual Financial Report

The discussion of financial reporting in the GASB *Codification* Sec. 2200 sets standards for the content of the comprehensive annual financial report of a state or local government reporting entity. A comprehensive annual financial report (CAFR) is the government's official annual report prepared and published as a matter of public record. In addition to the basic financial statements and other financial statements, the CAFR contains introductory material, an auditor's report, certain required supplementary information (RSI), schedules necessary to demonstrate legal compliance, and statistical tables. Illustration 1–2 reflects the major items included in the Comprehensive Annual Financial Report (CAFR). Chapter 2 presents an extensive discussion and illustration of the basic financial statements and the other major components of the CAFR.

Measurement Focus and Basis of Accounting

State and local governments prepare their financial reports using two general accounting methods. One method assumes an economic resources measurement focus and the accrual basis of accounting, and the other method assumes a flow of current

ILLUSTRATION 1–2 The Comprehensive Annual Financial Report

Introductory Section
  Letter of Transmittal
  Organization Chart
  List of Principal Officials
  Reproduction of Certificate of Achievement for Excellence in Financial Reporting
    (if applicable)

Financial Section
  Auditor's Report
  Management's Discussion and Analysis (MD&A)
  Basic Financial Statements
    Government-Wide Statements
      Statement of Net Assets
      Statement of Activities
    Fund Financial Statements
      Governmental Fund Statements
        Balance Sheet
        Statement of Revenues, Expenditures, and Changes in Fund Balances
      Proprietary Fund Statements
        Statement of Net Assets (or Balance Sheet)
        Statement of Revenues, Expenses, and Changes in Fund Net Assets
        Statement of Cash Flows
      Fiduciary Fund Statements
        Statement of Fiduciary Net Assets
        Statement of Changes in Fiduciary Net Assets
    Notes to the Financial Statements
  Required Supplementary Information Other than MD&A
    Budgetary Comparison Schedules
    Pension Schedules (when applicable)
    Information Required When Using Modified Approach for Reporting Infrastructure
    Information Required Regarding Risk Management Activities (when applicable)
  Other Supplementary Information
    Combining Statements of Nonmajor Funds
    Schedules

Statistical Section
  (Presents a number of tables, often presenting 10-year information on revenues, expenditures, debt levels, property values, demographic information, etc.)

financial resources measurement focus and modified accrual accounting. Each of these two methods is discussed below.

Economic Resources Measurement Focus and the Accrual Basis of Accounting

The government-wide statements and the fund statements for proprietary funds and fiduciary funds use the economic resources measurement focus and the accrual basis of accounting. In a governmental setting, these are two types of transactions:

(1) **exchange and exchange-like transactions** and (2) **nonexchange transactions.** GASB *Statement 33* indicates that an exchange transaction is one "in which each party receives and gives up essentially equal values." (Paragraph 1) An exchange-like transaction "is one in which the values exchanged, though related, may not be quite equal or in which the direct benefits may not be exclusively for the parties to the transaction." (Footnote 1) According to GASB *Statement 34,* "Revenues, expenses, gains, losses, assets, and liabilities resulting from exchange and exchange-like transactions should be recognized when the exchange takes place." (Paragraph 16) This, of course, is similar to accounting for business organizations.

In contrast, Paragraph 16 of GASB *Statement 34* indicates that "Revenues, expenses, gains, losses, assets, and liabilities resulting from nonexchange transactions should be recognized in accordance with the requirements of *Statement 33.*" Nonexchange transactions are defined in *Statement 33* as transactions "in which a government gives (or receives) value without directly receiving (or giving) equal value in exchange." (Paragraph 1) In summary, accounting for revenues, expenses, gains, losses, assets, and liabilities resulting from nonexchange transactions depends upon which of four types of nonexchange transaction has taken place. GASB has defined these four types as (1) derived tax revenues, (2) imposed nonexchange revenues, (3) government-mandated nonexchange transactions, and (4) voluntary nonexchange transactions. Accounting for nonexchange transactions is discussed more fully in Chapter 4.

Current Financial Resources Measurement Focus and the Modified Accrual Basis of Accounting The fund statements for governmental funds are presented using the current financial resources measurement focus and modified accrual basis of accounting. Many of the transactions in governmental funds are nonexchange in nature; that is, activities undertaken in response to the needs of the public. Activities reported in governmental funds are heavily financed by taxes and involuntary contributions from persons (and organizations) who do not receive services in proportion to the contribution they make. GASB standards provide that accounting systems of governmental funds are designed to measure (a) the extent to which financial resources obtained during a period are sufficient to cover claims incurred during that period against financial resources and (b) the net financial resources available for future periods. Thus, governmental funds are said to have a **flow of current financial resources measurement focus,** as distinguished from the government-wide, proprietary fund, and fiduciary fund statements which have a flow of economic resources measurement focus. Activities of governmental funds are said to be **expendable;** that is, the focus is on the receipt and expenditure of resources. These resources are further defined as expendable resources, generally but not totally restricted to current assets and liabilities.

Modified accrual accounting, as the term implies, is a modification of accrual accounting. As will be discussed much more fully in succeeding chapters, especially Chapters 4 and 5, revenues are generally recognized only when *measurable* and *available* to finance the expenditures of the current period. Expenditures (not expenses) are recognized in the period in which the fund liability is incurred.

Long-term assets, with minor exceptions, are not recognized; the same is true of most long-term debt. Fixed assets and long-term debt are not reported in governmental funds. It should be noted that governmental *funds* are reported using the modified accrual basis of accounting; governmental-type *activities* are reported in the government-wide statements using the accrual basis of accounting, including fixed assets and long-term debt. This apparent inconsistency will be explained further in later chapters.

Fund Structure for State and Local Government Accounting and Reporting

Traditionally, state and local government financial reporting has been based on **fund accounting.** Fund accounting and reporting permit governmental managers to demonstrate compliance with legal and contractual requirements. Fund accounting and the term **fund,** are defined by the GASB as follows:

> Governmental accounting systems should be organized and operated on a fund basis. A fund is defined as a **fiscal and accounting entity** with a self-balancing set of accounts recording cash and other financial resources, together with all related liabilities and residual equities or balances, and changes therein, which are segregated for the purpose of carrying on specific activities or attaining certain objectives in accordance with special regulations, restrictions, or limitations.[3]

Note that the definition of the word *fund* requires that two conditions must be met for a fund, in a technical sense, to exist: (1) there must be a **fiscal entity**—assets set aside for specific purposes, and (2) there must be a double-entry **accounting entity** created to account for the fiscal entity.

States and local governments use 11 fund types. These fund types are organized into three categories: governmental funds, proprietary funds, and fiduciary funds. These are discussed below.

Governmental Funds   Five fund types are classified as **governmental funds:**
1. The **General Fund** accounts for most of the basic services provided by the governmental unit. Technically, this fund accounts for all resources other than those required to be accounted for in other funds.
2. **Special revenue funds** account for resources that are legally restricted for current purposes, such as intergovernmental grants and for funds set aside in formal action by the governing body, such as for library expenditures. Accounting for the General Fund and special revenue funds is discussed in Chapters 3 and 4 of this text.
3. **Capital projects funds** account for financial resources intended for major capital projects other than those financed by proprietary or fiduciary funds. Accounting for capital projects funds is discussed in Chapter 5 of this text.
4. **Debt service funds** (also discussed in Chapter 5) account for the payment of principal and interest on general long-term debt.

---

[3] Governmental Accounting Standards Board, *Codification of Governmental and Financial Reporting Standards,* as of June 30, 2001 (Norwalk, CT, 2001), par. 1100.102.

5. **Permanent funds** report resources that are legally restricted so only earnings, not principal, may be expended, and for purposes to benefit the government and its citizenry. Permanent funds are also discussed in Chapter 5.

Proprietary Funds Two types of funds used by state and local governments are classified as **proprietary funds.** The term indicates that the funds are used to account for a government's ongoing organizations and activities that are similar to those often found in the commercial sector. Proprietary funds are discussed in Chapter 6. There are two types of proprietary funds:
1. **Enterprise funds** are used when resources are provided primarily through the use of sales and service charges to parties external to the government. Examples of enterprise funds include water and other utilities, airports, swimming pools, and transit systems.
2. **Internal service funds** account for services provided by one department of a government to another, generally on a cost-reimbursement basis. In some cases, these services are also provided to other governments. Examples of internal service funds include print shops, motor pools, and self-insurance funds.

Fiduciary Funds **Fiduciary funds,** sometimes known as **trust and agency funds,** account for resources for which the government is acting as a collecting/disbursing agent or as a trustee. Fiduciary funds are covered in Chapter 7. Four types of fiduciary funds exist:
1. **Agency funds** are used to account for situations in which the government is acting as a collecting/disbursing agent. An example would be a county tax agency fund, where the county collects and disburses property taxes for other taxing units within the county, such as independent school districts.
2. **Pension (and other employee benefit) trust funds** are used to account for pension and employee benefit funds for which the governmental unit is the trustee.
3. **Investment trust funds** account for the external portion of investment pools reported by the sponsoring government.
4. **Private-purpose trust funds** report all other trust arrangements under which principal and income benefit individuals, private organizations, or other governments.

Number of Funds Required

In the GASB Summary Statement of Principles, the principle that follows the definition of fund types and account groups is often overlooked. This principle states that *governmental units should establish and maintain those funds required by law and sound financial administration.* If in a specific governmental unit, state law and/or agreements with creditors do not require that the receipt of revenues that are raised solely for a defined purpose and if administrators do not feel that use of a separate fund is needed to be able to demonstrate that revenues that were raised solely for that particular purpose, the General Fund should be used.

Budgetary Accounting

GASB standards recognize that state laws generally require administrators of state agencies and of local governmental units to obtain the appropriate legislative body's formal approval of all plans to raise revenues and make expenditures. Additionally, it is common for state agencies to be given the responsibility for monitoring the financial plans and financial operations of local governmental units within the state. Therefore, GASB standards contain the following three-part budgetary principle:

1. An annual budget(s) should be adopted by every governmental unit.
2. The accounting system should provide the basis for appropriate budgetary control.
3. Budgetary comparisons should be included in the appropriate financial statements and schedules for governmental funds for which an annual budget has been adopted.

Part 1 of the principle is not an accounting or financial reporting principle, but it is a necessary precondition to parts 2 and 3. A budget, when adopted according to procedures specified in state laws, is binding upon the administrators of a governmental unit. Accordingly, a distinctive characteristic of governmental accounting resulting from the need to demonstrate compliance with laws governing the sources of revenues available to governmental units and laws governing the utilization of those revenues is the formal reporting of the legally approved budget compared with actual results for the General Fund and all major special revenue funds that have a legally adopted annual budget. This report is included as a part of required supplementary information (RSI) in the CAFR. The nature and operation of accounting and budgetary reporting are explained in appropriate detail in Chapter 3.

Accounting for Capital Assets, Including Infrastructure

GASB *Statement 34* requires that fixed (capital) assets be recorded at historical cost, including ancillary charges such as freight, site preparation, and professional fees. Donated capital assets should be reported at the estimated fair value at the date of acquisition, plus ancillary charges needed to place the asset in service. According to Paragraph 19 of *Statement 34:*

> The term *capital assets* includes land, improvements to land, easements, buildings, building improvements, vehicles, machinery, equipment, works of art and historical treasures, infrastructure, and all other tangible or intangible assets that are used in operations and that have initial useful lives extending beyond a single reporting period. *Infrastructure assets* are long-lived assets that normally are stationary in nature and normally can be preserved for a significantly greater number of years than most capital assets. Examples of infrastructure assets include roads, bridges, tunnels, drainage systems, water and sewer systems, dams, and lighting systems. . . .

The only exception to the requirement for capitalization is for works of art and historical treasures that are considered a **collection.** Governments are encouraged, but not required to capitalize collections. In order to be considered a collection, the following conditions must be met as outlined in Paragraph 27 of *Statement 34.* The collection must be:

1. Held for public exhibition, education, or research in furtherance of public service, rather than financial gain.
2. Protected, kept unencumbered, cared for and preserved.
3. Subject to an organizational policy that requires the proceeds from sales of collection items to be used to acquire other items for collections.

When not capitalized, the government is required to disclose a description of the collection and the reasons the collections are not capitalized. This exception is especially important for governmental colleges and museums.

Capitalized fixed assets will be reported in the government-wide Statement of Net Assets, classified as being a part of governmental activities, business-type activities, or component units. Capitalized fixed assets are *not reported* in the governmental fund financial statements but *are reported* in the proprietary fund financial statements.

With the exception of infrastructure assets reported under the modified approach, all capitalized assets are to be depreciated, using a generally accepted depreciation method, over estimated useful lives. This depreciation charge is included as an expense in the Statement of Activities in the government-wide financial statements and as an expense in the Statement of Revenues, Expenses, and Changes in Fund Net Assets in the proprietary fund financial statements.

Infrastructure assets *must* be capitalized. However, a government may choose to not depreciate infrastructure assets, choosing instead to use the **modified approach** established by GASB. If the modified approach is used, the government will expense expenditures to extend the lives of those assets. Additions and improvements will continue to be capitalized. The logic behind the modified approach is that, if infrastructure is maintained properly, the useful life is indefinite and depreciation charges would not be necessary. In order to choose the modified approach, two requirements must be met: (1) an asset management system must be established and (2) the government must document that the eligible fixed assets meet or exceed the condition level established and disclosed by the government. In order to meet the first requirement Paragraph 23 of *Statement 34* indicates that the asset management system should:

a. Have an up-to-date inventory of eligible infrastructure assets
b. Perform condition assessments of the eligible infrastructure assets and summarize the results using a measurement scale
c. Estimate each year the annual amount to maintain and preserve the eligible infrastructure assets at the condition level established and disclosed by the government.

In order to meet the second requirement, Paragraph 24 indicates that the government should document that:

a. Complete condition assessments of eligible infrastructure assets are performed in a consistent manner at least every three years.
b. The results of the three most recent complete condition assessments provide reasonable assurance that the eligible infrastructure assets are being preserved approximately at (or above) the condition level established and disclosed by the government.

Accounting for Long-Term Debt and Other Long-Term Liabilities

Long-term debt of state and local governments includes bonds, notes, loans, and leases payable. Other long-term liabilities include compensated absences, operating leases with scheduled rent increases, pensions, special termination benefits, landfill closure and postclosure care costs, and claims and judgments. Liabilities related to pensions are discussed in Chapter 7.

State and local governments are required to report all long-term debt and long-term liabilities in the Statement of Net Assets. This includes debt that is to be paid out of general government resources, such as general obligation (G.O.) debt, which is paid out of tax revenues. This debt is reflected in the governmental-type activities column of the statement. The Statement of Net Assets also includes debt paid from revenues raised by proprietary fund activities, which would be reported in the business-type activities column. Debt related to component units is reported in the component unit column of the government-wide Statement of Net Assets. When reporting long-term debt and other liabilities, a distinction must be made between that portion to be paid within one year and that portion to be paid in later years.

In addition, long-term debt paid from proprietary fund revenues is reported as a liability in the proprietary fund Statement of Net Assets (or Balance Sheet). Debt paid out of general revenues is *not* reflected in the governmental fund balance sheets, due to the current financial resources measurement focus of governmental funds.

In the government-wide statements, accounting for long-term debt generally parallels that found in the private sector. Interest expense is reported on the accrual basis, and premiums and discounts are amortized using the effective interest method. Governmental fund statements generally report debt service payments out of a debt service fund or, in some cases, the General Fund. Principal and interest expenditures are reported on the modified accrual basis, which means that those expenditures are recognized when due and that premiums and discounts on the bonds are not amortized. Accounting for debt paid from governmental funds is discussed in more detail in Chapter 5.

ADDITIONAL RESOURCES

Individuals interested in studying the original sources of GAAP may consult the GASB *Codification*.[4] The *Codification* lists GASB pronouncements by topic; alternatively, a person may consult the GASB *Original Pronouncements* that provide the information in statement order.[5] In addition to hard copies of the original sources, GASB markets a CD-ROM version called GARS (Governmental Accounting Research System). All of these sources can be accessed on the GASB website

---

[4] Governmental Accounting Standards Board. *Codification of Governmental Accounting and Financial Reporting Standards*. Norwalk, CT: GASB, 2001.
[5] Governmental Accounting Standards Board. *Original Pronouncements: Governmental Accounting and Financial Reporting Standards*. Norwalk, CT: GASB, 2001.

(www.gasb.org) which also provides information regarding current activities, exposure drafts, and links to governments that have adopted the reporting standards of GASB *Statement 34*.

The American Institute of Certified Public Accountants (AICPA) provides guidance regarding state and local governmental accounting and auditing, especially in its *Audit and Accounting Guide: State and Local Governmental Units*.[6] The AICPA website is www.aicpa.org.

The Government Finance Officers Association of the United States and Canada (GFOA) is the professional organization of the preparers of governmental financial statements. Detailed guidance is available in their publication, *Governmental Accounting, Auditing, and Financial Reporting*.[7] The GFOA website is www.gfoa.org.

Questions and Exercises

1–1. Obtain a copy of a recent Comprehensive Annual Financial Report (CAFR), which uses the reporting format outlined in GASB *Statement 34*. These may be obtained by writing the director of finance in a city or county of your choice. Your instructor may have one available for you, or you may obtain one from the GASB website: www.gasb.org/. It would be best, but not absolutely necessary, to use a CAFR that has a Certificate of Excellence in Financial Reporting from the Government Finance Officers Association. You will be answering questions related to the CAFR in Chapters 1 through 9. Answer the following questions related to your CAFR.

   a. What are the inclusive dates of the fiscal year?

   b. Write the name and address of the independent auditor. Is the auditor's opinion unqualified? If not, describe the qualification. Is the opinion limited to the basic financial statements, or does the opinion include combining and individual fund statements?

   c. Is the report separated into the three distinct sections: introductory, financial, and statistical? Does the report have a "single audit" section at the end? (A few CAFRs include their single audit report in the CAFR—see Chapter 13 for more detail of the single audit requirements.)

   d. Does the report contain an organization chart? A table of contents? A list of principal officials? A letter of transmittal? Is the letter of transmittal dated and signed by the chief financial officer? List the major items of discussion in the letter of transmittal.

   e. Does the report include a Management's Discussion and Analysis? List the major items of discussion.

---

[6] American Institute of Certified Public Accountants. *Audit and Accounting Guide: State and Local Governmental Units*. New York, AICPA, 2002.
[7] Stephen J. Gautier, *Governmental Accounting, Auditing, and Financial Reporting Using the GASB 34 Model*. Chicago: Government Finance Officers Association, 2001.

f. Does the report include the government-wide statements (Statement of Net Assets and Statement of Activities)?

g. Does the report reflect fund financial statements for governmental, proprietary, and fiduciary funds? List those statements. List the major governmental and propriety funds (the funds which have separate columns in the governmental and proprietary fund statements).

1–2. For each of the following, select the letter corresponding with the *best* answer:

1. The private sector organization that has been given primary authority to set accounting and financial reporting standards for state and local governments is the
    a. Financial Accounting Standards Board.
    b. Governmental Accounting Standards Board.
    c. Federal Accounting Standards Advisory Board.
    d. American Institute of Certified Public Accountants.

2. The private sector organization that has been given primary authority to set accounting and financial reporting standards for private sector, not-for-profit organizations is the:
    a. Financial Accounting Standards Board.
    b. Governmental Accounting Standards Board.
    c. Federal Accounting Standards Advisory Board.
    d. American Institute of Certified Public Accountants.

3. The organization that has been given primary authority to set accounting and financial reporting standards for the federal government and its agencies is the:
    a. Financial Accounting Standards Board.
    b. Governmental Accounting Standards Board.
    c. Federal Accounting Standards Advisory Board.
    d. American Institute of Certified Public Accountants.

4. The hierarchy of GAAP for all entities is established by the:
    a. Financial Accounting Standards Board.
    b. Governmental Accounting Standards Board.
    c. Federal Accounting Standards Advisory Board.
    d. American Institute of Certified Public Accountants.

5. Objectives of financial accounting and reporting have been established by the:
    a. Financial Accounting Standards Board.
    b. Governmental Accounting Standards Board.
    c. Federal Accounting Standards Advisory Board.
    d. All of the above.

6. The three main sections of a comprehensive annual financial report are:
   a. Basic statements, notes, and statistical.
   b. Introductory, main body, and conclusion.
   c. Introductory, financial, and statistical.
   d. Auditor's opinion, basic financial statements, and notes.
7. The government-wide financial statements include a:
   a. Statement of net assets and a statement of activities.
   b. Statement of net assets and a statement of changes in net assets.
   c. Statement of net assets and a statement of revenues, expenditures, and changes in fund balances.
   d. Balance sheet, an income statement, and a statement of cash flows.
8. Governmental funds include:
   a. General, internal service, debt service, capital projects, and permanent funds.
   b. General, special revenue, debt service, and capital projects funds.
   c. Enterprise and internal service funds.
   d. General, special revenue, debt service, capital projects, and permanent funds.
9. Governmental funds use the:
   a. Economic resources measurement focus and modified accrual basis of accounting.
   b. Current financial resources measurement focus and accrual basis of accounting.
   c. Economic resources measurement focus and accrual basis of accounting.
   d. Current financial resources measurement focus and modified accrual basis of accounting.
10. Which of the following is true regarding accounting for fixed assets of state and local governmental units?
    a. Fixed assets are to be recorded at historical cost, or if donated, at the fair value at date of donation.
    b. Fixed assets are to be reported and depreciated in the government-wide financial statements.
    c. Fixed assets are to be reported and depreciated in the proprietary fund financial statements but not in the governmental fund financial statements.
    d. All of the above are true.

1–3. For each of the following, select the letter corresponding to the best answer:
   1. Which of the following organizations would not have accounting and financial reporting principles established by the Financial Accounting Standards Board?

a. St. Mary's Catholic Hospital.
   b. Cook County Hospital.
   c. Yale University, a private institution.
   d. Boy Scouts of America.
2. Objectives adopted by the Governmental Accounting Standards Board include which of the following?
   a. Financial reporting plays an important role in fulfilling government's duty to be publicly accountable in a democratic society.
   b. Financial reports are used to compare actual financial results with the legally adopted budget.
   c. Financial reports are used to assess financial condition and results of operations.
   d. All of the above.
3. Which of the following would not be included in the financial section of a comprehensive annual financial report?
   a. Auditor's opinion.
   b. Notes to the financial statements.
   c. Letter of transmittal.
   d. Balance sheet—governmental funds.
4. Proprietary fund financial statements include:
   a. Statement of net assets, statement of revenues, expenses, and changes in fund net assets, and statement of cash flows.
   b. Statement of net assets, statement of revenues, expenditures, and changes in fund balances, and statement of cash flows.
   c. Statement of net assets and statement of changes in net assets.
   d. Statement of net assets and statement of revenues, expenditures, and changes in fund balances.
5. Which of the following statements would not be prepared using full accrual accounting?
   a. Government-wide statement of activities.
   b. Proprietary fund statement of revenues, expenses, and changes in fund net assets.
   c. Governmental fund statement of revenues, expenditures, and changes in fund balances.
   d. Fiduciary fund statement of changes in net assets.
6. Which of the following is not a governmental fund?
   a. General.
   b. Private-purpose.
   c. Special revenue.
   d. Debt service.

7. Which of the following fund types uses the same measurement focus and basis of accounting as the General Fund?
   a. Enterprise.
   b. Pension and other employee benefit.
   c. Internal service.
   d. Permanent.
8. Which of the following is not true regarding the reporting of infrastructure by state and local governmental units?
   a. Infrastructure must be recorded as fixed assets in the government-wide statements.
   b. Infrastructure includes such assets as roads, bridges, tunnels, and water and sewer systems.
   c. Infrastructure may be either depreciated or reported using the modified approach outlined by the GASB.
   d. None of the above; all are true.
9. Which of the following is not true regarding the recording of collections by state and local governments?
   a. Collections may or may not be capitalized.
   b. In order to be considered a collection, the assets must be: (1) held for public exhibition, education, or research in furtherance of public service, other than financial gain; (2) protected, kept unencumbered, cared for and protected; and (3) subject to an organizational policy that requires the proceeds from sales of collection items to be used to acquire other items for collections.
   c. When not capitalized, a government must disclose a description of the collection and the reasons the collections are not capitalized.
   d. None of the above; all are true.
10. Which of the following is not true regarding accounting and financial reporting for long-term debt and other long-term liabilities by state and local governmental units?
    a. Long-term debt and other long-term liabilities are to be reported in the government wide statement of net assets.
    b. Long-term debt and other long-term liabilities are to be reported in the proprietary fund statement of net assets.
    c. Long-term debt and other long-term liabilities are to be reported in the governmental fund balance sheet.
    d. None of the above; all are true.

1–4. Discuss the jurisdiction issue related to accounting and financial reporting for state and local governments, the federal government, and nongovernmental, not-for-profit organizations. Include in your answer: (a) the three organizations that set standards and how the standards-setting authority is divided, (b) the definition of a government, and (c) the hierarchy of GAAP.

THE GOVERNMENTAL REPORTING ENTITY

General-purpose governments such as states, counties, and large cities typically are complex organizations that include semiautonomous boards, commissions, and agencies created to accomplish projects or activities that, for one reason or another (generally restrictive clauses in state constitutions or statutes), may not be carried out by a government as originally constituted. For many years, separate annual reports were issued for each legal entity. The entity was usually consistent with governments as defined by the U.S. Bureau of the Census, which takes a census of governments every five years.

Current GASB pronouncements, however, require state and local governments to follow the standards set forth in GASB *Codification* Sec. 2100, *Defining the Reporting Entity,* and in Sec. 2600, *Reporting Entity and Component Unit Presentation and Disclosure,* as well as all other financial reporting standards relating to the presentation of the basic financial statements and the comprehensive annual financial report (CAFR). GASB standards assume that all functions of government are responsible to elected officials at the state or local levels and that the financial activities and condition of each governmental function should be reported at the lowest level of legislative authority consistent with the criteria set forth in the *Codification.*

For the purposes of this section, the following definitions are useful:

- A **financial reporting entity** is a primary government, organizations for which the primary government is financially accountable, and other organizations for which the nature and significance of their relationship with the primary government are such that exclusion would cause the reporting entity's financial statements to be misleading or incomplete. The nucleus of a financial reporting entity usually is a primary government. However, a governmental organization other than a primary government (such as a component unit, a joint venture, a jointly governed organization, or other stand-alone government) serves as the nucleus for its own reporting entity when it issues separate financial statements.
- A **primary government** is a state government or general-purpose local government. It is also a special purpose government that has a separately elected governing body, is legally separate, and is fiscally independent of other state or local governments.
- **Component units** are legally separate organizations for which the elected officials of the primary government are financially accountable. In addition, a component unit can be another organization for which the nature and significance of its relationship with a primary government are such that exclusion would cause the reporting entity's financial statements to be misleading or incomplete.

GASB standards provide two methods for including component unit financial information with that of primary governments. The first is known as **blending.** Blending involves combining the financial information of the component units with that of the primary government in the appropriate fund groups. For example, an enterprise activity of a component unit would become an enterprise fund of the reporting entity. Blending is done only when component units are "so intertwined with the primary government that they are, in substance, the same as the primary government and should be reported as part of the primary government." It should be noted that the General Fund of a component unit would normally be a special revenue fund of the reporting entity, and the General Fund of the primary government would be the General Fund of the reporting entity.

Most component units are incorporated through **discrete presentation.** These component units are presented in the government-wide statements as a separate column. Combining statements are provided for the component units, as necessary. Illustrations 2–1 and 2–2 provide examples of discrete presentation of component units.

OVERVIEW OF THE COMPREHENSIVE ANNUAL FINANCIAL REPORT (CAFR)

The Comprehensive Annual Financial Report (CAFR) is to include, according to *Codification* Sec. 2200, three major sections: introductory, financial, and statistical. The CAFR is to include blended component units and discretely presented component units. In addition, the CAFR includes an introductory section, management's discussion and analysis (MD&A), the basic financial statements, required supplementary information (RSI), combining and individual statements, schedules, and a statistical section. An outline of the CAFR follows:

Introductory section
    Table of contents
    Letter of transmittal
    List of principal officials
    Organization chart

Financial section
    Auditor's report
    Management's discussion and analysis
    Basic financial statements
        Government-wide statements
            Statement of net assets
            Statement of activities
        Fund financial statements
            Governmental funds
                Balance sheet
                Statement of revenues, expenditures, and changes in fund balances
            Proprietary funds
                Statement of fund net assets (or balance sheet)
                Statement of revenues, expenses, and changes in fund net assets

Statement of cash flows
Fiduciary funds (and component units that are fiduciary in nature)
Statement of fiduciary net assets
Statement of changes in fiduciary net assets
Notes to the financial statements
Required supplementary information other than MD&A
Schedule of funding progress of pension plans
Schedule of employer contributions of pension plans
Budgetary comparison schedules for the general and major special revenue funds (may be included as a basic financial statement)
Information about infrastructure assets using the modified approach (if applicable)
Schedules required for external risk financing pools (if applicable)
Combining statements for nonmajor funds and individual funds and schedules

Statistical section

INTRODUCTORY SECTION

The introductory section of a CAFR includes the table of contents, a letter of transmittal, a list of principal officials, and an organization chart. If a government received a Certificate of Achievement for Excellence in Financial Reporting from the Government Finance Officers Association in the prior year,[1] it will include a reproduction of that Certificate. The introductory section is not audited.

FINANCIAL SECTION

The financial section of a CAFR includes the auditor's report, management's discussion and analysis, the basic financial statements (government-wide, fund, and the notes), required supplementary information, and the combining and individual fund statements.

Auditor's Report

The auditor's report, placed at the beginning of the financial section, normally expresses an opinion on the basic financial statements. This opinion is expressed on *opinion units,* including the governmental activities, the business-type activities, the aggregate discretely presented component units, each major governmental and enterprise fund, and the aggregate remaining fund information. Alternatively, the

---

[1] The Government Finance Officers Association of the United States and Canada sponsors a Certificate of Achievement for Excellence in Financial Reporting program to encourage and promote excellent financial reporting. To receive that certificate, a government must have an unqualified audit opinion and have its report reviewed, using a multipage checklist, by independent reviewers who are experienced in financial reporting. See www.gfoa.org.

scope of the audit may result in an opinion on all individual funds as well as the government-wide statements. Audit opinions are discussed in more detail and are illustrated in Chapter 13.

Management's Discussion and Analysis (MD&A)

The MD&A provides an opportunity for the government to provide, in plain English terms, an overview of the government's financial activities. This section is considered **Required Supplementary Information,** which means that it is required and has some auditor involvement but not as much as the basic financial statements. Auditors review the material to establish that it is not misleading in relation to the basic statements but do not include the MD&A in the scope of the audit. A number of specific items must be included, as listed below, but governments are encouraged to avoid boilerplate language. This section should compare current year results with the prior year, with emphasis on the current year. The following are the basic requirements for MD&A:

1. A brief discussion of the financial statements.
2. Condensed financial information derived from the government-wide financial statements, comparing the current year with the prior year. A total of 14 items are listed in Paragraph 11 of *Statement 34,* including program revenues by major source, program expenses by major function, and total net assets, distinguishing between amounts invested in capital assets, net of related debt, restricted amounts, and unrestricted amounts.
3. An analysis of the government's overall financial position and results of operations to assist users in assessing whether financial position has improved or deteriorated as a result of the year's operations.
4. An analysis of balances and transactions of individual funds.
5. An analysis of significant variations between original and final budget amounts and between final budget amounts and actual budget results for the General Fund.
6. A description of significant capital asset and long-term debt activity during the year.
7. A discussion by governments that use the modified approach to report some or all of their infrastructure assets that would include (*a*) any changes in the condition of infrastructure, (*b*) a comparison of assessed condition with the condition level established by the government, and (*c*) significant differences between the amount needed to maintain infrastructure and the amount expended.
8. A description of any known facts, decisions, or conditions that would have a significant effect on the government's financial position or results of operations.

GASB *Statement 37* makes it clear that MD&A is limited to the preceding eight items.

Government-Wide Financial Statements

Statement 34 requires governments to prepare government-wide financial statements using the economic resources measurement focus and full accrual basis of accounting. The statements are: (1) Statement of Net Assets and (2) Statement of Activities. The following are some of the major features of the government-wide statements:

1. The statements reflect the government as a whole, with the exception of fiduciary activities. This includes the primary government and its component units. Governmental and business-type activities are reflected separately as are discretely presented component units. Governmental type activities include those activities normally reported in governmental funds and most internal service funds. Business-type activities are those normally reported in enterprise funds.
2. In addition to including a column in the government-wide statements, individual major component units may be reported in one of three ways. The first method is to present each major component unit in the Statement of Net Assets and Statement of Activities. The second method is to include combining statements (net assets and activities) of major component units in statements immediately following the fund financial statements. The third is to provide condensed financial statements in the notes.
3. Prior-year data may be presented but are not required.
4. Full accrual accounting is to be used, including depreciation of fixed assets. Exchange transactions are to be recognized when the exchange takes place. Nonexchange transactions are to be recognized in accord with the provisions of *Statement 33* (described in Chapter 4).
5. Use of the accrual basis requires adoption of private sector rules (FASB Statements, APB Opinions, and Accounting Research Bulletins issued on or before November 30, 1989, unless those pronouncements conflict with or supersede GASB pronouncements). Business-type activities may be reported applying FASB pronouncements issued after November 30, 1989, as described in Chapter 6 for enterprise funds.
6. Depreciation expense is to be reported, as described more fully below, in the section on the Statement of Activities. Infrastructure is to be capitalized and depreciated, unless the modified approach is used. (See the section on infrastructure in the following section.)
7. Works of art, historical treasures, and similar assets should be capitalized and depreciated unless those items qualify as **collections.** To qualify as a collection, such assets are "(*a*) held for public exhibition, education, or research in furtherance of public service, rather than financial gain; (*b*) protected, kept unencumbered, cared for and preserved; (*c*) subject to an organizational policy that requires the proceeds from sales of collection items to be used to acquire other items for collections." (*Statement 34,* Paragraph 27) Note that this is the same definition as that of FASB (described in Chapter 10 of this text).

Statement of Net Assets Illustration 2–1 reflects one of the *Statement 34* examples of a Statement of Net Assets for a municipality. Note that assets are generally reported in order of liquidity. Capital assets are reported net of depreciation. A classified approach may also be used, separating current and noncurrent assets. Noncurrent liabilities are reported separately, using either method. Net assets are reported in three categories: (*a*) invested in capital assets, net of related debt; (*b*) restricted; and (*c*) unrestricted.

Invested in capital assets, net of related debt is computed by taking the capital (fixed) assets less accumulated depreciation, less the debt outstanding that is

ILLUSTRATION 2–1

SAMPLE CITY
Statement of Net Assets
December 31, 2004

	Primary Government			
	Governmental Activities	Business-Type Activities	Total	Component Units
Assets				
Cash and cash equivalents	$ 13,597,899	$ 10,279,143	$ 23,877,042	$ 303,935
Investments	27,365,221	—	27,365,221	7,428,952
Receivables (net)	12,833,132	3,609,615	16,442,747	4,042,290
Internal balances	175,000	(175,000)	—	—
Inventories	322,149	126,674	448,823	83,697
Capital assets, net (Note 1)	170,022,760	151,388,751	321,411,511	37,744,786
Total assets	224,316,161	165,229,183	389,545,344	49,603,660
Liabilities				
Accounts payable	6,783,310	751,430	7,534,740	1,803,332
Deferred revenue	1,435,599	—	1,435,599	38,911
Noncurrent liabilities (Note 2):				
Due within one year	9,236,000	4,426,286	13,662,286	1,426,639
Due in more than one year	83,302,378	74,482,273	157,784,651	27,106,151
Total liabilities	100,757,287	79,659,989	180,417,276	30,375,033
Net assets				
Invested in capital assets, net of related debt	103,711,386	73,088,574	176,799,960	15,906,392
Restricted for:				
Capital projects	11,705,864	—	11,705,864	492,445
Debt service	3,020,708	1,451,996	4,472,704	—
Community development projects	4,811,043	—	4,811,043	—
Other purposes	3,214,302	—	3,214,302	—
Unrestricted (deficit)	(2,904,429)	11,028,624	8,124,195	2,829,790
Total net assets	$123,558,874	$ 85,569,194	$209,128,068	$19,228,627

Source: GASB *Statement 34*, p. 201.

related to capital assets. The deduction does not include other long-term debt, not related to the acquisition of capital assets. This equity amount may or may not be directly computed from the face of the Statement of Net Assets.

The term **restricted** is defined by GASB as "(*a*) externally imposed by creditors (such as through debt covenants), grantors, contributors, or laws or regulations of other governments, and (*b*) imposed by law through constitutional provisions or enabling legislation." According to Paragraph 34 of *Statement 34*, "enabling legislation, as the term is used in this Statement, authorizes the government to assess, levy, charge, or otherwise mandate payment of resources (from external resource providers) *and* includes a legally enforceable requirement that those resources be used only for the specific purposes stipulated in the legislation." Note that this definition of "restricted" is much broader than the FASB definition of "restricted" described in Chapter 10, which includes only contributions restricted by donors.

Unrestricted net assets is a "plug" figure, determined by deducting the other two categories (invested in capital assets, net of related debt and restricted) from the total net assets. GASB concluded that "designations" of net assets (by management of the government) should not be reported on the Statement of Net Assets.

Statement of Activities   Illustration 2–2 reflects the standard Statement of Activities for a municipality. Other possible formats exist, and some of these are illustrated in *Statement 34*.

Note the general format of the statement. Expenses, computed on the full accrual basis, are reported on a functional basis (public safety, general government, etc.). Revenues that can be directly associated with those functions are deducted, and a net expense or revenue is reflected to the right. These functions are classified as governmental activities, business-type activities, and component units. Then, general revenues are deducted from the net expenses (revenues). Special and extraordinary items are shown after the general revenues, as are transfers. The change in net assets is then reflected, after which the net assets for the beginning and end of the period are shown.

All governments are required to report direct expenses by function. If a government chooses to allocate some indirect expenses to functions, separate columns should show the direct, indirect, and total costs charged to each function. The direct expenses would include depreciation that can be directly charged to functional activities. Depreciation expense that applies to two or more functions should be allocated. Depreciation expense that serves all functions may be (1) allocated as an indirect expense, (2) charged to general government, or (3) charged as unallocated depreciation expense. Depreciation expense for general infrastructure assets should not be allocated but shown as either an expense of the function that normally is used for capital outlay (public works, for example) or as a separate line. Governments may choose not to depreciate infrastructure but charge expenditures that extend infrastructure life to expense, as described in Chapter 1.

Interest on long-term debt would be included in direct expenses if the interest is related to a single function. Most interest, however, cannot be identified with a separate function and should be shown separately, as is shown in Illustration 2–2. Interest incurred during construction is capitalized for business-type activities but not for governmental activities.

Program revenues include charges for services, operating grants and contributions, and capital grants and contributions (additional categories may be added). Charges for services, including charges by enterprise operations (water, sewer, golf courses, tolls, etc.) and fines and forfeits are reported with the programs that generate the revenue. Operating grants and contributions reflect nonexchange transactions with other governments that are restricted by the government; these are reported with the programs to which the grants and contributions are restricted.

General revenues include tax revenues and those other revenues that are not associated directly with a particular function or program. *All* taxes levied by the reporting government, including those restricted for a particular purpose (such as a motor fuel tax restricted for road repairs) are reported as general revenues. Taxes levied by other governments (for example, a state shared sales tax) are reported as program revenues.

Several items are reported separately, after general revenues. Contributions to term and permanent endowments and contributions to permanent fund principal (see Illustration 9–4, related to public colleges) are reported separately. Extraordinary items are those transactions that are both unusual in nature and infrequent in occurrence, in accord with Accounting Principles Board Opinion No. 20. Significant transactions or other events within the control of management that are *either* unusual in nature or infrequent in occurrence are shown as **special items.** An example would be the Gain on Sale of Park Land, shown in Illustration 2–2. Finally, transfers are shown in a separate line. These transfers reflect only transfers between governmental activities, business-type activities, and discretely presented component units.

The Statement of Activities is a consolidated statement, within columns. Services provided and used and transfers between governmental activities, business-type activities, and component units are not eliminated; those transactions within those categories are eliminated.

Fund Financial Statements

In addition to government-wide statements, GASB requires fund financial statements. These are presented separately for governmental, proprietary, and fiduciary funds. Governmental and the enterprise fund portion of the proprietary fund statements focus on **major funds** rather than on fund type. The General Fund is always a major fund. Other funds must be considered major when both of the following conditions exist: (*a*) total assets, liabilities, revenues, *or* expenditures/expenses of that individual governmental or enterprise fund constitute 10 percent of the governmental or enterprise category, *and* (*b*) total assets, liabilities, revenues, *or* expenditures/expenses are 5 percent of the total of the governmental and enterprise category. The 10 and 5 percent rules apply to each category (assets, liabilities, revenues, expenditures/expenses).[2] A government may designate any fund major if reporting that fund separately in the basic statements would be useful. In all fund statements, the nonmajor funds are aggregated and reported as a single column. Fiduciary fund financial statements and the internal service fund portion of proprietary fund statements are reported by fund type, not major fund, as is described later.

Governmental Funds—Balance Sheet Illustration 2–3 reflects a balance sheet for the governmental funds of a general purpose local government. Several features

---

[2] For example, look at the Community Redevelopment Fund in Illustration 2–3. Total assets of $13,616,035 exceed 10 percent of total governmental fund assets ($51,705,690). The total assets of $13,616,035 also exceed the 5 percent of total governmental ($51,705,690) and enterprise fund ($165,404,183 from Illustration 2–6) assets (total $217,109,873), which would be $10,855,493. As a result the Community Redevelopment Fund *must* be a major fund and reported separately on the governmental fund statements.

ILLUSTRATION 2–2 Statement of Activities

SAMPLE CITY
Statement of Activities
For the Year Ended December 31, 2004

Functions/Programs	Expenses	Program Revenues			Net (Expense) Revenue and Changes in Net Assets			
		Charges for Services	Operating Grants and Contributions	Capital Grants and Contributions	Primary Government			Component Units
					Govern-mental Activities	Business-Type Activities	Total	
Primary government:								
Governmental activities:								
General government	$ 9,571,410	$ 3,146,915	$ 843,617	$ —	$ (5,580,878)	$ —	$ (5,580,878)	$ —
Public safety	34,844,749	1,198,855	1,307,693	62,300	(32,275,901)	—	(32,275,901)	—
Public works	10,128,538	850,000	—	2,252,615	(7,025,923)	—	(7,025,923)	—
Engineering services	1,299,645	704,793	—	—	(594,852)	—	(594,852)	—
Health and sanitation	6,738,672	5,612,267	575,000	—	(551,405)	—	(551,405)	—
Cemetery	735,866	212,496	—	—	(523,370)	—	(523,370)	—
Culture and recreation	11,532,350	3,995,199	2,450,000	—	(5,087,151)	—	(5,087,151)	—
Community development	2,994,389	—	—	2,580,000	(414,389)	—	(414,389)	—
Education (payment to school district)	21,893,273	—	—	—	(21,893,273)	—	(21,893,273)	—
Interest on long-term debt	6,068,121	—	—	—	(6,068,121)	—	(6,068,121)	—
Total governmental activities	105,807,013	15,720,525	5,176,310	4,894,915	(80,015,263)	—	(80,015,263)	—

Business-type activities:							
Water	3,595,733	4,159,350	—	1,159,909	—	1,723,526	1,723,526
Sewer	4,912,853	7,170,533	—	486,010	—	2,743,690	2,743,690
Parking facilities	2,796,283	1,344,087	—	—	—	(1,452,196)	(1,452,196)
Total business-type activities	11,304,869	12,673,970	—	1,645,919	—	3,015,020	3,015,020
Total primary government	$117,111,882	$28,394,495	$5,176,310	$6,540,834	(80,015,263)	3,015,020	(77,000,243)
Component units:							
Landfill	$ 3,382,157	$ 3,857,858	$ —	$ 11,397			487,098
Public school system	31,186,498	705,765	3,937,083	—			(26,543,650)
Total component units	$ 34,568,655	$ 4,563,623	$3,937,083	$ 11,397			(26,056,552)

General revenues:			
Taxes:			
Property taxes, levied for general purposes	51,693,573	—	51,693,573
Property taxes, levied for debt service	4,726,244	—	4,726,244
Franchise taxes	4,055,505	—	4,055,505
Public service taxes	8,969,887	—	8,969,887
Payment from Sample City	—	—	—	21,893,273
Grants and contributions not restricted to specific programs	1,457,820	—	1,457,820	6,461,708
Investment earnings	1,958,144	601,349	2,559,493	881,763
Miscellaneous	884,907	104,925	989,832	22,464
Special item—Gain on sale of park land	2,653,488	—	2,653,488	—
Transfers	501,409	(501,409)	—	—
Total general revenues, special items, and transfers	76,900,977	204,865	77,105,842	29,259,208
Change in net assets	(3,114,286)	3,219,885	105,599	3,202,656
Net assets—beginning	126,673,160	82,349,309	209,022,469	16,025,971
Net assets—ending	$123,558,874	$85,569,194	$209,128,068	$19,228,627

Source: GASB *Statement 34*, pp. 208–9.

ILLUSTRATION 2–3 Balance Sheet—Governmental Funds

SAMPLE CITY
Balance Sheet
Governmental Funds
December 31, 2004

	General	HUD Programs	Community Redevelopment	Route 7 Construction	Other Governmental Funds	Total Governmental Funds
Assets						
Cash and cash equivalents	$3,418,485	$1,236,523	$ —	$ —	$ 5,606,792	$10,261,800
Investments	3,644,561	2,953,438	13,262,695	10,467,037	3,485,252	27,214,984
Receivables, net	1,370,757	—	353,340	11,000	10,221	6,972,560
Due from other funds						1,370,757
Receivables from other governments	—	119,059	—	—	1,596,038	1,715,097
Liens receivable	791,926	3,195,745	—	—	—	3,987,671
Inventories	182,821	—	—	—	—	182,821
Total assets	$9,408,550	$7,504,765	$13,616,035	$10,478,037	$10,698,303	$51,705,690
Liabilities and fund balances						
Liabilities:						
Accounts payable	$3,408,680	$129,975	$190,548	$1,104,632	$1,074,831	$5,908,666
Due to other funds	—	25,369	—	—	—	25,369
Payable to other governments	94,074	—	—	—	—	94,074
Deferred revenue	4,250,430	6,273,045	250,000	11,000	—	10,784,475
Total liabilities	7,753,184	6,428,389	440,548	1,115,632	1,074,831	16,812,584

Fund balances:					
Reserved for:					
Inventories	182,821	—	—	—	182,821
Liens receivable	791,926	—	—	—	791,926
Encumbrances	40,292	41,034	—	1,814,122	7,807,349
Debt service	—	—	5,792,587	3,832,062	3,832,062
Other purposes	—	—	—	1,405,300	1,405,300
Unreserved, reported in:					
General fund	640,327	—	—	—	640,327
Special revenue funds	—	1,035,342	—	1,330,718	2,366,060
Capital projects funds	—	—	13,056,173	1,241,270	17,867,261
Total fund balances	1,655,366	1,076,376	13,175,487	9,623,472	34,893,106
Total liabilities and fund balances	$9,408,550	$7,504,765	$13,616,035	$10,698,303	

Amounts reported for *governmental activities* in the statement of net assets are different because:

Capital assets used in governmental activities are not financial resources and therefore are not reported in the funds. 161,082,708

Other long-term assets are not available to pay for current-period expenditures and therefore are deferred in the funds.

Internal service funds are used by management to charge the costs of certain activities, such as insurance and telecommunications, to individual funds. The assets and liabilities of the internal service funds are included in governmental activities in the statement of net assets. 9,348,876

Long-term liabilities, including bonds payable, are not due and payable in the current period and therefore are not reported in the funds. 2,994,691

(84,760,507)

Net assets of governmental activities $123,558,874

Source: GASB *Statement 34*, pp. 220–1.

of this statement should be noted. First, a total column is required. Second, major funds are included, of all governmental fund types (general, special revenue, debt service, capital projects, permanent). Third, the other governmental funds are grouped together into a single column and are presented in a combining statement whenever a CAFR is prepared. Fourth, fund balances are broken down between reserved and unreserved categories. Separate lines are shown for unreserved fund balances by fund type. Finally, a reconciliation is shown between the total fund balances shown in this statement ($34,893,106) and the net assets shown in the government-wide Statement of Net Assets (Illustration 2–1; $123,558,874).

Governmental Funds—Statement of Revenues, Expenditures, and Changes in Fund Balances Illustration 2–4 reflects the operating statement for the governmental funds, reflecting the General Fund and other major funds also shown in the Balance Sheet. This statement is prepared using the current financial resources measurement focus and modified accrual basis of accounting. Revenues are reported by source and expenditures are reported by character (current, debt service, capital outlay) and by function (general government, public safety, etc.). Other financing sources and uses reflect proceeds of long-term debt, payment to a bond refund escrow agent, and transfers. Special and extraordinary items are shown separately, as was true for the government-wide statements. A reconciliation between this statement and the Statement of Activities (Illustration 2–2) is presented as Illustration 2–5.

Proprietary Funds—Statement of Net Assets, or Balance Sheet Illustration 2–6 reflects the Statement of Net Assets for proprietary funds (enterprise, internal service). In this example, note that both enterprise funds are major funds and that a total is shown for enterprise funds. Internal service funds do not follow the procedure where all major funds are in the statement; only one column for all internal service funds is shown with the detailed financial statements included later in the CAFR. A reconciliation to the government-wide statements is normally not necessary for proprietary fund statements, because the same measurement focus and basis of accounting (economic resources, accrual) is used.

A few things should be noted about Illustration 2–6. First, GASB requires a classified balance sheet with current and noncurrent assets and liabilities shown separately. Net assets are broken down in the same manner as in the government-wide statements: (1) invested in capital assets, net of related debt, (2) restricted, and (3) unrestricted. Finally, Illustration 2–6 is presented in a "net asset" format, so that assets − liabilities = net assets. The balance sheet format (assets = liabilities + net assets) is also acceptable, and an example is shown in *Statement 34*.

Proprietary Funds—Statement of Revenues, Expenses, and Changes in Fund Net Assets Illustration 2–7 reflects the Statement of Revenues, Expenses, and Changes in Fund Net Assets for a municipality in the format required by *Statement 34*. That is, operating revenues and expenses must be reported first, followed by an operating income figure. Next, nonoperating revenues and expenses are reported, followed by income (loss) before contributions and transfers. Note that depreciation is shown separately as an operating expense; interest expense is shown separately in the nonoperating category. The next section includes capital contributions, additions to permanent and term endowments, special and extraordinary items, and transfers. The economic resources measurement focus and accrual basis of accounting are used for this statement.

Proprietary Funds—Statement of Cash Flows Illustration 2–8 reflects the Statement of Cash Flows for the proprietary funds of a general-purpose local government. This statement is described in detail in Chapter 6. Several differences exist between the cash flow statement required by GASB and the cash flow statement required by FASB (illustrated in Chapter 10). First, the direct method is required for reporting cash flows from operations. Second, the reconciliation, appearing at the bottom of the statement, is from operating income (not net income) to cash flows from operations. Third, four categories of cash flows are used instead of three: cash flows from operating, noncapital financing, capital and related financing, and investing. Fourth, capital assets acquired through debt proceeds are reflected as decreases in cash flows from financing activities (noncapital or capital) instead of investing activities. Fifth, interest payments are reflected as financing activities, instead of operating activities. Finally, interest and dividends received are reflected as investing activities, not operating activities.

Fiduciary Funds—Statement of Fiduciary Net Assets and Statement of Changes in Fiduciary Net Assets Illustration 2–9 reflects the Statement of Fiduciary Net Assets and Statement of Changes in Fiduciary Net Assets for a general purpose local government. GASB requires that these statements be included for all trust and agency fund types and for component units that are similar in nature. GASB also requires, if separate GAAP basis financial reports are not issued for individual pension and other employee benefit plans, that those reports be reflected in the notes to the basic financial statements. If separate statements have been issued, the notes should indicate how they might be obtained. Note that agency funds are included in the Statement of Net Assets and not in the Statement of Changes in Net Assets because agency funds report only assets and liabilities. Note also that fiduciary funds are reported by fund type, not by major funds.

Notes to the Financial Statements

GASB recently issued *Statement 38,* revising the required note disclosures. *Statement 38* indicates that the notes must distinguish between the primary government and discretely presented component units. GASB *Codification* Sec. 2300.106 requires the following note disclosures:

- Summary of significant accounting policies, including:
    1. A description of the government-wide financial statements.
    2. A brief description of the component units of the financial reporting entity and their relationship to the primary government.
    3. A description of the activities accounted in each of the following columns—major funds, internal service funds, and fiduciary fund types—presented in the basic financial statements.

ILLUSTRATION 2–4 Balance Sheet—Governmental Funds

SAMPLE CITY
Statement of Revenues, Expenditures, and Changes in Fund Balances
Governmental Funds
For the Year Ended December 31, 2004

	General	HUD Programs	Community Redevelopment	Route 7 Construction	Other Governmental Funds	Total Governmental Funds
Revenues						
Property taxes	$51,173,436	$ —	$ —	$ —	$ 4,680,192	$ 55,853,628
Franchise taxes	4,055,505	—	—	—	—	4,055,505
Public service taxes	8,969,887	—	—	—	—	8,969,887
Fees and fines	605,946	—	—	—	—	606,946
Licenses and permits	2,287,794	—	—	—	—	2,287,794
Intergovernmental	6,119,938	2,578,191	—	—	2,830,916	11,529,045
Charges for services	11,374,460	—	—	—	30,708	11,405,168
Investment earnings	552,325	87,106	549,489	270,161	364,330	1,823,411
Miscellaneous	881,874	66,176	—	2,939	94	951,083
Total revenues	86,022,165	2,731,473	549,489	273,100	7,906,240	97,482,467
Expenditures						
Current:						
General government	8,630,835	—	—	16,700	121,052	9,186,401
Public safety	33,729,623	—	—	—	—	33,729,623
Public works	4,975,775	—	—	—	3,721,542	8,697,317
Engineering services	1,299,645	—	—	—	—	1,299,645
Health and sanitation	6,070,032	—	—	—	—	6,070,032
Cemetery	706,305	—	—	—	—	706,305
Culture and recreation	11,411,685	—	—	—	—	11,411,685
Community development	—	2,954,389	—	—	—	2,954,389
Education—payment to school district	21,893,273	—	—	—	—	21,893,273

Debt service:						
Principal	—	—	—	—	3,450,000	3,450,000
Interest and other charges	—	—	—	—	5,215,151	5,215,151
Capital outlay	—	2,246,671	—	—	3,190,209	16,718,649
Total expenditures	88,717,173	2,954,389	2,664,485	11,281,769	15,697,954	121,332,470
Excess (deficiency) of revenues over expenditures	(2,695,008)	(222,916)	(2,114,996)	11,298,469	(11,025,369)	(7,791,714)	(23,850,003)
Other financing sources (uses)						
Proceeds of refunding bonds	—	—	—	—	38,045,000	38,045,000
Proceeds of long-term capital-related debt	—	—	17,529,560	—	1,300,000	18,829,560
Payment to bond refunding escrow agent	—	—	—	—	(37,284,144)	(37,284,144)
Transfers in	129,323	—	—	—	5,551,187	5,680,510
Transfers out	(2,163,759)	(348,046)	(2,273,187)	—	(219,076)	(5,004,068)
Total other financing sources and uses	(2,034,436)	(348,046)	15,256,373	—	7,392,967	20,266,858
Special Item						
Proceeds from sale of park land	3,476,488	—	—	—	—	3,476,488
Net change in fund balances	(1,252,956)	(570,962)	13,141,377	(11,025,369)	(398,747)	(106,657)
Fund balances—beginning	2,908,322	1,647,338	34,110	20,387,774	10,022,219	34,999,763
Fund balances—ending	$1,655,366	$1,076,376	$13,175,487	$ 9,362,405	$ 9,623,472	$34,893,106

Source: GASB *Statement 34,* pp. 222–3.

ILLUSTRATION 2–5

SAMPLE CITY
Reconciliation of the Statement of Revenues, Expenditures, and Changes in Fund Balances of Governmental Funds to the Statement of Activities
For the Year Ended December 31, 2004

Net change in fund balances—total governmental funds	$ (106,657)
Amounts reported for *governmental activities* in the statement of activities are different because:	
Governmental funds report capital outlays as expenditures. However, in the statement of activities, the cost of those assets is allocated over their estimated useful lives as depreciation expense. This is the amount by which capital outlays exceeded depreciation in the current period.	14,039,717
In the statement of activities, only the *gain* on the sale of the park land is reported, whereas in the governmental funds, the proceeds from the sale increase financial resources. Thus, the change in net assets differs from the change in fund balance by the cost of the land sold.	(823,000)
Revenues in the statement of activities that do not provide current financial resources are not reported as revenues in the funds.	1,920,630
Bond proceeds provide current financial resources to governmental funds, but issuing debt increases long-term liabilities in the statement of net assets. Repayment of bond principal is an expenditure in the governmental funds, but the repayment reduces long-term liabilities in the statement of net assets. This is the amount by which proceeds exceeded repayments.	(16,140,416)
Some expenses reported in the statement of activities do not require the use of current financial resources and therefore are not reported as expenditures in governmental funds.	(1,245,752)
Internal service funds are used by management to charge the costs of certain activities, such as insurance and telecommunications, to individual funds. The net revenue (expense) of the internal service funds is reported with governmental activities.	(758,808)
Change in net assets of governmental activities.	$(3,114,286)

Source: GASB *Statement 34*, p. 224.

4. The measurement focus and basis of accounting used in the government-wide financial statements.
5. The revenue recognition policies used in the fund financial statements, including the length of time used to define *available* for purposes of revenue recognition in the governmental fund financial statements.
6. The policy for eliminating internal activity in the government-wide statement of activities.
7. The policy for capitalizing assets and for estimating the useful lives of those assets.
8. A description of the types of transactions included in program revenues and the policy for allocating indirect expenses to functions in the statement of activities.

9. The policy for defining operating and nonoperating revenues of proprietary funds.
10. The policy for applying FASB pronouncements issued after November 30, 1989, to business-type activities and to enterprise funds of the primary government.
11. The definition of cash and cash equivalents used in the statement of cash flows for proprietary funds.
12. The government's policy regarding whether to first apply restricted or unrestricted resources when an expense is incurred for purposes for which both restricted and unrestricted assets are available.

- Cash deposits with financial institutions.
- Investments.
- Significant contingent liabilities.
- Encumbrances outstanding.
- Significant effects of subsequent events.
- Annual pension cost and net pension obligations (NPO).
- Significant violations of finance-related legal and contractual provisions and actions taken to address such violations.
- Debt service requirements to maturity.
- Commitments under noncapitalized (operating) leases.
- Construction and other significant commitments.
- Required disclosures about capital assets.
- Required disclosures about long-term liabilities.
- Deficit fund balance or net assets of individual nonmajor funds.
- Interfund receivables and payables.
- For each major component unit, the nature and amount of significant transactions with other discretely presented component units or with the primary government.
- Disclosures about donor-restricted endowments.

Of course, the disclosures just listed are not required when they do not apply. For example, lease disclosures are not applicable if the government has no noncancelable leases. In addition, a government may choose to make additional disclosures.

Required Supplementary Information Other than MD&A

Chapter 7 indicates that GASB requires a Schedule of Funding Progress and a Schedule of Employer Contributions as Required Supplementary Information (RSI) when pension plans are reported. These schedules are illustrated in Chapter 7. In addition, GASB *Statement 10* requires certain RSI schedules for external risk financing pools, considered beyond the scope of this text. GASB *Statement 34* also requires RSI for two major areas: (1) budgetary comparison schedules and (2) information about infrastructure assets reporting using the modified approach, if applicable.

ILLUSTRATION 2–6 Statement of Net Assets—Proprietary Funds

SAMPLE CITY
Statement of Net Assets
Proprietary Funds
December 31, 2004

	Business-Type Activities—Enterprise Funds			Governmental Activities—Internal Service Funds
	Water and Sewer	Parking Facilities	Totals	
Assets				
Current assets:				
Cash and cash equivalents	$ 8,416,653	$ 369,168	$ 8,785,821	$ 3,336,099
Investments	—	—	—	150,237
Receivables, net	3,564,586	3,535	3,568,121	157,804
Due from other governments	41,494	—	41,494	—
Inventories	126,674	—	126,674	139,328
Total current assets	12,149,407	372,703	12,522,110	3,783,468
Noncurrent assets				
Restricted cash and cash equivalents	—	1,493,322	1,493,322	—
Capital assets:				
Land	813,513	3,021,637	3,835,150	—
Distribution and collection systems	39,504,183	—	39,504,183	—
Buildings and equipment	106,135,666	23,029,166	129,164,832	14,721,786
Less accumulated depreciation	(15,328,911)	(5,786,503)	(21,115,414)	(5,781,734)
Total noncurrent assets	131,124,451	21,757,622	152,882,073	8,940,052
Total assets	143,273,858	22,130,325	165,404,183	12,723,520

Liabilities

Current liabilities:

Accounts payable	447,427	304,003	751,430
Due to other funds	175,000	—	175,000
Compensated absences	112,850	8,827	121,677
Claims and judgments	—	—	—
Bonds, notes, and loans payable	3,944,609	360,000	4,304,609
Total current liabilities	4,679,886	672,830	5,352,716

Noncurrent liabilities:

Compensated absences	451,399	35,306	486,705
Claims and judgments	—	—	—
Bonds, notes, and loans payable	54,451,549	19,544,019	73,995,568
Total noncurrent liabilities	54,902,948	19,579,325	74,482,273
Total liabilities	59,582,834	20,252,155	79,834,989

Net assets

Invested in capital assets, net of related debt	72,728,293	360,281	73,088,574
Restricted for debt service	—	1,451,996	1,451,996
Unrestricted	10,962,731	65,893	11,028,624
Total net assets	$ 83,691,024	$ 1,878,170	$ 85,569,194

	780,570
	1,170,388
	237,690
	1,687,975
	249,306
	4,125,929
	—
	5,602,900
	5,602,900
	9,728,829
	8,690,746
	—
	(5,696,055)
	$ 2,994,691

Source: GASB *Statement 34*, p. 228.

43

ILLUSTRATION 2-7

SAMPLE CITY
Statement of Revenues, Expenses, and Changes in Fund Net Assets
Proprietary Funds
For the Year Ended December 31, 2004

	Business-Type Activities—Enterprise Funds			Governmental Activities—
	Water and Sewer	Parking Facilities	Totals	Internal Service Funds
Operating revenues:				
Charges for services	$11,329,883	$ 1,340,261	$12,670,144	$15,256,164
Miscellaneous	—	3,826	3,826	1,066,761
Total operating revenues	11,329,883	1,344,087	12,673,970	16,322,925
Operating expenses:				
Personal services	3,400,559	762,348	4,162,907	4,157,156
Contractual services	344,422	96,032	440,454	584,396
Utilities	754,107	100,726	854,833	214,812
Repairs and maintenance	747,315	64,617	811,932	1,960,490
Other supplies and expenses	498,213	17,119	515,332	234,445
Insurance claims and expenses	—	—	—	8,004,286
Depreciation	1,163,140	542,049	1,705,189	1,707,872
Total operating expenses	6,907,756	1,582,891	8,490,647	16,863,457
Operating income (loss)	4,422,127	(238,804)	4,183,323	(540,532)
Nonoperating revenues (expenses):				
Interest and investment revenue	454,793	146,556	601,349	134,733
Miscellaneous revenue	—	104,925	104,925	20,855
Interest expense	(1,600,830)	(1,166,546)	(2,767,376)	(41,616)
Miscellaneous expense	—	(46,846)	(46,846)	(176,003)
Total nonoperating revenue (expenses)	(1,146,037)	(961,911)	(2,107,948)	(62,031)
Income (loss) before contributions and transfers	3,276,090	(1,200,715)	2,075,375	(602,563)
Capital contributions	1,645,919	—	1,645,919	18,788
Transfers out	(290,000)	(211,409)	(501,409)	(175,033)
Change in net assets	4,632,009	(1,412,124)	3,219,885	(758,808)
Total net assets—beginning	79,059,015	3,290,294	82,349,309	3,753,499
Total net assets—ending	$83,691,024	$ 1,878,170	$85,569,194	$ 2,994,691

Source: GASB *Statement 34*, p. 229

Budgetary Comparison Schedules Statement 34 requires a budgetary comparison schedule, as a part of RSI, for the General Fund and for each major special revenue fund that has a legally adopted annual budget. This schedule is to include the original budget, the original appropriated budget, and actual results, computed on the budgetary basis. A variance column may or may not be used. The format may be that of the original budget document or in the format, terminology, and classifications in a statement of revenues, expenditures, and changes in fund balances. Information must be provided, either in this schedule or in notes to RSI, that provides a reconciliation from the budgetary basis to GAAP. In addition, notes to RSI must include any cases where actual expenditures exceed appropriations at the legal level of control. Illustration 2–10 presents one of the possible formats of this schedule included in *Statement 34*. Alternatively, a government may choose to prepare a budgetary comparison statement, as part of the basic financial statements.

Modified Approach for Reporting Infrastructure As mentioned earlier, governments have the option of not depreciating their infrastructure assets if they adopt a modified approach for recording infrastructure. Two requirements must be met to adopt this approach. First, the government must manage the eligible infrastructure assets using an asset management system that has certain characteristics. These characteristics include: (*a*) keeping an up-to-date inventory of infrastructure assets; (*b*) performing condition assessments of eligible infrastructure assets, and summarizing the results using a measurement scale; and (*c*) estimating the costs each year to preserve the infrastructure assets at the condition level established and disclosed by the government. Second, the government must document that the infrastructure assets have been preserved at the condition level prescribed by the government.

Two schedules and some disclosures, in notes to RSI, are required of governments that adopt the modified approach. The required schedules are reflected in Illustration 2–11, taken directly from *Statement 34*.

Combining and Individual Fund Statements and Schedules

A complete Comprehensive Annual Financial Report (CAFR) includes, in its financial section, combining financial statements to reflect its nonmajor funds. Whenever a nonmajor column is used in one of the fund financial statements, combining statements are required. The total column in the combining statements would be the same as the nonmajor funds column in the basic financial statements. The combining statements for nonmajor funds are required in each of the two categories: governmental and proprietary. Illustration 2–12 is an example of a combining balance sheet for nonmajor governmental funds for a municipality.

SPECIAL PURPOSE GOVERNMENTS

The reporting outlined above is for general-purpose governments, such as states, municipalities, and counties. However, many governments are special purpose, including school districts, sanitary districts, public employee retirement systems,

ILLUSTRATION 2–8 Statement of Cash Flows—Proprietary Funds

SAMPLE CITY
Statement of Cash Flows
Proprietary Funds
For the Year Ended December 31, 2004

	Business-Type Activities—Enterprise Funds			Governmental Activities–Internal Service Funds
	Water and Sewer	Parking Facilities	Totals	
Cash flows from operating activities:				
Receipts from customers	$11,400,200	$1,345,292	$12,745,492	$15,326,343
Payments to suppliers	(2,725,349)	(365,137)	(3,090,486)	(2,812,238)
Payments to employees	(3,360,055)	(750,828)	(4,110,883)	(4,209,688)
Internal activity—payments to other funds	(1,296,768)	—	(1,296,768)	—
Claims paid	—	—	—	(8,482,451)
Other receipts (payments)	(2,325,483)	—	(2,325,483)	1,061,118
Net cash provided by operating activities	1,692,545	229,327	1,921,872	883,084
Cash flows from noncapital financing activities:				
Operating subsidies and transfers to other funds	(290,000)	(211,409)	(501,409)	(175,033)
Cash flows from capital and related financing activities:				
Proceeds from capital debt	4,041,322	8,660,778	12,702,100	—
Capital contributions	1,645,919	—	1,645,919	—
Purchases of capital assets	(4,194,035)	(144,716)	(4,338,751)	(400,086)
Principal paid on capital debt	(2,178,491)	(8,895,000)	(11,073,491)	(954,137)
Interest paid on capital debt	(1,479,708)	(1,166,546)	(2,646,254)	41,616
Other receipts (payments)	—	19,174	19,174	131,416
Net cash (used) by capital and related financing activities	(2,164,993)	(1,526,310)	(3,691,303)	(1,264,423)

Cash flows from investing activities:

Proceeds from sales and maturities of investments			
Interest and dividends	454,793	143,747	15,684
			129,550
Net cash provided by investing activities	454,793	143,747	145,234
Net (decrease) in cash and cash equivalents	(307,655)	(1,364,645)	(411,138)
Balances—beginning of the year	8,724,308	3,227,135	3,747,237
Balances—end of the year	$ 8,416,653	$ 1,862,490	$ 3,336,099
Reconciliation of operating income (loss) to net cash provided (used) by operating activities:			
Operating income (loss)	$ 4,422,127	$ (238,804)	$ 4,183,323
Adjustments to reconcile operating income to net cash provided (used) by operating activities:			
Depreciation expense	1,163,140	542,049	1,705,189
Change in assets and liabilities:			
Receivables, net	653,264	1,205	654,469
Inventories	2,829	—	2,829
Accounts and other payables	(297,446)	(86,643)	(384,089)
Accrued expenses	(4,251,369)	11,520	(4,239,849)
Net cash provided by operating activities	$ 1,692,545	$ 229,327	$ 1,921,872

	598,540
	598,540
	(1,672,300)
	11,951,443
	$10,279,143

	31,941
	39,790
	475,212
	(831,199)
	$ 883,084

	1,707,872

Source: GASB *Statement 34*, p. 229

ILLUSTRATION 2–9 Statements of Fiduciary Net Assets

SAMPLE CITY
Statement of Fiduciary Net Assets
Fiduciary Funds
December 31, 2004

Assets	Employee Retirement Plan	Private-Purpose Trusts	Agency Funds
Cash and cash equivalents	$ 1,973	$ 1,250	$ 44,889
Receivables:			
Interest and dividends	508,475	760	—
Other receivables	6,826	—	183,161
Total receivables	515,301	760	183,161
Investments, at fair value:			
U.S. government obligations	13,056,037	80,000	—
Municipal bonds	6,528,019	—	—
Corporate bonds	16,320,047	—	—
Corporate stocks	26,112,075	—	—
Other investments	3,264,009	—	—
Total investments	65,280,187	80,000	—
Total assets	65,797,461	82,010	$228,050
Liabilities			
Accounts payable	—	1,234	—
Refunds payable and others	1,358	—	228,050
Total liabilities	1,358	1,234	$228,050
Net assets			
Held in trust for pension benefits and other purposes	$65,796,103	$80,776	

Source: GASB *Statement 34*, pp. 235–6.

tollway systems, and fire protection districts. How financial information is reported by special purpose governments depends on whether those governments are governmental or business-type in nature, or both. Paragraph 15 of *Statement 34* provides the following definitions:

> Governmental activities generally are financed through taxes, intergovernmental revenues, and other nonexchange revenues. These activities are usually reported in governmental funds and internal service funds. Business-type activities are financed in whole or in part by fees charged to external parties for goods or services. These activities are usually reported in enterprise funds.

Special purpose governments that have more than one governmental activity, or that have both governmental and business-type activities, are required to present both government-wide and fund reporting, as described previously. This reporting includes MD&A, the basic financial statements and notes, and RSI. Special purpose governments that have only one governmental program may combine the fund and government-wide statements, using separate columns and a reconciliation, or use other simplified approaches. See Illustrations 9–1 and 9–2 for examples. Special purpose governments that have only business-type activities should report only the financial statements required for enterprise funds. These would include:

ILLUSTRATION 2-9 (Continued)

SAMPLE CITY
Statement of Changes in Fiduciary Net Assets
Fiduciary Funds
For the Year Ended December 31, 2004

	Employee Retirement Plan	Private-Purpose Trusts
Additions		
Contributions:		
Employer	$ 2,721,341	$ —
Plan members	1,421,233	—
Total contributions	4,142,574	—
Investment earnings:		
Net (decrease) in fair value of investments	(272,522)	—
Interest	2,460,871	4,560
Dividends	1,445,273	—
Total investment earnings	3,633,622	4,560
Less investment expense	216,428	—
Net investment earnings	3,417,194	4,560
Total additions	7,559,768	4,560
Deductions		
Benefits	2,453,047	3,800
Refunds of contributions	464,691	—
Administrative expenses	87,532	678
Total deductions	3,005,270	4,478
Change in net assets	4,554,498	82
Net assets—beginning of the year	61,241,605	80,694
Net assets—end of the year	$65,796,103	$80,776

Source: GASB *Statement 34*, pp. 235–6.

- MD&A
- Statement of Net Assets, or Balance Sheet
- Statement of Revenues, Expenses, and Changes in Fund Net Assets
- Statement of Cash Flows
- Notes to the Financial Statements
- RSI, other than MD&A, as appropriate.

Special purpose governments that are fiduciary only in nature, such as public employee retirement systems (PERS), are to prepare only those statements required for fiduciary funds, including MD&A, a Statement of Fiduciary Net Assets, a Statement of Changes in Fiduciary Net Assets, and notes to the financial statements.

PUBLIC COLLEGES AND UNIVERSITIES

In November 1999 GASB issued *Statement 35, Basic Financial Statements—and Management's Discussion and Analysis—for Public Colleges and Universities*. *Statement 35* requires that public colleges and universities be folded into the reporting model of *Statement 34*. These institutions will be able to choose between

ILLUSTRATION 2–10 Budgetary Comparison Schedule

SAMPLE CITY
Schedule of Revenues, Expenditures, and Changes in Fund Balances—Budget and Actual
General Fund
For the Year Ended December 31, 2004

| | Budgeted Amounts | | Actual Amounts | Budget to GAAP | Actual Amounts |
	Original	Final	Budgetary Basis	Differences Over (Under)	GAAP Basis
REVENUES					
Property taxes	$52,017,833	$51,853,018	$51,173,436	$ —	$51,173,436
Other taxes—franchise and public service	12,841,209	12,836,024	13,025,392	—	13,025,392
Fees and fines	718,800	718,800	606,946	—	606,946
Licenses and permits	2,126,6000	2,126,600	2,287,794	—	2,287,794
Intergovernmental	6,905,898	6,571,360	6,119,938	—	6,119,938
Charges for services	12,392,972	11,202,150	11,374,460	—	11,374,460
Interest	1,015,945	550,000	552,325	—	552,325
Miscellaneous	3,024,292	1,220,991	881,874	—	881,874
Total revenues	91,043,549	87,078,943	86,022,165		86,022,165
EXPENDITURES					
Current:					
General government (including contingencies and miscellaneous)	11,837,534	9,468,155	8,621,500	(9,335) (1)	8,630,835
Public safety	33,050,966	33,983,706	33,799,709	70,086 (1)	33,729,623
Public works	5,215,630	5,025,848	4,993,187	17,412 (1)	4,975,775
Engineering services	1,296,275	1,296,990	1,296,990	(2,655) (1)	1,299,645
Health and sanitation	5,756,250	6,174,653	6,174,653	104,621 (1)	6,070,032
Cemetery	724,500	724,500	706,205	—	706,305
Culture and recreation	11,059,140	11,368,070	11,289,146	(122,539) (1)	11,411,685
Education—payment to school district	22,000,000	22,000,000	21,893,273	—	21,893,273
Total expenditures	90,940,295	90,041,922	88,774,763	57,590	88,717,173

Excess (deficiency) of revenues over expenditures	103,254	(2,962,979)	(2,752,598)	57,590	(2,695,008)
OTHER FINANCING SOURCES (USES)					
Transfers in	939,525	130,000	129,323	—	129,323
Transfers out	(2,970,256)	(2,163,759)	(2,163,759)	—	(2,163,759)
Total other financing sources and uses	(2,030,731)	(2,033,759)	(2,034,436)	—	(2,034,436)
SPECIAL ITEM					
Proceeds from sale of park land	1,355,250	3,500,000	3,476,488	—	3,476,488
Net change in fund balance	(572,227)	(1,496,738)	(1,310,546)	57,590	(1,252,956)
Fund balances—beginning	3,528,750	2,742,799	2,742,799	165,523	2,908,322
Fund balances—ending	$ 2,956,523	$ 1,246,061	$ 1,432,253 (2)	$ 223,113	$ 1,655,366

Explanation of differences:

1. The City budgets for claims and compensated absences only to the extent expected to be paid, rather than on the modified accrual basis. (129,100)

   Encumbrances for equipment and supplies ordered but not received are reported in the year *the orders are placed* for budgetary purposes, but are reported in the year the equipment and supplies are received for GAAP purposes. 186,690

   Net increase in fund balance—budget to GAAP $ 57,590

2. The amount reported as "fund balance" on the budgetary basis of accounting derives from the basis of accounting used in preparing the City's budget. This amount differs from the fund balance reported in the statement of revenues, expenditures, and changes in fund balances (Section 2200, paragraph .915, C-2) because of the cumulative effect of transactions such as those described above.

Source: [*GASBS 34*, ¶477, Illustrations G–1–G–4].

ILLUSTRATION 2–11 Condition Rating of the City's Street System

	Percentage of Lane-Miles in Good or Better Condition		
	2004	2003	2002
Main arterial	93.2%	91.5%	92.0%
Arterial	85.2	81.6	84.3
Secondary	87.2	84.5	86.8
Overall system	87.0	85.5	87.3

	Percentage of Lane-Miles in Substandard Condition		
	2004	2003	2002
Main arterial	1.7%	2.6%	3.1%
Arterial	3.5	6.4	5.9
Secondary	2.1	3.4	3.8
Overall system	2.2	3.6	3.9

Comparison of Needed-to-Actual Maintenance/Preservation (in Thousands)					
	2004	2003	2002	2001	2000
Main arterial:					
Needed	$2,476	$2,342	$2,558	$2,401	$2,145
Actual	2,601	2,552	2,432	2,279	2,271
Arterial:					
Needed	1,485	1,405	1,535	1,441	1,287
Actual	1,560	1,531	1,459	1,367	1,362
Secondary:					
Needed	990	937	1,023	960	858
Actual	1,040	1,021	972	911	908
Overall system:					
Needed	4,951	4,684	5,116	4,802	4,290
Actual	5,201	5,104	4,863	4,557	4,541
Difference	250	420	(253)	(245)	251

Note: The condition of road pavement is measured using the XYZ pavement management system, which is based on a weighted average of six distress factors found in pavement surfaces. The XYZ pavement management system uses a measurement scale that is based on a condition index ranging from zero for a failed pavement to 100 for a pavement in perfect condition. The condition index is used to classify roads in good or better condition (70–100), fair condition (50–69), and substandard condition (less than 50). It is the City's policy to maintain at least 85 percent of its street system at a good or better condition level. No more than 10 percent should be in a substandard condition. Condition assessments are determined every year.

Source: GASB *Statement 34*, page 277.

reporting as business-type activities (only), governmental activities (only) or as governmental and business-type activities. The latter would most likely be chosen by community colleges with the power to tax. Most other institutions will likely choose the alternative to report as business-type activities. Illustrative financial statements are provided in *Statement 35*. Accounting for public colleges and universities is discussed, along with accounting for other governmental not-for-profit organizations, in Chapter 9.

ILLUSTRATION 2–12 Combining Balance Sheet

SAMPLE CITY
Combining Balance Sheet
Nonmajor Governmental Funds
December 31, 2004

	Special Revenue Funds				Debt Service Funds			Capital Projects Fund	Permanent Fund	Total Nonmajor Governmental Funds
	Impact Fees	Local Gas Tax	Historic District	Total	Central City Development	Community Redevelopment	Total	Bridge	Cemetery Care	
Assets										
Cash and cash equivalents	$371,413	$1,999,819	$189,880	$2,561,112	$ 677,143	$ 164,861	$ 842,004	$1,141,648	$1,062,028	$ 5,606,792
Investments	—	—	—	—	941,510	2,200,470	3,141,980	—	343,272	3,485,252
Receivables, net	—	10,221	—	10,221	—	—	—	—	—	10,221
Receivable from other governments	—	129,883	4,836	134,719	—	—	—	1,461,319	—	1,596,038
Total assets	$371,413	$2,139,923	$194,716	$2,706,052	$1,618,653	$2,365,331	$3,983,984	$2,602,967	$1,405,300	$10,698,303
Liabilities and fund balances										
Liabilities:										
Accounts payable	$ 61,165	$ 170,615	$ 4,836	$ 236,616	$ 151,922	$ —	$ 151,922	$ 686,293	$ —	$ 1,074,831
Total liabilities	61,165	170,615	4,836	236,616	151,922	—	151,922	686,293	—	1,074,831
Fund balances:										
Reserved for:										
Encumbrances	176,487	962,231	—	1,138,718	—	—	—	675,404	—	1,814,122
Debt service	—	—	—	—	1,466,731	2,365,331	3,832,062	—	—	3,832,062
Other purposes	—	—	—	—	—	—	—	—	1,405,300	1,405,300
Unreserved	133,761	1,007,077	189,880	1,330,718	—	—	—	1,241,270	—	2,571,988
Total fund balances	310,248	1,969,308	189,880	2,469,436	1,466,731	2,365,331	3,832,062	1,916,674	1,405,300	9,623,472
Total liabilities and fund balances	$371,413	$2,139,923	$194,716	$2,706,052	$1,618,653	$2,365,331	$3,983,984	$2,602,967	$1,405,300	$10,698,303

Source: *GASB Statement 34*, pp. 280–281.

OTHER GOVERNMENTAL NOT-FOR-PROFIT ORGANIZATIONS

Certain not-for-profit organizations may be determined to be governmental in nature for accounting purposes, under the definition outlined in Chapter 1. This might include foundations of public colleges and universities, public schools, and other governmental units. Museums, performing arts organizations, and public health organizations might also be considered governmental. The general rule is the same as it is for public colleges and universities and for special governmental units. Required reports would depend on whether the entity is considered governmental, business-type, or governmental and business-type in nature. An exception is made for certain not-for-profit governmental units that had been following the provisions of GASB *Statement 29*. Not-for-profit governmental entities using prior accounting and reporting principles under AICPA Statement of Position 78–10 or under the AICPA Audits of Voluntary Health and Welfare Guide (see Chapter 10) may choose to report as business-type activities, even if the criteria are not met. This is to avoid requiring those governmental not-for-profits to create modified accrual accounting statements.

Questions and Exercises

2–1. Using the Comprehensive Annual Financial Report obtained for Exercise 1–1, answer the following questions.

   a. Compare the items discussed in the MD&A in your CAFR with the list of items in this chapter. Which topics listed in this chapter are not in your CAFR? Which topics are in your CAFR that are not listed in this chapter? Do you feel your CAFR has a reasonably complete discussion?

   b. From the MD&A in your report, write a short summary of (1) the financial condition of your government, (2) a comparison of revenues compared with the prior year, (3) a comparison of expenses compared with the prior year, and (4) a comparison of budgeted and actual activity.

   c. From the Statement of Net Assets, write down the following: (1) unrestricted net assets—governmental activities; (2) unrestricted net assets—business-type activities; (3) restricted net assets by restriction—governmental activities; (4) restricted net assets by restriction—business-type activities; and (5) unrestricted and restricted net assets—component units.

   d. From the Statement of Activities, write down the following: (1) net program expense (or revenue)—governmental activities; (2) net program expense (or revenue)—business-type activities; (3) net program expense (or revenue)—component units; (4) change in net assets—governmental activities; (5) change in net assets—business-type activities; and (6) change in net assets—component units. Do the ending net asset figures in this statement agree with the net asset figures in the Statement of Net Assets?

e. From the Statement of Revenues, Expenditures, and Changes in Fund Balances for Governmental Funds, write the names of the major governmental funds. Write down the net change in fund balance for each major fund.

f. From the governmental fund statements, take one major fund (other than the General Fund) and prove, using the 10 percent and 5 percent criteria described in this chapter, that the fund is required to be reported as a major fund. From the Statement of Revenues, Expenses, and Changes in Fund Net Assets (or Statement of Changes in Net Assets), list the major enterprise funds. For each, write down (1) the operating income, (2) the net income (loss) before contributions and transfers, and (3) the change in net assets.

2–2. For each of the following, select the letter corresponding with the *best* answer.

1. Which of the following is not part of the basic financial statements?
   a. Government-wide Statement of Net Assets.
   b. Proprietary Funds Statement of Revenues, Expenses, and Changes in Fund Net Assets.
   c. Combining Balance Sheet–Nonmajor Governmental Funds.
   d. Notes to the Financial Statements.

2. Which of the following could be a component unit?
   a. The State of Illinois.
   b. The City of DeKalb.
   c. The Police Department of the City of DeKalb.
   d. The DeKalb Public Library.

3. Which of the following is true regarding the Management's Discussion & Analysis (MD&A) section of a Comprehensive Annual Financial Report?
   a. The MD&A is considered Required Supplementary Information.
   b. The MD&A is normally included in the audit scope.
   c. The MD&A is part of the Introductory Section of the CAFR.
   d. The MD&A has no specific content requirements; the content is entirely up to the management of the reporting government.

4. Which of the following is true regarding the government-wide financial statements?
   a. The government-wide financial statements include the Statement of Net Assets and Statement of Activities.
   b. The government-wide financial statements are to be prepared using the economic resources measurement focus and accrual basis of accounting.

c. The government-wide financial statements include information for governmental activities, business-type activities, the total primary government, and component units.
d. All of the above are true.

5. In the government-wide Statement of Net Assets:
   a. Assets and liabilities must be reported as classified between current and long term.
   b. Net assets are categorized as reserved and unreserved.
   c. Designations of net assets may not be presented.
   d. Prior-year information must be presented.

6. In the Statement of Activities:
   a. All expenses are subtracted from all revenues to get net income.
   b. It is possible to determine the net program expense (revenue) for major functions and programs of the primary government and component units.
   c. Some internally generated tax revenues are considered program revenues and others are considered general revenues.
   d. Extraordinary items are those that are either unusual in nature or infrequent in occurrence.

7. Fund financial statements are to be prepared for which of the following fund categories?
   a. Governmental
   b. Fiduciary
   c. Proprietary
   d. All of the above

8. In the governmental funds Statement of Revenues, Expenditures, and Changes in Fund Balances:
   a. Net assets are categorized as invested in plant, net of related debt, restricted, and unrestricted.
   b. Expenditures are classified as current, debt service, and capital outlay.
   c. Columns are presented for all governmental funds.
   d. The end (bottom) of the statement reflects the change in net assets of all funds.

9. Which of the following are the statements required for proprietary funds?
   a. Balance Sheet and Statement of Revenues, Expenditures, and Changes in Fund Balances.
   b. Statement of Fund Net Assets (or Balance Sheet), Statement of Revenues, Expenses, and Changes in Fund Net Assets, and Statement of Cash Flows.

c. Statement of Net Assets (or Balance Sheet), Statement of Revenues, Expenditures, and Changes in Fund Balances, and Statement of Cash Flows.

d. Statement of Net Assets (or Balance Sheet) and Statement of Revenues, Expenses, and Changes in Net Assets.

10. Which of the following is true regarding financial reporting under GASB *Statement 34*?

   a. A comparison of budget and actual revenues and expenditures for the General Fund is required as part of the basic financial statements.

   b. Infrastructure must be recorded and depreciated as part of the Statement of Activities in the basic financial statements.

   c. Public colleges and universities are to report in exactly the same manner as private colleges and universities.

   d. Special purpose governments that have only business-type activities are permitted to report only the financial statements required for enterprise funds.

2–3. For each of the following, select the letter corresponding with the *best* answer.

1. Which of the following is not part of the basic financial statements?

   a. Governmental funds Statement of Revenues, Expenditures, and Changes in Fund Balances.

   b. Budgetary Comparison Schedules—General and Special Revenue Funds. Required Supplementary

   c. Government-wide Statement of Activities.

   d. Notes to the financial statements.

2. Which of the following is *not* true regarding GASB requirements pertaining to the financial reporting entity?

   a. In order to be considered a component unit, an entity must be legally separate from its primary government. T

   b. The two methods specified for reporting component units are blending and discrete presentation. T

   c. An example of a reporting entity might be when a county is considered to be a component unit of a state, the primary government. F

   d. A component unit might be considered the nucleus for its own reporting entity when it issues its own financial statements. T

3. Which of the following is *not* true regarding the organization of the Comprehensive Annual Financial Report (CAFR)?

   a. The three major sections are introductory, financial, and statistical.

   b. The Management's Discussion and Analysis (MD&A) is considered to be part of the Introductory Section.

   c. The auditor's report is considered to be part of the financial section.

d. Basic financial statements include the government-wide statements, the fund financial statements, and the notes to the financial statements.

4. Which of the following is *not* true regarding the government-wide financial statements?
   a. The government-wide financial statements include the Statement of Net Assets and the Statement of Activities.
   b. The government-wide financial statements are prepared on the current financial resources measurement focus for governmental activities and the economic resources measurement focus for business-type activities.
   c. Prior-year data may be presented but are not required.
   d. Works of art, historical treasures, and similar assets may or may not be capitalized, depending on whether or not those assets are determined to be collections.

5. Which of the following would be considered "restricted" in the government-wide Statement of Net Assets?
   a. A contribution to a public university restricted by a donor.
   b. A state grant to a municipality restricted by state legislation.
   c. A local tax, restricted by local legislation to a specific purpose.
   d. All of the above.

6. With regard to recording infrastructure by state and local governments
   a. Infrastructure must be recorded and depreciated, unless a modified approach is used, in which case, depreciation is not required.
   b. Infrastructure must be recorded and depreciated in all cases.
   c. Infrastructure is not to be recorded and depreciated.
   d. State and local governments have the option, but are not required, to record and depreciate infrastructure.

7. With regard to determining "major" funds for the fund financial statements
   a. The general fund is always considered major.
   b. Other funds are considered major if both of the following conditions exist: (1) total assets, liabilities, revenues, expenditures/expenses of that individual governmental or enterprise fund constitute 10 percent of the governmental or enterprise category, and (2) total assets, liabilities, revenues, expenditures/expenses are 5 percent of the total of the governmental and enterprise category.
   c. A government may choose to reflect a fund as major even if it does not meet the criteria for major funds.
   d. All of the above are true.

8. The fund statements required for fiduciary funds include:
   a. Balance Sheet, Statement of Activities.

b. Statement of Net Assets, Statement of Revenues, Expenses, and Changes in Net Assets, and Statement of Cash Flows.
   c. Statement of Fiduciary Net Assets and Statement of Changes in Fiduciary Net Assets.
   d. None of the above; statements are not required for fiduciary funds.
9. Which of the following is *not* true regarding the notes to the financial statements?
   a. Notes are considered part of the basic financial statements.
   b. The notes must include a summary of significant accounting policies.
   c. The notes include disclosure of the information necessary to use the modified approach for infrastructure.
   d. None of the above; all are true regarding the notes to the financial statements.
10. Regarding special purpose governments:
   a. Special purpose governments that have more than one governmental activity or that have both governmental and business-type activities are required to present both government-wide and fund reporting.
   b. Special purpose governments that have only business-type activities are permitted to report only those statements required for enterprise funds.
   c. Special purpose governments that are fiduciary only in nature, such as an independent pension plan, are to prepare only those statements required for fiduciary funds.
   d. All of the above are true.

2–4. With regard to GASB rules for the financial reporting entity, answer the following:
   a. Define the financial reporting entity.
   b. Define and give an example of a primary government.
   c. Define and give an example of a component unit.
   d. Define and describe the two methods of reporting the primary government and component units in the financial reporting entity.

2–5. With regard to the Comprehensive Annual Financial Report (CAFR):
   a. What are the three major sections?
   b. List the government-wide statements. Indicate the measurement focus and basis of accounting used for the government-wide statements.
   c. List the governmental fund statements. Indicate the measurement focus and basis of accounting used for the governmental fund statements.
   d. List the proprietary fund statements. Indicate the measurement focus and basis of accounting used for the proprietary fund statements.
   e. List the fiduciary fund statements. Describe the measurement focus and basis of accounting used for the fiduciary fund statements.

f. Outline the reports and schedules to be reported as required supplementary information.

2–6. Look at the HUD Programs Fund, reported as a major fund in Illustrations 2–3 and 2–4. Prove that the HUD Programs Fund is required to be a major fund.

  a. First, apply the 10 percent test to assets, liabilities, revenues, and expenditures for governmental funds.

  b. For those categories that survive the first step, apply the 5 percent test by looking at totals for governmental and enterprise funds. Enterprise funds are shown in Illustrations 2–6 and 2–7, if applicable.

2–7. The following information is available for the preparation of the government-wide financial statements for the City of Southern Springs as of April 30, 2004:

Cash and cash equivalents, governmental activities	$ 1,880,000
Cash and cash equivalents, business-type activities	850,000
Receivables, governmental activities	459,000
Receivables, business-type activities	1,330,000
Inventories, business-type activities	520,000
Capital assets, net, governmental activities	12,500,000
Capital assets, net, business-type activities	10,340,000
Accounts payable, governmental activities	650,000
Accounts payable, business-type activities	559,000
Noncurrent liabilities, governmental activities	5,350,000
Noncurrent liabilities, business-type activities	3,210,000
Net assets, invested in capital assets, net, governmental activities	8,123,000
Net assets, invested in capital assets, net, business-type activities	7,159,000
Net assets, restricted for debt service, governmental activities	654,000
Net assets, restricted for debt service, business-type activities	323,000

From the preceding information, prepare, in good form, a Statement of Net Assets for the City of Southern Springs as of April 30, 2004. Include the unrestricted net assets, which is to be computed from this information. Include a total column.

2–8. The following information is available for the preparation of the government-wide financial statements for the City of Northern Pines for the year ended June 30, 2004:

Expenses:	
General government	$10,300,000
Public safety	23,900,000
Public works	11,290,000
Health and sanitation	6,210,000
Culture and recreation	4,198,000
Interest on long-term debt, governmental type	621,000
Water and sewer system	11,550,000
Parking system	419,000

Revenues:
Charges for services, general government	1,110,000
Charges for services, public safety	210,000
Operating grant, public safety	698,000
Charges for services, health and sanitation	2,555,000
Operating grant, health and sanitation	1,210,000
Charges for services, culture and recreation	2,198,000
Charges for services, water and sewer	11,578,000
Charges for services, parking system	398,000
Property taxes	27,112,000
Sales taxes	20,698,000
Investment earnings, business-type	319,000
Special item—gain on sale of unused land, Governmental type	1,250,000
Transfer from governmental activities to Business-type activities	688,000
Net assets, July 1, 2003, governmental activities	13,222,000
Net assets, July 1, 2003, business-type activities	22,333,000

From the previous information, prepare, in good form, a Statement of Activities for the City of Northern Pines for the year ended June 30, 2004. Northern Pines has no component units.

2–9. The following general fund information is available for the preparation of the financial statements for the City of Eastern Shores for the year ended September 30, 2004:

Revenues:	
Property taxes	$16,000,000
Sales taxes	23,216,000
Fees and fines	1,124,000
Licenses and permits	1,921,000
Intergovernmental	868,000
Investment earnings	654,000
Expenditures:	
Current:	
General government	8,192,000
Public safety	24,444,000
Public works	6,211,000
Health and sanitation	1,193,000
Culture and recreation	2,154,000
Debt service—principal	652,000
Debt service—interest	821,000
Proceeds of long-term, capital-related debt	1,210,000
Transfer to special revenue fund	1,119,000
Special item—proceeds from sale of land	821,000
Fund balance, October 1, 2003	13,211,000

From the information given above, prepare, in good form, a General Fund Statement of Revenues, Expenditures, and Changes in Fund Balances for the City of Eastern Shores General Fund for the Year Ended September 30, 2004.

2–10. The following water and sewer fund information is available for the preparation of the financial statements for the City of Western Sands for the year ended December 31, 2004:

Operating revenues—charges for services	$18,387,000
Operating expenses:	
Personal services	6,977,000
Contractual services	2,195,000
Utilities	888,000
Repairs and maintenance	1,492,000
Depreciation	5,922,000
Interest revenue	129,000
Interest expense	934,000
Capital contributions	1,632,000
Transfer to general fund	1,965,000
Net assets, January 1, 2004	13,219,000

From the information given above, prepare, in good form, a Water and Sewer Fund column for the proprietary fund Statement of Revenues, Expenses, and Changes in Fund Net Assets for the year ended December 31, 2004.

2–11. Go to the website for the Government Finance Officers Association (www.gfoa.org.). You will need to go to the "Awards Programs" and "GFOA Forms" addresses to answer the following questions:

   a. Give a general description of the GFOA Certificate of Achievement for Excellence in Financial Reporting Program. What percentage of municipalities and counties over 50,000 in population participate in the program? How many states participate? How many reports were submitted to the 2000 (or whatever year is presented) awards program?

   b. If possible, list at least three award winners from your state.

   c. If possible, list at least three members of the review committee from your state.

   d. Verify that question 5–1 of the GFOA Questionnaire for the new reporting model requires the same basic financial statements as listed in this text. Access to Adobe Acrobat reader is necessary to answer this question. Access through "forms."

Continuous Problem

2–C. Open a general journal for the Street and Highway Fund, a special revenue fund. Use two pages of 8½-by-11 loose-leaf ledger paper or its equivalent. Use the format illustrated in Problem 1–C. Also, open a general ledger for the Street and Highway Fund, using the format shown in Problem 1–C. Use three pages of the ledger paper, allowing six lines for each of the following accounts. Post the beginning balances of the balance sheet accounts from the prior-year balance sheet. The use of account numbers in optional. The following account numbers are all preceded by an "02," indicating the Street and Highway Fund.

Cash (02-101)
Investments (02-111)
Due from State Government (02-141)
Accounts Payable (02-201)
Fund Balance Reserved for Encumbrances (02-311)
Fund Balance—Unreserved (02-321)
Revenues Control (02-400)
Expenditures Control (02-500)
Estimated Revenues Control (02-600)
Appropriations Control (02-700)
Encumbrances Control (02-800)
Budgetary Fund Balance (02-900)
Budgetary Fund Balance Reserved for Encumbrances (02-950)

CITY OF EVERLASTING SUNSHINE
Street and Highway Fund Balance Sheet
As of December 31, 2003

Assets

Cash	$ 6,500
Investments	55,000
Due from state government	200,000
Total assets	$261,500

Liabilities and Fund Equity

Liabilities:	
Accounts payable	$ 6,300
Fund equity:	
Fund balance—unreserved	255,200
Total liabilities and fund equity	$261,500

Chapter Three

Budgetary Accounting for the General and Special Revenue Funds

The financial reporting model reflected in Chapter 2 requires, as a part of Required Supplementary Information (RSI), budgetary comparison schedules for the General Fund (see Illustration 2–10) and for all major special revenue funds for which an annual budget is legally adopted. Alternatively, Budgetary Comparison Statements may be prepared. This chapter illustrates how governments record the budget in the accounts to produce these schedules (or statements). In addition, this chapter discusses the budgetary process, suggests how one revenue source—the property tax—is planned, and provides an introduction to detailed revenue and expenditure accounting.

The General Fund of a state or local governmental unit is the entity that accounts for all the assets and resources used for financing the general administration of the unit and the traditional services provided to the people. GASB standards require that each governmental reporting entity display only *one* General Fund in its basic financial statements.

A typical governmental unit now engages in many activities that, for legal and historical reasons, are financed by sources other than those available to the General Fund. Whenever a tax or other revenue source is authorized by a legislative body to be used for a specified purpose only, a governmental unit availing itself of that source may create a special revenue fund in order to be able to demonstrate that all revenue from that source was used for the specified purpose. A common example of a special revenue fund is one used to account for state gasoline tax receipts distributed to a local government; in many states, the use of this money is restricted to the construction and maintenance of streets, highways, and bridges. Special revenue funds are commonly used, also, to account for federal and state grants and for libraries and other activities supported by special taxes. Accounting and financial reporting standards applicable to special revenue funds are identical to those applicable to the General Fund.

BUDGETS AS LEGAL DOCUMENTS

The General Fund, special revenue funds, and all other fund types classified as governmental funds are created in conformity with legal requirements. A governmental unit may raise revenues only from sources allowed by law. Laws commonly set a maximum amount that may be raised from each source or set a maximum rate that may be applied to the base used in computation of revenue from a given source. Revenues to be raised pursuant to law during a budget period are set forth in an **Estimated Revenues** budget. Revenues are raised to finance governmental activities, but revenues may be expended only for purposes and in amounts approved by the legislative branch in compliance with laws of competent jurisdictions—this is known as the **appropriations process.** An **appropriations** budget, when enacted into law, is *the legal authorization for the administrators of the governmental unit to incur liabilities during the budget period for purposes specified in the appropriations statute or ordinance and not to exceed the amount specified for each purpose.* When a purchase order or contract is issued as authorized by an appropriation, the appropriation is said to be **encumbered.** When a liability is incurred as authorized by an appropriation, the appropriation is said to be **expended.** At the end of the budget period unencumbered, unexpended appropriations lapse; that is, administrators no longer have the authority to incur liabilities under the lapsed appropriation. Appropriations that are encumbered may or may not carry forward to the next accounting period; if they do carry forward, the encumbrances are said to **not lapse** at year-end; if they do not and must be appropriated for the following year, the encumbrances are said to **lapse.** In nearly all cases, administrators continue to have the authority to disburse cash in payment of liabilities legally incurred in a prior period.

BALANCE SHEET AND OPERATING STATEMENT ACCOUNTS

The General Fund, special revenue funds, and all other fund types classified as governmental funds account only for cash and those other assets that may be expected to be converted into cash in the normal operations of the governmental unit. Similarly, the General Fund or a special revenue fund accounts only for those liabilities that will be liquidated by use of fund assets. General fixed assets and general long-term debt are not reported in governmental funds; only in the government-wide statements.

The arithmetic difference between total fund assets and total fund liabilities is the **Fund Balance.** Residents of the governmental unit have no legal claim on any excess of fund assets over fund liabilities; therefore, the Fund Balance is not analogous to the capital of an investor-owned entity. In order to disclose to readers of the financial statements that a portion of the Fund Balance as of balance sheet date is, for reasons to be explained later, not available for appropriation, **reserve** accounts are established; the portion of equity that is available for appropriation at year-end is disclosed in an account called **Fund Balance—Unreserved.**

In addition to the Balance Sheet accounts just described, the General Fund and special revenue funds account for financial activities during a fiscal year in accounts such as Revenues, Other Financing Sources, Expenditures, and Other Financing Uses. **Revenues** are defined as increases in fund financial resources other than from interfund transfers and debt proceeds. Revenues include taxes, fees, charges for services, and resources provided by other governments. Transfers received from another fund and debt proceeds received by a fund are classified as **Other Financing Sources.** Accounting standards specify that the revenues of all fund types classified as **governmental funds** (the General Fund, special revenue funds, capital projects funds, debt service funds, and permanent funds) be recognized on the *modified accrual* basis, meaning that governmental fund revenues should be recognized in the fiscal year in which they are available for expenditure. See Chapter 4 for a detailed explanation of modified accrual accounting.

Expenditure is a term that replaces both the terms **costs** and **expenses** used in accounting for profit-seeking entities. Expenditures are defined as decreases in fund financial resources other than through interfund transfers. Transfers out of a fund to other funds are classified as **Other Financing Uses.** Under the modified accrual basis, an expenditure is recognized when a liability to be met from fund assets is incurred. An expenditure may be for salaries (an operating item), for supplies (a current asset), for a long-lived capital asset, such as land, buildings, or equipment, or for debt service principal or interest.

An example of the use of transfer accounts occurs in those jurisdictions in which a portion of the taxes recognized as revenue by the general fund of a unit is transferred to a debt service fund that will record expenditures for payment of interest and principal of general obligation debt. The General Fund would record the amounts transferred as Transfers Out; the debt service fund would record the amount received as Transfers In. Thus, use of the transfer accounts achieves the desired objective that revenues be recognized in the fund that levied the taxes and expenditures be recognized in the fund that expends the revenue. Other Financing Sources and Other Financing Uses accounts are closed to Fund Balance in the same manner as Revenues and Expenditures but are disclosed separately in the Combined Statement of Revenues, Expenditures, and Changes in Fund Balances, as shown in Illustration 2–4.

BUDGETS AND BUDGETARY ACCOUNTS

The fact that budgets are legally binding upon administrators has led to the incorporation of budgetary accounts in the General Fund and in special revenue funds for which annual budgets are adopted.

As indicated earlier, governments are required to report budget-actual comparisons as schedules in Required Supplementary Information. Governments may elect instead to provide those comparisons as one of the basic statements rather than as a schedule. The schedule (or statement) must provide the original budget, the final budget, and actual amounts of revenues, expenditures, and other financing sources and uses. A variance column between the final budget and actual is encouraged, but not required. A government may also choose to provide a variance column between the original and revised budgets. The format of the schedule (or statement) may be that of the budget document, or in the form used for the Statement of Revenues, Expenditures, and Changes in Fund Balances (see Illustration 2–10). The latter approach will be illustrated in this chapter.

Whichever approach is used, *the amounts in the Actual column are to be reported on the basis required by law for budget preparation, even if that basis differs from the basis provided in GASB standards.* For example, in some states revenues must be budgeted on the cash basis. If the Budget and Actual columns of the budget-actual comparison schedule differ from GASB standards, the heading of the statement should so indicate.

Budgetary practices of a government may differ from GAAP accounting practices in respects other than basis. GASB standards identify **timing, entity,** and **perspective** differences. Discussion of these differences is beyond the scope of this text; it is sufficient to emphasize that GASB standards require that the amounts shown in the Actual column of the budgetary comparison schedule conform in all respects with practices used to develop the amounts shown in the Budget column of the schedule, so there is a true comparison. Standards further require that, either on the face of the budgetary comparison schedule or in a separate schedule, the amounts in the Actual column of the budgetary comparison schedule must be reconciled with the amounts shown in the Combined Statement of Revenues, Expenditures, and Changes in Fund Balances prepared in conformity with GAAP. Reconciliation of the amounts shown in the two statements is discussed and illustrated in a later section of this chapter.

In order to facilitate preparation of budgets and preparation of the budgetary comparison schedule, accounting systems of governmental funds that are required by law should incorporate **budgetary accounts.** The general ledger control accounts needed to provide appropriate budgetary control are **Estimated Revenues, Appropriations, Encumbrances, Budgetary Fund Balance,** and **Budgetary Fund Balance Reserved for Encumbrances.** Budgeted interfund transfers and proceeds from issuance of debt may be recorded in **Estimated Other Financing Sources** and **Estimated Other Financing Uses** control accounts supported by subsidiary accounts as needed.

At the beginning of the budget period, the Estimated Revenues control account is debited for the total amount of revenues expected to be recognized, as provided in the Revenues budget. The amount of revenue expected from each source specified in the Revenues budget is recorded in a subsidiary ledger account so that the total of subsidiary ledger detail agrees with the debit to the control account, and both agree with the adopted budget. If a separate entry is to be made to record the Revenues budget, the general ledger debit to the Estimated Revenues control account is offset by a credit to Budgetary Fund Balance. The credit balance of the Budgetary Fund Balance account, therefore, is the total amount expected to be available to finance appropriations. Consequently, the accounting entry to record the legally approved appropriations budget is a debit to Budgetary Fund Balance and a credit to Appropriations for the total amount appropriated for the activities accounted for by the fund. The Appropriations control account is supported by a subsidiary ledger kept in the same detail as provided in the appropriations ordinance, so that the total of the subsidiary ledger detail agrees with the credit to the Appropriations control account, and both agree with the adopted budget. The use of the Encumbrances and Budgetary Fund Balance Reserved for Encumbrance account is explained in a following section.

RECORDING THE BUDGET

In order to illustrate entries in journal form to record a budget, assume that the amounts used in the following example have been legally approved as the budget for the General Fund of a certain governmental unit for the fiscal year ending December 31, 2004. As of January 1, 2004, the first day of the fiscal year, the total Estimated Revenues should be recorded in the General Fund general ledger accounts, and the amounts that are expected to be recognized during 2004 from each revenue source specified in the budget should be recorded in the subsidiary ledger accounts. If the budget provided for other financing sources, such as transfers in, Entry 1 would indicate a debit to Estimated Other Financing Sources. An appropriate entry would be as follows:

	General Ledger		Subsidiary Ledger	
	Debits	Credits	Debits	Credits
1. Estimated Revenues Control	1,350,000			
Budgetary Fund Balance		1,350,000		
Revenues Ledger:				
Taxes			$882,500	
Licenses and permits			125,500	
Intergovernmental revenues			200,000	
Charges for services			90,000	
Fines and forfeits			32,500	
Miscellaneous revenues			19,500	

The total Appropriations legally approved for 2004 for the General Fund of the same governmental unit should also be recorded in the General Fund general ledger accounts, and the amounts that are appropriated for each function itemized in the budget should be recorded in subsidiary ledger accounts. An appropriate entry would be as follows:

	General Ledger		Subsidiary Ledger	
	Debits	Credits	Debits	Credits
2. Budgetary Fund Balance	1,300,000			
Appropriations Control		1,225,500		
Estimated Other Financing Uses Control		74,500		
Appropriations Ledger:				
General government				$129,000
Public safety				277,300
Highways and streets				84,500
Sanitation				50,000
Health				47,750
Welfare				51,000
Culture and recreation				44,500
Education				541,450
Other Financing Uses Ledger:				
Transfers out				74,500

It is acceptable to combine the two entries illustrated and make one General Fund entry to record Estimated Revenues, Appropriations, and Estimated Other Financing Uses; in this case there would be a credit to Budgetary Fund Balance for $50,000 (the amount by which Estimated Revenues exceeds Appropriations and Estimated Other Financing Uses).

ACCOUNTING FOR REVENUES

During a fiscal year, actual revenues should be recognized in the general ledger accounts of governmental funds by credits to the Revenues Control account (offset by debits to receivable accounts for revenues susceptible to accrual or by debits to Cash for revenues that are recognized on the cash basis). The general ledger Revenues Control account supported by Revenues subsidiary ledger accounts is kept in exactly the same detail as kept for the Estimated Revenues subsidiary ledger accounts. For example, assume that the General Fund of the governmental unit for which budgetary entries are illustrated in the preceding section collected revenues in cash from the following sources in these amounts:

	General Ledger		Subsidiary Ledger	
	Debits	Credits	Debits	Credits
3. Cash	1,314,500			
Revenues Control		1,314,500		

Revenues Ledger:	
Taxes	$881,300
Licenses and permits	103,000
Intergovernmental revenues	186,500
Charges for services	91,000
Fines and forfeits	33,200
Miscellaneous revenues	19,500

Comparability between Estimated Revenues subsidiary accounts and Revenues subsidiary accounts is necessary so that, periodically throughout the fiscal year, actual revenues from each source can be compared with estimated revenues from that source. Illustration 3–1 shows a form of Revenues subsidiary ledger in which the debit column is subsidiary to the Estimated Revenues general ledger control account and the credit column is subsidiary to the Revenues general ledger control account. Normally, during a fiscal year the amount of revenue budgeted from each source will exceed the amount of revenue from that source realized to date; consequently the Balance column will have a debit balance and may be headed Estimated Revenues Not Yet Realized.

ACCOUNTING FOR ENCUMBRANCES AND EXPENDITURES

An appropriation, when enacted into law, is an authorization for administrators to incur on behalf of the governmental unit liabilities in the amounts specified in the appropriation ordinance or statute for the purposes set forth in that ordinance or statute, during the period of time specified. An appropriation is considered to be **expended** when the authorized liabilities are incurred. Because penalties may be imposed by law on an administrator who incurs liabilities for any amount in excess

ILLUSTRATION 3–1 Revenues Ledger

NAME OF GOVERNMENTAL UNIT Revenues Ledger General Fund					
Year: 2004				Class: Licenses and Permits	
Transactions	Item	Reference	Estimated Revenues DR.	Revenues CR.	Balance DR. (CR.)
2004					
January 2	Budget estimate	(1)	$125,500		$125,500
Various	Collections	(3)		$103,000	22,500
December 31	Budget Revision	(7)	(22,500)		–0–

of that appropriated or for any purpose not covered by an appropriation, prudence dictates that each purchase order and each contract be reviewed before it is signed to determine that a valid and sufficient appropriation exists to which the expenditures can be charged when goods or services are received. Purchase orders and contracts will result in liabilities when the purchase orders are filled and the contracts executed. Such expected liabilities are called **encumbrances.** In order to keep track of purchase orders and contracts outstanding, it is recommended that the Encumbrance Control account (and the subsidiary account for the specific appropriation encumbered) be debited and the Budgetary Fund Balance—Reserved for Encumbrances account credited for the amount of each purchase order or contract issued. When goods or services are received, two entries are necessary: (1) Budgetary Fund Balance—Reserved for Encumbrances is debited, and Encumbrances Control (and the proper subsidiary account) is credited for the amount entered in these accounts when the encumbrance documents were issued; and (2) Expenditures Control (and the proper subsidiary account) is debited and a liability account is credited for the amount to be paid to the creditor. In order to accomplish the necessary matching of Encumbrances and Expenditures, it is necessary that subsidiary ledger classifications of all three correspond exactly. Note that no subsidiary accounts need be kept for Budgetary Fund Balance—Reserved for Encumbrances. At year-end, budgetary authority expires; therefore, the balances of the Expenditures and Encumbrances accounts are closed to Fund Balance—Unreserved. In many jurisdictions, however, the government continues to have authority in subsequent years to receive and pay for goods and services ordered under purchase orders and contracts outstanding at the previous year-end.

The following entries illustrate accounting for Encumbrances and Expenditures for the General Fund of the governmental unit for which entries are illustrated in previous sections of this chapter. Entry 4 reflects purchase orders issued pursuant to the authority contained in the General Fund appropriations; assumed amounts chargeable to each function for which purchase orders are issued on this date are shown in the debits to the Encumbrances subsidiary accounts.

	General Ledger		Subsidiary Ledger	
	Debits	Credits	Debits	Credits
4. Encumbrances Control	500,100			
Budgetary Fund Balance—				
Reserved for Encumbrances		500,100		
Encumbrances Ledger:				
General government			$ 73,200	
Public safety			115,100	
Highways and streets			34,600	
Sanitation			29,300	
Health			16,500	
Welfare			18,700	

Culture and recreation	14,800
Education	197,900

Entries 5a and 5b illustrate entries required to record the receipt of some of the items for which purchase orders were recorded in Entry 4. Note that Entry 4 is made for the amounts estimated at the time purchase orders or other commitment documents are issued. When the purchase orders are filled, the actual amount approved by the governmental unit for payment to the supplier often differs from the estimated amount recorded in the Encumbrances account (and subsidiary ledger accounts) because the quantity of goods actually received differs from the quantity ordered, prices of items have changed, and so on. Since the Encumbrances Control account was debited in Entry 4 for the estimated amount, the Encumbrances Control account must be credited for the same estimate to the extent that purchase orders are filled (or canceled). The balance remaining in the Encumbrances Control account, therefore, is the estimated dollar amount of purchase orders outstanding. Entry 5a shows the entry necessary on the assumption that most purchase orders recorded in Entry 4 have now been filled but purchase orders for general government and education remain outstanding. Expenditures, however, should be recorded at the actual amount the governmental unit agrees to pay the vendors who have filled the purchase orders. Entry 5b shows the entry necessary to record the liability for invoices approved for payment. The fact that estimated and actual amounts differ causes no accounting difficulties as long as goods or services are received in the same fiscal period as ordered. The accounting treatment required when encumbrances outstanding at year-end are filled or canceled in a following year is illustrated in Chapter 4.

	General Ledger		Subsidiary Ledger	
	Debits	Credits	Debits	Credits
5a. Budgetary Fund Balance—Reserved for Encumbrances	492,300			
Encumbrances Control		492,300		
Encumbrances Ledger:				
General government				$ 68,300
Public safety				115,100
Highways and streets				34,600
Sanitation				29,300
Health				16,500
Welfare				18,700
Culture and recreation				14,800
Education				195,000
5b. Expenditures Control	491,800			
Accounts Payable		491,800		

Expenditures Ledger:

General government	$ 69,100
Public safety	115,100
Highways and streets	34,400
Sanitation	29,300
Health	16,600
Welfare	18,700
Culture and recreation	14,800
Education	193,800

The encumbrance procedure is not always needed to make sure that appropriations are not overexpended. For example, although salaries and wages of governmental employees must be chargeable against valid and sufficient appropriations in order to give rise to legal expenditures, many governmental units do not find it necessary to encumber the departmental personal services appropriations for estimated payrolls of recurring, relatively constant amounts. Departments having payrolls that fluctuate greatly from one season to another may follow the encumbrance procedure to make sure that the personal service appropriation is not overexpended. Entry 6 shows the recording of expenditures of appropriations for salaries and wages not previously encumbered, assuming that gross pay is vouchered.

	General Ledger		Subsidiary Ledger	
	Debits	Credits	Debits	Credits
6. Expenditures	663,600			
Accounts Payable		663,600		
Expenditures Ledger:				
General government			$ 47,805	
Public safety			143,295	
Highways and streets			51,000	
Sanitation			26,950	
Health			27,900	
Welfare			28,100	
Culture and recreation			26,100	
Education			312,450	

Illustration 3–2 shows a form of subsidiary ledger that supports all three general ledger control accounts: Appropriations, Expenditures, and Encumbrances. Note that at all times the available balance equals the appropriations less the open encumbrances and the total expenditures. Note also that the available balance is reduced when encumbrances are incurred; it is adjusted when the amount of the purchase order and related expenditure differ; and it is reduced when expenditures are incurred without corresponding purchase orders (such as for salaries).

ILLUSTRATION 3-2

NAME OF GOVERNMENTAL UNIT
Appropriations, Expenditures, and Encumbrances Ledger
General Fund

Year: 2004   Function: Public Safety

		Encumbrances			Expenditures		Appro-priations	Available
Transactions	Reference	Debit	Credit	Open	Debit	Cumulative Total	Credit	Balance
(2)	Budget						$277,300	$277,300
(4)	Purchase Orders Issued	$115,100		$115,100				162,200
(5a)	Invoices							
(5b)	Approved for Payment		$115,100		$115,100	$115,100		162,200
(6)	Payrolls				143,295	258,395		18,905

BUDGET REVISIONS

In most cases, governmental units will prepare and adopt budget revisions. Assume the governmental unit in this example decided to revise the Estimated Revenues budget downward by $36,000 and the Appropriations Budget upward by $8,000:

	General Ledger		Subsidiary Ledger	
	Debits	Credits	Debits	Credits
7. Budgetary Fund Balance	44,000			
Estimated Revenues Control		36,000		
Appropriations Control		8,000		
Revenues Ledger:				
Licenses and permits				$22,500
Intergovernmental revenues				13,500
Appropriations Ledger:				
Highways and streets				1,000
Sanitation				7,000

Budget revisions would require adjustments to the budgetary accounts and balances in the subsidiary ledgers (Illustrations 3–1 and 3–2).

BUDGETARY COMPARISON SCHEDULE

Illustration 3–3 presents a budgetary comparison schedule as it might be prepared by the government in the example. Assume a transfer out in the amount of $74,500 as provided in the budget. This schedule would be included as a part of Required Supplementary Information, or could be prepared as a basic financial statement.

GASB requires a reconciliation between the amount shown as GAAP Expenditures in the basic financial statements and the amount shown in the budgetary comparison schedule. That reconciliation is shown directly in the budgetary comparison schedule or in a separate schedule. Often the only difference relates to the encumbrances that are combined with expenditures in the budgetary comparison schedule. See Illustration 2–10 for an example of a reconciliation.

CLASSIFICATION OF ESTIMATED REVENUES AND REVENUES

In order for administrators to determine whether proposed expenditures can be financed by resources available to the budgeting jurisdiction, a revenue budget should be prepared. The budget should include all sources, including interfund transfers and bond issue proceeds as well as taxes, licenses and permits, fees, forfeits, and

ILLUSTRATION 3-3

NAME OF GOVERNMENTAL UNIT
Budgetary Comparison Schedule
General Fund
For the Year Ended December 31, 2004

	Budgeted Amounts		Actual Amounts (Budgetary Basis)	Variance with Final Budget Positive (Negative)
	Original	Final		
Revenues:				
Taxes	$ 882,500	$ 882,500	$ 881,300	$ (1,200)
Licenses and permits	125,500	103,000	103,000	—
Intergovernmental revenues	200,000	186,500	186,500	—
Charges for services	90,000	90,000	91,000	1,000
Fines and forfeits	32,500	32,500	33,200	700
Miscellaneous revenues	19,500	19,500	19,500	—
Total revenues	1,350,000	1,314,000	1,314,500	500
Expenditures and Encumbrances:				
General government	129,000	129,000	121,805	7,195
Public safety	277,300	277,300	258,395	18,905
Highways and streets	84,500	85,500	85,400	100
Sanitation	50,000	57,000	56,250	750
Health	47,750	47,750	44,500	3,250
Welfare	51,000	51,000	46,800	4,200
Culture and recreation	44,500	44,500	40,900	3,600
Education	541,450	541,450	509,150	32,300
Total Expenditures and Encumbrances	1,225,500	1,233,500	1,163,200	70,300
Excess (Deficiency) of revenues over expenditures and encumbrances	124,500	80,500	151,300	70,800
Other financing sources (uses): transfers out	(74,500)	(74,500)	(74,500)	—
Net change in fund balance	50,000	6,000	76,800	70,800
Fund balance—beginning	332,000	350,000	350,000	—
Fund balance—ending	$ 382,000	$ 356,000	$ 426,800	$70,800

other revenue sources. It should be emphasized that a governmental unit may raise revenues only from sources that are available to it by law.

The primary classification of governmental revenue is by **fund**. Within each fund the major classification is by **source**. Within each major source class it is desirable to have as many secondary classes as are needed to facilitate revenue budgeting and accounting. Commonly used major revenue source classes are:

Taxes	Charges for services
Licenses and permits	Fines and forfeits
Intergovernmental revenues	Miscellaneous revenues

In addition to the revenue source classes listed, an additional revenue source, special assessments, is sometimes utilized. In some jurisdictions, services normally financed by the General Fund or by a special revenue fund may be extended to property owners outside the normal service area of the government or may be provided at a higher level or at more frequent intervals than for the general public to property owners who pay additional fees (special assessments). In such cases, the Special Assessments revenue source class would be utilized by the General Fund or by a special revenue fund, as appropriate.

In order to determine during a fiscal year that revenues are being realized from each budgeted source in amounts consistent with the budget, actual revenues should be accounted for on the same classification system as used in the Estimated Revenues budget. A separate control account, Estimated Other Financing Sources, should be used for interfund transfers and bond issue proceeds.

AD VALOREM TAXES

Ad valorem (based on value) property taxes are a major source of revenue for many local units of government. Property taxes may be imposed against real (e.g., land and buildings) or personal (e.g., motor vehicles) property. When a property tax is imposed (*levied* is the technical term), it is to finance the budget of a particular period. Under accrual accounting, property (or ad valorem) tax revenues should be recognized in the period *for which* they are levied, regardless of when cash is received. Property taxes received before the period for which they are levied should be reported as deferred revenues. Under modified accrual accounting, revenues may not exceed the amount received during a fiscal year plus the amount expected to be received during the first 60 days after the end of the fiscal year. See Chapter 4 for details.

The amount of a property tax levy depends on two factors: (1) the assessed valuation of the property being taxed and (2) the tax rate. The valuation of each parcel of taxable real property and of the taxable property owned by each taxpayer is assigned by a legal process known as **property assessment.** The assessment process differs state by state and, in some states, by jurisdictions within the state. The tax rate is set by one of two widely different procedures: (1) the governmental body simply multiplies the assessed valuation of property in its jurisdiction by a flat rate—either the maximum rate allowable under state law or a rate determined by policy—or (2) the property tax is treated as a residual source of revenue. In the latter event, revenues to be recognized from all sources other than property taxes must be budgeted; the total of those sources must be compared with the total appropriations in order to determine the amount to be raised from property taxes. Illustration

ILLUSTRATION 3–4

CITY OF ANYWHERE
Computation of Amount to Be Raised by Property Taxes for 2004
July 31, 2003

Requirements:		
Estimated expenditures, August 1–December 31, 2003		$ 3,500,000
Proposed appropriations for 2004		8,000,000
Estimated working balance required for beginning of 2005		600,000
Estimated total requirements		$12,100,000
Resources other than tax levy for 2004:		
Actual balance, July 31, 2003	$ 750,000	
Amount to be received from second installment of 2003 taxes	2,000,000	
Miscellaneous receipts expected during balance of 2003	1,600,000	
Revenues expected from sources other than property taxes during 2004	4,300,000	
Estimated total resources other than property tax levy		8,650,000
Amount required from property taxes in 2004		$ 3,450,000

3–4 shows the computation of the total amount of revenues to be raised from property taxes under the assumption that property taxes are a residual source of revenues.

The computation of the amount of revenue to be raised from property taxes is one step in determining the tax levy for the year. A second step is the determination from historical data and economic forecasts of the percentage of the tax levy that is expected to be collectible. (Even though property taxes are a lien against the property, personal property may be removed from the taxing jurisdiction and some parcels of real property may not be salable for enough for the taxing jurisdiction to recover accumulated taxes against the property.) Therefore, the levy must be large enough to allow for estimated uncollectible taxes. For example, assume that the City of Anywhere can reasonably expect to collect only 97 percent of the 2004 levy. Thus, if tax revenue is to be $3,450,000 (per Illustration 3–4), the gross levy must be $3,450,000 ÷ 0.97, or $3,556,701.

When the gross levy is known, the tax rate may be computed on the basis of the assessed valuation of taxable property lying within the taxing jurisdiction. The term **taxable property** is used in the preceding sentence in recognition of the fact that property owned by governmental units and property used by religious and charitable organizations is often not taxable by the local government. Additionally, senior citizens, war veterans, and others may have statutory exemption from taxation for a limited portion of the assessed valuation of property. Continuing the City of Anywhere example, assume that the net assessed valuation of property taxable by that city is $205,500,000. In that case, the gross property tax levy ($3,556,701) is divided by the net assessed valuation ($205,500,000) to determine the property tax rate. The rate would be expressed as "$1.73 per $100 assessed valuation," or "$17.31 per $1,000 assessed valuation"—rounding up the actual decimal fraction (0.017307) to two places to the right of the decimal, as is customary.

CLASSIFICATION OF APPROPRIATIONS AND EXPENDITURES

Recall that an appropriation, when enacted into law, is an authorization to incur liabilities on behalf of the governmental unit for goods, services, and facilities to be used for purposes specified in the appropriation ordinance, or statute, in amounts not in excess of those specified for each purpose. When liabilities authorized by an appropriation have been incurred, the appropriation is said to be expended. Classification by fund is, of course, essential. Within each fund one or more of the following classification schemes are used to meet the needs of financial statement users: (1) function or program, (2) organization unit, (3) activity, (4) character, and (5) object. Common terminology and classifications should be used consistently throughout the budget, the accounts, and the financial reports of each fund.

Examples of classifications by **function** are general government, public safety, and highways and streets. While most governmental units report by function, others report by **program,** such as protection of persons and property and environmental protection. Programs are often performed by more than one department; consequently, program expenditures often cross departmental lines. Examples of classification by **department,** which is useful for budgetary control, are the Mayor's Office and the Police Department. **Activities** are specific and distinguishable lines of work performed by organizational units. Examples of activities are solid waste collection and solid waste disposal, both in the Public Works Department. Classification by **character** deals with the time period involved and includes current expenditures, capital outlays, and debt service. Classification by **object** reports the inputs, or the item or service received, such as personal services, supplies, other services and charges, capital outlays, and debt service. Generally, more detailed object classes are used for each of the major categories.

Questions and Exercises

3–1. Using the annual report obtained for Exercise 1–1, answer the following questions.

   a. Look at the Statement of Revenues, Expenditures, and Changes in Fund Balances for the governmental funds. List the revenue source classes. Do they agree with those sources discussed in this chapter? Are expenditures reported by character? List the functional classifications under the current character classification. Do those classifications agree with those listed in the example shown in this chapter? Are Other

Financing Sources and Uses separately presented? Does your report show transfers in? transfers out? capital leases? proceeds of bonds?

  b. Look at the Budgetary Comparison Schedule in the RSI section of your annual Report (or Budgetary Comparison Statement, if that is used by your government) for the General Fund. Is the budgetary format used, or is the schedule in the format used for the Statement of Revenues, Expenditures, and Changes in Fund Balances? Does the report reflect the original budget, revised budget, and actual figures? Are variance columns presented comparing the actual with the revised budget? comparing the original with the revised budget? Is a reconciliation between the budgetary basis of accounting and GAAP presented on the budgetary comparison schedule or in a separate schedule? What are the major differences, if any? Are budgetary comparison schedules (or statements) presented for special revenue funds? Are all special revenue funds included?

  c. Look at the note that describes the basis of budgeting (usually in the Summary of Significant Accounting Policies). Is the budget prepared on the GAAP basis or some other basis? Are the differences, if any, between the budgetary basis and GAAP clearly explained? Does the note indicate that encumbrance accounting is used? Do unexpended encumbrances lapse at year-end? If unexpended encumbrances lapse, are they normally reappropriated in the following year? Do the notes describe the budget calendar (a separate note may have this information)? Do the notes describe the legal level of budgetary control and the levels at which certain budget revisions might be made? Were budget revisions necessary during the year?

3-2. For each of the following, select the letter corresponding with the *best* answer:

  1. Which of the following in the acquisition of goods and services occurs first?
     a. Expenditure.
     b. Encumbrance.
     c. Appropriation.
     d. Cash payment.

  2. Which of the following is true regarding the term *expenditures?*
     a. Expenditures are decreases in fund financial resources other than through interfund transfers.
     b. Expenditures may be for current, capital outlay, or debt service purposes.
     c. Expenditures are generally recognized when goods and services are received.
     d. All of the above.

3. Debt issue proceeds received by a governmental fund would be recorded as:
   a. a revenue.
   b. an other financing source.
   c. a liability.
   d. none of the above.

4. Which of the following is true regarding governmental budgetary reporting?
   a. Governments must prepare budget-actual statements for all funds.
   b. The budget-actual statement for the general and special revenue funds must be one of the basic financial statements.
   c. The budget-actual schedule (or statement) must provide information on the original as well as the revised budget.
   d. All of the above.

5. Which of the following would be an example of expenditure reporting by character?
   a. Public safety.
   b. Salaries.
   c. Current.
   d. Fire protection.

6. The Board of Commissioners of the City of Belvedire's adopted budget for the year ending July 31, 2004, indicated revenues of $1,000,000 and appropriations of $970,000. When the budget is formally integrated into the accounting records, what is the required journal entry?

		Debits	Credits
a.	Memorandum entry only		
b.	Estimated Revenues Control	1,000,000	
	Appropriations Control		970,000
	Budgetary Fund Balance		30,000
c.	Appropriations Control	1,000,000	
	Estimated Revenues Control		970,000
	Budgetary Fund Balance		30,000
d.	Revenues Receivable	1,000,000	
	Estimated Expenditures		970,000
	General Fund Balance		30,000

7. When a purchase order is issued for the General Fund, which of the following entries would be prepared, assuming the purchase order amount is $500?

	Debits	Credits
a. Encumbrances Control	500	
Budgetary Fund Balance Reserved for Encumbrances		500
b. Expenditures Control	500	
Vouchers Payable		500
c. Memorandum entry only		
d. Budgetary Fund Balance Reserved for Encumbrances	500	
Encumbrances Control		500

8. Assume the following facts for the City of Evanston Police Department for the month of July, 2003, the first month of the fiscal year:

   The appropriation for the year was passed, amounting to $10,000,000. Purchase orders and contracts were issued in the amount of $300,000. Of the purchase orders already mentioned, $250,000 were filled, with invoices amounting to $260,000. Salaries, not encumbered, amounted to $500,000.

   What is the available balance at the end of July 2003?
   a. $9,200,000
   b. $9,240,000
   c. $9,190,000
   d. $9,210,000

9. Which of the following refers to an actual cost rather than an estimate?
   a. expenditure
   b. appropriation
   c. budget
   d. encumbrance

10. The Encumbrances Control account would be decreased when:
    a. Purchase orders are issued.
    b. Goods, related to purchase orders, are received.
    c. Payment is made for goods received.
    d. Budget revisions are made, decreasing Appropriations.

3–3. For each of the following, select the letter corresponding with the *best* answer:
   1. The Fire Department of a certain city received an appropriation in the amount of $13,000,000 for the fiscal year ended June 30, 2004. During the month ended July 31, 2003, the following transactions occurred: (*a*) purchase orders were issued in the amount of $600,000; (*b*) purchase orders, related to (*a*) above, were filled in the amount of $585,000; the related invoice amount was $587,000; invoices were paid in the amount of $540,000; (*c*) salaries were accrued in the amount of

$630,000. The balance available for the Fire Department as of July 31, 2003 is
a. $11,770,000.
b. $11,768,000.
c. $11,830,000.
d. $11,783,000.

2. The City of X adopted an appropriations ordinance in the amount of $23,000,000 for the General Fund for a certain fiscal year. Revenues other than property taxes amounted to $9,000,000. The total market value of taxable property in City X amounted to $1.2 billion. The assessment ratio (assessment percentage of market value) was 33⅓ percent. Homestead, veterans, and other exemptions amounted to $10,000,000, based on assessed value. It is estimated that 2 percent of the assessed taxes will not be collected. The property tax rate per $100 net assessed value would be (rounded to the nearest penny):
a. $3.66.
b. $3.57.
c. $3.59.
d. $3.50.

3. An example of an expenditure classified by object would be:
a. Police Department.
b. Public Safety.
c. Current.
d. Salaries.

4. A certain government passed its budget for the fiscal year ended June 30, 2004. Estimated Revenues amounted to $12,000,000; Appropriations amounted to $11,300,000; Estimated Other Financing Sources amounted to $600,000; and Estimated Other Financing Uses amounted to $700,000. In the budgetary entry, Budgetary Fund Balance would be:
a. Debited for $600,000.
b. Debited for $800,000.
c. Credited for $600,000.
d. Credited for $800,000.

5. When goods, which had previously been encumbered, are received, and the invoice amount is different than the purchase order amount:
a. Budgetary Fund Balance—Reserved for Encumbrances would be credited for the purchase order amount.
b. Encumbrances Control would be debited for the purchase order amount.
c. Encumbrances Control would be credited for the invoice amount.

d. Budgetary Fund Balance—Reserved for Encumbrances would be debited for the purchase order amount.

6. Which of the following is true regarding the Budgetary Comparison Schedule?
   a. Columns are required for the original budget, the revised budget, and the actual amount.
   b. The Budgetary Comparison Schedule is presented as a part of Required Supplementary Information.
   c. The Budgetary Comparison Schedule may be presented as one of the basic financial statements.
   d. All of the above.

7. Which of the following is true regarding the Budgetary Comparison Schedule?
   a. A variance column may be presented but is not required.
   b. The Schedule is required for the General Fund and all major special revenue funds that have a legally adopted annual budget.
   c. The actual presented must be on the budgetary basis, even if the budgetary basis is different than GAAP.
   d. All of the above.

8. If Budgetary Fund Balance is debited in the process of recording a budget in the General Fund, it can be assumed that:
   a. Estimated Revenues and Other Financing Sources exceeded Appropriations and Other Financing Uses.
   b. Estimated Revenues and Other Financing Sources exceeded actual Revenues and Other Financing Sources.
   c. Appropriations and Estimated Other Financing Uses exceeded Estimated Revenues and Other Financing Sources.
   d. Revenues and Other Financing Sources exceeded Estimated Revenues and Estimated Other Financing Sources.

9. Under accrual accounting, property tax revenue, net of estimated uncollectibles is recognized:
   a. For no more than is collected during the fiscal year.
   b. For no more than is collected during the fiscal year plus the amount collected during the first 60 days of the next fiscal year.
   c. Immediately upon the levy, regardless of the date.
   d. In the year for which the tax is levied.

10. Under modified accrual accounting, an expenditure is recognized:
    a. When an appropriation is enacted.
    b. When a purchase order is issued.
    c. When goods or services are received.
    d. When payment is made for the goods or services.

3–4. The City of South Dundee appropriations ordinance for the fiscal year ended June 30, 2004, included an appropriation for the police department in the amount of $18,000,000. During the month of July 2003, the following transactions occurred (in summary):

Purchase orders were issued in the amount of $600,000.
Of the $600,000 in purchase orders, $580,000 were filled, with invoices amounting to $575,000.
Salaries, not encumbered, amounted to $898,000.
A budget appropriations reduction in the amount of $20,000 was approved by the city council.

Prepare an appropriations expenditure ledger for the police department for the month of July, in a format similar to Illustration 3–2.

3–5. Prepare budgetary entries, using general ledger accounts only, for each of the following unrelated situations:
  a. Anticipated revenues are $10 million; anticipated expenditures and encumbrances are $9.8 million.
  b. Anticipated revenues are $9.8 million; anticipated expenditures and encumbrances are $10 million.
  c. Anticipated revenues are $10 million; anticipated transfers from other funds are $1.3 million; anticipated expenditures and encumbrances are $9.8 million; anticipated transfers to other funds are $1.2 million.
  d. Anticipated revenues are $9.8 million; anticipated transfers from other funds are $1.2 million; anticipated expenditures and encumbrances are $10 million; anticipated transfers to other funds are $1.3 million.

3–6. The Baker Independent School District passed an appropriations ordinance for the General Fund for a certain fiscal year in the amount of $50 million. Revenues were anticipated from sources other than the property tax in the amount of $24 million. The total market value of property in the school district amounts to $2 billion, but $200 million is exempt from taxation for religious and other reasons. The assessment ratio (assessment percentage of market value) for all school districts in the state is 33⅓ percent. Owners of property have filed for and received household, old age, and other exemptions in the amount of $80 million. It is anticipated that 2 percent of the assessed taxes will not be collected.
  a. Compute the amount to be raised from property taxes.
  b. Compute the gross levy required to raise revenue in the amount you computed for requirement (*a*). Round the computation to the nearest dollar.
  c. Compute the property tax rate per $100 net assessed valuation.
  d. Compute the property tax rate per $1,000 net assessed valuation (this rate is often called the *millage*). Round fractional cents to the next higher whole cent.

e. You own a home with a market value of $180,000. Compute the gross assessed valuation. You are eligible for a homestead exemption of $2,000; deduct this amount from the gross assessed valuation to determine the net assessed valuation of your house. Multiply the NAV in thousands of dollars by the property tax rate computed in part (d) of this problem to determine the property tax payable on your house.

3–7. For each of the summarized transactions for the Village of Sycamore General Fund, prepare the general ledger journal entries. The year is January 1–December 31, 2004.

   a. The budget was formally adopted, providing for estimated revenues of $1,000,000 and appropriations of $980,000.
   b. Revenues were received, all in cash, in the amount of $1,010,000.
   c. Purchase orders were issued in the amount of $500,000.
   d. Of the $500,000 in (c), purchase orders were filled in the amount of $470,000; the invoice amount was $480,000.
   e. Expenditures, not encumbered, amounted to $460,000.
   f. Closing entries were made. This includes: (1) a reversal of the budgetary entry, (2) closing of the nominal accounts to Fund Balance—Unreserved, and (3) closing of the Budgetary Fund Balance Reserved for Encumbrances to the equity account, Fund Balance—Reserved for Encumbrances. Note that this entry is not illustrated in this chapter.

3–8. Presented here are several transactions and events of the General Fund of Johnson County. All transactions and events relate to calendar year 2004.

   1. Estimated revenues from the following sources were legally budgeted for 2004.

Sales taxes	$ 6,000,000
Fines and forfeits	2,000,000
Licenses and permits	1,750,000
Intergovernmental revenues	350,000
Total	$10,100,000

   2. Appropriations for the following functions were legally budgeted for 2004.

General government	$2,100,000
Public safety	3,890,000
Culture and recreation	700,000
Health and welfare	3,000,000
Total	$9,690,000

   3. During the year, revenues were received in cash from the following sources:

Budgetary Accounting for the General and Special Revenue Funds

Sales taxes	$ 5,930,000
Fines and forfeits	1,990,000
Licenses and permits	1,740,000
Intergovernmental revenues	385,000
Total	$10,045,000

4. During the year, contracts and purchase orders were issued as follows:

General government	$ 450,000
Public safety	800,000
Culture and recreation	280,000
Health and welfare	500,000
Total	$2,030,000

5. Goods and services (ordered in transaction 4) were received, as follows:

	Estimated	Actual
General government	$ 450,000	$ 452,000
Public safety	500,000	510,000
Culture and recreation	275,000	276,000
Health and welfare	500,000	500,000
Total	$1,725,000	$1,738,000

6. A budget revision was approved by the County Commission. Estimated revenues for intergovernmental revenues were increased by $35,000. Appropriations for general government were increased by $100,000.

7. Vouchers were issued for items not previously encumbered, primarily personal services, in the following amounts:

General government	$1,747,000
Public safety	3,080,000
Culture and recreation	418,000
Health and welfare	2,500,000
Total	$7,745,000

a. Record the previous transactions in general journal form. Include subsidiary accounts as illustrated in this chapter.

b. Open budgetary, revenue, expenditure, and encumbrance general ledger control accounts and post the transactions to T-accounts.

c. Open Revenue and Appropriations, Expenditures, and Encumbrances subsidiary ledgers. Post the transactions. Prove that the control account balances agree with the related subsidiary ledger accounts.

d. Assume a beginning Fund Balance—Unreserved of $150,000. Prepare a budgetary comparison schedule for the General Fund. Include encumbrances with expenditures. Use Illustration 3–3 as an example.

e. Assuming that encumbered appropriations do *not* lapse at the end of the budget year, how much of the 2004 appropriations, by function, did lapse at the end of 2004? Show computations in good form.

3–9. The City of Grafton's records reflected the following budget and actual data for the General Fund for the fiscal year ended June 30, 2004.

1. Estimated Revenues:

Taxes	$3,000,000
Licenses and permits	800,000
Intergovernmental revenues	300,000
Miscellaneous revenues	200,000

2. Revenues:

Taxes	$3,000,000
Licenses and permits	801,320
Intergovernmental revenues	293,000
Miscellaneous revenues	198,000

3. Appropriations:

General government	$ 900,000
Public safety	2,000,000
Health and welfare	1,400,000

4. Expenditures of 2004 Appropriations:

General government	$ 880,000
Public safety	1,949,000
Health and welfare	1,398,000

5. Encumbrances of 2004 Appropriations, outstanding as of June 30, 2004.

General government	$18,000
Public safety	50,000

6. Transfer to Debt Service Fund:

Budget	$600,000
Actual	600,000

7. Budget revisions approved by the city council:

Estimated Revenues:	
Decrease intergovernmental revenues	$10,000
Decrease miscellaneous revenues	3,000
Appropriations:	
Decrease general government	2,000

8. Fund Balance—Unreserved, July 1, 2003 $1,038,000

   Prepare a budgetary comparison schedule for the City of Grafton for the fiscal year ended June 30, 2004. Use Illustration 3–3 as an example. Include outstanding encumbrances with expenditures.

3–10. Go to the website of the Government Finance Officers Association (www.gfoa.org) and select "Award Programs." Look for the Distinguished Budget Presentation Award (Budget Awards Program) and answer the following questions:
   a. When was the program first established? During FY 2001 (or the year covered, if later), how many governments participated in the program?
   b. List three award winners from your state, if possible.
   c. List three reviewers from your state, if possible.
   d. Download the form by going to "forms" site. Answer the following questions: (1) What are the four major categories listed in the document? (2) List the mandatory requirements for the "Budget as a Financial Plan." (Do not list the questions after the requirements.) Note that Adobe Acrobat reader is required for this step.

Continuous Problem

3–C. This portion of the continuous problem continues the General Fund and special revenue fund examples started in Problems 1–C and 2–C by requiring the recording and posting of the budgetary entries. In order to reduce clerical effort required for the solution, subsidiary accounts are not required in the continuous problem. However, keep in mind that subsidiary revenue and appropriations expenditure ledgers would (in practice) be maintained for the general fund and all major special revenue funds that have legally adopted annual budgets, in the manner illustrated in this chapter and in Exercise 3–8.

   a. As of January 1, 2004, the City Council approved and the mayor signed a budget calling for $10,700,000 in property tax and other revenue, $9,300,000 in appropriations for expenditures, and $1,280,000 to be transferred to two debt service funds for the payment of principal and interest. Record the budget in the general journal for the General Fund and post to the ledger.

   b. Also as of January 1, 2004, the City Council approved and the mayor signed a budget for the Street and Highway Fund that provided for estimated revenues from the state government in the amount of $950,000 and appropriations of $925,000. Record the budget in the general journal and post to the ledger.

Chapter Four

Accounting for the General and for Special Revenue Funds

In Chapter 3, the use of budgetary accounts (Estimated Revenues, Estimated Other Financing Sources, Appropriations, Estimated Other Financing Uses, Encumbrances, Budgetary Fund Balance, Budgetary Fund Balance Reserved for Encumbrances) and related operating statement accounts (Revenues, Transfers In, Expenditures, Transfers Out) are illustrated. The necessity for subsidiary ledgers supporting the budgetary accounts and related operating statement accounts is also discussed in Chapter 3. In this chapter, common transactions and events in the operation of the General Fund and of a special revenue fund of a hypothetical local government unit, the Village of Elizabeth, are discussed. Appropriate accounting entries and fund financial statements are also illustrated. In this chapter, subsidiary ledgers are not illustrated for the budgetary and operating statement accounts, but keep in mind that subsidiary accounts, as described in Chapter 3, would be required in actual situations.

In order to understand the accounting for the General and special revenue funds, three topics must first be understood. These are (1) accounting for nonexchange transactions, (2) modified accrual accounting, and (3) interfund transactions.

ACCOUNTING FOR NONEXCHANGE TRANSACTIONS

Nonexchange transactions are defined in GASB *Statement 33* as transactions "in which a government gives (or receives) value without directly receiving (or giving) equal value in exchange." Nonexchange transactions are contrasted from exchange and exchange-like transactions "in which each party receives and gives up essentially equal values." By their nature, governmental funds, including the General Fund and special revenue funds, are engaged in nonexchange transactions. GASB Statement 33, *Accounting and Financial Reporting for Nonexchange Transactions*, presumes that an entity is using full accrual accounting, as would be the case for government-wide statements. When preparing fund financial statements (as will be done in this chapter) the provisions of *Statement 33* would be modified to meet the requirements of modified accrual accounting. The next section will describe those modifications.

Classes of Nonexchange Transactions

GASB *Statement 33* separates nonexchange transactions into four classes, based on the nature of the underlying transactions. Accounting for each nonexchange transaction is then determined by which of the four classes applies. The four classes are (1) derived tax revenues, (2) imposed nonexchange revenues, (3) government-mandated nonexchange transactions, and (4) voluntary nonexchange transactions. A nonexchange revenue is considered to be an increase in unrestricted net assets unless that revenue is restricted by the grantor, donor, or legislation. For example, motor fuel tax revenues in many states are restricted (for local governments) to road repair and maintenance. Governments would normally account for motor fuel taxes as special revenue funds. Purpose restrictions do not affect the timing of revenues and expenditures.

Eligibility Requirements

A number of **eligibility requirements** must be met before revenues and assets may be recognized. The requirements are:

1. **Required Characteristics of Recipients.** The recipient must have the characteristics specified by the provider. For example, a state may provide funding on a per student basis to public schools. In order to recognize a revenue or an asset, a recipient must be a public school as defined in state statutes and regulations.
2. **Time Requirements.** If time requirements (for expenditure) are specified by the resource provider or legislation, those time requirements must be met. For example, if a state indicates that funds are appropriated to park districts for the fiscal year ending June 30, 2004, then neither the asset nor revenue would be recognized by the park districts until that fiscal year, unless resources were provided before that fiscal year. If received in advance, the asset would be offset by Deferred Revenues, a liability. If the resource provider does not specify time requirements, then no condition exists, and the revenue and asset would be recognized. For example, if a donor pledged $100,000 to a public university at some unspecified time in the future but did not specify when the funds could be expended, then the entire $100,000 would be recognized as a receivable and as a revenue at the time of the pledge.
3. **Reimbursements.** For those grants and gifts that are payable only upon the incurrence of qualifying outlays permissible under the grant, receivables and revenues would be recognized only when the expenditures have been incurred.
4. **Contingencies.** Resources pledged that have a contingency attached are not to be recognized until the contingency has been met. For example, if a donor indicates that $100,000 will be donated to build an addition to the city library when funds in an equal amount have been pledged by others, that receivable and revenue would be recognized only after the $100,000 has been raised from others.

Recognition Requirements for the Four Classes of Nonexchange Transactions

Definitions, examples, and revenue and asset recognition requirements for each of the four classes of nonexchange revenues are now discussed. **Derived tax revenues** result from taxes assessed on exchange transactions. Examples include sales taxes, income taxes, and motor fuel taxes. *Statement 33* requires that assets be recognized when the tax is imposed or when the resources are received, whichever occurs first. The tax is considered "imposed" when the underlying transaction takes place. Revenue should be recognized at the same time as the asset, provided the underlying transaction has taken place. If resources are received before the underlying transaction has taken place, the asset will be offset by Deferred Revenues, a liability.

Imposed nonexchange transactions are taxes and other assessments imposed by governments that are not derived from underlying transactions. Examples include property taxes, special assessments, and fines and forfeits. Assets from imposed nonexchange transactions should be recognized when an enforceable legal claim exists, or when the resources are received, whichever occurs first. In the case of property taxes, this would normally be specified in the enabling legislation, such as the lien or assessment date. Revenues for property taxes should be recognized, net of estimated refunds and estimated uncollectible taxes, in the period for which the taxes are levied. All other imposed nonexchange revenues should be recognized as revenues at the same time as the assets, or as soon as use is first permitted.

Government-mandated nonexchange transactions exist when the providing government, such as the federal government or a state government, requires the receiving government to expend the funds for a program mandated by the providing government. In addition, certain specific requirements, possibly including some eligibility requirements, such as described above under "reimbursements," may exist. Receiving governments should record both assets and revenues when eligibility requirements, as described above, are met.

Voluntary nonexchange transactions include grants and entitlements from one government to another where the providing government does *not* mandate a particular program. It also includes voluntary contributions from individuals, other nongovernmental entities, and governmental entities to recipient governmental entities. Voluntary nonexchange transactions may or may not have purpose restrictions. An example of this type of transaction would be a gift of cash from a private donor to a municipality, for purposes of expanding the book collection of the city library. The recognition of assets and revenues would be the same as for government-mandated nonexchange transactions; all eligibility requirements must be met before either an asset or revenue can be recognized. Cash received before eligibility requirements have been met would be offset by Deferred Revenues, a liability.

Other Features of GASB *Statement 33*

If there is a difference between a provider government's fiscal year and the recipient government's fiscal year, for the purpose of determining eligibility requirements, the providing government's fiscal year applies. If the providing government has a biennial appropriation, the amount recognized would be split equally, based on the providing government's fiscal year, unless legislation provides otherwise. All of the asset and revenue recognition requirements listed above for receiving governments also apply to the liability and expenditure (expense) recognition for providing governments. Illustration 4–1 reflects the classes and timing of recognition of nonexchange transactions.

ILLUSTRATION 4–1 Classes and Timing of Recognition of Nonexchange Transactions

Class	Recognition
Derived tax revenues Examples: sales taxes, personal and corporate income taxes, motor fuel taxes, and similar taxes on earnings or consumption	**Assets*** Period when *underlying exchange has occurred* or when resources are received, whichever is first. **Revenues** Period when *underlying exchange has occurred*. (Report advance receipts as deferred revenues.) When modified accrual accounting is used, resources also should be "available." See Paragraphs 16 and 30a of *Statement 33*.
Imposed nonexchange revenues Examples: property taxes, most fines and forfeitures	**Assets*** Period when an *enforceable legal claim has arisen* or when resources are received, whichever is first. **Revenues** Period when *resources are required to be used* or first period that use is permitted (for example, for property taxes, the *period for which levied*). When modified accrual accounting is used, resources also should be "available." (For property taxes, apply NCGA Interpretation 3, as amended.) See Paragraphs 17, 18, 30b, and 30c of *Statement 33*.
Government-mandated nonexchange transactions Examples: federal government mandates on state and local governments **Voluntary nonexchange transactions** Examples: certain grants and entitlements, most donations	**Assets* and liabilities** Period when *all eligibility requirements have been met* or (for asset recognition) when resources are received, whichever is first. **Revenues and expenses or expenditures** Period when *all eligibility requirements have been met*. (Report advance receipts or payments for use in the following period as deferred revenues or advances, respectively. However, when a provider precludes the sale, disbursement, or consumption of resources for a specified number of years, until a specified event has occurred, or permanently (for example, permanent and term endowments), report revenues and expenses or expenditures when the resources are, respectively, received or paid and report resulting net assets, equity, or fund balance as restricted.) When modified accrual accounting is used for revenue recognition, resources *also* should be "available." See Paragraphs 19 through 25 and 30d of *Statement 33*.

*If there are purpose restrictions, report restricted net assets (or equity or fund balance) or, for governmental funds, a reservation of fund balance.

Source: GASB *Statement 33*, p. 48.

MODIFIED ACCRUAL ACCOUNTING

Governmental fund financial statements are to be prepared on the **modified accrual** basis of accounting. As the term implies, certain modifications are made to the accrual basis of accounting, which is used for business enterprises and for proprietary and fiduciary funds. Modified accrual accounting can be described by looking at revenue recognition and expenditure recognition.

Revenue Recognition

Under modified accrual accounting, revenues are recognized when they become both **measurable** and **available** to finance expenditures of the current period. The term *measurable* means that the government is able to determine or reasonably estimate the amount. For example, property taxes are measurable before collection, because the government determines the amount to be collected. According to GASB *Codification* Sec. 1600.106, "Available means collectible within the current period or soon enough thereafter to be used to pay liabilities of the current period." Revenues that may be recognized prior to collection include property taxes, charges for inspections, intergovernmental grants, and sales and income taxes. Other revenues, such as fines and forfeits, are typically recognized when cash is received.

A special rule applies to property taxes. The term *available* means that property taxes collected more than 60 days after the end of the fiscal year cannot be recognized in that fiscal year. If property taxes receivable are recognized but the revenue cannot be recognized, Deferred Revenues, a liability account, is credited. A government may choose to defer all property taxes not collected at year-end, but is permitted to recognize those collected up to 60 days after year-end. This concept is illustrated in the Village of Elizabeth example. Except for property taxes, governments are to establish a policy and disclose (e.g., number of days) regarding what is considered available.

Expenditure Recognition

The term *expenditure* rather than *expense* is used in modified accrual accounting. **Expenditures** are decreases in net financial resources and are generally recognized when the related liability is incurred. Expenditures may be for current purposes, such as salaries or supplies, for capital outlay, or for debt service principal or interest. GASB *Interpretation 6, Recognition and Measurement of Certain Liabilities and Expenditures in Governmental Fund Financial Statements*, clarifies when expenditures should be recognized when using modified accrual accounting.

In the absence of a modification, expenditures are recorded and fund liabilities are recognized when goods and services are received, regardless of whether or not resources are available in the fund. The most important modification is that debt service expenditures for principal and interest are recorded when *due*. This means that debt service expenditures are not accrued but are recognized and fund liabilities are recorded on the maturity date. If a government has a debt service due date no more than one month after the end of a fiscal year and has the resources available, then it is permitted to record expenditures and a fund liability for the debt service. This concept is illustrated in Chapter 5.

According to *Interpretation 6*, expenditures for claims and judgments, compensated absences, special termination benefits, and landfill closure and postclosure care costs of governmental funds should be recognized to the extent that the liabilities are going to be paid with available resources; additional amounts are reported as long-term liabilities in the government-wide statements.

INTERFUND TRANSACTIONS

Interfund transactions are transactions between individual funds. GASB *Statement 34* requires that interfund transactions be classified into two categories, each with two subcategories. Journal entries to record interfund transactions are based on these classifications. **Reciprocal interfund activity** is the internal counterpart to exchange and exchange-like transactions and includes **interfund loans** and **interfund services provided and used.** Nonreciprocal interfund activity includes **interfund transfers** and **interfund reimbursements.**

Interfund Loans

Interfund loans are resources provided from one fund to another with the requirement for repayment. The fund providing the resources records an interfund receivable (Due from Other Funds) and the fund receiving the resources records an interfund payable (Due to Other Funds). Long-term loans use the terms *Advance to* and *Advance from.* Interfund loans affect only asset and liability accounts.

Interfund Services Provided and Used

Interfund services provided and used represent transactions involving sales and purchases of goods and services between funds. An example is the sale of water from a water utility (enterprise) fund to the General Fund. In these transactions, one fund records a revenue (enterprise, in this example) and the other fund records an expenditure or expense (the General Fund). Earlier standards used the term **quasi-external transactions,** reflecting that these transactions are reported as if they were transactions with parties outside the government. Interfund services provided and used are illustrated later in this chapter.

Interfund Transfers

Interfund transfers represent flows of cash or other assets without a requirement for repayment. An example would be an annual transfer of resources from the General to a debt service fund. Interfund transfers act (in terms of debits and credits) as if they are revenues or expenditures (expenses) but are classified differently, as other financing sources (the debt service fund) and other financing uses (the General Fund). Interfund transfers are also illustrated later in this chapter.

Interfund Reimbursements

Interfund reimbursements represent repayments to the funds that initially recorded expenditures or expenses by the funds responsible. For example, assume the General Fund had previously debited expenditures to acquire some supplies, but the supplies should have been charged to a special revenue fund. The reimbursement entry would have one fund (the special revenue fund) debit an expenditure (or expense) and the other fund (the General Fund) credit an expenditure or expense. Additional examples of interfund transactions are provided in Chapter 7.

GENERAL FUND ACCOUNT STRUCTURE

Illustration 4–2 presents a Governmental Fund Account Structure that can be used as a guide when studying the following illustrative case and other journal entries in Chapters 4 and 5.

ILLUSTRATIVE CASE—GENERAL FUND

Assume that at the beginning of fiscal year 2004, the Village of Elizabeth's General Fund had the following balances in its accounts:

	Debits	Credits
Cash	$100,000	
Taxes Receivable—Delinquent	400,000	
Estimated Uncollectible Delinquent Taxes		$ 40,000
Interest and Penalties Receivable on Taxes	25,000	
Estimated Uncollectible Interest and Penalties		10,000
Accounts Payable		135,000
Deferred Revenues—Property Taxes		20,000
Due to Federal Government		30,000
Fund Balance—Reserved for Encumbrances		45,000
Fund Balance—Unreserved		245,000
Totals	$525,000	$525,000

ILLUSTRATION 4–2   Governmental Funds Account Structure

Real (Balance Sheet) Accounts
Current Assets (DR)
Current Liabilities (CR)
Fund Balance (Fund Equity) (CR)
  Reserved (Encumbrances, Inventories, etc.) (CR)
  Unreserved (CR)
    Designated (CR)
    Undesignated (CR)

Nominal (Operating Statement) Accounts
Revenues Control (CR)
Other Financing Sources Control (CR)
  (Transfers In)
  (Bond Issue Proceeds)
Expenditures Control (DR)
Other Financing Uses Control (DR)
  (Transfers Out)

Budgetary Accounts
Estimated Revenues Control (DR)
Estimated Other Financing Sources
  Control (DR)
Appropriations Control (CR)
Encumbrances Control (DR)
Estimated Other Financing Uses
  Control (CR)
Budgetary Fund Balance (DR) (CR)
Budgetary Fund Balance Reserved
  for Encumbrances (CR)

The Deferred Revenues—Property Taxes account reflects the portion of the $400,000 in taxes receivable that have not yet been recognized as a revenue. The Fund Balance—Reserved for Encumbrances account represents the amount of purchase orders and contracts, related to the prior year, that are open at the beginning of 2004.

Recording the Budget

At the beginning of fiscal year 2004, it is necessary to record the budget (assuming that all legal requirements have been met). If the total estimated revenue budget for 2004 is $6,200,000, the total appropriations are $5,200,000, the total planned transfer to debt service funds is $204,000, and a planned transfer to establish an internal service fund is $596,000, the necessary entry to record the budget would be as follows (keeping in mind that appropriate subsidiary ledger detail would be required in actual situations):

	Debits	Credits
1. Estimated Revenues Control	6,200,000	
Appropriations Control		5,200,000
Estimated Other Financing Uses Control		800,000
Budgetary Fund Balance		200,000

Assume the appropriations budget includes $45,000 to honor the purchase orders outstanding at the beginning of the year. This might have been done (1) by adding $45,000 to the 2004 budgets of the departments involved or (2) by requiring the departments to cover the $45,000 out of the budgeted funds for 2004.

Re-establishment of Encumbrances

Assuming the $45,000 in purchase orders at the beginning of the year will be honored, it is necessary to re-establish the encumbrances. Also, the Fund Balance—Reserved for Encumbrances account is no longer needed.

2a. Encumbrances Control	45,000	
Budgetary Fund Balance Reserved for Encumbrances		45,000
2b. Fund Balance—Reserved for Encumbrances	45,000	
Fund Balance—Unreserved		45,000

Recording Prior Year Property Taxes as Revenues

GASB standards for property tax revenue recognition under the modified accrual basis of accounting provide that revenue should not be recognized for property taxes expected to be collected more than 60 days beyond the end of the fiscal year. In fact, some governments defer all of their property taxes receivable at year-end. At the end of 2003, the Village of Elizabeth deferred $20,000 in property taxes, and that amount is reflected in the beginning trial balance. Entry 3 recognizes that amount as a revenue for 2004 (see entry 27 for the 2004 deferral):

	Debits	Credits
3. Deferred Revenues—Property Taxes	20,000	
Revenues Control		20,000

Tax Anticipation Notes Payable

In the trial balance of the General Fund of the Village of Elizabeth, liabilities (Accounts Payable and Due to Federal Government) total $165,000. Cash of the General Fund on the date of the trial balance amounts to $100,000. Although some collections of delinquent taxes receivable are expected early in the year, payrolls and other liabilities are incurred and must be paid before substantial amounts of cash will be collected; accordingly, it is desirable to arrange a short-term loan. The taxing power of the Village is ample security for a short-term debt; local banks customarily meet the working capital needs of governmental units by accepting a "tax anticipation note" (a short-term note) from the government officials. If the amount of $200,000 is borrowed at this time the necessary entry is as follows:

4. Cash	200,000	
Tax Anticipation Notes Payable		200,000

Payment of Liabilities as Recorded

Checks were drawn to pay the accounts payable and the amount due to the federal government as of the end of 2003:

5. Accounts Payable	135,000	
Due to Federal Government	30,000	
Cash		165,000

Encumbrance Entry

In addition to the $45,000 outstanding at the beginning of the year, purchase orders for materials and supplies are issued in the amount of $800,000. The general ledger entry to record the encumbrances for the purchase orders is as follows (subsidiary ledger detail is omitted from this example but should be recorded by an actual governmental unit):

6. Encumbrances Control	800,000	
Budgetary Fund Balance—Reserved for Encumbrances		800,000

Recording Property Tax Levy

Assume that the budgeted revenue from real property taxes, included in the total Estimated Revenues recorded in entry 1 of this chapter, was $3,200,000, excluding the 20,000 in entry 3. Assume further that 2 percent of these taxes are estimated to be uncollectible due to tax collection policy and local economic conditions. In order to generate revenues of $3,200,000, the gross levy must be in the amount of $3,265,306 ($3,200,000 ÷ 0.98). Therefore, when the taxes are levied, the following entry should be made:

	Debits	Credits
7. Taxes Receivable—Current	3,265,306	
Estimated Uncollectible Current Taxes		65,306
Revenues Control		3,200,000

Keep in mind that the account Revenues Control is a control account in the General Fund general ledger. It is supported by a subsidiary ledger in the manner illustrated in Chapter 3. Taxes Receivable—Current is also a control account and is supported by a subsidiary ledger organized by parcels of property according to their legal descriptions. In many cases, this subsidiary ledger is maintained by the county officer responsible for collecting property taxes as agent for all funds and governmental units within the county.

Collection of Delinquent Taxes

Delinquent taxes are subject to interest and penalties that must be paid at the time the tax bill is paid. It is possible for a government to record the amount of the penalties at the time that the taxes become delinquent. Interest may be computed and recorded at year-end so that financial statements report the account on the accrual basis. Interest must also be computed and recorded for the period from the date of last recording to the date when a taxpayer pays the delinquent taxes. In the current year, the Village of Elizabeth collected delinquent taxes in the amount of $330,000, on which interest and penalties of $20,000 had been accrued at the end of 2003; further $3,000 additional interest was collected for the period from the first day of 2004 to the dates on which the delinquent taxes were collected. Entry 8a records the additional interest as revenue of 2004; entry 8b records the collection of the delinquent taxes and the total interest and penalties owed on them.

8a. Interest and Penalties Receivable on Taxes	3,000	
Revenues Control		3,000
8b. Cash	353,000	
Taxes Receivable—Delinquent		330,000
Interest and Penalties Receivable on Taxes		23,000

Collection of Current Taxes

Collections during 2004 of property taxes levied are $2,700,000. Since the revenue was recognized at the time the receivable was recorded, the following entry would be made:

	Debits	Credits
9. Cash	2,700,000	
Taxes Receivable—Current		2,700,000

Revenue Recognized on Cash Basis

Revenue from licenses and permits, fines and forfeits, and other sources not susceptible to accrual is recognized on the cash basis. Collections during the year 2004 are $2,800,000.

	Debits	Credits
10. Cash	2,800,000	
Revenues Control		2,800,000

Repayment of Tax Anticipation Notes

As tax collections begin to exceed current disbursements, it becomes possible for the Village of Elizabeth to repay the local bank for the money borrowed in tax anticipation notes (entry 4). Just as borrowing money did not involve the recognition of revenue, the repayment of the principal is merely the extinguishment of short-term debt of the General Fund and not an expenditure. Payment of interest, however, must be recognized as the expenditure of an appropriation. Assuming the interest is $5,000, the entry is as follows:

	Debits	Credits
11. Tax Anticipation Notes Payable	200,000	
Expenditures Control	5,000	
Cash		205,000

Recognition of Expenditures for Encumbered Items

Some of the materials and supplies ordered last year and this year (see entries 2a and 6) were received. Invoices for the items received totaled $820,300; related purchase orders totaled $795,000. After inspection of the goods and supplies and preaudit of the invoices, the invoices were approved for payment. Since the purchase orders had been recorded as encumbrances against the appropriations, it is necessary to reverse the encumbered amount and record the expenditure in the amount of the actual liability:

	Debits	Credits
12. Budgetary Fund Balance—Reserved for Encumbrances	795,000	
Encumbrances Control		795,000
Expenditures Control	820,300	
Accounts Payable		820,300

The net effect of entry 12 on the departmental appropriations accounts is a $25,300 reduction in total available balances.

Payrolls and Payroll Taxes

The gross pay of employees of General Fund departments amounted to $3,345,000. The Village of Elizabeth does not use the encumbrance procedure for payrolls. Deductions from gross pay for the period amount to $256,000 for employees' share of FICA tax and Medicare tax; $430,000 for employees' federal withholding tax; and $78,000 for employees' state withholding tax. The first two have to be remitted by the Village to the federal government, and the last item has to be remitted to the state government. The gross pay is chargeable to the appropriations of the individual departments. Assuming the liability for net pay is vouchered, the entry is as follows:

	Debits	Credits
13a. Expenditures Control	3,345,000	
Due to Federal Government		686,000
Due to State Government		78,000
Accounts Payable		2,581,000

Payment of the vouchers for the net pay results in the following entry:

13b. Accounts Payable	2,581,000	
Cash		2,581,000

Inasmuch as the Village is liable for the employer's share of FICA tax and Medicare tax ($256,000) and for contributions to additional retirement funds established by state law, assumed to amount to $167,000 for the year, the Village's liabilities for its contributions must be recorded:

14. Expenditures Control	423,000	
Due to Federal Government		256,000
Due to State Government		167,000

Payment of Vouchers and Other Items

Payment is made on $770,000 of the outstanding accounts payable, and the amounts due the state and federal governments are paid in full:

15. Accounts Payable	770,000	
Due to Federal Government	942,000	
Due to State Government	245,000	
Cash		1,957,000

Correction of Errors

No problems arise in the collection of current taxes if they are collected as billed; the collections are debited to Cash and credited to Taxes Receivable—Current. Sometimes, even in a well-designed and well-operated system, errors occur and must be corrected. If, for example, duplicate tax bills totaling $1,200 were sent out for the same piece of property, the following entry would be required. (The error also caused a slight overstatement of the credit to Estimated Uncollectible Current Taxes in entry 7, but the error in that account is not considered material enough to correct.)

	Debits	Credits
16. Revenues Control	1,200	
Taxes Receivable—Current		1,200

Postaudit may disclose errors in the recording of expenditures during the current year or during a prior year. If the error occurred during the current year, the Expenditures Control account and the proper subsidiary ledger account can be debited or credited as needed to correct it. If the error occurred in a prior year, however, the Expenditures account in error has been closed to Fund Balance—Unreserved, so theoretically the correcting entry should be made to that account. As a practical matter, immaterial changes resulting from corrections of prior period errors in expenditures may be recorded in the current period Revenues or Expenditures accounts.

Amendment of the Budget

Comparisons of budgeted and actual revenues by sources and comparisons of departmental or program appropriations with expenditures and encumbrances, as well as an interpretation of information that was not available at the time the budgets were originally adopted, may indicate the desirability or necessity of legally amending the budget during the fiscal year. For example, assume that the revenues budget was increased by $50,000 in the Charges for Services source category and that the appropriation for the Public Works Department was increased by $100,000. The amendments to the budget would be recorded when they were legally approved, as shown in entry 17:

17. Estimated Revenues Control	50,000	
Budgetary Fund Balance	50,000	
Appropriations Control		100,000

Corresponding changes would be made in the subsidiary ledger accounts as illustrated in Chapter 3.

Interfund Transactions

Interfund services provided and used Interfund services provided and used are recognized as revenues or expenditures (or expenses in the case of proprietary funds) of the funds involved just as they would be recognized as revenues and expenditures (or expenses) if the transactions involved organizations external to the governmental unit.

Water utilities ordinarily provide a city with fire hydrants and water service for fire protection at a flat annual charge. A government-owned water utility expected to support the cost of its operations by user charges should be accounted for as an enterprise fund. Fire protection is logically budgeted as an activity of the fire department, a General Fund department. Assuming that the amount charged by the water utility to the General Fund for hydrants and water service was $80,000, the General Fund entry would be as follows:

	Debits	Credits
18. Expenditures Control	80,000	
Due to Water Utility Fund		80,000

The enterprise fund would also record this transaction (see enterprise fund entry 1 in Chapter 6).

Government-owned utility property is not assessed for property tax purposes, but a number of government utilities make an annual contribution to the General Fund of the governmental unit in recognition of the fact that the utility does receive police and fire protection and other services. If the water utility of the Village of Elizabeth agrees to contribute $60,000 to the General Fund in lieu of taxes, which is approximately equal to the service provided, the General Fund entry is as follows:

19. Due from Water Utility Fund	60,000	
Revenues Control		60,000

See enterprise fund entry 15 in Chapter 6.

Another common transaction for the General Fund is the receipt of supplies or services from an internal service fund established to provide purchasing and distribution services to other government departments. Assume that the General Fund received $377,000 in supplies from the Supplies Fund and later made a partial payment of $322,000 in cash. The entries would be as follows:

20a. Expenditures Control	377,000	
Due to Supplies Fund		377,000
20b. Due to Supplies Fund	322,000	
Cash		322,000

The internal service fund would also record this (see internal service fund entries 5b and 7 in Chapter 6).

Interfund transfers Some transactions are labeled as "other financing sources (uses)—transfers" in order to avoid reporting revenues and expenditures more than once in the governmental unit. Assuming that the General Fund made the budgeted transfer to a Debt Service Fund for the payment of debt service, the General Fund entry would be as follows:

	Debits	Credits
21a. Other Financing Uses—Transfers Out Control	204,000	
Due to Debt Service Fund		204,000

When the cash is transferred, the entry would be as follows:

21b. Due to Debt Service Fund	204,000	
Cash		204,000

See debt service entry 19 in Chapter 5.

Other transfers are nonroutine transactions, often made to establish or liquidate a fund. Assume that the General Fund made a permanent transfer of $596,000 to establish an internal service fund. The General Fund entry would be as follows:

22. Other Financing Uses—Transfers Out Control	596,000	
Cash		596,000

See internal service fund entry 1 in Chapter 6.

Interfund Reimbursements Assume that $20,000 of the expenditures in entry 12 related to supplies used for road maintenance that should have been charged to the Motor Fuel Tax Fund, a special revenue fund. It was decided that $20,000 cash would be transferred from the Motor Fuel Tax Fund and that the transaction be treated as an interfund reimbursement. Accordingly, $20,000 is charged to the Motor Fuel Tax Fund (see entry 3 in the Special Revenue Fund section of this chapter) and General Fund expenditures are reduced by $20,000.

23. Cash	20,000	
Expenditures Control		20,000

Write-off of Uncollectible Delinquent Taxes

Just as officers of profit-seeking entities should review aged schedules of receivables periodically in order to determine the adequacy of allowance accounts and to authorize the write-offs of items judged to be uncollectible, so should officers of a governmental unit review aged schedules of taxes receivable and other receivables. Although the levy of property taxes creates a lien against the underlying property in the amount of tax, accumulated taxes may exceed the market value of the property, or in the case of personal property, the property may be removed from the jurisdiction of the governmental unit. When delinquent taxes are deemed to be uncollectible, the related interest and penalties must also be written off. If the treasurer of the Village of Elizabeth received approval to write off delinquent taxes totaling $30,000 and related interest and penalties of $3,000, the entry would be as follows:

	Debits	Credits
24. Estimated Uncollectible Delinquent Taxes	30,000	
Taxes Receivable-Delinquent		30,000
Estimated Uncollectible Interest and Penalties	3,000	
Interest and Penalties Receivable on Taxes		3,000

When delinquent taxes are written off, the tax bills are retained in the files, although they are no longer subject to general ledger control, because changes in conditions may make it possible to collect the amounts in the future. If collections of write-off taxes are made, it is highly desirable to return the tax bills to general ledger control by making an entry that is the reverse of the write-off entry, so that the procedures described in entries 8a and 8b may be followed.

Reclassification of Current Taxes

Assuming that all property taxes levied by the Village of Elizabeth for 2004 were to have been paid by property owners before the end of the year, any balance of taxes receivable at year-end is properly classified as delinquent, rather than current. The related allowance for estimated uncollectible taxes also should be transferred to the delinquent classification. A review should be made at this time to ensure that the estimated uncollectible amount is reasonable in relation to the delinquent taxes. Assuming the estimate is reasonable, the entry would be as follows:

25. Taxes Receivable—Delinquent	564,106	
Taxes Receivable—Current		564,106
Estimated Uncollectible Current Taxes	65,306	
Estimated Uncollectible Delinquent Taxes		65,306

Accrual of Interest and Penalties

Delinquent taxes are subject to interest and penalties, as discussed previously. The amount of interest and penalties earned in 2004 by the General Fund of the Village of Elizabeth and not yet recognized is $56,410, but it is expected that only $39,490 of that can be collected. The entry would be as follows:

26. Interest and Penalties Receivable on Taxes	56,410	
Estimated Uncollectible Interest and Penalties		16,920
Revenues Control		39,490

Deferral of Property Tax Revenue

A review of the taxes receivable subsidiary ledger indicated that approximately $40,000 would probably be received more than 60 days beyond the end of the fiscal year. GASB standards require that the $40,000 be deferred:

	Debits	Credits
27. Revenues Control	40,000	
Deferred Revenues—Property Taxes		40,000

Special Item

GASB requires that extraordinary items and special items be reported separately after other financing sources and uses. Extraordinary items are significant transactions or other events that are both unusual and infrequent. **Special items** are significant transactions or other events that are *either* unusual or infrequent but *within* the control of management. Assume the Village sold land for $300,000.

	Debits	Credits
28. Cash	300,000	
Special Item—Proceeds from Sale of Land		300,000

The reduction in the land account would be reported in the government-wide financial statements.

Preclosing Trial Balance

Assuming that the illustrated entries for the transactions and events pertaining to the year 2004 for the Village of Elizabeth have been made and posted, the following trial balance shows the General Fund general ledger accounts before closing entries:

VILLAGE OF ELIZABETH
General Fund
Trial Balance
As of December 31, 2004

	Debits	Credits
Cash	$ 443,000	
Taxes Receivable—Delinquent	604,106	
Estimated Uncollectible Delinquent Taxes		$ 75,306
Interest and Penalties Receivable on Taxes	58,410	
Estimated Uncollectible Interest and Penalties		23,920
Due from Water Utility Fund	60,000	
Accounts Payable		50,300
Due to Water Utility Fund		80,000
Due to Supplies Fund		55,000
Deferred Revenues—Property Taxes		40,000
Budgetary Fund Balance Reserved for Encumbrances		50,000

	Debits	Credits
Fund Balance—Unreserved		290,000
Estimated Revenues Control	6,250,000	
Revenues Control		6,081,290
Appropriations Control		5,300,000
Estimated Other Financing Uses Control		800,000
Budgetary Fund Balance		150,000
Expenditures Control	5,030,300	
Encumbrances Control	50,000	
Other Financing Uses—Transfers Out Control	800,000	
Special Item—Proceeds from Sale of Land		300,000
	$13,295,816	$13,295,816

Closing Entries

The essence of the closing process for the General Fund or special revenue funds of a state or local governmental unit is the transfer of the balances of the operating statement accounts and the balances of the budgetary accounts for the year to the Fund Balance—Unreserved account. Note that the first closing entry has the effect of reversing the entry to record the budget (entry 1) and the entry to amend the budget (entry 17). After the closing entries are posted, the Fund Balance—Unreserved account represents the net amount of resources available for appropriation.

		Debits	Credits
29.	Appropriations Control	5,300,000	
	Estimated Other Financing Uses Control	800,000	
	Budgetary Fund Balance	150,000	
	Estimated Revenues Control		6,250,000
30.	Revenues Control	6,081,290	
	Special Items—Proceeds from Sale of Land	300,000	
	Expenditures Control		5,030,300
	Other Financing Uses—Transfers Out Control		800,000
	Encumbrances Control		50,000
	Fund Balance—Unreserved		500,990
31.	Budgetary Fund Balance Reserved for Encumbrances	50,000	
	Fund Balance—Reserved for Encumbrances		50,000

Year-End Financial Statements

The Balance Sheet for the General Fund of the Village of Elizabeth as of the end of 2004 is shown in Illustration 4–3. Note that the amount due *from* the Water Utility Fund has been offset against the amount due *to* the Water Utility Fund. (It should be emphasized, however, that it is not acceptable to offset a receivable from one fund against a payable to a different fund.)

ILLUSTRATION 4–3

VILLAGE OF ELIZABETH
General Fund Balance Sheet
As of December 31, 2004

Assets

Cash		$ 443,000
Taxes Receivable—Delinquent	$604,106	
Less: Estimated Uncollectible	75,306	528,800
Interest and Penalties Receivable on Taxes	58,410	
Less: Estimated Uncollectible	23,920	34,490
Total Assets		$1,006,290

Liabilities and Fund Equity

Liabilities:		
Accounts Payable	$ 50,300	
Due to Water Utility Fund	20,000	
Due to Supplies Fund	55,000	
Deferred Revenues—Property Taxes	40,000	
Total Liabilities		$ 165,300
Fund Equity:		
Fund Balance—Reserved for Encumbrances	50,000	
Fund Balance—Unreserved	790,990	
Total fund equity		840,990
Total liabilities and fund equity		$1,006,290

A second financial statement that should be presented in the year-end comprehensive annual financial report is a Statement of Revenues, Expenditures, and Changes in Fund Balance (see Illustration 4–4). Illustration 4–4 presents the actual revenues and actual expenditures that resulted from transactions illustrated in this chapter. Note that the expenditures do not include the current encumbrances of $50,000, because GASB standards specify that encumbrances are not to be reported as expenditures (except in statements on schedules prepared in conformity with budgetary practices instead of GAAP).

Information shown in Illustration 4–4 would be presented in columnar form in the Statement of Revenues, Expenditures, and Changes in Fund Balances for governmental funds (see Chapter 5).

ILLUSTRATIVE CASE—SPECIAL REVENUE FUND

Special revenue funds are needed when legal or policy considerations require that separate funds be created for current purposes. Such purposes exclude debt service, capital expenditures, and proprietary or fiduciary activities. Examples of special revenue funds are State Motor Fuel Tax, Emergency 911 Access Fees, and Library

ILLUSTRATION 4–4

VILLAGE OF ELIZABETH
General Fund
Statement of Revenues, Expenditures, and Changes in Fund Balance
For the Year Ended December 31, 2004

Revenues (Amounts Assumed):		
Property Taxes	$3,178,800	
Interest and Penalties on Delinquent Taxes	42,490	
Sales Taxes	1,410,000	
Licenses and Permits	540,000	
Fines and Forfeits	430,000	
Intergovernmental Revenue	350,000	
Charges for Services	100,000	
Miscellaneous Revenues	30,000	
Total Revenues		$6,081,290
Expenditures (Amounts Assumed):		
General Government	810,000	
Public Safety	2,139,500	
Public Works	630,000	
Health and Welfare	480,100	
Parks and Recreation	527,400	
Contribution to Retirement Funds	423,000	
Miscellaneous Expenditures	20,300	
Total Expenditures		(5,030,300)
Excess of Revenues over Expenditures		1,050,990
Other financing uses:		
Transfers Out		(800,000)
Special Item:		
Proceeds from Sale of Land		300,000
Net Change in Fund Balance		550,990
Fund Balance, January 1, 2004		290,000
Fund Balance, December 31, 2004		$ 840,990

Operating. The first two are created for legal reasons; the Library Operating Fund might be created due to a special tax levy or simply the desire of the governing board to have a separate fund to account for an activity that differs from other governmental activities. Governmental units should attempt to keep the number of special revenue and other funds to a minimum; often, a functional classification in the General Fund will provide as much information as is needed.

Assume the Village of Elizabeth maintains a Motor Fuel Tax Fund, as required by state law. Revenues include state motor fuel tax receipts and state reimbursement grants. Expenditures are incurred for road repairs and maintenance. A legally adopted annual budget is not required or used. Assume, at the beginning of 2004, the Motor Fuel Tax Fund has cash of $212,500 offset by unreserved fund balance in the same amount.

Motor Fuel Tax Revenues

During 2004, the State notified the Village that $650,000 in motor fuel taxes will be awarded. Records show $575,000 was received in cash; the remainder is due from the state. Motor fuel taxes are a derived tax revenue; under modified accrual accounting, the amount that can be recognized is the amount that is measurable and available.

		Debits	Credits
1.	Cash	575,000	
	Due from State Government	75,000	
	Revenues Control		650,000

Expenditures for Road Repairs

Also during 2002, expenditures for road repairs amounted to $605,000, of which $540,000 was paid in cash. Note that encumbrance accounting might be used but is omitted for the sake of brevity.

2.	Expenditures Control	605,000	
	Cash		540,000
	Accounts Payable		65,000

Reimbursement to General Fund

Entry 23 in the General Fund example related to a charge, originally charged by the General Fund, that was for road repairs and should be charged to the motor fuel tax fund. The corresponding interfund reimbursement entry to charge the motor fuel tax fund and to reimburse cash to the General Fund is

3.	Expenditures Control	20,000	
	Cash		20,000

Reimbursement Grant Accounting

Assume the State awarded the Village a grant of $450,000 for major repairs to three Village intersections. The funds will be released by the State only as work is completed, as a reimbursement. GASB *Statement 33* considers this to be an eligibility requirement. Accordingly, grant revenues and receivables would be recognized as expenditures are incurred. During 2004, expenditures in the amount of $350,000 were incurred, of which $280,000 were paid. The State had remitted $300,000 cash as of the end of 2004.

	Debits	Credits
4. Expenditures Control	350,000	
Cash		280,000
Accounts Payable		70,000
5. Due from State Government	350,000	
Revenues Control		350,000
6. Cash	300,000	
Due from State Government		300,000

Closing Entry

At year-end, the Motor Fuel Tax Fund would prepare the following closing entry:

7. Revenues Control	1,000,000	
Expenditures Control		975,000
Fund Balance—Unreserved		25,000

Year-End Financial Statements

Illustrations 4–5 and 4–6 reflect the Balance Sheet and the Statement of Revenues, Expenditures, and Changes in Fund Balances for the Motor Fuel Tax Fund.

RECOGNITION OF INVENTORIES IN GOVERNMENTAL FUNDS

Generally, supplies inventories are insignificant relative to governmental fund balances. In any case, GAAP permit two methods of accounting for inventories. Under the **consumption method** of accounting for inventories, an asset is debited when inventories are acquired, and the account Expenditures is debited and the asset credited when inventories are consumed, the same as in business accounting.

Under the **purchases method** of accounting for inventories, the Expenditures account is debited when supplies are received. If inventories are significant, GAAP require that a year-end adjustment be made in which an asset account is debited and an equal amount set aside as a fund balance reserve. For example, assume a government decided to begin recording the year-end inventory in the General Fund, and the amount is $150,000. The following adjusting entry would be made.

Inventory of Supplies	150,000	
Fund Balance—Reserved for Inventory of Supplies		150,000

ILLUSTRATION 4–5

VILLAGE OF ELIZABETH
Motor Fuel Tax Fund Balance Sheet
As of December 31, 2004

Assets

Cash	$247,500
Due from State Government	125,000
Total Assets	$372,500

Liabilities and Fund Equity

Liabilities:	
Accounts Payable	$135,000
Fund Equity:	
Fund Balance—Unreserved	237,500
Total Liabilities and Fund Equity	$372,500

ILLUSTRATION 4–6

VILLAGE OF ELIZABETH
Motor Fuel Tax Fund
Statement of Revenues, Expenditures, and Changes in Fund Balances
For the Year Ended December 31, 2004

Revenues:	
Motor Fuel Taxes	$ 650,000
State Reimbursement Grant	350,000
Total Revenues	1,000,000
Expenditures:	
Public Works	975,000
Net Change in Fund Balance	25,000
Fund Balance, January 1, 2004	212,500
Fund Balance, December 31, 2004	$ 237,500

During the next year, all acquisitions of inventory would be debited to Expenditures. If, at year-end, an inventory indicates that the ending balance is $130,000, the following entry would be made:

	Debits	Credits
Fund Balance—Reserved for Inventory of Supplies	20,000	
Inventory of Supplies		20,000

GAAP also permit, but do not require, governments to record (and reserve Fund Balance for) prepaid items, such as prepaid insurance and prepaid rent, in the same manner as the purchases method for inventories.

Questions and Exercises

4–1. Using the annual financial report obtained for Exercise 1–1, answer the following questions:

  a. Look at the General Fund column of the Balance Sheet for governmental funds. What are the major assets? Liabilities? What reserves have been established for fund balance? Are any designations shown? Are taxes receivable offset by Deferred Revenues? Are the amounts the same? (If so, this would indicate cash accounting for property taxes.)

  b. Look at the General Fund column of the governmental funds Statement of Revenues, Expenditures, and Changes in Fund Balances. Prepare a schedule showing percentages of revenues by source. Prepare a schedule showing percentages of expenditures by function. Does your government have significant transfers in or out? Can you tell the fund that provides or receives these resources? Does your government have any other financing sources or uses? Special and/or extraordinary items?

  c. Does your government report any special revenue funds as major funds in the governmental fund statements? What are they? What are the major revenue sources? Expenditure functions?

  d. Review the notes to the financial statements to determine the measurement focus and basis of accounting used to prepare the governmental fund financial statements. Do the notes describe modified accrual accounting in a manner consistent with this book? Which revenue sources are subject to accrual? Are expenditures generally recognized when goods and services are received? Which specific modifications to accrual accounting are mentioned in the notes?

  e. Look at the General Fund column of the governmental fund statements from the point of view of a financial analyst. Is the Fund Balance as of the balance sheet date larger or smaller than at the beginning of the year? Are reasons for the change apparent from the statements? Compute a ratio of fund balance/general fund revenues and compare with your class members.

4–2. For each of the following, select the letter corresponding with the *best* answer.

  1. Which of the following would *not* be an example of a nonexchange transaction?
     a. Property taxes
     b. Fines and forfeits
     c. Charges for services
     d. Sales taxes

  2. Which of the following would be an example of a derived tax revenue?
     a. Sales taxes.
     b. Income taxes.

114 Chapter 4

    c. Both of the above.
    d. Neither of the above.

3. Which of the following would be an example of a voluntary nonexchange transaction?
    a. A grant from the state that is accompanied by legislation requiring certain expenditures from the grant.
    b. A grant from the state, not accompanied by legislation, that requires grant resources be expended for certain purposes.
    c. Both of the above.
    d. Neither of the above.

4. Which of the following is true regarding nonexchange transactions?
    a. If a donor specifies that a contribution is not to be expended until a future year, then that contribution would not be recognized as a revenue until that future year.
    b. If a donor attaches a contingency to a gift that has not yet been met, then a revenue would not be recognized until that contingency is met.
    c. Both of the above.
    d. Neither of the above.

5. Which of the following is true regarding nonexchange transactions?
    a. Nonexchange transactions are written with the assumption that modified accrual accounting is used.
    b. Grants and gifts that are payable only on the incurrence of expenditures are not recognized as revenue until the expenditure occurs.
    c. Both of the above.
    d. Neither of the above.

6. Which of the following is true regarding recognition of sales taxes, using accrual accounting?
    a. Assets should be recognized when the tax is imposed or when the resources are received, whichever occurs first.
    b. Revenue should be recognized at the same time as the receivable, providing the underlying transaction has taken place.
    c. Both of the above.
    d. Neither of the above.

7. Which of the following is true regarding the recognition of property taxes, using accrual accounting?
    a. Assets should be recognized when an enforceable legal claim exists or when the resources are received, whichever occurs first.
    b. Revenues should be recognized in the year for which the taxes are levied.
    c. Both of the above.
    d. Neither of the above.

8. Which of the following is true regarding modified accrual accounting?
   a. Modified accrual accounting is required for all fund financial statements.
   b. Modified accrual accounting requires that all expenditures be recognized on the accrual basis.
   c. Both of the above are true.
   d. Neither of the above are true.
9. Which of the following is true regarding modified accrual accounting?
   a. Expenditures should generally be recognized for activities normally paid out of governmental fund resources even if those resources are not available at the present time.
   b. Expenditures for compensated absences should be computed on the accrual basis and the entire amount shown as a governmental fund liability.
   c. Both of the above are true.
   d. Neither of the above are true.
10. Which of the following is true regarding modified accrual accounting?
    a. Debt service expenditures for principal and interest are generally recorded when due and are not accrued at year-end.
    b. If a government has resources available in a debt service fund at year-end, an expenditure may be accrued as long as the maturity date is no longer than one month from the end of the year.
    c. Both of the above are true.
    d. Neither of the above are true.

4–3. For each of the following, select the letter corresponding with the *best* answer.

1. The City of Evansville's governing body adopted a budget consisting of anticipated revenues of $30,000,000, anticipated expenditures and encumbrances of $29,000,000, anticipated transfers in of $200,000, and anticipated transfers out of $900,000. To complete the budget entry:
   a. Fund Balance—Unreserved would be credited in the amount of $1,000,000.
   b. Fund Balance—Unreserved would be credited in the amount of $300,000.
   c. Budgetary Fund Balance would be credited in the amount of $300,000.
   d. Budgetary Fund Balance would be credited in the amount of $1,700,000.

2. For the budgetary year ending December 31, 2004, Johnson County's General Fund expects the following inflow of resources:

Property taxes, licenses, and fines	$7,000,000
Proceeds of debt issue	2,000,000
Interfund transfer from enterprise fund	600,000

In the budgetary entry, what amount should Johnson record for Estimated Revenues?
a. $9,600,000
b. $7,000,000
c. $9,000,000
d. $7,600,000

3. During the fiscal year ended June 30, 2004, Allison Township issued purchase orders totaling $8,000,000, which were properly charged to Encumbrances Control at that time. Allison received goods and related invoices at the encumbered amounts totaling $7,600,000 before year-end. The remaining goods of $400,000 were not received until after year-end. The related invoices amounted to $7,650,000, and Allison paid $7,500,000 of those invoices prior to the end of the year. What amount of Allison's encumbrances were outstanding on June 30, 2004?
a. $400,000
b. $450,000
c. $350,000
d. $500,000

4. The City of Elmwood reported the following for the fiscal year ended December 31, 2004:

Purchase orders authorized by 2004 appropriations and outstanding as of December 31, 2004	$ 300,000
Expenditures authorized by 2004 appropriations	2,900,000
Expenditures authorized by 2003 appropriations	200,000
Unencumbered and unexpended balance of 2004 appropriations	500,000

Assume that appropriations do not lapse.

What amount would be reported for Expenditures (and Encumbrances, if appropriate) in the Statement of Revenues, Expenditures and Changes in Fund Balances?
a. $2,900,000
b. $3,100,000
c. $3,200,000
d. $3,400,000

Items 5 and 6 are based on the following information relating to property taxes levied by Western Oaks Village for the calendar year 2004:

Collections during 2004	$800,000
Expected collections during the first 60 days of 2005	100,000
Expected collections during the balance of 2005	50,000
Expected collections during January 2006	30,000
Estimated to be uncollectible	20,000
Total levy	$1,000,000

5. What is the maximum amount Western Oaks can report for 2004 property tax revenues, using accrual accounting, in the government-wide statements?
   a. $1,000,000.
   b. $980,000.
   c. $800,000.
   d. $900,000.
6. What is the maximum amount Western Oaks can report for 2004 property tax revenues, using modified accrual accounting, in the governmental fund Statement of Revenues, Expenditures, and Changes in Fund Balances?
   a. $1,000,000.
   b. $980,000.
   c. $800,000.
   d. $900,000.
7. West Bend County created a special revenue fund, the Summer Employment Grant Fund, to account for the proceeds of a federal grant for summer youth employment. During the year ended June 30, 2004, the County received an award for this reimbursement grant in the amount of $1,000,000. Grant expenditures were in June 2004, $300,000; in July 2004, $350,000; and in August 2004, $350,000. The cash was received from the federal government on August 31, 2004. How much revenue should be recognized in the special revenue fund for the year ended June 30, 2004?
   a. $0
   b. $1,000,000
   c. $300,000
   d. $650,000
8. The Encumbrance Control account of a governmental unit is credited when:
   a. The budget is recorded.
   b. A purchase order is approved.
   c. Goods are received.
   d. Payment is made.
9. A Budgetary Fund Balance—Reserved for Encumbrances (current year) in excess of a balance of Encumbrances Control indicates:
   a. An excess of Vouchers Payable over Encumbrances Control.
   b. An excess of purchase orders over invoices received.
   c. An excess of Appropriations Control over Encumbrances Control.
   d. A recording error.

10. A municipality had the following preclosing account balances as of June 30, 2004:

Revenues	$9,000,000
Expenditures	8,300,000
Encumbrances	400,000
Transfers In	700,000
Transfers Out	1,000,000

In the closing entries, the Fund Balance—Unreserved account would be:

a. Credited for $400,000
b. Credited for $700,000
c. Debited for $700,000
d. Unchanged

4–4. a. Distinguish between (1) exchange and (2) nonexchange transactions.
b. Identify and describe the four eligibility requirements listed in GASB *Statement 33*.
c. GASB *Statement 33* classifies nonexchange transactions into four categories. List the four categories, give an example of each, and outline asset and revenue recognition criteria for each.

4–5. a. Outline revenue recognition criteria under modified accrual accounting. Include specific requirements for property tax revenue.
b. Outline expenditure recognition criteria under modified accrual accounting. Include the general case, recognition of debt service expenditures, and recognition of expenditures for items such as compensated absences.

4–6. On January 1, 2004, the first day of its fiscal year, the City of Carter received notification that a federal grant in the amount of $450,000 was approved. The grant was categorical; that is, it was restricted for the payment of wages to teenagers for summer employment. The terms of the grant permitted reimbursement only after payment was made; the grant could be used over a two-year period. The following data pertain to operations of the Summer Employment Grant Fund, a special revenue fund of the City of Carter, during the year ended December 31, 2004.

Show entries in general journal form to record the following events and transactions in the accounts of the Summer Employment Grant Fund:

1. The budget for fiscal year 2004 was recorded. It provided for Estimated Revenues for the year in the amount of $255,000, and for Appropriations in the amount of $255,000.
2. A temporary loan of $250,000 was received from the General Fund.

3. During the year, teenagers earned and were paid $246,000 under terms of the Summer Employment program. Recognize the receivable and revenue.
4. A properly documented request for reimbursement was sent to the federal government; a check for $246,000 was received.
5. Necessary closing entries were made.

4–7. The Town of Quincy's fiscal year ends on June 30. The following data relate to the property tax levy for the fiscal year ended June 30, 2005.
Prepare journal entries for each of the dates as indicated.

   a. On July 1, 2004, property taxes in the amount of $10,000,000 were levied. It was estimated that 3 percent would be uncollectible. The property taxes were intended to finance the expenditures for the year ended June 30, 2005.
   b. On October 31, 2004, $4,600,000 in property taxes were collected.
   c. On December 31, 2004, $4,800,000 in additional property taxes were collected.
   d. On January 1, 2005, the uncollected property taxes became delinquent.
   e. On June 30, 2005, the entire balance of taxes receivable, net of the estimated uncollectible amount, $300,000, was transferred from Revenues Control to Deferred Revenues.
   f. On July 1, 2005, the $300,000 was recognized as a revenue in a reversing entry.
   g. On October 31, 2005, $300,000 in delinquent property taxes were collected.
   h. On November 1, 2005, the remaining delinquent property taxes were written off.

4–8. The City of Brownstown has an October 1—September 30 fiscal year.
   1. During the year ended September 30, 2004, goods and services were ordered in the amount of $990,000.
   2. During the year, goods and services ordered in the amount of $960,000 were received; related invoices amounted to $961,000.
   3. Make closing entries related to the encumbrances and expenditures as of September 30, 2004. Debit Fund Balance—Unreserved for the full amount of the encumbrances and expenditures, recognizing that revenues will offset that debit in another closing entry not related in this problem. Remember to establish the Fund Balance—Reserved for Encumbrances.
   4. At the beginning of the fiscal year ended September 30, 2005, close the fund balance reserve and re-establish the encumbrances.
   5. During the fiscal year ended September 30, 2005, the remaining goods related to the prior year purchase orders were received, along with invoices in the same amount.

4–9. The following information was abstracted from the accounts of the General Fund of the City of Rom after the books had been closed for the fiscal year ended June 30, 2004.

	Postclosing Trial Balance June 30, 2003	Transactions July 1, 2003 to June 30, 2004		Postclosing Trial Balance June 30, 2004
		Debits	Credits	
Cash	$700,000	$1,820,000	$1,852,000	$668,000
Taxes Receivable	40,000	1,870,000	1,828,000	82,000
	$740,000			$750,000
Allowance for Uncollectible Taxes	$ 8,000	$ 8,000	$ 10,000	$ 10,000
Accounts Payable	132,000	1,852,000	1,840,000	120,000
Fund Balance:				
Reserved for Encumbrances	—		70,000	70,000
Unreserved	600,000	50,000		550,000
	$740,000			$750,000

The budget for the fiscal year ended June 30, 2004, provided for estimated revenues of $2,000,000 and appropriations of $1,940,000. During the year, purchase orders were placed in the amount of $1,070,000. These purchase orders were filled in the amount of $1,000,000 leaving $70,000 open at year-end. Rom follows the procedures outlined in this text for encumbrances. Prepare journal entries to record the budgeted and actual transactions for the fiscal year ended June 30, 2004. Include closing entries.

(AICPA, adapted)

4–10. The Village of Maple Park had a beginning inventory balance in the amount of $200,000, which was considered material and properly recorded as of July 1, 2004, the beginning of the fiscal year. The following transactions took place during the fiscal year ended June 30, 2005:
1. Supplies were received during the year and paid for in the amount of $1,000,000.
2. Supplies were consumed in the amount of $980,000.
3. An ending inventory confirmed that the ending balance of inventory was $220,000.

Required

a. Record the above transactions, assuming Maple Park uses the purchases method to record inventories.

b. Record the above transactions, assuming Maple Park uses the consumption method to record inventories.

4–11. The General Fund trial balance of the City of Cordes as of January 1, 2004 was as follows:

	Debits	Credits
Cash	$20,000	
Taxes Receivable—Delinquent	77,200	
Estimated Uncollectible Taxes—Delinquent		$ 9,200
Accounts Payable		16,000
Fund Balance—Reserved for Encumbrances		8,000
Fund Balance—Unreserved		64,000
	$97,200	$97,200

The following data pertain to General Fund operations for the City of Cordes for the fiscal year ended December 31, 2004:

1. Budget adopted:

    Revenues:
Property Taxes	$420,800
Fines, Forfeits, and Penalties	160,000
Miscellaneous Revenues	20,000
	$600,800

    Expenditures and Other Financing Uses:
Public Safety	$390,000
General Government	120,000
Culture and Recreation	54,000
Transfers Out	30,000
	$594,000

2. Encumbrances outstanding at the end of 2003 were reestablished (see Village of Elizabeth example).
3. Property taxes were levied at an amount that would result in revenues of $420,800 after deduction of 4 percent of the tax levy as uncollectible. Round computations to the nearest dollar.
4. Purchase orders issued in 2004:

Public Safety	$152,000	
General Government	80,000	
Culture and Recreation	54,000	
		$286,000

5. Cash collections and transfers:

Delinquent Taxes	$ 39,200	
Current Taxes	368,000	
Fines, Forfeits, and Penalties	154,000	
Miscellaneous Revenues	20,000	
Transfers In	18,000	
		$599,200

6. Purchase orders issued in 2004 were filled in the following amounts:

	Estimated	Actual
Public Safety	$148,000	$148,400
General Government	80,000	80,000
Culture and Recreation	54,000	54,000
	$282,000	$282,400

7. Purchase orders issued in 2003 in the following amounts were filled in 2004:

	Estimated	Actual
Public Safety	$8,000	$8,200

8. Additional accounts payable for salaries and wages (not encumbered):

Public Safety	$230,000
General Government	40,000
	$270,000

9. Accounts paid amounted to $570,000; the transfer out, $30,000, was made in cash.
10. Reclassify Taxes Receivable—Current and Estimated Uncollectible Taxes—Current as delinquent.

Required:

a. Prepare journal entries to record the effects of the foregoing data. Omit explanations and subsidiary accounts.
b. Prepare closing entries.
c. Prepare for the General Fund of the City of Cordes
   (1) a Balance Sheet as of December 31, 2004.
   (2) a Statement of Revenues, Expenditures, and Changes in Fund Balance for the year ended December 31, 2004.

Continuous Problem

4–C. *Part 1.* Presented here are a number of transactions of the General Fund of the City of Everlasting Sunshine for which the budget was prepared in Continuous Problem 3–C.

Required:

a. Record in the general journal the following transactions for FY 2004. Make any computations to the nearest dollar. Subsidiary accounts and explanations are not required.
   (1) Encumbrances outstanding at the end of 2003 were reestablished (see Village of Elizabeth example).

(2) The 1/1/2004 balance of $20,000 in Deferred Revenues relates to property taxes levied for 2004, but collected in 2003. This amount should be recognized as 2004 revenues (debit Deferred Revenues and credit Revenues Control).

(3) A general tax levy in the amount of $6,700,000 was made. It is estimated that 3 percent of the tax will be uncollectible.

(4) Tax anticipation notes in the amount of $500,000 were issued.

(5) Goods and supplies related to all encumbrances outstanding as of 12/31/03 were received, along with invoices amounting to $30,000; the invoices were approved for payment.

(6) All vouchers and the amount due other funds were paid.

(7) The General Fund collected the following in cash: delinquent taxes, $180,000; interest and penalties receivable on taxes, $16,500; current taxes, $6,400,000; $330,000 due from the state government; licenses and permits, $800,000; sales taxes, $3,115,000; and miscellaneous revenues, $235,000. (The last three items had not been accrued.)

(8) Purchase orders, contracts, and other commitment documents were issued in the amount of $4,266,000.

(9) Payrolls for the General Fund totaled $4,600,000. Of that amount $506,000 were withheld for employees' federal income taxes and $361,100 were withheld for employees' FICA and Medicare tax liability; the balance was paid in cash. The encumbrance system is not used for payrolls.

(10) The liability for the city's share of FICA and Medicare taxes, $361,100, was recorded as was the liability for state unemployment taxes in the amount of $35,000.

(11) Invoices for most of the supplies and services ordered in transaction 8 were received in the amount of $4,037,300 and approved for payment. The related commitment documents amounted to $4,038,200.

(12) Tax anticipation notes were paid at maturity, along with interest in the amount of $22,000.

(13) Notification was received that an unrestricted state grant in the amount of $288,000 would be received during the first month of 2005.

(14) The General Fund recorded a liability to the Water and Sewer Fund for services in the amount of $45,000 and to the Stores and Services Fund for supplies in the amount of $313,200; $300,000 of the amount due the Stores and Services Fund was paid.

(15) The General Fund recorded an amount due of $35,000 from the Water and Sewer Fund as a contribution in lieu of taxes.

(16) The General Fund paid vouchers in the amount of $3,980,000 and paid the amounts due the federal and state governments. The General Fund also transferred to the debt service funds cash in the amount of $1,256,000 for the recurring payment of principal and interest.

(17) All required legal steps were accomplished to increase appropriations by the net amount of $360,000. Estimated revenues were increased by $330,000.

(18) The City Council authorized a write-off of $30,000 in delinquent property taxes and corresponding interest and penalties amounting to $4,000.

(19) Current taxes receivable were transferred to the delinquent classification. Interest and penalties receivable on taxes were accrued in the amount of $33,000; $5,000 of this amount is expected to be uncollectible.

(20) It is estimated that $50,000 of the delinquent taxes receivable will be collected more than 60 days beyond the fiscal year-end.

b. Post to the general ledger and prepare a trial balance. Remember to include the beginning balances.

c. Prepare and post the closing entries for the General Fund.

d. Prepare in good form a Balance Sheet for the General Fund as of the end of fiscal year, 12/31/04. Net the amounts due from and due to the Water and Sewer Fund.

e. Prepare a Statement of Revenues, Expenditures, and Changes in Fund Balance for the year ended December 31, 2004. Assume the following detail:

Revenues		Expenditures	
Property Taxes	$ 6,469,000	General Government	$1,692,300
Sales Taxes	3,115,000	Public Safety	3,258,700
Interest and Penalties on Taxes	28,000	Highways and Streets	1,441,400
Licenses and Permits	800,000	Sanitation	591,400
Intergovernmental Revenue	288,000	Health	723,600
Miscellaneous Revenue	270,000	Welfare	373,800
		Culture and Recreation	916,800
		Capital Outlay	445,600
Total	$10,970,000	Total	$9,443,600

Part 2. What follows are a number of transactions of the Street and Highway Fund for the City of Everlasting Sunshine for which the budget was prepared in Part 1 of Continuous Problem 3–C.

Required:

a. Record in the general journal the following transactions. Make any computations to the nearest dollar. Subsidiary accounts and explanations are not required.

(1) The state government notified the City that $975,000 will be available during 2004. The funds are not considered reimbursement-type as defined by GASB standards.
(2) Cash in the total amount of $950,000 was received from the state government.
(3) Contracts, all eligible for payment from the Street and Highway Fund, were signed in the amount of $923,000.
(4) Contractual services (see transaction 3) were received; the related contracts amounted to $891,500. Invoices amounting to $896,000 for these items were approved for payment. The goods and services all were for highways and streets.
(5) Investment revenue of $4,000 was earned and received.
(6) Vouchers were paid in the amount of $898,000.
(7) All required legal steps were accomplished to increase appropriations in the amount of $2,500.

b. Post to the general ledger and prepare a trial balance.
c. Prepare and post the necessary closing entries for the Street and Highway Fund.
d. Prepare a Balance Sheet for the Street and Highway Fund as of December 31, 2004.
e. Prepare a Statement of Revenues, Expenditures, and Changes in Fund Balances for the Street and Highway Fund for the fiscal year ended December 31, 2004.

Chapter Five

Accounting for Other Governmental Fund Types: Capital Projects, Debt Service, and Permanent

Chapters 3 and 4 illustrate accounting and financial reporting for the General Fund and for special revenue funds. GASB provides for three additional governmental fund types: capital projects, debt service, and permanent. This chapter describes and illustrates the accounting for each of these fund types, continuing the Village of Elizabeth example. Governmental fund statements are then presented for the Village of Elizabeth, including all five governmental fund types: General, special revenue, capital projects, debt service, and permanent. All of these governmental fund types use the current financial resources measurement focus and the modified accrual basis of accounting.

Governmental fund types account for revenues, other financing sources, expenditures, and other financing uses that are for capital outlay and debt service purposes, as well as for current purposes. General fixed assets that are acquired with governmental fund resources are not recorded as expenditures in the governmental funds but are displayed as fixed assets in the government-wide financial statements. Similarly, the proceeds of general long-term debt incurred for governmental activities (and paid back with governmental resources) are recorded as other financing sources (and expenditures) in governmental funds but the liability is displayed as long-term debt in the government-wide statements. Capital projects funds and debt service funds, in particular, are used to acquire major fixed assets and to issue and service long-term debt, although the General Fund may also be used for these purposes. Adjustments needed to record the general fixed assets and long-term debt transactions prior to preparing the government-wide statements are covered briefly in this chapter but illustrated more fully in Chapter 8 of this text. The general fixed assets and long-term debt for the Village of Elizabeth are included in the government-wide statements illustrated in Chapter 8.

Permanent funds reflect resources that are legally restricted so that principal may not be expended; earnings are used to benefit the government or its citizenry. In this chapter, a cemetery perpetual care fund is used to illustrate permanent funds.

CAPITAL PROJECTS FUNDS

A major source of funding for capital projects funds is the issuance of long-term debt. In addition to proceeds of issues of long-term debt, capital projects funds may receive grants from other governmental units, transfers from other funds, gifts from individuals or organizations, or a combination of several of these sources. Capital projects funds may also be used to account for the acquisition by a governmental unit of general fixed assets under capital lease agreements.

Capital projects funds differ from general and special revenue funds in that a capital projects fund exists only for the duration of the project for which it is created. In some jurisdictions, governments are allowed to account for all capital projects within a single Capital Projects Fund. In other jurisdictions, laws require each project to be accounted for by a separate capital projects fund. Even in jurisdictions that permit the use of a single fund, managers may prefer to use separate funds in order to enhance control over each project. In such cases, a fund is created when a capital project or a series of related projects is legally authorized; it is closed when the project or series is completed.

GASB standards require the same modified accrual basis of accounting for capital projects funds as for all other governmental funds. Proceeds of debt issues should be recognized by a capital projects fund at the time the debt is actually incurred, rather than at the time it is authorized, because authorization of an issue does not guarantee its sale. Proceeds of debt issues are recorded as **Proceeds of Bonds** or **Proceeds of Long-Term Notes** rather than as Revenues, and are reported in the Other Financing Sources section of the Statement of Revenues, Expenditures, and Changes in Fund Balances. Similarly, revenues raised by the General Fund or a special revenue fund and transferred to a capital projects fund are recorded as Transfers In and reported in the Other Financing Sources section of the operating statement. Taxes or other revenues raised specifically for a capital projects fund are recorded as Revenues of the capital projects fund. Grants, entitlements, or shared revenues received by a capital projects fund from another governmental unit are considered revenues of the capital projects fund as is interest earned on temporary investments of the capital projects fund.

Expenditures of capital projects funds generally are reported in the capital outlay character classification in the Governmental Funds Statement of Revenues, Expenditures, and Changes in Fund Balances. Capital outlay expenditures result in additions to the general fixed assets reported in the government-wide Statement of Net Assets. Even though budgetary accounting is not required for capital projects funds, encumbrance accounting is used; outstanding contracts and purchase orders are reported as reservations of fund balances in the governmental funds Balance Sheet.

Illustrative Case

In the following illustration of accounting for representative transactions of a capital projects fund, it is assumed that early in 2004 the Village Council of the Village of Elizabeth authorized an issue of $1,200,000 of 8 percent 10-year regular serial tax-supported bonds to finance construction of a fire station addition. The total cost of the fire station addition was expected to be $2,000,000, with $600,000 to be financed by grants from other governmental units and $200,000 to be transferred from an enterprise fund of the Village of Elizabeth. The project, to utilize land already owned by the Village, was to be done partly by a private contractor and partly by the Village's own working force. Completion of the project was expected within the year. Transactions and entries are illustrated next. For economy of time and space, vouchering of liabilities and entries in subsidiary ledger accounts are not illustrated.

The $1,200,000 bond issue, which had received referendum approval by taxpayers, was officially approved by the Village Council. No formal entry is required. A memorandum entry may be made to identify the approved project and the means of financing it.

The sum of $100,000 was borrowed from the National Bank for defraying engineering and other preliminary costs incurred before bonds could be sold. The notes will be repaid in the current period and are recorded as a liability in the capital project fund.

		Debits	Credits
1.	Cash	100,000	
	Bond Anticipation Notes Payable		100,000

The receivables from the enterprise fund and the other governmental units were recorded; receipt was expected during 2004.

		Debits	Credits
2.	Due from Other Funds	200,000	
	Due from Other Governmental Units	600,000	
	Other Financing Sources—Transfers In		200,000
	Revenues Control		600,000

Total purchase orders and other commitment documents issued for supplies, materials, items of minor equipment, and labor required for the project amounted to $245,698.

		Debits	Credits
3.	Encumbrances Control	245,698	
	Fund Balance—Reserved for Encumbrances		245,698

A contract was issued for the major part of the work to be done by a private contractor in the amount of $1,500,000.

		Debits	Credits
4.	Encumbrances Control	1,500,000	
	Fund Balance—Reserved for Encumbrances		1,500,000

Note that entries 3 and 4 differ from the entries illustrated in Chapters 3 and 4 to record encumbrances of the General or special revenue funds in that those fund types normally operate under annual budgets. In Chapters 3 and 4, a Budgetary Fund Balance Reserved for Encumbrances account was used as a part of the budgetary process. In this chapter, the credit is directly to the equity account Fund Balance—Reserved for Encumbrances.

Special engineering and miscellaneous preliminary costs that had not been encumbered were paid in the amount of $97,500.

5.	Construction Expenditures	97,500	
	Cash		97,500

When the project was approximately half finished, the contractor submitted billing for a payment of $750,000. The following entry records conversion of a commitment (recorded in Fund Balance—Reserved for Encumbrances) to a firm liability, eligible for payment upon proper authentication. Contracts Payable records the status of a claim under a contract between the time of presentation and verification for vouchering or payment.

6.	Fund Balance—Reserved for Encumbrances	750,000	
	Construction Expenditures	750,000	
	Encumbrances Control		750,000
	Contracts Payable		750,000

The transfer was received from the enterprise fund, and $300,000 was received from the other governmental units.

7.	Cash	500,000	
	Due from Other Funds		200,000
	Due from Other Governmental Units		300,000

The bond issue, dated January 2, was sold at a premium of $12,000 on that date. Under modified accrual accounting, bond premiums and discounts are not amortized. In this example, as is generally true, the premium must be used for debt service and is not available for use by the capital projects fund; therefore, the premium is transferred to the debt service fund. Entry 8a records the receipt by the capital projects fund of the par value of the bonds sold, and 8b records the transfer to the debt service fund.

	Debits	Credits
8a. Cash	1,212,000	
Other Financing Sources—Proceeds of Bonds		1,200,000
Other Financing Sources—Premium on Bonds		12,000
8b. Other Financing Uses—Transfers Out	12,000	
Cash		12,000

If bonds were sold at a discount, either the difference would be made up by a transfer from another fund, or the capital projects fund would have fewer resources available for the project. Generally, bond issue costs would be involved and would be recorded as expenditures.

If bonds were sold between interest dates, the governmental unit would collect from the purchaser the amount of interest accrued to the date of sale, because a full six months' interest would be paid on the next interest payment date. Interest payments are made from debt service funds; therefore, cash in the amount of accrued interest sold at the time of bond issuance should be recorded in the Debt Service Fund.

When the Village of Elizabeth's Capital Projects Fund pays the bond anticipation notes and interest (assumed to amount to $2,500), entry 9 is made:

9. Bond Anticipation Notes Payable	100,000	
Interest Expenditures	2,500	
Cash		102,500

The contractor's initial claim (see entry 6) was paid, less a 5 percent retention. Retention of a contractually stipulated percentage from payments to a contractor is common until the construction is completed and has been inspected for conformity with specifications and plans.

10. Contracts Payable	750,000	
Cash		712,500
Contracts Payable—Retained Percentage		37,500

Upon final acceptance of the project, the retained percentage is paid. In the event that the governmental unit finds it necessary to spend money on correction of deficiencies in the contractor's performance, the payment is charged to Contracts Payable—Retained Percentage.

Disbursements for items ordered at an estimated cost of $215,000 (included in the amount recorded by entry 3) amounted to $216,500.

		Debits	Credits
11.	Fund Balance—Reserved for Encumbrances	215,000	
	Construction Expenditures	216,500	
	Encumbrances Control		215,000
	Cash		216,500

Assume the contractor completes construction of the fire station and bills the Village of Elizabeth for the balance on the contract:

		Debits	Credits
12.	Fund Balance—Reserved for Encumbrances	750,000	
	Construction Expenditures	750,000	
	Encumbrances Control		750,000
	Contracts Payable		750,000

Assume the amount remaining from other governmental units was received:

		Debits	Credits
13.	Cash	300,000	
	Due from Other Governmental Units		300,000

Invoices for goods and services previously encumbered in the amount of $30,698 were received and approved for payment in the amount of $32,000. Additional construction expenditures, not encumbered, amounted to $115,000. The entire amount was paid in cash.

		Debits	Credits
14.	Fund Balance—Reserved for Encumbrances	30,698	
	Construction Expenditures	147,000	
	Encumbrances Control		30,698
	Cash		147,000

Assuming that inspection revealed only minor imperfections in the contractor's performance, and upon correction of these, the contractor's bill and the amount previously retained were paid, entry 15 should be made:

		Debits	Credits
15.	Contracts Payable—Retained Percentage	37,500	
	Contracts Payable	750,000	
	Cash		787,500

After entry 15 is recorded, $36,500 in cash remained in the capital projects fund. That amount was transferred to a debt service fund for the payment of bonds:

	Debits	Credits
16. Other Financing Uses—Transfers Out	36,500	
Cash		36,500

Prior to year-end, the closing entry was made:

	Debits	Credits
17. Revenues Control	600,000	
Other Financing Sources—Transfers In	200,000	
Other Financing Sources—Proceeds of Bonds	1,200,000	
Other Financing Sources—Premium on Bonds	12,000	
Construction Expenditures		1,961,000
Interest Expenditures		2,500
Other Financing Uses—Transfers Out		48,500

Financial statements for the Fire Station Addition Capital Projects Fund are presented as part of the Governmental Funds Balance Sheet (Illustration 5–1) and the Governmental Funds Statement of Revenues, Expenditures, and Changes in Fund Balances (Illustration 5–2).

The addition to the fire station, excluding interest, will be capitalized and shown as an addition to the capital assets in the government-wide financial statements. In addition, the $1,200,000 in bonds will be recorded as a liability in the government-wide statements. See Chapter 8 for the adjustments necessary as a result of this project.

ACQUISITION OF GENERAL FIXED ASSETS BY LEASE AGREEMENTS

FASB *SFAS No. 13* defines and establishes accounting and financial reporting standards for a number of forms of leases including **operating leases** and **capital leases**. GASB *Codification* Sec. L20.107 accepts the *SFAS No. 13* definitions of these two forms of leases and prescribes accounting and financial reporting for lease agreements of state and local governmental units. If a particular lease meets any one of the following criteria, it is a **capital** lease:
1. The lease transfers ownership of the property to the lessee by the end of the lease term.
2. The lease contains an option to purchase the leased property at a bargain price.
3. The lease term is equal to or greater than 75 percent of the estimated economic life of the leased property.
4. The present value of rental or other minimum lease payments equals or exceeds 90 percent of the fair value of the leased property less any investment tax credit retained by the lessor.

If none of the criteria are met, the lease is classified as an **operating** lease by the lessee. Rental payments under an operating lease for assets used by the governmental funds are recorded by the governmental funds as expenditures of the period. The

GASB has issued specific guidelines for state and government entities with operating leases with scheduled rent increases (*Codification* Sec. L20.108-112). Discussion of this special case is beyond the scope of this text.

If a governmental unit acquires general fixed assets under a capital lease agreement, the asset should be recorded in the government-wide financial statements at the inception of the agreement at the lesser of (1) the present value of the rental and other minimum lease payments or (2) the fair value of the leased property. For example, assume a governmental unit signs a capital lease agreement to pay $10,000 on January 1, 2004, the scheduled date of delivery of certain equipment to be used by an activity accounted for by a special revenue fund. The lease calls for annual payments of $10,000 at the beginning of each year thereafter; that is, January 1, 2005, January 1, 2006, and so on, through January 1, 2013. There are 10 payments of $10,000 each, for a total of $100,000, but GASB standards require entry in the accounts of the **present value** of the stream of annual payments, not their total. Since the initial payment of $10,000 is paid at the inception of the lease, its present value is $10,000. The present value of the remaining nine payments must be determined from present value tables, using the rate "the lessee would have incurred to borrow over a similar term the funds necessary to purchase the leased asset." Assuming the rate to be 10 percent, tables show that the present value of payments 2 through 10 is $57,590. The present value of the 10 payments is, therefore, $67,590. Assuming the fair value of the leased property to be more than $67,590, the asset should be recorded in the government-wide statement at $67,590, and the liability for $57,590 should also be recorded in the government-wide statements. GASB standards also require a governmental fund be used to record the following entry at the inception of the capital lease:

	Debits	Credits
Expenditures—Capital Outlay	67,590	
Other Financing Sources—Capital Lease Agreements		57,590
Cash		10,000

Rental payments during the life of the capital lease are recorded in a governmental fund as illustrated later in this chapter.

CONSTRUCTION OF GENERAL FIXED ASSETS FINANCED BY SPECIAL ASSESSMENT DEBT

A special assessment is a special tax levy that is assessed only against certain taxpayers—those taxpayers who are deemed to benefit from the service or project paid for by the proceeds of the special assessment levy. Special assessments may be either **service types** or **construction types.** Service-type special assessments, such as an assessment to downtown businesses for special garbage removal or police protection, would be accounted for in the appropriate fund, often the General or a special revenue fund.

Construction-type special assessment projects account for longer-term projects that often require debt financing. For example, assume that a government issued $500,000 in debt to install street lighting and build sidewalks in a newly annexed subdivision. Five-year special assessment bonds were issued to finance the project, which is administered by the city. Since city law requires that the provision of lighting and sidewalks is the responsibility of property owners, a special assessment is levied against the property owners in that subdivision for a five-year period. The proceeds of the assessment are used to pay the principal and interest on the debt.

Special assessment projects may be accounted for in one of two ways. First, if the governmental unit is either primarily or secondarily liable for the payment of debt principal and interest, the project is accounted for as if it were a governmental project. A capital projects fund should account for the proceeds of the debt and the construction expenditures, as illustrated for other capital projects in this chapter. The capitalized cost will be recorded in the government-wide statements. The debt should be recorded in the government-wide statements, and the levy and debt service expenditures should be recorded in a debt service fund, as illustrated for general government debt in this chapter.

Second, if the government is not liable for the special assessment debt directly or through guarantee, the special assessment is accounted for in an agency fund. Accounting for agency and other fiduciary funds is discussed and illustrated in Chapter 7.

DEBT SERVICE FUNDS

The principal of long-term debt incurred to finance the construction or purchase of general fixed assets, or other general long-term debt and interest on that debt is sometimes paid from collections of tax levies specifically designated for debt service. A second source would be from general taxes levied by the General Fund and transferred for that purpose. A third source of revenue may be from special assessments levied against property deemed to be particularly benefited by the fixed assets constructed or acquired, as described in the preceding section.

GASB standards provide a fund type called, unsurprisingly, the **debt service fund** type to account for revenue and other financing sources raised to service long-term debt, and for expenditures for debt service. Debt service funds are not created for debt issues of proprietary funds because debt service activities of such funds are accounted for within those funds. Earlier in this century, governmental issues of long-term debt commonly matured in total on a given date. In that era, bond indentures often required the establishment of a sinking fund, sometimes operated on an actuarial basis. Some sinking fund term bond issues are still outstanding, but they are dwarfed in number and amount by serial bond issues, in which the principal matures in installments.

If taxes and/or special assessments for payment of interest and principal on long-term debt are levied specifically for the debt service fund, they are recognized as revenues of the debt service fund. If taxes and/or special assessments are levied by another fund and transferred to the debt service fund, they will be recorded as revenues by the fund that levies the taxes or special assessments (often the General Fund) and as transfers to the debt service fund. The debt service fund should record transfers from other funds as well as revenues that it will raise directly or that will be earned on its investments. Similarly, as illustrated earlier in this chapter, if capital projects are completed with total expenditures less than total revenues and other financing sources, the cash is ordinarily transferred to the appropriate debt service fund. Because the timing and amounts of payments are predictable, encumbrance accounting is not used by debt service funds.

The Modified Accrual Basis—Meaning for Debt Service

GASB standards require debt service accounting to be on the same modified accrual basis of accounting as General, special revenue, and capital project funds. One peculiarity of the modified accrual basis as applied to debt service accounting is that interest on long-term debt is not accrued; it is recognized as an expenditure in the year in which the interest is legally due. For example, if the fiscal year of a government ends on December 31, 2003, and the interest on its bonds is payable on April 1 and October 1 of each year, interest payable on January 1, 2004, would not be reported as a liability in the Balance Sheet of the Debt Service Fund prepared as of December 31, 2003. The rationale is that, since interest is not legally due until April 1, 2004, resources need not be expended until 2004. The same reasoning applies to principal amounts that mature in the next fiscal year; expenditures and liabilities are recognized in the debt service fund in the year for which the principal is legally due. The only exception permitted by GASB is that if a government has resources available for payment in a debt service fund and the period of time until interest or principal payment is due is no more than one month, then the interest or principal payment may be accrued.

Additional Uses of Debt Service Funds

Debt service funds may be required to service, in addition to term bonds and serial bonds, debt arising from the use of notes or warrants having a maturity more than one year after the date of issue. Although each issue of long-term or intermediate-term debt is a separate obligation and may have legal restrictions and servicing requirements that differ from other issues, all debts to be serviced from tax revenues may be accounted for by a single debt service fund, if permitted by state laws and covenants with creditors. If more than one debt service fund is required by law, as few funds of this type should be created as possible. Subsidiary records of a debt service fund can provide needed assurance that restrictions and requirements relating to each debt issue are properly budgeted and accounted for.

If a governmental unit enters into a lease agreement that meets the criteria of a capital lease, a debt service fund may be used to account for the payments required by the lease agreement. Accounting for capital lease payments is discussed in a later section of this chapter.

In some jurisdictions, there are no statutes that require the debt service function to be accounted for by a debt service fund. Whether or not required by statute or local ordinance, bond indentures or other agreements with creditors are often construed as requiring the use of a debt service fund. Unless the debt service function is very simple, it may be argued that good financial management would dictate the establishment of a debt service fund even though not legally required. If neither law nor sound financial administration require the use of debt service funds, the function may be performed within the accounting and budgeting framework of the General Fund. In such cases, the accounting and financial reporting standards discussed in this chapter should be followed for the debt service activities of the General Fund.

Debt Service Accounting for Serial Bonds

Accounts recommended for use by debt service funds that are created to account for resources to be used for the payment of interest and principal of serial bond issues are similar to those recommended for use by General and special revenue funds, with the exception of budgetary accounts. Usually the government designates a bank as fiscal agent to handle interest and principal payments for each debt issue. The assets of a debt service fund may, therefore, include Cash with Fiscal Agent, and the appropriations, expenditures, and liabilities may include amounts for the service charges of fiscal agents.

There are four types of serial bonds: regular, deferred, annuity, and irregular. If the total principal of an issue is repayable in a specified number of equal installments over the life of the issue, it is a **regular** serial bond issue. If the first installment is delayed for a period of more than one year after the date of the issue, but thereafter installments fall due on a regular basis, the bonds are known as **deferred** serial bonds. If the amount of annual principal repayments is scheduled to increase each year by approximately the same amount that interest payments decrease (interest decreases, of course, because the amount of outstanding bonds decreases) so that the total debt service remains reasonably level over the term of the issue, the bonds are called **annuity** serial bonds. **Irregular** serial bonds may have any pattern of repayment that does not fit the other three categories.

Illustrative Case—Regular Serial Bonds

Accounting for regular serial bonds is illustrated by a debt service fund created to pay principal and interest for the fire station project for the Village of Elizabeth discussed earlier in this chapter. Recall that, early in 2004, the Village Council of the Village of Elizabeth authorized an issue of $1,200,000 of 8 percent tax-supported bonds. At the time of authorization, no formal entry is required in the capital projects fund; at that time, a memorandum entry may be made in the capital projects fund and provision made to account for debt service of the new debt issue in a debt service fund.

Assume that the bonds in this example are dated January 2, 2004, that interest payment dates are June 30 and December 31, and that the first of the 10 equal annual principal payments will be on December 31, 2004.

The bonds were sold on January 2, 2004, at a premium of $12,000, which was recorded in the capital projects fund (see entry 8a of this chapter). The premium was transferred to the debt service fund (see entry 8b):

	Debits	Credits
18. Cash	12,000	
Other Financing Sources—Transfers In		12,000

While GASB standards do not require the reporting of budget-actual schedules for debt service funds, prudence would dictate internal budgetary planning. Assuming the $12,000 amount was known at the time of budgetary planning, the following would reflect debt service needs related to this project:

Interest, June 30 ($1,200,000 × .08 × ½)	$ 48,000
Interest, December 31 ($1,200,000 × .08 × ½)	48,000
Principal, December 31 ($1,200,000/10)	120,000
Total Cash Needed	216,000
Less: Premium	12,000
Cash Needs (Net)	$204,000

Assume cash was transferred from the General Fund in the amount of $204,000 (see entries 21a and 21b of Chapter 4):

19. Cash	204,000	
Other Financing Sources—Transfers In		204,000

On June 30, $48,000 was paid to a local bank to make the first interest payment. An expenditure and a liability were also recorded:

20a. Cash with Fiscal Agent	48,000	
Cash		48,000
20b. Expenditures—Bond Interest	48,000	
Matured Interest Payable		48,000

When the fiscal agent reports that checks have been issued to all bondholders, entry 21 is made:

	Debits	Credits
21. Matured Interest Payable	48,000	
Cash with Fiscal Agent		48,000

On December 31, the next interest payment of $48,000 is due; also on that date, a principal payment of $120,000 is due. The debt service fund pays $168,000 to the local bank for payment and records the expenditures and liabilities for principal and interest:

	Debits	Credits
22a. Cash with Fiscal Agent	168,000	
Cash		168,000
22b. Expenditures—Bond Principal	120,000	
Expenditures—Bond Interest	48,000	
Matured Bonds Payable		120,000
Matured Interest Payable		48,000

The bank reported that all payments had been made as of December 31, 2004:

	Debits	Credits
23. Matured Bonds Payable	120,000	
Matured Interest Payable	48,000	
Cash with Fiscal Agent		168,000

It should be noted that, if principal and/or interest payment dates were other than the end of the fiscal year, for example, May 1 and November 1, accruals would *not* be made for the fund financial statements, following modified accrual accounting. However, accruals for interest would be made when preparing the government-wide financial statements.

Entry 16 of the capital projects fund illustration in this chapter reflected a transfer of $36,500 to the debt service fund, representing the unused construction funds. The corresponding entry is made in the debt service fund:

	Debits	Credits
24. Cash	36,500	
Other Financing Sources—Transfers In		36,500

At year-end, the debt service fund would reflect the following closing entry:

	Debits	Credits
25. Other Financing Sources—Transfers In	252,500	
Expenditures—Bond Principal		120,000
Expenditures—Bond Interest		96,000
Fund Balance—Reserved for Debt Service		36,500

Financial statements for the Fire Station Addition Debt Service Fund are presented as part of the Governmental Funds Balance Sheet (Illustration 5–1) and the Governmental Funds Statement of Revenues, Expenditures, and Changes in Fund Balances (Illustration 5–2).

Debt Service Accounting for Deferred Serial Bonds

If a government issues bonds other than regular serial bonds, debt service fund accounting is somewhat more complex than just illustrated. A government that issues deferred serial bonds will normally have several years without principal repayment during which, if it is fiscally prudent, amounts will be accumulated in the debt service fund for payment when the bonds mature. If this is the case, debt service fund cash should be invested in order to earn interest revenues. Material amounts of interest receivable on investments should be accrued at year-end.

Debt Service Accounting for Term Bonds

Term bond issues mature in their entirety on a given date, in contrast to serial bonds, which mature in installments. Term bond debt service requirements may be determined on an actuarial basis or on less sophisticated bases designed to produce approximately level contributions during the life of the issue. The annuity tables used for an actuarial basis assume that the investments of a debt service fund earn interest at a given percentage. Accounting for a term bond debt service fund would be similar to the method of accounting for a deferred serial bond issue.

Debt Service Accounting for Capital Lease Payments

Earlier in this chapter, the section headed "Acquisition of General Fixed Assets by Lease Agreements" gave an example of the necessary entry in a governmental fund at the inception of a capital lease.

Commonly, governmental units use the General or a debt service fund to record capital lease payments. Like an annuity serial bond, part of each lease payment is interest at a constant rate on the unpaid balance of the lease obligation, and part is a payment on the principal. Each annual payment on the capital lease in this example amounts to $10,000; for the payment on January 1, 2005, assuming $5,759 is payment of interest ($57,590 × .10) and $4,241 is payment on principal, the entry in the Debt Service Fund would be as follows:

	Debits	Credits
Expenditures—Interest	5,759	
Expenditures—Principal	4,241	
Cash		10,000

As indicated earlier in this chapter, a worksheet entry would be made for the government-wide statements, recording the fixed asset and capital lease obligation at the present value of lease payments. As a result of the above transaction, the capital lease obligation would be reduced by $4,241.

For the payment on January 1, 2006, the interest would be ($57,590 − $4,241 = $53,349) × .10, or $5,335 (rounded), and the principal expenditure would be $4,665.

Bond Refundings

Governments often refund bonds, that is, issue new debt to replace old debt. This may be to obtain better interest rates, to escape onerous debt covenants, or to change the maturity of the debt. A **current refunding** exists when new debt is issued, and the proceeds are used to call in the existing debt. When recording a current refunding, the debt proceeds would be reported as an Other Financing Source with a descriptor such as "Refunding of Existing Debt." An **advance refunding** exists when the proceeds are placed in an escrow account pending the call date or the maturity date of the existing debt. In this case, the debt is said to be **defeased** for accounting purposes. That means that the old debt is not reported in the financial statements and is replaced by the new debt. For advance refundings, the journal entry would be (assuming $10,000,000 in debt):

	Debits	Credits
Other Financing Uses—Payment to Bond Refunding Agent	10,000,000	
Other Financing Sources—Refunding Bonds Issued		10,000,000

Extensive note disclosures are required for both current and advance refundings.

Permanent Funds

Permanent funds are governmental funds that report resources that are legally restricted so that principal cannot be expended. Earnings from investments are to be expended for purposes that benefit the government and its citizens. (Similar funds whose earnings benefit individuals, private organizations, or other governments are *private purpose trust funds,* discussed in Chapter 7.) An example of a permanent fund is a cemetery perpetual care fund, which provides resources for the ongoing maintenance of a public cemetery.

Assume that, early in 2004, Richard Lee, a citizen of the Village of Elizabeth, drove by the Village Cemetery and was distressed by the poor level of maintenance. He entered into an agreement with Village officials on April 1, 2004, to provide $300,000 to the Village, with the stipulation that the $300,000 be invested, the principal never be expended, and the earnings be used to maintain the Village Cemetery. Accordingly, the Lee Cemetery Perpetual Care Fund was established, and the following entry was made:

26. Cash	300,000	
Revenues—Additions to Permanent Endowments		300,000

The funds were immediately invested in ABC Company bonds, which were selling at par. The bonds carried an annual interest rate of 8 percent and paid interest on April 1 and October 1:

	Debits	Credits
27. Investments—Bonds	300,000	
Cash		300,000

On October 1, $12,000 interest was received:

28. Cash	12,000	
Revenues—Investment Income—Interest		12,000

During 2004, $11,000 was expended for cemetery maintenance:

29. Expenditures—Cemetery	11,000	
Cash		11,000

Modified accrual accounting permits interest revenues to be accrued at year-end. The amount is $6,000 ($300,000 × .08 × 3/12):

30. Accrued Interest Receivable	6,000	
Revenues—Investment Income—Interest		6,000

GASB *Statement 31* requires that investments with determinable fair values be recorded at fair value. On December 31, 2004, it was determined that the ABC Company bonds had a fair value of $302,000, excluding accrued interest:

31. Investments—Bonds	2,000	
Revenue—Net Increase in Fair Value of Investments		2,000

As of December 31, 2004, the books were closed for the Lee Cemetery Perpetual Care Fund:

32. Revenues—Additions to Permanent Endowments	300,000	
Revenues—Investment Income—Interest	18,000	
Revenues—Investment Income—		
Net Increase in Fair Value of Investments	2,000	
Expenditures—Cemetery		11,000
Fund Balance—Reserved for Other Purposes		309,000

Financial statements for the Lee Cemetery Perpetual Care Fund are presented as part of the Governmental Funds Balance Sheet (Illustration 5–1) and the Governmental Funds Statement of Revenues, Expenditures, and Changes in Fund Balances (Illustration 5–2).

FINANCIAL REPORTING FOR GOVERNMENTAL FUNDS

GASB *Statement 34* requires two financial statements for the General Fund and other governmental funds. Both report separate columns for major funds and a column for nonmajor funds, as well as a total column. The General Fund must always be considered a major fund. Other governmental funds are considered major if both the following criteria exist (from Paragraph 76 of *Statement 34*):
1. Total assets, liabilities, revenues, *or* expenditures of that individual government fund are at least 10 percent of the corresponding total (assets, liabilities, and so forth) for all governmental funds.
2. Total assets, liabilities, revenues, *or* expenditures of the individual governmental fund are at least 5 percent of the corresponding total for all governmental and enterprise funds combined.

In addition, the government may *choose* to include any other governmental fund in these statements. See Chapter 2 for an example calculation of a major fund. In the Village of Elizabeth example, we assume that a decision is made to include all governmental funds in the basic governmental funds statements.

Balance Sheet—Governmental Funds

Illustration 5–1 presents the Balance Sheet for the governmental funds for the Village of Elizabeth. This Balance Sheet includes the General Fund and special revenue fund illustrated in Chapter 4 as well as the debt service and permanent funds illustrated in this chapter. Note that the capital projects fund does not have a column because all accounts were closed when the project was completed. Major capital projects funds continuing into future periods would be included in this statement.

Note that Fund Balances are separated into reserved and unreserved components. Reserved fund balances represent those balances that are committed (such as encumbrances) or that are legally set aside for specific purposes (debt service, other purposes—for permanent funds). The unreserved fund balances are broken down by fund type. In the General Fund, the unreserved fund balance represents the amount available for appropriation.

Statement of Revenues, Expenditures, and Changes in Fund Balances—Governmental Funds

Illustration 5–2 presents the Statement of Revenues, Expenditures, and Changes in Fund Balances. This statement includes the funds in Illustration 5–1 plus the capital project fund illustrated in this chapter. In the Village of Elizabeth example, students should be able to trace the transactions in the illustrative problems to this statement.

ILLUSTRATION 5-1

VILLAGE OF ELIZABETH
Balance Sheet
Governmental Funds
December 31, 2004

	General	Motor Fuel Tax	Fire Station Addition Debt Service	Lee Cemetery Perpetual Care	Total Governmental Funds
Assets					
Cash	$ 443,000	$247,500	$ 36,500	$ 1,000	$ 728,000
Investments				302,000	302,000
Interest receivable, net	34,490			6,000	40,490
Taxes receivable, net	528,800				528,800
Due from state government		125,000			125,000
Total Assets	$1,006,290	$372,500	$ 36,500	$309,000	$1,724,290
Liabilities and Fund Balances					
Liabilities:					
Accounts payable	$ 50,300	$135,000			$ 185,300
Due to other funds	75,000				75,000
Deferred revenues	40,000				40,000
Total Liabilities	165,300	135,000	–0–	–0–	$ 300,300
Fund Balances:					
Reserved for:					
Encumbrances	50,000				50,000
Debt service			36,500		36,500
Other purposes				309,000	309,000
Unreserved, reported in:					
General fund	790,990				790,990
Special revenue funds		237,500			237,500
Total Fund Balances	840,990	237,500	36,500	309,000	1,423,990
Total Liabilities and Fund Balances	$1,006,290	$372,500	$ 36,500	$309,000	$1,724,290

ILLUSTRATION 5–2

VILLAGE OF ELIZABETH
Statement of Revenues, Expenditures, and Changes in Fund Balances
Governmental Funds
For the Year Ended December 31, 2004

	General	Motor Fuel Tax	Fire Station Addition Debt Service	Fire Station Addition Capital Projects	Lee Cemetery Perpetual Care	Total Governmental Funds
Revenues						
Property taxes	$3,178,800	$	$	$		$3,178,800
Motor fuel taxes		650,000				650,000
Sales taxes	1,410,000					1,410,000
Interest and penalties on taxes	42,490					42,490
Licenses and permits	540,000					540,000
Fines and forfeits	430,000					430,000
Intergovernmental revenue	350,000	350,000		600,000		1,300,000
Charges for services	100,000					100,000
Addition to permanent endowment					300,000	300,000
Investment income—interest					18,000	18,000
Investment income—net increase in fair value of investments					2,000	2,000
Miscellaneous	30,000					30,000
Total Revenues	6,081,290	1,000,000		600,000	320,000	8,001,290

144

Expenditures				
Current:				
General government	$ 810,000	$	$	$ 810,000
Public safety	2,139,500			2,139,500
Public works	630,000	975,000		1,605,000
Health and welfare	480,100			480,100
Cemetery			11,000	11,000
Parks and recreation	527,400			527,400
Contribution to retirement				
funds	423,000			423,000
Miscellaneous	20,300			20,300
Debt Service				
Principal		120,000		120,000
Interest		96,000		96,000
Capital Outlay			1,963,500	1,963,500
Total Expenditures	5,030,300	975,000	1,963,500	8,195,800
Excess (Deficiency) of Revenues				
over Expenditures	1,050,990	25,000	(1,363,500)	(194,510)
Other financing sources (uses)				
Proceeds of bonds			1,200,000	1,200,000
Premium on bonds			12,000	12,000
Transfers in		252,500	200,000	452,500
Transfers out	(800,000)		(48,500)	(848,500)
Total Other Financing Sources				
(Uses)	(800,000)	252,500	1,363,500	816,000
Special item				
Proceeds from sale of land	300,000	-0-	-0-	300,000
Net Change in Fund Balances	550,990	25,000	36,500	309,000
Fund Balances—Beginning	290,000	212,500	-0-	502,500
Fund Balances—Ending	$ 840,990	$ 237,500	$ 36,500	$1,423,990

Questions and Exercises

5–1. Using the annual financial report obtained for Exercise 1–1, answer the following questions:

    a. Look at the governmental fund financial statements. Are any major capital projects funds included? If so, list them. Attempt to find out the nature and purpose of the projects from the letter of transmittal, the notes, or MD&A. What are the major sources of funding, such as bond sales, intergovernmental grants, and transfers from other funds? Were the projects completed during the year?

    b. Again looking at the governmental fund financial statements, are any major debt service funds included? If so list them. What are the sources of funding for these debt service payments?

    c. Does your report include supplemental information including combining statements for nonmajor funds? If so, are any capital projects and debt service funds included? If so, list them. Indicate the major revenue and other financing source categories for these funds.

    d. Look at the governmental fund Statement of Revenues, Expenditures, and Changes in Fund Balances, specifically the expenditure classification. Compute a ratio of capital outlay/total expenditures. Again, compute a ratio of debt service/total expenditures. Compare those with your classmates. Comment on the possible meaning of these ratios.

    e. Look at the notes to the financial statements, specifically the note (in the summary of significant accounting policies) regarding the definition of modified accrual accounting. Does the note specifically indicate that modified accrual accounting is used for capital projects and debt service funds? Does the note indicate that debt service payments, both principal and interest, are recorded as an expenditure when due?

    f. Does your government report capital leases payable in the government-wide Statement of Net Assets? If so, can you determine if new capital leases were initiated during the year? Can you trace the payments related to capital leases?

    g. Does your government report any permanent funds, either major or nonmajor? If so, list them. What are the amounts of the permanent resources available for governmental purposes? What is/are the governmental purpose(s)?

5–2. For each of the following, select the letter that represents the *best* answer.

    1. Which of the following fund types use modified accrual accounting?
       a. Capital projects.
       b. Debt service.
       c. Permanent.
       d. All of the above.

    2. Financing for the renovation of Fir City's municipal park, begun and completed during 2004, came from the following sources:

Grant from State Government	$400,000
Proceeds from General Obligation Bond Issue	500,000
Transfer from Fir's General Fund	100,000

In its 2004 Statement of Revenues, Expenditures, and Changes in Fund Balances, how should Fir report these amounts (choose one of the following options)?

	Revenues	Other Financing Sources
a.	$1,000,000	$ 0
b.	900,000	100,000 ✓
c.	400,000	600,000
d.	0	1,000,000

3. Which of the following is true regarding capital projects funds?
   a. Encumbrance accounting is often employed.
   b. Budgetary accounts (Estimated Revenues, Appropriations, etc.) are normally employed to facilitate the preparation of the Budgetary Comparison Schedule required by the GASB to be in RSI.
   c. Both of the above.
   d. Neither of the above.

4. When a government enters into a capital lease for the use of street cleaning equipment, which of the following is true?
   a. A governmental fund must debit an expenditure and credit an "other financing source" for the present value of the future lease payments.
   b. In future years, as payments are made, a governmental fund must record expenditures for principal and interest.
   c. Both of the above.
   d. Neither of the above.

5. Stone City, which is legally obligated to maintain a debt service fund, issued the following general obligation bonds on July 1, 2004:

Term of Bonds	10 years
Face Amount	$1,000,000
Issue Price	101
Stated Interest Rate	6%

Interest is payable January 1 and July 1. What amount of bond premium should be amortized in Wood's debt service fund for the year ended December 31, 2004?
   a. $1,000
   b. $500
   c. $250
   d. $0

Items 6–9 are based on the following information: The City of X, which has a calendar fiscal year, issued $1,000,000 in 6% general obligation bonds on October 1, 2003, at 101. Interest is payable on April 1 and October 1, and the first of 10 equal annual principal payments is due October 1, 2004. All payments are to be funded by General Fund transfers.

6. What would be the amount of debt service expenditures for the year ended December 31, 2003?
   a. $0
   b. $30,000
   c. $60,000
   d. $160,000

7. What would be the proper accounting for the $10,000 bond premium?
   a. The bond premium would normally be recorded as a revenue in a capital projects fund.
   b. The bond premium would normally be amortized over the life of the bond issue.
   c. The bond premium would normally be recorded as an other financing source in a capital projects fund.
   d. None of the above.

8. What would be the amount of the debt service expenditures for the year ended December 31, 2004?
   a. $0
   b. $60,000
   c. $130,000
   d. $160,000

9. What would be the amount of the debt service expenditures for the year ended December 31, 2005?
   a. $160,000
   b. $157,000
   c. $154,000
   d. $54,000

10. What would be an example of a permanent fund?
    a. A cemetery perpetual care fund.
    b. A gift given, to be invested permanently, with the proceeds to benefit retired firefighters.
    c. A pension trust fund.
    d. All of the above.

5-3. For each of the following, select the letter that represents the *best* answer.
   1. Which of the following funds are classified as *governmental* by the GASB?
      a. General, special revenue, capital projects, debt service.

b. General, special revenue.
c. General, special revenue, capital projects, debt service, permanent.
d. General, special revenue, capital projects, debt service, proprietary, fiduciary.

2. General fixed assets constructed through capital projects funds would be reported in the:
   a. Capital projects fund only.
   b. Government-wide statements only.
   c. Capital projects fund and government-wide statements.
   d. General Fixed Asset Account Group (under *Statement 34*).

Items 3–7 are based on the following information: During the fiscal year ending December 31, 2004, the City of X issued 6% general obligation bonds in the amount of $2,000,000 at par and used $1,990,000 of the proceeds to construct a police station. The remaining $10,000 was transferred to a debt service fund. The bonds were dated November 1, 2004, and paid interest on May 1 and November 1. The first of 20 equal annual principal payments was due on November 1, 2005.

3. How would the $2,000,000 bond sale be recorded?
   a. As a liability of the debt service fund.
   b. As a revenue in a capital projects fund.
   c. As another financing source in a debt service fund.
   d. As another financing source in a capital projects fund.

4. The amount of capital outlay expenditures to be reported by a capital projects fund would be:
   a. $2,000,000
   b. $1,990,000
   c. $2,010,000
   d. $0

5. How would the government account for the $10,000 unused funds?
   a. As a revenue in a debt service fund and as an expenditure in a capital projects fund.
   b. As an asset in a capital projects fund and as a liability in a debt service fund.
   c. As another financing source in a capital projects fund and as another financing use in a debt service fund.
   d. As another financing source in a debt service fund and as another financing use in a capital projects fund.

6. What would be the amount recorded as expenditures by a debt service fund in the year ended December 31, 2004?
   a. $0
   b. $20,000

c. $53,333
d. $60,000

7. What would be the amount recorded as expenditures by a debt service fund in the year ended December 31, 2005?
   a. $0
   b. $120,000
   c. $220,000
   d. $320,000

8. Modified accrual accounting requires that expenditures for debt service be recorded when principal and interest payments are legally due. An exception is made sometimes when a government has resources at year-end. What is the exception?
   a. The resources may be held in any governmental fund, and the payment must be due within one month of the fiscal year-end.
   b. The resources must be held in a debt service fund; payment must be due within three months.
   c. The resources must be held in a debt service fund; payment must be due within one month.
   d. The resources may be held in any governmental fund; payment must be due within six months.

9. Which financial statements are required for the General and other major governmental funds?
   a. Balance Sheet, Statement of Activities.
   b. Balance Sheet, Statement of Revenues, Expenses, and Changes in Net Assets.
   c. Balance Sheet, Statement of Revenues, Expenditures, and Changes in Fund Balances.
   d. Statement of Net Assets, Statement of Activities.

10. Which of the following is true regarding permanent funds?
    a. Permanent funds must use modified accrual accounting.
    b. Permanent funds must include resources that cannot be expended.
    c. The income from permanent funds must benefit the government and/or its citizens.
    d. All of the above are true.

5-4. a. Armstrong County established a County Office Building Construction Fund to account for a project that was expected to take less than one year to complete. Record the following transactions in that Construction Fund. The County's fiscal year ends on June 30.
   (1) On July 1, 2004, bonds were sold at par in the amount of $9,000,000 for the project.
   (2) On July 5, 2004, a contract was signed with the Sellers Construction Company in the amount of $8,800,000.

(3) On December 30, 2004, a progress bill was received from Sellers in the amount of $6,000,000. The bill was paid, except for a 5 percent retainage.

(4) On June 1, 2005, a final bill was received in the amount of $2,800,000 from Sellers, which was paid, except for the 5 percent retainage. An appointment was made between the County Engineer and Bill Sellers to inspect the building and to develop a list of items that needed to be corrected.

(5) On the day of the meeting, the County Engineer discovered that Sellers had filed for bankruptcy and moved to Florida to establish a new construction firm. The City incurred a liability in the amount of $450,000 to have the defects corrected by the Baker Construction Company. (Charge the excess over the balance of Contracts Payable—Retained Percentage to Construction Expenditures.)

(6) All accounts (from 5 above) were paid; remaining cash was transferred to the Debt Service Fund.

(7) The accounts of the County Office Building Construction Fund were closed.

b. Prepare a separate Statement of Revenues, Expenditures, and Changes in Fund Balances for the County Office Building Construction Fund for the year ended June 30, 2005.

5–5. The Village of Harvard issued $5,000,000 in 6 percent general obligation, tax-supported bonds on July 1, 2003 at 101. Record the following transactions on the books of the Village of Harvard Debt Service Fund. A fiscal agent is not used. Resources for principal and interest payments are to come from the General Fund, in amounts exactly equal to the required payments. Interest payment dates are December 31 and June 30. The first of 20 annual principal payments is to be made June 30, 2004. Harvard has a calendar fiscal year.

1. The bonds were issued. A capital projects fund transferred $50,000 to the debt service fund, to be used for the first principal payment.
2. On December 31, 2003, funds in the amount of $150,000 were received from the General Fund, and the first interest payment was made.
3. On December 31, 2003, the books were closed.
4. On June 30, 2004, funds in the amount of $350,000 were received from the General Fund, and the second interest and the first principal payments were made. Remember to use the $50,000 from the premium.
5. On December 31, 2004, funds in the amount of $142,500 were received from the General Fund, and the interest payment was made.
6. On December 31, 2004, the books were closed.

5–6. On July 1, 2003, the City of Irwin issued $10,000,000 in 6 percent tax-supported regular serial bonds at par. The bonds pay interest on July 1 and January 1 of each year. The first of 10 equal annual principal payments is due on July 1, 2004. Funding is to come from General Fund transfers, the first day of each fiscal year, in an amount equal to the required payments. Irwin does not accrue interest at year-end. Closing entries are not required.

    a. Assuming Irwin's fiscal year ends on June 30, prepare the entries for the Debt Service Fund for the fiscal years ending June 30, 2004, and June 30, 2005.

    b. Assuming Irwin's fiscal year ends on September 30, prepare the entries for the Debt Service Fund for the fiscal years ending September 30, 2003, and September 30, 2004.

5–7. The Village of Budekville, which has a fiscal year July 1 to June 30, sold $1,000,000 in 6 percent tax-supported bonds at par to construct an addition to its police station. The bonds were dated and issued on July 1, 2003. Interest is payable semiannually on January 1 and July 1, and the first of 10 equal annual principal payments was made on July 1, 2004. The village used a capital projects fund to account for the project, which was completed at a total cost of $995,000 on June 15, 2004. You are to record the following transactions on the books of Budekville's: (*a*) Capital Projects Fund; and (*b*) Debt Service Fund. Remember that interest during construction is not capitalized.

1. The bonds were sold on July 1, 2003.
2. The General Fund transferred an amount equal to the first interest payment on December 31, 2003. The Debt Service Fund made the payment as of January 1, 2004.
3. The project was completed on June 15, 2004. You may omit encumbrance entries.
4. The remaining balance was transferred to the Debt Service Fund from the Capital Projects Fund for the eventual payment of principal.
5. The books were closed as of June 30, 2004.
6. The General Fund transferred an amount equal to the payments due as of July 1, 2004.
7. The payments were made as required by the Debt Service Fund.

5–8. On July 1, 2003, a five-year agreement is signed between the City of Genoa and the Computer Leasing Corporation for the use of computer equipment not associated with proprietary funds activity. The cost of the lease, excluding executory costs, is $15,000 per year. The first payment is to be made by a capital projects fund at the inception of the lease. Subsequent payments, beginning July 1, 2004, are to be made by a debt service fund. The present value of the lease payments, including the first payment, is $68,189. The interest rate implicit in the lease is 5 percent.

    a. Assuming the agreement meets the criteria for a capital lease under the provisions of *SFAS No. 13,* make the entries required in (1) the capital projects fund and (2) the debt service fund on July 1, 2003 and July 1, 2004.

b. Comment on where the fixed asset and long-term liability associated with this capital lease would be recorded and the impact of the journal entries recorded for (*a*).

5–9. The Town of McHenry has $6,000,000 in general obligation bonds outstanding and maintains a single debt service fund for all debt service transactions. On July 1, 2004, a refunding took place in which $6,000,000 in new general obligation bonds were issued. Record the transaction on the books of the debt service fund under each of the following assumptions:

   a. A current refunding.
   b. An advance refunding.

5–10. The City of Sharpesburg received a gift of $1,000,000 from a local resident on June 1, 2004, and signed an agreement that the funds would be invested permanently and that the income would be used to purchase books for the city library. The following transactions took place during the year ended December 31, 2004:

   1. The gift was recorded on June 1.
   2. On June 1, ABC Company bonds were purchased in the amount of $1,000,000, at par. The bonds carry an annual interest rate of 8 percent, payable semiannually on December 1 and June 1.
   3. On December 1, the semiannual interest payment was received. Round to the nearest dollar.
   4. From December 1 through December 31, $37,500 in book purchases were made; full payment was made in cash.
   5. On December 31, an accrual was made for interest.
   6. Also, on December 31, a reading of the financial press indicated that the ABC bonds had a fair value of $1,005,000, exclusive of accrued interest.
   7. The books were closed.

   Required:
   a. Record the transactions on the books of the Library Book Permanent Fund.
   b. Prepare a separate Statement of Revenues, Expenditures, and Changes in Fund Balances for the Library Book Permanent Fund for the Year Ended December 31, 2004.

Continuous Problem

5–C. *Part 1.* The voters of the City of Everlasting Sunshine approved the issuance of tax-supported bonds in the face amount of $4,000,000 for the construction and equipping of a new annex to the City Hall. Architects were to be retained, and construction was to be completed by outside contractors. In addition to the bond proceeds, a $500,000 grant was expected from the state government. You are required to do the following:

154 Chapter 5

a. Open a general journal for the City Hall Annex Construction Fund. Record the following transactions, as necessary. Use account titles listed under requirement *b*.
   (1) On January 1, 2004, the total face amount of bonds bearing an interest rate of 8 percent was sold at a $50,000 premium. The bonds are to mature in blocks of $200,000 each year over a 20-year period commencing January 1, 2005. Interest payment dates are July 1 and January 1. The first interest payment will be July 1, 2004. The premium was transferred to the City Hall Annex Debt Service Fund for the future payment of principal on the bonds.
   (2) The receivable from the state government was recorded.
   (3) Legal and engineering fees early in the project were paid in the amount of $53,000. This amount had not been encumbered.
   (4) Architects were engaged at a fee of $210,000.
   (5) Preliminary plans were approved, and the architects were paid 20 percent of the fee.
   (6) The complete plans and specifications were received from the architects and approved. A liability in the amount of $126,000 to the architects was approved and paid.
   (7) Bids were received and opened in public session. After considerable discussion in City Council, the low bid from Hardhat Construction Company in the amount of $3,800,000 was accepted, and a contract was signed.
   (8) The contractor required partial payment of $2,000,000. Payment was approved and vouchered with the exception of a 5 percent retainage.
   (9) Cash in the full amount of the grant was received from the state government.
   (10) Furniture and equipment for the annex were ordered at a total cost of $400,000.
   (11) Payment was made to the contractor for the amount vouchered (see transaction 8).
   (12) The contractor completed construction and requested payment of the balance due on the contract. After inspection of the work, the amount, including the past retainage, was vouchered and paid.
   (13) Furniture and equipment were received at a total actual installed cost of $405,550. Invoices were approved for payment.
   (14) The remainder of the architects' fees was approved for payment.
   (15) The City Hall Annex Construction Fund paid all outstanding liabilities on December 31, 2004.

b. Open a general ledger for the City Hall Annex Construction Fund. Use the following account titles. Allow five lines unless indicated otherwise. Post the entries to the City Hall Annex Construction Fund general ledger.

> Cash (03–101)—11 lines
> Due from State Government (03–141)
> Accounts Payable (03–201)—11 lines
> Contracts Payable—Retained Percentage (03–202)
> Fund Balance—Reserved for Encumbrances (03–311)—12 lines
> Fund Balance—Unreserved (03–321)
> Revenues Control (03–400)
> Other Financing Sources—Proceeds of Bonds (03–450)
> Other Financing Sources—Premium on Bonds (03–451)
> Construction Expenditures (03–510)—10 lines
> Other Financing Uses—Transfers Out (03–560)
> Encumbrances Control (03–800)

c. Prepare a preclosing trial balance. Then, prepare and post an entry closing all nominal accounts to Fund Balance. Prepare an entry transferring remaining cash to the City Hall Annex Debt Service Fund. Finally, prepare an entry closing the City Hall Annex Construction Fund completely.

Part 2. The City Hall Debt Service Fund of the City of Everlasting Sunshine has been open for five years; it was created to service an $8,000,000, 6 percent tax-supported bond issue. As of December 31, 2003, this serial bond issue had a balance of $6,000,000. Semiannual interest payments are made on January 1 and July 1, and a principal payment of $400,000 is due on January 1 of each year. As this is a regular serial bond debt service fund, the only accounts with balances as of January 1, 2004, were Cash with Fiscal Agent and Fund Balance—Reserved for Debt Service, each with balances of $580,000. (Revenues were raised and collected in cash in 2003 in order to be able to pay bond principal and interest due on January 1, 2004.) The government chose not to accrue interest payable.

a. Open a general journal for the City Hall Debt Service Fund and prepare journal entries for the following transactions. Use account titles listed under requirement *b*.

   (1) The fiscal agent reported that $180,000 in checks had been mailed to bondholders for interest due on January 1, and $400,000 in checks were mailed for bonds maturing that day.

   (2) Cash in the amount of $168,000 was received from the General Fund on June 30 and was transferred to the fiscal agent.

   (3) The fiscal agent reported that checks dated July 1 had been mailed to bondholders for interest due that day.

   (4) Cash in the amount of $568,000 was received from the General Fund on December 31 and transferred to the fiscal agent to be used for the interest and principal payments due on January 1, 2005. The government elected to not accrue the interest and principal at year-end.

b. Open a general ledger for the City Hall Debt Service Fund. Use the following account titles. Allow five lines for each account. Enter the beginning balances. Post the entries made for requirement *a* to the ledger accounts.

   Cash (041–101)
   Cash with Fiscal Agent (041–102)
   Fund Balance—Reserved for Debt Service (041–312)
   Other Financing Sources—Transfers In (041–460)
   Expenditures—Bond Principal (041–521)
   Expenditures—Bond Interest (041–522)

c. Prepare a preclosing trial balance. Then prepare and post an entry closing all nominal accounts to Fund Balance.

Part 3. On the advice of the city attorney, a City Hall Annex Debt Service Fund is opened to account for debt service transactions related to the bond issue sold on January 1, 2004 (see Part 1).

a. Open a general journal for the City Hall Annex Debt Service Fund. Record the following transactions, as necessary. Use account titles listed under requirement *b*.

   (1) The premium described in transaction 1 of Part 1 was received as a transfer from the capital projects fund.
   (2) Cash in the amount of $160,000 was received from the General Fund on June 30 and was transferred to the fiscal agent.
   (3) The fiscal agent reported that checks dated July 1 had been mailed to bondholders for interest due that day.
   (4) The transfer described in part (c) of Part 1 was received.
   (5) Cash in the amount of $360,000 was received from the General Fund on December 31 and transferred to the fiscal agent to be used for interest and principal payments due on January 1, 2005. The remaining cash on hand was invested. The government elected to not accrue the interest at year-end.

b. Open a general ledger for the City Hall Annex Debt Service Fund. Use the following account titles. Allow five lines for each account, unless indicated otherwise. Post the entries made for requirement *a* to the ledger accounts.

   Cash (042–101)—7 lines
   Cash with Fiscal Agent (042–102)
   Investments (042–111)
   Fund Balance—Reserved for Debt Service (042–312)
   Other Financing Sources—Transfers In (042–460)
   Expenditures—Bond Interest (042–522)

c. Prepare a preclosing trial balance. Then prepare and post an entry closing all nominal accounts to fund balance.

Part 4.

a. Prepare a Balance Sheet for the governmental funds for the City of Everlasting Sunshine as of December 31, 2004. Include the General Fund, the Street and Highway Fund (P4–C), the City Hall Annex Construction Fund, the City Hall Debt Service Fund, and the City Hall Annex Debt Service Fund. Use the balances computed in Chapter 4 for the General Fund and special revenue fund portions of this statement.

b. Prepare a Statement of Revenues, Expenditures, and Changes in Fund Balances for the governmental funds for the City of Everlasting Sunshine for the Year Ended December 31, 2004. Include the same funds as listed in requirement *a*.

Chapter Six

Proprietary Funds

All of the funds discussed in previous chapters (General, special revenue, capital projects, debt service, and permanent) are classified as governmental funds, and owe their existence to legal constraints placed upon the raising of revenue and/or the use of resources for the provision of services to the public and the acquisition of facilities to aid in the provision of services. Funds discussed in previous chapters record only current financial resources and liabilities that will be settled with current financial resources. Fixed assets and long-term debt are not accounted for in governmental funds, but are presented in government-wide statements. Governmental funds recognize revenues and expenditures, not revenues and expenses.

A second fund classification, **proprietary funds,** describes funds that are used to account for activities similar to those often engaged in by profit-seeking businesses. That is, users of goods or services produced by a proprietary fund are charged amounts directly related to the costs of providing the goods or services. Thus, in the pure case, proprietary funds are self-supporting. Revenues and *expenses* (not expenditures) are recognized on the full accrual basis, so that financial statements of proprietary funds are similar in many respects to those of business organizations. Fixed assets used in fund operations and long-term debt serviced from fund revenues are recorded in the accounts of each proprietary fund. Depreciation on fixed assets is recognized as an expense, and other accruals and deferrals common to business accounting are recorded in proprietary funds. Budgets should be prepared for proprietary funds to facilitate management of fund activities, but GASB standards do not require or encourage budget-actual reporting.

The use of full accrual accounting permits financial statement users to observe whether proprietary funds are operated at a profit or a loss. The full accrual basis of accounting requires revenues to be recognized when earned and expenses to be recognized when incurred. Operating revenues and expenses are to be distinguished from nonoperating revenues and expenses.

Two types of funds are classified as proprietary funds: internal service funds and enterprise funds. Internal service funds provide, on a user charge basis, services to other government departments. Enterprise funds provide, on a user charge basis, services to the general public.

Three financial statements are required for proprietary funds: a Statement of Net Assets (or Balance Sheet), a Statement of Revenues, Expenses, and Changes in Fund Net Assets, and a Statement of Cash Flows. As is true for governmental funds, enterprise funds are reported by major fund, with nonmajor funds presented in a separate column. However, internal service funds are reported in a single column. These statements will be discussed in more detail and illustrated later in this chapter.

GASB *Codification* Sec. P80 provides guidance regarding the application of private sector accounting pronouncements to the accounting and reporting for proprietary funds. All FASB Statements and Interpretations, Accounting Principles Board Opinions, and Accounting Research Bulletins issued on or before November 30, 1989, that do not contradict GASB pronouncements are presumed to apply. In addition, for enterprise funds (but not for internal service funds), governments have the option to apply (or not apply) FASB Statements and Interpretations that are issued after November 30, 1989, and that apply to business organizations (not to not-for-profit organizations). The option chosen must be disclosed in the notes.

INTERNAL SERVICE FUNDS

As governmental units become more complex, efficiency can be improved if services used by several departments or funds or even by several governmental units are combined in a single administrative unit. Purchasing, computer services, transportation services, and risk management activities are common examples. Activities that produce goods or services to be provided to *other departments* or *other governmental units* on a cost-reimbursement basis are accounted for by internal service funds.

Internal service funds recognize revenues and expenses on the full accrual basis. They account for all fixed assets used in their operations and for long-term debt to be serviced from revenues generated from their operations, as well as for all current assets and current liabilities. Net assets are to be reported in three categories: (1) invested in capital assets, net of related debt; (2) restricted, and (3) unrestricted.

Establishment and Operation of Internal Service Funds

The establishment of an internal service fund is normally subject to legislative approval. The original allocation of resources to the fund may be derived from a transfer of assets of another fund, such as the General Fund or an enterprise fund, intended as a **transfer** not to be repaid or as a loan that is in the nature of a long-term **advance** to be repaid by the internal service fund over a period of years.

Because internal service funds are established to improve the management of resources, they should be operated and accounted for on a business basis. For example, assume that administrators request the establishment of a fund for the purchasing, warehousing, and issuing of supplies used by a number of funds and departments. A budget should be prepared for the internal service fund (but not recorded in the accounts) to demonstrate that fund management has realistic plans to generate sufficient revenues to cover the cost of goods issued and such other expenses, including depreciation, that the governing body intends fund operations to recover. Departments and units expected to purchase goods and services from internal service funds should include in their budgets the anticipated outlays for goods and services. During the year, as supplies are issued or services are rendered, the internal service fund records operating revenues (Charges for Services is an account title commonly used instead of Sales). Since the customer is another department of the government, the using departments typically accounted for by governmental funds record expenditures. Periodically and at year-end, an operating statement should be prepared for each internal service fund to compare revenues and related expenses; these operating statements, called Statements of Revenues, Expenses, and Changes in Fund Net Assets, are similar to income statements prepared for investor-owned businesses.

Illustrative Case—Supplies Fund

Assume that the administrators of the Village of Elizabeth obtain approval from the Village Council in early 2004 to centralize the purchasing, storing, and issuing functions and to administer and account for these functions in a Supplies Fund. A payment of $596,000 cash is made from the General Fund which is not to be repaid by the Supplies Fund. Of the $596,000, $290,000 is to finance capital acquisitions and $306,000 is to finance noncapital acquisitions. Additionally, a long-term advance of $200,000 is made from the Water Utility Fund for the purpose of acquiring capital assets. The advance is to be repaid in 20 equal annual installments, with no interest. The receipt of the transfer in and the liability to the Water Utility Fund would be recorded in the Supplies Fund accounts in the following manner:[1]

	Debits	Credits
1. Cash	796,000	
Transfers In		596,000
Advance from Water Utility Fund		200,000

To provide some revenue on funds not needed currently, $50,000 is invested in marketable securities:

	Debits	Credits
2. Investments	50,000	
Cash		50,000

Assume that early in 2004, a satisfactory warehouse building is purchased for $350,000; $80,000 of the purchase price is considered as the cost of the land. Necessary warehouse machinery and equipment is purchased for $100,000. Delivery equipment is purchased for $40,000. If the purchases are made for cash, the acquisition of the assets would be recorded in the books of the Supplies Fund as follows:

---

[1] The corresponding entry in the General Fund is entry 22 in Chapter 4. The corresponding entry in the Water Utility Fund is entry 3 in the "Illustrative Case—Water Utility Fund" section later in this chapter.

	Debits	Credits
3. Land	80,000	
Building	270,000	
Machinery and Equipment—Warehouse	100,000	
Equipment—Delivery	40,000	
Cash		490,000

Supplies are ordered to maintain inventories at a level commensurate with expected usage. No entry is needed because proprietary funds accounted for in conformity with GASB standards are not required to record encumbrances. During 2004, it is assumed that supplies are received and related invoices are approved for payment in the amount of $523,500; the entry needed to record the asset and the liability is as follows:

	Debits	Credits
4. Inventory of Supplies	523,500	
Accounts Payable		523,500

Governmental funds that maintain relatively minor inventories of supplies usually account for them on the physical inventory basis, as illustrated in Chapter 4 (the purchases method). The Supplies Fund, however, should account for its inventories on the perpetual inventory basis because the information is needed for proper performance of its primary function. Accordingly, when supplies are issued, the Inventory Account must be credited for the cost of the supplies issued. Because the using fund will be charged an amount in excess of the inventory carrying value, the Receivable and Revenue accounts must reflect the selling price. The markup above cost should be determined on the basis of budgeted expenses and other items to be financed from net income. If the budget for the Village of Elizabeth's Supplies Fund indicates that a markup of 30 percent on cost is needed, issues to General Fund departments of supplies costing $290,000 would be recorded by the following entries:

	Debits	Credits
5a. Operating Expenses—Cost of Sales and Services	290,000	
Inventory of Supplies		290,000
5b. Due from General Fund	377,000	
Operating Revenues—Charges for Sales and Services		377,000

During the year, it is assumed that purchasing expenses totaling $19,000, warehousing expenses totaling $12,000, delivery expenses totaling $13,000, and administrative expenses totaling $11,000 are incurred. The government has chosen to separate operating expenses into three categories: (1) costs of sales and services, (2) administration, and (3) depreciation. If all liabilities are vouchered before payment, the entry would be as follows:

		Debits	Credits
6.	Operating Expenses—Costs of Sales and Services	44,000	
	Operating Expenses—Administration	11,000	
	Accounts Payable		55,000

If collections from the General Fund during 2004 total $322,000, the entry would be as follows (see Chapter 4, entries 20a and 20b for General Fund entries corresponding to entries 5b and 7):

		Debits	Credits
7.	Cash	322,000	
	Due from General Fund		322,000

Assuming that payment of vouchers during the year totals the $567,500, the following entry is made:

		Debits	Credits
8.	Accounts Payable	567,500	
	Cash		567,500

The advance from the Water Utility Fund is to be repaid in 20 equal annual installments; repayment of one installment at the end of 2004 is recorded as follows:

		Debits	Credits
9.	Advance from Water Utility Fund	10,000	
	Cash		10,000

At the time depreciable assets are acquired, the warehouse building has an estimated useful life of 20 years; the warehouse machinery and equipment have an estimated useful life of 10 years; the delivery equipment has an estimated useful life of 10 years; and none of the assets is expected to have any salvage value at the expiration of its useful life. Under these assumptions, straight-line depreciation of the building would be $13,500 per year; depreciation of machinery and equipment, $10,000 per year; and depreciation of delivery equipment, $4,000 per year. (Since governmental units are not subject to income taxes, there is no incentive to use any depreciation method other than straight line.)

	Debits	Credits
10. Operating Expenses—Depreciation	27,500	
Accumulated Depreciation—Building		13,500
Accumulated Depreciation—Machinery and Equipment—Warehouse		10,000
Accumulated Depreciation—Equipment—Delivery		4,000

Organizations that keep perpetual inventory records must adjust the records periodically to reflect shortages, overages, and out-of-condition stock disclosed by physical inventories. Adjustments to the Inventory account are also considered to be adjustments to the warehousing expenses of the period. In this illustrative case, it is assumed that no adjustments are found to be necessary at year-end.

Interest income is earned and received in cash on the investments purchased at the beginning of the year:

	Debits	Credits
11. Cash	3,000	
Nonoperating Revenues—Interest		3,000

Assuming that all revenues, expenses, and transfers applicable to 2004 have been properly recorded by the entries illustrated, the nominal accounts should be closed as of December 31, 2004:

	Debits	Credits
12. Operating Revenues—Charges for Sales and Services	377,000	
Nonoperating Revenues—Interest	3,000	
Transfers In	596,000	
Operating Expenses—Costs of Sales and Services		334,000
Operating Expenses—Administration		11,000
Operating Expenses—Depreciation		27,500
Net Assets—Invested in Capital Assets—Net of Related Debt		272,500
Net Assets: Unrestricted		331,000

Note that the account, Net Assets, is separated into two components: (1) Invested in Capital Assets, Net of Related Debt and (2) Unrestricted. The first component of net assets ($272,500) is computed by taking the fixed assets (entry 3—$490,000) less accumulated depreciation (entry 10—$27,500) less the amount due to the enterprise fund (entry 1—$200,000 less entry 9 − $10,000 = $190,000). The remaining $331,000 is unrestricted; no restrictions exist on the remaining funds.

The Balance Sheet, Statement of Revenues, Expenses, and Changes in Fund Net Assets, and Statement of Cash Flows for the Supplies Fund are included in the proprietary funds statements (Illustrations 6–1, 6–2, and 6–3).

A NOTE ABOUT RISK MANAGEMENT ACTIVITIES

In recent years, governments have been turning to self-insurance for part or all of their risk financing activities. If a government decides to use a single fund to accumulate funds and make payments for claims, it must use either the General Fund or an internal service fund. Many use the internal service fund type.

When using internal service self-insurance funds, interfund premiums are treated as interfund services provided and used (see Chapter 4). Thus, revenues are recognized in the internal service fund for interfund charges, and an expenditure or expense, as appropriate, is recognized in the contributing fund. When claims are paid or accrued, an operating expense is recorded in the internal service fund.

Charges should be based on anticipated charges or on a long-range plan to break even over time, such as an actuarial method. Payments by contributing funds in excess of the amount required to break even are recorded as transfers. If an internal service fund has a material deficit at year-end, that deficit should be made up over a reasonable period of time and should be disclosed in the notes to the financial statements.

ENTERPRISE FUNDS

Enterprise funds are used by governmental units to account for services provided *to the general public* on a user-charge basis. Under GASB *Statement 34,* enterprise funds *must* be used in the following circumstances:

- When debt is backed solely by fees and charges.
- When a legal requirement exists that the cost of providing services for an activity, including capital costs, be recovered through fees or charges.
- When a government has a policy to establish fees and charges to cover the cost of providing services for an activity.

The most common examples of governmental enterprises are public utilities, notably water and sewer utilities. Electric and gas utilities, transportation systems, airports, ports, hospitals, toll bridges, produce markets, parking lots, parking garages, liquor stores, municipal sports facilities, and public housing projects are other examples frequently found.

Enterprise funds are to be reported using the economic resources measurement focus and accrual basis of accounting. Fixed assets and long-term debt are included in the accounts. As indicated earlier in this chapter, enterprise funds are to use accounting and reporting standards provided for business enterprises issued on or before November 30, 1989 (unless that guidance conflicts with GASB guidance) and may use guidance by the FASB for businesses issued after that date. As a result, accounting is similar to that for business enterprises and includes depreciation, accrual of interest payable, amortization of discounts and premiums on debt, and so on.

Governmental enterprises often issue debt, called **revenue bonds,** that is payable solely from the revenues of the enterprise. These bonds are recorded directly in the accounts of the enterprise fund. On the other hand, **general obliga-**

tion bonds are often issued for governmental enterprises, in order to provide greater security by pledging the full faith and credit of the government in addition to enterprise revenues. If payment is to be paid from enterprise revenues, these general obligation bonds would also be reflected in the accounts of enterprise funds.

Budgetary accounts should be used only if required by law. Debt service and construction activities of a governmental enterprise are accounted for within an enterprise fund, rather than by separate debt service and capital project funds. Thus, the reports of enterprise funds are self-contained; and creditors, legislators, or the general public can evaluate the performance of a governmental enterprise by the same criteria as they can the performance of investor-owned enterprises in the same industry.

By far the most numerous and important enterprise services rendered by local governments are public utilities. In this chapter, therefore, the example used is that of a water utility fund.

Illustrative Case—Water Utility Fund

It is assumed that the Village of Elizabeth is located in a state that permits enterprise funds to operate without formal legal approval of their budgets. Accordingly, the budget is not recorded in enterprise accounts.

Assume that as of December 31, 2003, the accountants for the Village of Elizabeth prepared the postclosing trial balance shown here:

VILLAGE OF ELIZABETH
Water Utility Fund
Postclosing Trial Balance
December 31, 2003

	Debits	Credits
Cash	$ 406,400	
Customer Accounts Receivable	72,500	
Accumulated Provision for Uncollectible Accounts		$ 2,175
Materials and Supplies	37,500	
Restricted Assets	115,300	
Utility Plant in Service	4,125,140	
Accumulated Provision for Depreciation of Utility Plant		886,500
Construction Work in Progress	468,125	
Accounts Payable		73,700
Customer Advances for Construction		25,000
Customer Deposits		35,300
Revenue Bonds Payable		2,700,000
Net Assets—Invested in Capital Assets, Net of Related Debt		1,006,765
Net Assets—Restricted for Debt Service		55,000
Net Assets—Unrestricted		440,525
Totals	$5,224,965	$5,224,965

It is common for governmental enterprises, especially utilities, to report "restricted assets." In this example, the restricted assets include customer advances for construction ($25,000), customer deposits ($35,300), and $55,000 set aside for future debt service payments in accord with a revenue bond indenture (see balance of Net Assets—Restricted for Debt Service).

When utility customers are billed during the year, appropriate revenue accounts are credited. Assuming that during 2004 the total bills to nongovernmental customers amounted to $975,300, bills to the Village of Elizabeth General Fund amounted to $80,000, and all revenue was from sales of water, the following entry summarizes the results:

		Debits	Credits
1.	Customer Accounts Receivable	975,300	
	Due from General Fund	80,000	
	Operating Revenues—Charges for Sales and Services		1,055,300

If collections from nongovernmental customers totaled $968,500 for water billings, entry 2 is needed:

		Debits	Credits
2.	Cash	968,500	
	Customer Accounts Receivable		968,500

During 2004, the Village of Elizabeth established a Supplies Fund, and the Water Utility Fund advanced $200,000 to the Supplies Fund as a long-term loan. The entry by the Supplies Fund is illustrated in entry 1 in the "Illustrative Case—Supplies Fund" section of this chapter. The following entry should be made by the Water Utility Fund:

		Debits	Credits
3.	Long-Term Advance to Supplies Fund	200,000	
	Cash		200,000

Materials and supplies in the amount of $231,500 were purchased during the year by the Water Utility Fund, and vouchers in that amount were recorded as a liability:

		Debits	Credits
4.	Materials and Supplies	231,500	
	Accounts Payable		231,500

When materials and supplies are issued to the functional departments of the Water Utility Fund, operating expenses are charged for the cost of materials and supplies. Materials and supplies issued for use for construction projects are capitalized temporarily as Construction Work in Progress. (Entry 9 illustrates the entry required when a capital project is completed.)

		Debits	Credits
5.	Operating Expenses—Costs of Sales and Services	110,400	
	Construction Work in Progress	127,600	
	Materials and Supplies		238,000

Payrolls for the year were chargeable to the accounts in the following entry. Taxes were accrued and withheld in the amount of $90,200, and the remainder was paid in cash.

		Debits	Credits
6.	Operating Expenses—Costs of Sales and Services	253,600	
	Operating Expenses—Administration	92,900	
	Operating Expenses—Sales	17,200	
	Construction Work in Progress	58,900	
	Payroll Taxes Payable		90,200
	Cash		332,400

Bond interest in the amount of $189,000 was paid:

		Debits	Credits
7.	Nonoperating Expenses—Interest	189,000	
	Cash		189,000

Bond interest in the amount of $17,800 was considered to be properly charged to construction:

		Debits	Credits
8.	Construction Work in Progress	17,800	
	Nonoperating Expenses—Interest		17,800

Construction projects on which costs totaled $529,300 were completed and the assets placed in service. Utility Plant in Service summarizes the investment in fixed assets used for utility purposes. In an actual case, detail would be presented to disclose the cost of fixed assets used for each of the principal functions of the utility.

		Debits	Credits
9.	Utility Plant in Service	529,300	
	Construction Work in Progress		529,300

To receive service from a utility, potential customers often have to deposit with the utility an amount set by a regulatory commission, to be held by the utility as security against nonpayment of bills by the customer. Customers' deposits amounting to $5,920 were refunded by check to customers discontinuing service (entry 10a). Deposits totaling $6,350 were received from new customers (entry 10b). Note that resources held for customer deposits are a part of restricted assets and the related liability is recorded in the account, Customer Deposits.

	Debits	Credits
10a. Customer Deposits	5,920	
Restricted Assets		5,920
10b. Restricted Assets	6,350	
Customer Deposits		6,350

Customers owing bills totaling $3,510 left the Village of Elizabeth and could not be located. These customers had paid deposits to the water utility totaling $1,530; the customer deposit liability was applied to the bills, and the unpaid remainder was charged to the accumulated provision for uncollectible accounts (entry 11a). The $1,530 is transferred from the restricted asset account to cash (entry 11b):

	Debits	Credits
11a. Customer Deposits	1,530	
Accumulated Provision for Uncollectible Accounts	1,980	
Customer Accounts Receivable		3,510
11b. Cash	1,530	
Restricted Assets		1,530

Customers requesting services from the utility that necessitated additions to the utility plant had advanced $25,000 to the Water Utility Fund as of December 31, 2003. During 2004 the construction was completed, and service to these customers commenced. In accord with the agreement with the customers, advances in the amount of $12,500 were applied to their water bills. The remainder of the advance was contributed to the Water Utility Fund, and the Capital Contributions account was credited. Note that Capital Contributions is a nominal account that will increase Net Assets but is reported separately (see Illustration 6–2).

	Debits	Credits
12. Customer Advances for Construction	25,000	
Customer Accounts Receivable		12,500
Capital Contributions		12,500

As indicated immediately after the trial balance on page 165, the $25,000 was held in restricted assets at the beginning of the current year. The $25,000 is now transferred to the general cash account, as it is no longer required to be set aside:

	Debits	Credits
13. Cash	25,000	
Restricted Assets		25,000

Payment of accounts totaled $275,600, and payments of payroll taxes amounted to $81,200.

	Debits	Credits
14. Accounts Payable	275,600	
Payroll Taxes Payable	81,200	
Cash		356,800

The Water Utility Fund agreed to contribute $60,000 to the Village General Fund in lieu of property taxes. The amount approximated the amount of services provided by General Fund departments to the Water Utility Fund (if not, the difference would be covered by transfers). The entry in the General Fund is illustrated in Chapter 4 (see Chapter 4, entry 19). The following entry records the event on the books of the Water Utility Fund, assuming the charges are of an administrative nature:

	Debits	Credits
15. Operating Expenses—Administration	60,000	
Due to General Fund		60,000

Near the end of 2004, the Water Utility Fund received $10,000 cash from the Supplies Fund as partial payment of the long-term advance (see Supplies Fund, entry 9).

	Debits	Credits
16. Cash	10,000	
Long-Term Advance to Supplies Fund		10,000

During the year, the Water Utility Fund made a transfer of $200,000 to the Fire Station Addition Capital Projects Fund (see entry 2 in Chapter 5):

	Debits	Credits
17. Transfers Out	200,000	
Cash		200,000

At year-end, several adjustments are necessary. First, depreciation is recorded as an operating expense:

	Debits	Credits
18. Operating Expenses—Depreciation	122,800	
Accumulated Provision for Depreciation of Utility Plant		122,800

Provision is made for bad debts from utility customers. In accord with a recent Question and Answer (Q&A) Guide issued by GASB, the bad debt provision is a revenue deduction, not an expense:

	Debits	Credits
19. Operating Revenues—Charges for Sales and Services	2,200	
Accumulated Provision for Uncollectible Accounts		2,200

In accord with the revenue bond indenture, $55,000 was transferred from operating cash to the Restricted Assets category. The transfer required a reclassification of net assets:

	Debits	Credits
20a. Restricted Assets	55,000	
Cash		55,000
20b. Net Assets—Unrestricted	55,000	
Net Assets—Restricted for Debt Service		55,000

Revenue, expense, transfer, and capital contributions accounts for the year were closed to the Unrestricted Net Assets account:

	Debits	Credits
21. Operating Revenues—Charges for Sales and Services	1,053,100	
Capital Contributions	12,500	
Operating Expenses—Costs of Sales and Services		364,000
Operating Expenses—Administration		152,900
Operating Expenses—Depreciation		122,800
Operating Expenses—Sales		17,200
Nonoperating Expenses—Interest		171,200
Transfers Out		200,000
Net Assets—Unrestricted		37,500

Each year, it is necessary to adjust the Net Assets—Invested in Capital Assets, Net of Related Debt by providing for increases in capital assets, decreases due to depreciation, and increases or decreases due to debt associated with capital assets. For 2004, the adjustments would be as follows:

Additions to Construction Work in Progress (Entries 5, 6, 8)	$ 204,300
Deduction—Due to Increase in Accumulated Provision for Depreciation (Entry 18)	(122,800)
Increase	$81,500

Entry 9 had no effect on this reclassification, as the $529,300 was a reclassification of capital asset accounts. No revenue bonds were sold or redeemed during the year. Accordingly, entry 22 would be made.

	Debits	Credits
22. Net Assets—Unrestricted	81,500	
Net Assets—Invested in Capital Assets, Net of Related Debt		81,500

The financial statements for the water utility fund are included in Illustrations 6–1, 6–2, and 6–3.

Accounting for Municipal Solid Waste Landfills

Many of the solid waste landfills in the United States are operated by local governmental units. The GASB requires that certain postclosure costs be estimated and accrued during the period the landfills receive solid waste.

The federal government requires that owners and operators of solid waste landfills estimate the cost of closure, including the cost of equipment used, the cost of the landfill cover, and the cost of caring for the site for a period of 30 years after closure, or whatever period is required by regulations. These costs are called **current costs**, in that the costs are estimated as if they were incurred at the time of estimate.

The GASB requires that a portion of those future estimated costs be charged as an expense and a liability of the landfill operation on a units-of-production method (based on capacity used divided by total capacity) as waste is accepted. For example, if the total estimated costs for closure and postclosure were $10 million, and the landfill accepted 10 percent of its anticipated capacity (cubic yards) in a given year, the charge and liability for that year would be $1 million. Each year, revisions would be made, if necessary, for changes in cost estimates, landfill capacity, and inflation.

If the landfill is operated as an enterprise fund, the entries would be made directly in the enterprise fund, in accord with full accrual accounting. If the landfill is operated as a governmental fund, then modified accrual principles would apply, and the fund expenditure and liability would be limited to the amount to be paid with available financial resources. The remainder would be reflected as a liability in the government-wide financial statements.

For example, assume a landfill is operated as an enterprise fund. The total estimated closure and postclosure costs were $30 million. Total estimated capacity of the landfill is 10 million tons. During 2004, the first year of operations, the landfill accepted 2 million tons, or 20 percent of its capacity. A $6 million charge would be made during 2004:

	Debits	Credits
Operating Expenses—Estimated Landfill Closure and Postclosure Costs	6,000,000	
Accrued Liability for Estimated Landfill Closure and Postclosure Costs		6,000,000

The purpose of the charge is to match the estimated costs with the revenues during the period of time waste is accepted. Adjustments should made yearly or whenever estimates for capacity or costs change. When the landfill is closed, and closure and postclosure costs are incurred, those costs will be charged to the liability account.

PROPRIETARY FUND FINANCIAL STATEMENTS

Governments are required to report the following proprietary fund financial statements: (1) Statement of Net Assets (or Balance Sheet), (2) Statement of Revenues, Expenses, and Changes in Fund Net Assets, and (3) Statement of Cash Flows. As was true for governmental funds, *major* enterprise funds are to be presented, along with columns for nonmajor funds and total enterprise funds, where appropriate. On the other hand, a single column is to include all internal service funds. Illustrations 6–1, 6–2, and 6–3 reflect the proprietary funds statements for the Village of Elizabeth, which is assumed to have only one enterprise fund and one internal service fund.

Statement of Net Assets

The Statement of Net Assets for the proprietary funds for the Village of Elizabeth is presented as Illustration 6–1. GASB permits either this statement or a Balance Sheet where Assets = Liabilities + Net Assets. GASB requires a classified format, where current assets, noncurrent assets, current liabilities, and noncurrent liabilities are presented separately. Net assets are segregated into the three categories used for the government-wide Statement of Net Assets. First, Invested in Capital Assets, Net of Related Debt reflects the cost of the fixed assets less accumulated depreciation less the debt associated with the acquisition of fixed assets. In the Village of Elizabeth example, the various fixed asset and accumulated depreciation accounts were combined to present a single net figure for each fund. It was assumed that all long-term debt was for capital assets.

Second, net assets that are restricted are presented separately. According to GASB *Statement 34,* restricted net assets are those which are the result of constraints either:
1. Externally imposed by creditors (such as through debt covenants), grantors, contributors, or laws or regulations of other governments.
2. Imposed by law through constitutional provisions or enabling legislation.

In the water utility fund of the Village of Elizabeth, it is assumed that the $110,000 was restricted through a bond covenant.

Third, net assets may be unrestricted. This number is important to financial analysts and other users of financial statements, as it is considered not only unrestricted but expendable. GASB prohibits the display of designated, unrestricted net assets.

Finally, note the current asset, Due from General Fund in the amount of $20,000. When a single fund has both a receivable from and a payable due to the same fund, GASB permits those amounts to be netted. In this case, the $20,000 is the net between the $80,000 receivable in entry 1 and the $60,000 payable in entry 2. GASB does not permit receivables and payables from different funds to be offset.

Statement of Revenues, Expenses, and Changes in Fund Net Assets

The Statement of Revenues, Expenses, and Changes in Fund Net Assets for the proprietary funds of the Village of Elizabeth is presented as Illustration 6–2. GASB requires that operating revenues and operating expenses be shown separately from

ILLUSTRATION 6-1

VILLAGE OF ELIZABETH
Statement of Net Assets
Proprietary Funds
December 31, 2004

	Business-Type Activities— Enterprise Funds— Water Utility	Governmental Activities— Internal Service Funds
Assets		
Current assets:		
Cash	$ 78,230	$ 3,500
Investments		50,000
Accounts receivable (net)	60,895	
Due from general fund	20,000	55,000
Materials and supplies	31,000	233,500
Total current assets	190,125	342,000
Noncurrent assets:		
Restricted assets	144,200	
Long-term advance to supplies fund	190,000	
Capital assets, net of accumulated depreciation	3,788,265	462,500
Total noncurrent assets	4,122,465	462,500
Total assets	4,312,590	804,500
Liabilities		
Current liabilities:		
Accounts payable	29,600	11,000
Customer deposits	34,200	
Taxes payable	9,000	
Total current liabilities	72,800	11,000
Noncurrent liabilities:		
Advance from water utility fund		190,000
Revenue bonds payable	2,700,000	
Total noncurrent liabilities	2,700,000	190,000
Total liabilities	2,772,800	201,000
Net Assets		
Invested in capital assets, net of related debt	1,088,265	272,500
Restricted for Debt Service	110,000	
Unrestricted	341,525	331,000
Total net assets	$1,539,790	$603,500

and prior to nonoperating revenues and expenses. Operating income must be displayed. Operating revenues should be displayed by source. Operating expenses may be reported by function, as shown in Illustration 6–2, or may be reported by object classification, such as personal services, supplies, travel, etc.

ILLUSTRATION 6-2

VILLAGE OF ELIZABETH
Statement of Revenues, Expenses, and Changes in Fund Net Assets
Proprietary Funds
For the Year Ended December 31, 2004

	Business-Type Activities— Enterprise Funds— Water Utility	Governmental Activities— Internal Service Funds
Operating revenues:		
Charges for sales and services	$1,053,100	$377,000
Operating expenses:		
Cost of sales and services	364,000	334,000
Administration	152,900	11,000
Sales	17,200	
Depreciation	122,800	27,500
Total operating expenses	656,900	372,500
Operating income	396,200	4,500
Nonoperating revenues (expenses):		
Interest revenue		3,000
Interest expense	(171,200)	
Total nonoperating revenues (expenses)	(171,200)	3,000
Income before contributions and transfers	225,000	7,500
Capital contributions	12,500	
Transfers in		596,000
Transfers out	(200,000)	
Change in net assets	37,500	603,500
Net assets—January 1, 2004	1,502,290	–0–
Net assets—December 31, 2004	$1,539,790	$603,500

ILLUSTRATION 6-3

VILLAGE OF ELIZABETH
Statement of Cash Flows
Proprietary Funds
For the Year Ended December 31, 2004

	Business-Type Activities— Enterprise Funds— Water Utility	Governmental Activities— Internal Service Funds
Cash flows from operating activities:		
Cash received from customers and departments	$968,500	$ 322,000
Cash paid to suppliers and employees	(502,700)	(567,500)
Cash provided by customer deposits	430	
Net cash provided (used) by operating activities	466,230	(245,500)

ILLUSTRATION 6–3 (continued)

Cash flows from noncapital financing activities:		
Transfer from general fund for working capital		306,000
Transfer to capital projects fund	(200,000)	
Net cash provided (used) by noncapital financing activities	(200,000)	306,000
Cash flows from capital and related financing activities:		
Advance from water utility fund		200,000
Transfer from general fund for capital assets		290,000
Acquisition and construction of capital assets	(204,300)	(490,000)
Interest paid on long-term debt	(171,200)	
Partial repayment of advance from water utility fund		(10,000)
Net cash (used) by capital and related financing activities	(375,500)	(10,000)
Cash flows from investing activities:		
Advance to supplies fund	(200,000)	
Partial repayment of advance by supplies fund	10,000	
Purchase of investments		(50,000)
Interest received		3,000
Net cash (used) by investing activities	(190,000)	(47,000)
Net increase (decrease) in cash and cash equivalents	(299,270)	3,500
Cash and cash equivalents—beginning of year	521,700	–0–
Cash and cash equivalents—end of year	$222,430	$3,500
Reconciliation of operating income to net cash provided (used) by operating activities		
Operating income (loss)	396,200	4,500
Adjustments to reconcile operating income (loss) to net cash provided (used) by operating activities:		
Depreciation expense	122,800	27,500
Change in assets and liabilities:		
Decrease in customer accounts receivable	9,430	
Increase in interfund receivables	(20,000)	(55,000)
(Increase) decrease in inventory	6,500	(233,500)
Increase (decrease) in accounts payable	(44,100)	11,000
Customer advances applied to customer accounts receivable	(12,500)	
Decrease in customer deposits	(1,100)	
Increase in accrued liabilities	9,000	
Net Cash provided (used) by operating activities	$466,230	$(245,500)

Capital contributions, extraordinary and special items, and transfers should be shown separately, after nonoperating revenues and expenses. GASB requires the all-inclusive format, which reconciles to the ending net asset figures, as shown in Illustration 6–2. Note that the ending net asset figures shown in Illustration 6–2 are the same as the total net assets shown in the Statement of Net Assets (Illustration 6–1).

Statement of Cash Flows

The Statement of Cash Flows for the proprietary funds for the Village of Elizabeth is presented as Illustration 6–3. GASB requires the direct method to report cash flows from operating activities. Other differences exist between GASB requirements and the requirements by FASB for businesses and nongovernmental, not-for-profit organizations.

First, cash flow statements for proprietary funds of government have four categories, rather than the three presented under FASB standards. The four categories are (1) operating, (2) noncapital financing activities, (3) capital and related financing activities, and (4) investing activities.

Cash flows from **operating activities** include receipts from customers, payments to suppliers, payments to employees, and receipt and payment of cash for quasi-external transactions (interfund services provided and used) with other funds. Cash flows from **noncapital financing activities** include proceeds and repayment of debt not clearly related to capital outlay, grants received from and paid to other governments for noncapital purposes, transfers to and from other funds, and the payment of interest associated with noncapital debt. Illustration 6–3 makes the assumption that $306,000 of the initial contribution from the General Fund to the internal service fund was for working capital.

Cash flows from **capital and related financing activities** include proceeds and repayment of debt related to capital acquisition, the receipt of and payment of grants related to capital acquisition, the payment of interest on debt related to capital acquisition, and the purchase or construction of capital assets. Cash flows from **investing activities** include cash used to acquire investments, whether directly or through investment pools, the interest received on such investments, and cash received from the sale or redemption of investments. Note that cash flows from investing activities do not include acquisition of capital assets, as is the case with FASB requirements.

A reconciliation is required between the Statement of Revenues, Expenses, and Changes and Fund Net Assets and the Cash Flow Statement. The reconciliation should be between operating income and cash flows from operating activities. See Illustration 6–3 for an example.

In summary, GASB standards for the Statement of Cash Flows differ from FASB standards in four primary ways. First, GASB requires the direct method; FASB permits either the direct or indirect method. Second, GASB requires four classifications instead of the three required by FASB. Third, GASB standards provide some different classifications, primarily in interest receipts and payments and in the acquisition of capital assets. Fourth, the reconciliation is between operating income and cash flows from operating activities, rather than between net income and cash flows for operating activities, which is the FASB requirement.

Note that the figure for cash and cash equivalents includes the restricted assets, as is customary in practice. From Illustration 6–1, cash of $78,230 plus restricted assets of $144,200 equals the cash and cash equivalents of $222,430 (Illustration 6–3).

Questions and Exercises

6–1. Using the annual financial report obtained for Exercise 1–1, answer the following questions:

   a. Find the Statement of Net Assets for the proprietary funds. Is the Net Asset or the Balance Sheet format used? List the major enterprise funds from that Statement. Is the statement classified between current and noncurrent assets and liabilities? Are net assets broken down into the three classifications shown in your text? Is a separate column shown for internal service funds?

   b. Find the Statement of Revenues, Expenses, and Changes in Net Assets for the proprietary funds. Is the "all-inclusive" format used? Are revenues reported by source? Are expenses (not expenditures) reported by function or by object classification? Is depreciation reported separately? Is operating income, or a similar title displayed? Are nonoperating revenues and expenses shown separately after operating income? Are capital contributions, extraordinary and special items, and transfers shown separately? List any extraordinary and special items.

   c. Find the Statement of Cash Flows for the proprietary funds. List the four categories of cash flows. Are they the same as shown in the text? Are interest receipts reported as cash flows from investing activities? Are interest payments shown as financing activities? Is the direct method used? Is a reconciliation shown from operating income to net cash provided by operations? Are capital assets acquired from financing activities shown as decreases in cash flows from financing activities? Does the ending cash balance agree with the cash balance shown in the Statement of Net Assets (note that restricted assets may be included)?

   d. If your government has a CAFR, look to any combining statements and list the nonmajor enterprise funds. List the internal service funds.

   e. Look at the financial statements from the point of view of a financial analyst. Write down the unrestricted net asset balances for each of the major enterprise funds, and (if you have a CAFR) the nonmajor enterprise funds and internal service funds. Look at the long-term debt of major enterprise funds. Can you tell from the statements or the notes whether the debt is general obligation or revenue in nature? Write down the income before contributions, extraordinary items, special items, and transfers for each of the funds. Compare these numbers with prior years, if the information is provided in your financial statements. Look at the transfers. Can you tell if the general government is subsidizing or is subsidized by enterprise funds?

6–2. For each of the following, select the letter with the best answer:
  1. Which of the following would *not* be an example of an internal service fund?
     a. A print shop.
     b. An airport.
     c. A motor pool.
     d. A stores and services fund.
  2. Which is true regarding FASB accounting and financial reporting for enterprise funds, as long as FASB standards do not conflict with GASB standards?
     a. All FASB accounting principles prescribed for business organizations must be followed.
     b. FASB accounting principles prescribed for business organizations on or before November 30, 1989, must be followed; FASB accounting principles issued after that date may or may not be followed, as long as a government applies those accounting principles consistently.
     c. FASB accounting principles may or may not be followed, without any consideration of date.
     d. FASB accounting principles may not be followed in any case.
  3. Which of the following is true regarding the Statement of Net Assets for proprietary funds?
     a. Either the net asset format or the balance sheet format may be used.
     b. Major enterprise and internal service funds are to be reported separately.
     c. Net assets are to be displayed in two categories: reserved and unreserved.
     d. A government may report assets in order of liquidity or as classified between current and noncurrent.
  4. Which of the following is true regarding the Statement of Revenues, Expenses, and Changes in Fund Net Assets for proprietary funds?
     a. Revenues must be reported by source and expenses must be reported by function.
     b. An operating income figure must be displayed.
     c. Depreciation is normally shown as a nonoperating expense.
     d. Extraordinary items, special items, transfers, and capital contributions are reported as nonoperating revenues and expenses.
  5. Which of the following is true regarding the Statement of Cash Flows for proprietary funds?
     a. Three categories are required: operating, financing, and investing.
     b. Interest receipts and interest payments are to be reported as cash flows from operating activities.

c. Either the direct or indirect method may be used.
d. A reconciliation must be presented that illustrates the differences between operating income and cash flows from operating activities.

6. Which of the following is true regarding proprietary fund reporting?
   a. The economic resources measurement focus and accrual basis of accounting is required.
   b. When general obligation bonds are issued for proprietary fund purposes, the debt is shown in the combined statements only, not in the proprietary fund Statement of Net Assets.
   c. Fixed assets are reported in proprietary fund financial statements, but depreciation charges are optional.
   d. Long-term debt is shown only in the combined statements, not in proprietary fund statements.

Items 7 and 8 are based on the following information:

During the year ended December 31, 2004, Johnson City received a state grant of $600,000 to finance the purchase of buses and an additional grant of $200,000 to aid in the financing of bus operations in 2004. This is a reimbursement grant. Only $400,000 of the capital grant was used in 2004 for the purchase of buses, but the entire operating grant of $200,000 was expended in 2004.

7. If Johnson City's bus transportation system is accounted for as part of the city's General Fund, how much should Johnson City report as grant **revenues** for the year ended December 31, 2004?
   a. $200,000
   b. $400,000
   c. $600,000
   d. $800,000

8. If Johnson City's bus transportation system is accounted for as part of an enterprise fund, how much should Johnson City report as grant **revenues** for the year ended December 31, 2004?
   a. $200,000
   b. $400,000
   c. $600,000
   d. $800,000

9. The County of Sinasonville operated a landfill as an enterprise fund. The closure and postclosure care costs are estimated to be $30,000,000. It is estimated that the capacity of the landfill is 10 million tons of waste and that waste will be accepted for 10 years. During 2002, 1.2 million tons of waste was accepted. The charge for closure and postclosure care costs would be:
   a. $0.
   b. $3,000,000.

c. $3,600,000.
d. Impossible to determine based on the information given.

10. Which of the following is true regarding proprietary funds?
    a. Proprietary funds include internal service and enterprise funds.
    b. Proprietary funds are all reported as business-type activities in the government-wide statements.
    c. Both of the above.
    d. Neither of the above.

6–3. For each of the following, select the letter with the best answer:
1. Proprietary fund statements include:
    a. Statement of Net Assets (or Balance Sheet), Statement of Revenues, Expenses, and Changes in Retained Earnings, and Statement of Cash Flows.
    b. Statement of Net Assets (or Balance Sheet), Statement of Revenues, Expenditures, and Changes in Fund Balances, and Statement of Cash Flows.
    c. Statement of Net Assets (or Balance Sheet), Statement of Revenues, Expenses, and Changes in Fund Net Assets, and Statement of Cash Flows.
    d. Statement of Net Assets (or Balance Sheet) and Statement of Revenues, Expenses, and Changes in Net Assets only.

2. Which of the following would *not* be an example of an enterprise fund?
    a. Water utility fund.
    b. Self-insurance fund.
    c. Airport fund.
    d. Parking lot fund.

3. Which of the following is true regarding internal service funds?
    a. When an internal service fund charges a General Fund department for services, the internal service fund reports a Transfer In and the General Fund reports a Transfer Out.
    b. Internal service funds report fixed assets and record depreciation expense.
    c. Major internal service funds are reported in the proprietary fund Statement of Net Assets.
    d. Internal service funds are normally reported in the proprietary funds statements as business-type activities.

4. Which of the following is (are) true regarding the proprietary fund Statement of Net Assets?
    a. The Statement of Net Assets must report assets and liabilities classified as current and noncurrent.

b. The Statement of Net Assets reports net assets classified as: (1) contributed capital and (2) retained earnings.
c. Both of the above.
d. Neither of the above.

5. Which of the following is (are) true regarding the proprietary fund Statement of Revenues, Expenses, and Changes in Fund Net Assets?
   a. Capital contributions are to be reported separately after nonoperating revenues and expenses.
   b. Operating expenses may be reported either by function or by object classification.
   c. Both of the above.
   d. Neither of the above.

6. Which of the following is (are) true regarding the proprietary fund Statement of Cash Flows?
   a. Either the direct or indirect method may be used.
   b. When the direct method is used, a schedule must be prepared, illustrating the differences between net income and the cash flows from operations.
   c. Both of the above.
   d. Neither of the above.

7. When the General Fund purchases water from an enterprise fund:
   a. The General Fund would debit Expenditures and the enterprise fund would credit an operating revenue account such as Charges for Sales and Services.
   b. The General Fund would debit Transfers Out and the enterprise fund would credit Transfers In.
   c. The General Fund would debit Expenditures and the enterprise fund would credit a nonoperating revenue account.
   d. The General Fund would debit Fund Balance and the enterprise fund would credit Capital Contributions.

8. Which of the following is (are) true regarding risk management activities accounted for as internal service funds?
   a. Contributions from the General Fund and any other funds are treated as interfund services provided and used.
   b. Self-insurance funds with material deficits at year-end should be made up over a reasonable period of time and should be disclosed in the notes to the financial statements.
   c. Both of the above.
   d. Neither of the above.

9. When must an enterprise fund be used to account for an activity?
   a. When debt is backed solely by fees and charges.

b. When a legal requirement exists that the cost of providing services for an activity, including capital costs, be recovered through fees and charges.
   c. When a government has a policy to establish fees and charges to cover the cost of providing services for an activity.
   d. When any one of the above conditions exist.
10. Which of the following is (are) true regarding enterprise funds?
   a. Fixed assets are maintained in the accounts, and depreciation is recorded.
   b. Long-term debt paid from enterprise fund resources is recorded directly in the accounts; interest and principal payments are reported as expenditures.
   c. Both of the above.
   d. Neither of the above.

6–4. The City of Davidson decided to open a motor pool to provide transportation service for all departments. During the first year, July 1, 2003, through June 30, 2004, only passenger cars will be available, and a uniform mileage rate will be charged. A permanent contribution of $1,500,000 cash was received from the General Fund and a $1,000,000 long-term loan was received from the Enterprise Fund to support the purchase of fixed assets. Interest at the rate of 6 percent per year is to be paid on the unpaid balance of the loan; principal in the amount of $200,000 is to be repaid each year.

At the beginning of the first year, the following are purchased for cash: land, $100,000; buildings (30-year life), $300,000; equipment (10-year life), $150,000; automobiles (4-year life), $1,600,000; and fuel and supplies, $100,000. Depreciation expense is to be computed by the straight-line method, assuming no salvage value.

During the first year, salaries are expected to amount to $265,000, and the cost of fuel and supplies used is expected to amount to $250,000.

Prepare a budget on the full accrual basis for the City of Davidson Motor Pool Fund. Compute the mileage charge needed to permit the Motor Pool to break even on operations and to make the required principal payment of $200,000, assuming the automobiles will travel 3,750,000 miles during the year.

6–5. This exercise continues Exercise 6–4. Record the following transactions for the year for the City of Davidson Motor Pool Fund:
   1. The cash transfer was received from the General Fund and cash in the full amount of the long-term loan was received from the Enterprise Fund.
   2. The land, building, automobiles, equipment, and fuel and supplies were purchased for cash. (See Exercise 6–4 for amounts.)
   3. A total of 3,800,000 miles was driven and charged to other funds during the year.

4. Fuel and supplies were purchased on account in the amount of $200,000.
5. $850,000 cash was received from other funds in payment of mileage charges.
6. Salaries were paid in the amount of $260,000.
7. During the year, fuel and supplies were consumed in the amount of $270,000.
8. Accounts payable were paid in the amount of $185,000.
9. Interest charges were paid to the Enterprise Fund. In addition, a $200,000 repayment was made on the long-term advance.
10. Depreciation charges were recorded for the year.
11. Closing entries were made.

   a. Record the transactions just listed in the general journal of the City of Davidson Motor Pool Fund.
   b. Prepare a Statement of Net Assets for the Motor Pool Fund as of June 30, 2004.
   c. Prepare a Statement of Revenues, Expenses, and Changes in Fund Net Assets for the Motor Pool Fund for the Year Ended June 30, 2004.
   d. Prepare a Statement of Cash Flows for the Motor Pool Fund for the Year Ended June 30, 2004. Assume $350,000 of the Transfer from the General Fund was for working capital needs and the rest was for capital items.

6–6. The Town of Wilson has a Water Utility Fund with the following trial balance as of July 1, 2003, the first day of the fiscal year:

	Debit	Credit
Cash	$ 80,000	
Customer Accounts Receivable	300,000	
Accumulated Provision for Uncollectible Accounts		$ 10,000
Materials and Supplies	120,000	
Restricted Assets	300,000	
Utility Plant in Service	7,100,000	
Accumulated Provision for Depreciation—Utility Plant		2,600,000
Construction Work in Progress	100,000	
Accounts Payable		130,000
Accrued Expenses		80,000
Revenue Bonds Payable		3,500,000
Net Assets—Invested in Capital Assets, Net of Related Debt		1,100,000
Net Assets—Restricted		300,000
Net Assets—Unrestricted		280,000
Totals	$8,000,000	$8,000,000

During the year ended June 30, 2004, the following transactions and events occurred in the Town of Wilson Water Utility Fund:

1. Accrued expenses at July 1, 2003 were paid in cash.
2. Billings to nongovernmental customers for water usage for the year amounted to $1,310,000; billings to the General Fund amounted to $53,000.
3. Liabilities for the following were recorded during the year:

Materials and supplies	$215,000
Costs of sales and services	343,400
Administrative expenses	200,000
Construction work in progress	212,200

4. Materials and supplies were used in the amount of $265,700, all for costs of sales and services.
5. $8,000 of old accounts receivable were written off.
6. Accounts receivable collections totaled $1,450,000 from nongovernmental customers and $48,400 from the General Fund.
7. $1,035,000 of accounts payable were paid in cash.
8. One year's interest in the amount of $245,000 was paid.
9. Construction was completed on plant assets costing $135,000; that amount was transferred to Utility Plant in Service.
10. Depreciation was recorded in the amount of $235,000.
11. Interest in the amount of $25,000 was charged to Construction Work in Progress.
12. The Accumulated Provision for Uncollectible Accounts was increased by $13,100.
13. Cash in the amount of $100,000 was transferred to Restricted Assets for eventual redemption of the bonds. As required by the loan agreement, Net Assets in the amount of Restricted Assets was restricted.
14. Accrued expenses, all related to costs of sales and services amounted to $15,600.
15. Nominal accounts for the year were closed to Net Assets—Unrestricted.
16. Necessary adjustments were made to the Net Assets—Invested in Capital Assets—Net of Related Debt.

    a. Record the transactions for the year in general journal form.
    b. Prepare a Statement of Net Assets as of June 30, 2004.
    c. Prepare a Statement of Revenues, Expenses, and Changes in Fund Net Assets for the Year Ended June 30, 2004.
    d. Prepare a Statement of Cash Flows for the Year Ended June 30, 2004. Assume all debt and interest are related to capital outlay. Assume the entire $212,200 construction work in progress liability (see

item 3) was paid in entry 7. Include restricted assets as cash and cash equivalents.

6–7. The City of Sandwich purchased a swimming pool from a private operator as of April 1, 2004, for $500,000. Of the $500,000, $200,000 was provided by a one-time contribution from the General Fund, and $300,000 was provided by a loan from the First National Bank, secured by a note. The loan has an annual interest rate 6 percent, payable semiannually on October 1 and April 1; principal payments of $100,000 are to be made annually, beginning on April 1, 2005. The city has a calendar year as its fiscal year. During the year ended December 31, 2004, the following transactions occurred, related to the City of Sandwich Swimming Pool:

1. The amounts were received from the City General Fund and the First National Bank.
2. A short-term loan was provided in the amount of $100,000 from the Water Utility Fund.
3. The purchase of the pool was recorded. Based on an appraisal, it was decided to allocate $100,000 to the land, $300,000 to improvements other than buildings (the pool), and $100,000 to the building. There is a 10-year life for both the pool and the building, and depreciation is to be recorded annually, based on monthly allocations (do not record depreciation until entry 10).
4. Charges to patrons during the season amounted to $240,000, all received in cash.
5. Salaries paid to employees amounted to $130,000, all paid in cash. $100,000 was cost of services, and $30,000 was administration.
6. Supplies purchased amounted to $30,000; all but $5,000 were used. Cash was paid for the supplies, all of which were for cost of sales and services.
7. Administrative expenses amounted to $12,000, paid in cash.
8. The first interest payment was made to the First National Bank.
9. The short-term loan was repaid to the Water Utility Fund.
10. Depreciation was accrued for the year. Record 9/12 of the annual amounts.
11. Interest was accrued for the year.
12. Closing entries were prepared. First, revenues, expenses, and transfers were closed to Net Assets—Unrestricted. Second, an appropriate amount was transferred to Net Assets—Invested in Capital Assets, Net of Related Debt.

Required:
a. Prepare entries to record the transactions.
b. Prepare a Statement of Revenues, Expenses, and Changes in Fund Net Assets for the Year Ended December 31, 2004, for the City of Sandwich Swimming Pool Fund.

c. Prepare a Statement of Net Assets as of December 31, 2004, for the City of Sandwich Swimming Pool Fund.

d. Prepare a Statement of Cash Flows for the Year Ended December 31, 2004, for the City of Sandwich Swimming Pool Fund.

6–8. The Village of Parry reported the following for its Print Shop Fund for the year ended April 30, 2004:

VILLAGE OF PARRY—PRINT SHOP FUND
Statement of Revenues, Expenses, and Changes in Net Assets
For the Year Ended April 30, 2004

Operating Revenues:		
Charges for Services		$1,000,000
Operating Expenses:		
Salaries and Benefits	$500,000	
Depreciation	200,000	
Supplies Used	200,000	
Utilities	70,000	970,000
Income from Operations		30,000
Nonoperating Income (Expenses):		
Interest Revenue	30,000	
Interest Expense	(50,000)	(20,000)
Net Income before Transfers		10,000
Transfers In		180,000
Changes in Net Assets		190,000
Net Assets—Beginning		1,120,000
Net Assets—Ending		$1,310,000

The Print Shop Fund records also revealed the following:

1. Contribution from Water Utility Fund for Working Capital Needs .... $ 80,000
2. Contribution from General Fund for Purchase of Equipment 100,000
3. Loan from Water Utility Fund for Purchase of Equipment 300,000
4. Purchase of Equipment .... (450,000)
5. Purchase of One-Year Investments .... (100,000)

The following balances were observed in current asset and current liability accounts. ( ) denote credit balances:

	5/1/03	4/30/04
Cash	$100,000	$233,000
Accrued Interest Receivable	5,000	10,000
Due from Other Funds	40,000	50,000
Accrued Salaries and Benefits	(20,000)	(30,000)
Utility Bills Payable	(4,000)	(5,000)
Accounts Payable	(30,000)	(25,000)
Accrued Interest Payable	(5,000)	(7,000)

Prepare a Statement of Cash Flows for the Village of Parry Print Shop Fund for the Year Ended April 30, 2004. Include the reconciliation of operating income to net cash provided by operating activities. Assume all interest expense relates to capital needs.

6–9. *a.* Outline GASB standards for accounting and reporting when internal service funds are to be used for self-insurance activities of governmental units.

b. Outline GASB standards for accounting and reporting when a government uses an enterprise fund to account for a municipal solid waste landfill.

Continuous Problem

6–C *Part 1.* The Stores and Service Fund of the City of Everlasting Sunshine had the following account balances as of January 1, 2004:

	Debits	Credits
Cash	$ 12,000	
Due from Other Funds	25,000	
Inventory of Supplies	50,000	
Land	15,000	
Buildings	44,000	
Accumulated Depreciation—Buildings		$ 11,000
Equipment	21,000	
Accumulated Depreciation—Equipment		10,500
Accounts Payable		7,500
Advance from Water Utility Fund		30,000
Net Assets—Invested in Capital Assets, Net of Related Debt		28,500
Net Assets—Unrestricted		79,500
Totals	$167,000	$167,000

a. Open a general journal for the City of Everlasting Sunshine Stores and Service Fund and record the following transactions. Use the account titles in requirement *b.*

(1) A budget was prepared for FY 2004. It was estimated that supplies would be issued in the amount of $300,000, at cost. Operating expenses, including depreciation, were estimated to be $48,000. Issue prices of supplies were set to achieve a breakeven for the year. Assume a uniform markup percentage; compute the markup on cost.

(2) The amount due from other funds as of January 1, 2004, was collected in full.

(3) During the year, supplies were ordered and received in the amount of $285,000. This amount was vouchered.

(4) $10,000 of the advance from the Water Utility Fund, originally provided for construction, was repaid. No interest is charged.

(5) During the year, supplies costing $270,000 were issued to the General Fund, and supplies costing $50,000 were issued to the Water Utility Fund.

(6) Operating expenses, exclusive of depreciation, were recorded in accounts payable as follows: Purchasing, $10,100; Warehousing, $15,300; Delivery, $13,200; and Administrative, $7,300.

(7) Cash was received from the General Fund in the amount of $300,000 and from the Water Utility Fund in the amount of $50,000.

(8) Accounts payable were paid in the amount of $330,000.

(9) Depreciation in the amount of $2,200 was recorded for buildings and $2,100 for equipment.

b. Open a general ledger and enter January 1, 2004, balances given in the problem. Post the entries for requirement *a* to the general ledger. Use five lines each for the following accounts:

Cash (21–101)
Due from Other Funds (21–131)
Inventory of Supplies (21–151)
Land (21–161)
Buildings (21–162)
Accumulated Depreciation—Buildings (21–172)
Equipment (21–163)
Accumulated Depreciation—Equipment (21–173)
Accounts Payable (21–201)
Advance from Water Utility Fund (21–231)
Net Assets—Invested in Capital Assets, Net of Related Debt (21–351)
Net Assets—Unrestricted (21–353)
Operating Revenues—Charges for Sales and Services (21–410)
Operating Expenses—Costs of Sales and Services (21–510)
Operating Expenses—Administration (21–512)
Operating Expenses—Depreciation (21–513)

c. Prepare a preclosing trial balance.

d. Prepare and post closing entries. First, close revenues and expenses to Net Assets—Unrestricted. Then adjust for the change in Net Assets—Invested in Capital Assets, Net of Related Debt.

Part 2. The City of Everlasting Sunshine maintains a Water and Sewer Fund to provide utility services to its citizens. As of January 1, 2004, the

City of Everlasting Sunshine Water and Sewer Fund had the following account balances:

	Debits	Credits
Cash	$ 35,100	
Customer Accounts Receivable	113,000	
Accumulated Provision for Uncollectible Accounts		$ 2,260
Materials and Supplies	72,400	
Advance to Stores and Services Fund	30,000	
Restricted Assets	211,100	
Utility Plant in Service	4,135,200	
Construction Work in Progress	215,000	
Accumulated Provision for Depreciation of Utility Plant		692,600
Accounts Payable		116,000
Customer Deposits		61,100
Customer Advances for Construction		15,000
Revenue Bonds Payable		2,300,000
Net Assets—Invested in Capital Assets, Net of Related Debt		1,357,600
Net Assets—Restricted		135,000
Net Assets—Unrestricted		132,240
Totals	$4,811,800	$4,811,800

a. Open a general journal for the City of Everlasting Sunshine Water and Sewer Utility Fund and record the following transactions. Use the account titles in requirement b.

(1) During the year, sales of water to nonmunicipal customers amounted to $910,600, and sales of water to the General Fund amounted to $45,000.

(2) Collections from nonmunicipal customers amounted to $875,000.

(3) The Stores and Services Fund repaid $10,000 of the long-term advance to the Water and Sewer Fund.

(4) Materials and supplies in the amount of $235,000 were received. A liability in that amount was recorded.

(5) Materials and supplies were issued and were charged to the following accounts: cost of sales and services, $135,000; sales, $15,000; administration, $29,000; construction work in progress, $59,000.

(6) Payroll expense for the year totaled $416,200. Of that amount, $351,900 was paid in cash, and the remainder was withheld for taxes. In addition, taxes that are expenses of the utility amounted to $34,200. The $450,400 was distributed as follows: cost of sales and services, $240,800; sales, $24,900; administration, $91,400; construction work in progress, $93,300.

(7) Bond interest in the amount of $184,000 was paid.

(8) Interest in the amount of $13,100 was charged to Construction Work in Progress.

(9) Construction projects were completed in the amount of $250,000, and the assets were placed in service.

(10) The Water and Sewer Fund agreed to pay $35,000 to the General Fund as a contribution in lieu of taxes; the amount was charged to administration and was approximately equal to services rendered.

(11) Collection efforts were discontinued on bills totaling $5,820. The customers owing the bills had paid deposits totaling $4,260 to the utility; the deposits were applied to the bills, and the unpaid remainder was charged to the Accumulated Provision for Uncollectible Accounts. $4,260 was transferred from restricted assets to cash.

(12) Customers' deposits amounting to $3,590 were refunded by check to customers discontinuing service. Deposits totaling $4,140 were received from new customers. Customer's deposits are held in the restricted asset account.

(13) Payment of accounts payable amounted to $217,000. Payments of payroll taxes totaled $95,200.

(14) Customers' advances for construction in the amount of $5,000 were applied to their water bills. $5,000 was transferred from restricted assets to cash.

(15) Supplies transferred from the Stores and Services Fund amounted to $58,000. Cash in the amount of $50,000 was paid to the Stores and Services Fund for supplies.

(16) Depreciation expense for 2004 was computed to be $210,000.

(17) The provision for uncollectible accounts for 2004 amounted to $4,160.

(18) In accord with the revenue bond indenture, $15,000 cash was transferred from operating cash to restricted assets. The transfer requires a restriction of net assets in an equal amount.

b. Open a general ledger and enter January 1, 2004, balances given in the problem. Post the entries for requirement a to the general ledger. Allow 6 lines for each of the following accounts except cash, which requires 11 lines:

Cash (22–101)
Customer Accounts Receivable (22–111)
Accumulated Provision for Uncollectible Accounts (22–112)
Due from General Fund (22–131)
Materials and Supplies (22–151)
Advance to Stores and Services Fund (22–155)
Utility Plant in Service (22–165)

    Construction Work in Progress (22–166)
    Accumulated Provision for Depreciation of Utility Plant (22–175)
    Restricted Assets (22–181)
    Accounts Payable (22–201)
    Payroll Taxes Payable (22–202)
    Customer Advances for Construction (22–206)
    Customer Deposits (22–207)
    Due to General Fund (22–211)
    Due to Stores and Services Fund (22–215)
    Revenue Bonds Payable (22–251)
    Net Assets—Invested in Capital Assets, Net of Related Debt (22–351)
    Net Assets—Restricted (22–352)
    Net Assets—Unrestricted (22–353)
    Operating Revenues—Charges for Sales and Services (22–410)
    Operating Expenses—Costs of Sales and Services (22–510)
    Operating Expenses—Selling (22–511)
    Operating Expenses—Administration (22–512)
    Operating Expenses—Depreciation (22–513)
    Nonoperating Expenses—Interest (22–521)

c. Prepare a preclosing trial balance.

d. Prepare and post closing entries. First, close revenues and expenses to Net Assets—Unrestricted. Then adjust for the change in Net Assets—Invested in Capital Assets, Net of Related Debt.

Part 3. Prepare, in good form, for the proprietary funds accounted for in Parts 1 and 2, the following:

(1) A statement of Net Assets, as of December 31, 2004. Net the amounts due to and due from the General Fund.

(2) A statement of Revenues, Expenses, and Changes in Fund Net Assets for the Year Ended December 31, 2004.

(3) A Statement of Cash Flows for the Year Ended December 31, 2004. Include restricted assets as a part of cash and cash equivalents for this statement.

Chapter Seven

Fiduciary Funds, Interfund Transactions

Fiduciary funds are used to account for assets held by a governmental unit acting as a trustee or agent for entities external to the governmental unit: individuals, organizations, and other governmental units. (Assets held in trust for other governmental funds or for purposes of the governmental unit would be reported as special revenue funds, if expendable, and as permanent funds, if nonexpendable.) For this reason, fiduciary funds are often identified in governmental financial reports as Trust and Agency Funds. Trust relationships are generally established through formal trust agreements, while agency relationships are not. Generally, governments have more of a degree of involvement in decision-making for trust agreements than for agency relationships.

Authoritative pronouncements distinguish four types of fiduciary funds: (1) agency funds, (2) private-purpose trust funds, (3) investment trust funds, and (4) pension (and other employee benefit) trust funds. An **agency fund** accounts for assets held by a governmental unit temporarily as agent for individuals, organizations, or other governmental units. A **private-purpose trust fund** results when a contributor and a government agree that the principal and/or income of trust assets is for the benefit of individuals, organizations, or other governments. An **investment trust fund** exists when the government is the sponsor of a multigovernment investment pool and accounts for the external portion of those trust assets. Finally, a **pension (or other employee benefit) trust fund** exists when the government is the trustee for a defined benefit pension plan, defined contribution pension plan, other postemployment benefit plan, or other employee benefit plan.

Fiduciary funds use the economic resources measurement focus and accrual basis of accounting, with two exceptions. First, agency funds do not report revenues, expenses, or net assets; however, changes in assets and liabilities are recognized on the accrual basis. Second, certain liabilities of defined benefit pension plans and certain postemployment health care plans are recognized in accord with the requirements of GASB *Statements 25* and *26*. We describe these later in the chapter. The terms **additions** and **deductions** are used in trust fund reporting in lieu of revenues and expenses. However, additions and deductions are measured on the full accrual basis.

Fiduciary funds are reported by fund type: pension (and other employee benefit) trust funds, investment trust funds, private-purpose trust funds, and agency funds.

Two statements are required: the **Statement of Fiduciary Net Assets** and the **Statement of Fiduciary Changes in Net Assets** (see Illustration 2–9). Agency funds are not included in the Statement of Changes in Net Assets as no revenues (additions) or expenses (deductions) exist. In addition, two schedules are required for pension (and other employee benefit) trust funds as required supplementary information (RSI): the **Schedule of Funding Progress** and the **Schedule of Employer Contributions.** Fiduciary funds are *not* included in the government-wide financial statements.

This chapter discusses and illustrates agency, private-purpose trust, investment trust, and pension (and other employee benefit) trust funds. In addition, employer accounting for pensions is presented. Village of Elizabeth examples are provided for private-purpose and pension (and other employee benefit) trust funds. Finally, this chapter reviews and illustrates the four types of interfund transactions.

AGENCY FUNDS

Agency funds are used to account for assets held by a governmental unit acting as agent for one or more other governmental units or for individuals or private organizations. Assets accounted for in an agency fund belong to the party or parties for which the governmental unit acts as agent. Therefore, *agency fund assets are offset by liabilities equal in amount; no fund equity exists.* Agency fund assets and liabilities are to be recognized at the time the government becomes responsible for the assets. Additions and deductions are not recognized in the accounts of agency funds.

Unless use of an agency fund is mandated by law, by GASB standards, or by decision of the governing board of a governmental unit, an agency relationship may be accounted for within governmental and/or proprietary funds. For example, local governmental units must act as agents of the federal and state governments in the collection of employees' withholding taxes, retirement contributions, and (in many instances) social security taxes. In the absence of contrary requirements or administrative decisions, it is perfectly acceptable to account for the withholdings and the remittance to federal and state governments within the funds that account for the gross pay of the employees.

Only rarely is the use of a certain fund type mandated by GASB standards, rather than by law or by decision of the governing board of a government. However, GASB standards mandate that a governmental unit should account for special assessment activities in an agency fund if the government has no obligation to assume responsibility for debt payments, in the event of property owners default. GASB decided that only an agency relationship exists, even though the government may perform the functions of billing property owners for the assessments, collecting installments from the property owners, and making the principal and interest payments. (On the other hand, if the government *is* liable for payment of special assessment debt, in the event of default by the property owners, the transactions are handled as any other general government debt, normally through a debt service fund.)

Tax Agency Funds

An activity that often results in the creation of an agency fund is the collection of taxes and other revenues by an official of one governmental unit for other governmental units. State governments commonly collect sales taxes, gasoline taxes, and many other taxes that are apportioned to state agencies and to local governmental units within the state. At the local government level, it is common for an elected county official to serve as collector for all property taxes owed by persons or businesses owning property within the county. Taxes levied by all funds and units within the county are certified to the county collector for collection. The county collector is required by law to make periodic distributions of tax collections for each year to each fund or unit in the proportion the levy for that fund or unit bears to the total levy for the year.

Accounting for Tax Agency Funds

Assume that, for a given year, a county government levies for its General Fund the amount of $2,000,000 in property taxes, from which it expects to realize $1,960,000. For the same year, there is certified to it the amount of $3,000,000 in property taxes for the consolidated school district and $1,000,000 in property taxes for a village within the county. The county General Fund levy would be recorded in the accounts of the county General Fund in the same manner as in Chapter 4:

	Debits	Credits
Taxes Receivable—Current	2,000,000	
Estimated Uncollectible Current Taxes		40,000
Revenues Control		1,960,000

Each unit using the Tax Agency Fund would record its own levy in the manner just illustrated.

The Tax Agency Fund entry for recording levies of other governments certified to it, in this example totaling $4,000,000, would be as follows:

1. Taxes Receivable for Other Governments—		
Current	4,000,000	
Due to Other Governments		4,000,000

Note that the *gross* amount of the tax levy for all funds and units, not the net amount expected to be collected, should be recorded in the Tax Agency Fund as a receivable, because the county collector is responsible for attempting to collect all taxes as billed. Note also that the receivable is offset in total by the liability.

If collections of taxes during a certain portion of the year amounted to $1,600,000 for other governments and $800,000 for the County, the entry for the Tax Agency Fund would be:

	Debits	Credits
2. Cash	1,600,000	
Taxes Receivable for Other Governments—Current		1,600,000

The County General Fund would make the following journal entry:

	Debits	Credits
Cash	800,000	
Taxes Receivable—Current		800,000

In an actual case the tax collections must be identified with the parcels of property against which the taxes are levied, because the location of each parcel determines the governmental units and funds that should receive the tax collections. Assume for the sake of simplicity that the collections for the period represent collections of 40 percent of the taxes levied against each parcel in the county and that the County General Fund is given 1 percent of all collections for other governments as reimbursement for the cost of operating the Tax Agency Fund:

	Taxes Collected (40 Percent of Levy)	Collection Fee (Charged) Received	Cash to Be Distributed
County	$ 800,000	$ 16,000	$ 816,000
Village	400,000	(4,000)	396,000
School District	1,200,000	(12,000)	1,188,000
	$2,400,000	$ –0–	$2,400,000

If cash is not distributed as soon as the previous computation is made, the entry by the Tax Agency Fund to record the liability to other governments would be as follows:

	Debits	Credits
3. Due to Other Governments	1,600,000	
Due to County General Fund		16,000
Due to Village		396,000
Due to Consolidated School District		1,188,000

The entry made by the County General Fund to record the 1 percent fee would be:

	Debits	Credits
Due from County Tax Agency Fund	16,000	
Revenues Control		16,000

At the same time, the entry made by the Village General Fund would be:

	Debits	Credits
Due from County Tax Agency Fund	396,000	
Expenditures Control	4,000	
Taxes Receivable—Current		400,000

A similar entry would be made by the General Fund of the consolidated school district. When cash was transferred, the assets and liabilities to and from the specific funds would be extinguished.

If, as is likely, collections during a current year include collections of taxes that were levied for preceding years, computations must be made to determine the appropriate distribution of collections for each tax year to each government that levied taxes against the property for which collections have been received. It may also be necessary for a Tax Agency Fund to account for interest and penalties on delinquent taxes and advance collections.

Financial Reporting for Agency Funds

The assets and liabilities of agency funds should be included in the fiduciary funds Statement of Fiduciary Net Assets. However, since agency relationships do not generate revenues, expenditures, or expenses for the reporting entity, the operations of agency funds are not included in the Statement of Changes in Fiduciary Net Assets. The Comprehensive Annual Financial Report should include a Combining Statement of Changes in Assets and Liabilities—All Agency Funds. This statement is shown as Illustration 7–1.

PRIVATE-PURPOSE TRUST FUNDS

Private-purpose trust funds are created to account for trust agreements where principal and/or income benefit individuals, private organizations, or other governments. In some cases, these trusts are created when individuals or organizations contribute resources with the agreement that principal and/or income will be used to benefit others. For example, a government may agree to be trustee for a community foundation, where awards are made to not-for-profit organizations. In some cases, the principal of those gifts may be *nonexpendable*, in which case an **endowment** has been created. In other cases, the principal of those gifts may be expendable. In either case, management of the trust may involve significant investments.

Accounting for Investments

GASB Statement 31, *Accounting and Financial Reporting for Certain Investments and for External Investment Pools,* applies to (1) interest-earning investment contracts (CDs, time deposits, etc.), (2) external investment pools, (3) open-end mutual funds, (4) debt securities, and (5) equity securities that have readily determinable fair values. These investments are to be reported in the balance sheet at fair value, which is defined as the "amount at which an investment could be exchanged in a

ILLUSTRATION 7-1

NAME OF GOVERNMENTAL UNIT
Combining Statement of Changes in Assets and Liabilities—All Agency Funds
For Fiscal Year Ended December 31, 2004

	Balance January 1, 2003	Additions	Deductions	Balance December 31, 2004
Property Tax Fund				
Assets:				
Cash	$ 25,800	$ 800,000	$ 725,000	$100,800
Taxes Receivable	174,200	1,205,800	800,000	580,000
Total Assets	$200,000	$2,005,800	$1,525,000	$680,800
Liabilities:				
Due to Other Taxing Units:				
County	$180,000	$1,085,220	$652,500	$612,720
Special District	20,000	120,580	72,500	68,080
Total Liabilities	$200,000	$1,205,800	$ 725,000	$680,800
Student Activity Fund				
Assets:				
Cash	$ 1,600	$ 1,900	$ 1,650	$ 1,850
Liabilities:				
Due to Student Groups	$ 1,600	$ 1,900	$ 1,650	$ 1,850
Totals—All Agency Funds				
Assets:				
Cash	$ 27,400	$ 801,900	$ 726,650	$102,650
Taxes Receivable	174,200	1,205,800	800,000	580,000
Total Assets	$201,600	$2,007,700	$1,526,650	$682,650
Liabilities:				
Due to Other Taxing Units	200,000	1,205,800	725,000	680,800
Due to Student Groups	1,600	1,900	1,650	1,850
Total Liabilities	$201,600	$1,207,700	$ 726,650	$682,650

Source: Adapted from GASB *Codification* Sec. 2200.910.

current transaction between willing parties, other than in a forced or liquidation sale." When a quoted market price is available, that price should be used. *Statement 31* does not apply to investments of pension funds, which for purposes of this text have essentially the same requirements. Fair value, then, is to be reported for these investments in all funds of state and local governmental units. Investments not covered by *Statement 31* are to follow other accounting principles currently in effect. For example, investments in bonds without determinable fair values would be reported at amortized cost. Also, if a government has sufficient investments in a company to justify the equity method of accounting (see an intermediate accounting text), then the equity method of accounting would be followed.

As a result, according to *Statement 31*, "all investment income, including changes in the fair value of investments, should be recognized as revenue in the operating statement (or other statement of activities). When identified separately as an element of investment income, the change in the fair value of investments should be captioned *net increase (decrease) in the fair value of investments*." GASB does not permit separate display of the realized and unrealized components of the change in fair value, with the exception of external investment pools. However, GASB does permit note disclosure of the amount of realized gains. Other major disclosures include (1) methods and assumptions used to determine fair value, if other than quoted market prices and (2) the policy for determining which investments would be accounted for at amortized cost.

The provisions of *Statement 31* are illustrated in connection with the following discussion of private-purpose trust funds; however, it should be noted that the concepts apply to the accounting and reporting for all fund types.

Illustrative Case—Private-Purpose Trust Funds

Assume that, on January 2, 2004, a wealthy individual contributed $500,000 to the Village of Elizabeth and signed a trust agreement specifying that the principal amount be held intact and invested. The income is to be used to provide selected graduates from the Village's two high schools (one public and one private) scholarships to the colleges of their choice. On January 2, the gift was recorded in the newly created Scholarship Fund:

	Debits	Credits
1. Cash	500,000	
Additions—Contributions		500,000

On the same day, Village administrators purchased AB Company bonds, as an investment, in the amount of $480,000 plus accrued interest. The bonds carry an annual rate of interest of 6 percent, payable semiannually on May 1 and November 1. As of that date, accrued interest amounted to $4,800 ($480,000 $\times$ .06 $\times$ $\frac{2}{12}$):

2. Investment in AB Bonds	480,000	
Accrued Interest Receivable	4,800	
Cash		484,800

On May 1, 2004, the Scholarship Fund received interest in the amount of $14,400, of which $4,800 was a return on the original investment:

3. Cash	14,400	
Accrued Interest Receivable		4,800
Additions—Investment Earnings—Interest		9,600

On May 31, $9,000 in scholarships were awarded:

	Debits	Credits
4. Deductions—Scholarship Awards	9,000	
Cash		9,000

On November 1, 2004, interest in the amount of $14,400 was received:

5. Cash	14,400	
Additions—Investment Earnings—Interest		14,400

As of December 31, an interest accrual was made for November and December:

6. Accrued Interest Receivable	4,800	
Additions—Investment Earnings—Interest		4,800

GASB *Statement 31* requires that investments with determinable fair values be reported at fair value. It was determined that the AB Company bonds had a fair value of $482,000 on December 31, exclusive of accrued interest:

7. Investment in AB Bonds	2,000	
Additions—Investment Earnings—		
Net Increase in Fair Value of Investments		2,000

Finally, a closing entry was prepared for the Scholarship Fund:

8. Additions—Contributions	500,000	
Additions—Investment Earnings—Interest	28,800	
Additions—Investment Earnings—		
Net Increase in the Fair Value of Investments	2,000	
Deductions—Scholarship Awards		9,000
Net Assets Held in Trust for Scholarship Benefits		521,800

Financial statements for the Scholarship Private—Purpose Trust Fund are included in the Village of Elizabeth Statement of Fiduciary Net Assets (Illustration 7–3) and Statement of Changes in Fiduciary Net Assets (Illustration 7–4).

A Note about Escheat Property

In many cases, state governments obtain property in the absence of legal claimants or heirs. For example, if property is abandoned or if legal owners cannot be found, the property is turned over to state governments until the legal owners can be found. This property is known as **escheat property.** Some escheat property is ultimately claimed by rightful owners; other escheat property never is claimed and is eventually used by the government in some way.

GASB standards for the recording of escheat property are included in Statement 37, *Basic Financial Statements—and Management's Discussion and Analysis—for State and Local Governments: Omnibus. Statement 37,* paragraph 4 states in part, "Escheat property generally should be reported as an asset in the governmental or proprietary fund to which the property ultimately escheats." For example, a state might have legislation that requires the residual value of unclaimed property be dedicated to the state education fund. In this case, the resources might be reported in a special revenue fund dedicated to education. The value of unclaimed property expected to be paid out to claimants would either be reported as a liability in that fund or in an agency or private-purpose trust fund. If the second option is chosen, amounts ultimately payable to other governments would be reported in an agency fund (offset by liabilities), and amounts expected to be paid to individuals would be reported in a private-purpose trust fund (offset by fund balance).

INVESTMENT TRUST FUNDS

GASB Statement 31, *Accounting and Financial Reporting for Certain Investments and for External Investment Pools* provides requirements for investment pools. First, internal investment pools, which account for investments of the reporting entity, are to be spread out to the funds providing the resources, when preparing financial statements. For example, if a reporting government has $900 million in investments, which are pooled for management purposes, and those investments came one-third each from the General, an enterprise, and a private-purpose trust fund, then each fund would report $300 million of investments in the Balance Sheet or Statement of Net Assets. Likewise, income earned on the investments would be reported directly in those funds.

On the other hand, many governments participate in **external investment pools,** where investments for several governments are maintained. For example, a county government might, through the County Treasurer, maintain an investment pool for all governments situated within the county. For governments that maintain the multigovernment investment pool, the *external portion* is to be maintained in an *investment trust fund,* a fiduciary fund. The internal portion is to be spread out among the funds say, for the county (i.e., the county's portion) as described in the preceding paragraph.

Investment trust funds are to be reported, as fiduciary funds, using the economic resources measurement focus and accrual basis of accounting. Investment trust funds are reported, by fund type, in the fiduciary funds Statement of Fiduciary Net Assets and Statement of Changes in Fiduciary Net Assets. Investments are to be reported at fair value, as described earlier in this chapter. In addition, a number of note disclosures are required for investment trust funds.

PUBLIC EMPLOYEE RETIREMENT SYSTEMS (PENSION TRUST FUNDS)

State and local governmental units commonly provide pension plans for their employees. Statewide plans often exist for teachers, state government employees, local government general employees, local government police and fire department employees, and legislators. In addition, many local governments maintain their own pension plans.

For local governments, a statewide multiemployer plan may be either an **agency plan** or a **cost-sharing plan**. An agency plan is one in which each contributing employer, such as a local government, has a separate account; in this plan, each local government is required to keep its own contributions up to date. A cost-sharing plan is a statewide plan in which separate accounts are not kept for each employer; in this plan, unfunded actuarial liabilities are made up on a statewide basis; that is, the state applies extra charges to all participating governments to eliminate the actuarial deficiency. Employer disclosure requirements are more extensive for single-employer and agency plans than for cost-sharing plans.

A pension plan may be either *contributory* or *noncontributory*, depending on whether employees are required to contribute. A plan also may be defined benefit or defined contribution. A **defined benefit** plan is one in which the plan is required to pay out a certain sum (for example, 2 percent times the average salary over the past four years times the number of years worked), regardless of the amount available in the plan. A **defined contribution plan** is required only to pay out the amount that has been accumulated for each employee. As a result, defined benefit plans may have unfunded actuarial liabilities, whereas defined contribution plans do not.

Pension plans for governments are often called **Public Employee Retirement Systems** (PERS). When a PERS is a part of the reporting entity of a government, whether state or local, a pension trust fund is created and included in the Comprehensive Annual Financial Report. The pension trust fund data will be included in the fiduciary fund statements—the Statement of Fiduciary Net Assets and Statement of Changes in Fiduciary Net Assets. The fiduciary fund type is actually called pension (and other employee benefit) trust funds and includes other postemployment plans and any other employment benefit plans, including any IRS 457 Deferred Compensation plans (see section below).

Whether or not the PERS is a part of the reporting entity, certain employer disclosures are required in the notes to the statements. Full treatment of accounting and reporting requirements for both governmental employers and PERS is beyond the scope of this book. This section introduces the topic and presents a general overview of current standards.

Accounting and Reporting for Defined Benefit Pension Plans

The material in this section applies to stand-alone pension plans (for example, statewide pension plans for teachers) and to pension trust funds that are found in CAFRs of state or local governmental units (for example, a local government police retirement system). This material applies to single-employer plans, agent multiemployer plans, and cost-sharing multiemployer plans.

Financial reporting requirements include two statements and two schedules. The schedules are reported as **required supplementary information** immediately after the notes to the financial statements:

1. Statement of Plan Net Assets. This statement provides information about the fair value of plan assets, liabilities, and the net assets held in trust for benefits. This statement does *not* provide information about the actuarial status of the plan. In the CAFR of a government with a single employer plan reported as a trust fund, this information would be included in the fiduciary funds Statement of Net Assets.
2. Statement of Changes in Plan Net Assets. This statement provides information about additions to and deductions from net assets. When included in the reporting entity, it would be included in the fiduciary funds Statement of Changes in Net Assets.
3. Schedule of Funding Progress. This schedule provides information about the actuarial status of the plan from an ongoing long-term perspective.
4. Schedule of Employer Contributions. This schedule provides historical trend information about the **annual required contributions (ARC)** and the actual contributions made by employers.

In addition, certain note disclosures are required. The statements, schedules, and notes will be illustrated through an example of financial reporting for the Village of Elizabeth Public Employees Retirement Fund, assuming the reporting is made only through a pension trust fund section of a CAFR.

Assume that the Public Employees Retirement Fund had the following Statement of Plan Net Assets as of December 31, 2003 (shown in Illustration 7–2).

During the year ended December 31, 2004, the following events and transactions that affected the Village of Elizabeth's Public Employees Retirement Fund took place:

ILLUSTRATION 7-2

VILLAGE OF ELIZABETH
Public Employees Retirement Fund
Statement of Plan Net Assets
December 31, 2003

Assets	
Cash	$ 30,500
Accrued Interest Receivable	50,000
Investments, at Fair Value:	
Bonds	3,200,000
Common Stocks	2,100,000
Commercial Paper and Repurchase Agreements	500,000
Total Assets	5,880,500
Liabilities	
Accounts Payable and Accrued Expenses	30,000
Net Assets Held in Trust for Pension Benefits	$5,850,500

Accrued interest receivable as of January 1, 2004, was collected:

	Debits	Credits
1. Cash	50,000	
Accrued Interest Receivable		50,000

Member contributions in the amount of $210,000 and employer contributions in the amount of $210,000 were received in cash:

	Debits	Credits
2. Cash	420,000	
Additions—Contributions—Plan Members		210,000
Additions—Contributions—Employer		210,000

Annuity benefits in the amount of $110,000 and disability benefits in the amount of $15,000 were recorded as liabilities:

	Debits	Credits
3. Deductions—Annuity Benefits	110,000	
Deductions—Disability Benefits	15,000	
Accounts Payable and Accrued Expenses		125,000

Accounts payable and accrued expenses paid in cash amounted to $140,000:

	Debits	Credits
4. Accounts Payable and Accrued Expenses	140,000	
Cash		140,000

Terminated employees whose benefits were not vested were refunded $50,000 in cash:

	Debits	Credits
5. Deductions—Refunds to Terminated Employees	50,000	
Cash		50,000

Investment income received in cash amounted to $410,000, of which $210,000 was dividends and $200,000 was interest; additionally, $70,000 interest income was accrued at year-end:

	Debits	Credits
6. Cash	410,000	
Accrued Interest Receivable	70,000	
Additions—Investment Earnings—Interest		270,000
Additions—Investment Earnings—Dividends		210,000

Commercial paper and repurchase agreements carried at a cost of $200,000 matured, and cash in that amount was received:

	Debits	Credits
7. Cash	200,000	
Commercial Paper and Repurchase Agreements		200,000

Common stock carried at a fair value of $1,250,000 was sold for $1,300,000; $500,000 was reinvested in common stock and the remainder in bonds. An additional amount of $800,000 was also invested in bonds:

	Debits	Credits
8a. Cash	1,300,000	
Investments in Common Stock		1,250,000
Additions—Investment Earnings—		
Net Increase in Fair Value of Investments		50,000
8b. Investments in Bonds	1,600,000	
Investments in Common Stock	500,000	
Cash		2,100,000

Administrative expenses for the year totaled $80,000, all paid in cash:

	Debits	Credits
9. Deductions—Administrative Expenses	80,000	
Cash		80,000

During the year, the fair value of common stock increased $40,000; the fair value of bonds decreased $30,000:

	Debits	Credits
10. Investments in Common Stock	40,000	
Investments in Bonds		30,000
Additions—Investment Earnings—Net Increase		
in Fair Value of Investments		10,000

Nominal accounts for the year were closed:

	Debits	Credits
11. Additions—Contributions—Plan Members	210,000	
Additions—Contributions—Employer	210,000	
Additions—Investment Earnings—Interest	270,000	
Additions—Investment Earnings—Dividends	210,000	
Additions—Investment Earnings—		
Net Increase in Fair Value of Investments	60,000	

	Debits	Credits
Deductions—Annuity Benefits		110,000
Deductions—Disability Benefits		15,000
Deductions—Refunds to Terminated Employees		50,000
Deductions—Administrative Expenses		80,000
Net Assets Held in Trust for Pension Benefits		705,000

Illustration 7–3 reflects the Statement of Fiduciary Net Assets for the fiduciary funds, including the private-purpose trust fund and the Public Employees Retirement Fund as of December 31, 2004.

Illustration 7–4 presents the Statement of Changes in Net Assets for the fiduciary funds, including the private-purpose trust fund and the Public Employee Retirement System for the Year Ended December 31, 2004. It should be noted that the GASB standards do not allow the realized and unrealized gains on investments to be reported separately.

A Schedule of Funding Progress is required for all defined benefit pension plans. It presents, for at least the past six fiscal years, the actuarial valuation date, the actuarial value of plan assets, the actuarial liability, the total unfunded actuarial liability, the funded ratio, the annual covered payroll, and the ratio of the unfunded actuarial liability to the annual covered payroll. Illustration 7–5 reflects a Schedule of Funding Progress using assumed figures for the Village of Elizabeth.

ILLUSTRATION 7–3

VILLAGE OF ELIZABETH
Statement of Fiduciary Net Assets
Fiduciary Funds
December 31, 2004

	Public Employee Retirement Fund	Private-Purpose Trust
Assets		
Cash	$ 40,500	$ 35,000
Accrued interest receivable	70,000	4,800
Investments, at fair value:		
Bonds	4,770,000	482,000
Common stocks	1,390,000	
Commercial paper and repurchase agreements	300,000	
Total investments	6,460,000	482,000
Total assets	6,570,500	521,800
Liabilities		
Accounts payable and accrued expenses	15,000	–0–
Net Assets		
Held in trust for pension benefits and other purposes	$6,555,500	$521,800

ILLUSTRATION 7-4

VILLAGE OF ELIZABETH
Statement of Changes in Fiduciary Net Assets
Fiduciary Funds
For the Year Ended December 31, 2004

	Public Employee Retirement Fund	Private-Purpose Trust
Additions:		
Contributions:		
Employer	$ 210,000	
Plan members	210,000	
Individuals		$500,000
Total contributions	420,000	500,000
Investment earnings		
Interest	270,000	28,800
Dividends	210,000	
Net increase in fair value of investments	60,000	2,000
Total investment earnings	540,000	30,800
Total additions	960,000	530,800
Deductions:		
Annuity benefits	110,000	
Refunds to terminated employees	50,000	
Administrative expenses	80,000	
Disability benefits	15,000	
Scholarship awards		9,000
Total deductions	255,000	9,000
Change in net assets	705,000	521,800
Net assets—beginning of the year	5,850,500	–0–
Net assets—end of the year	$6,555,500	$521,800

A Schedule of Employer Contributions is also required to present six-year information. For each of the past six fiscal years, the Schedule should present the annual required employer contribution and the percentage contributed. Illustration 7–6 reflects the information for the Village of Elizabeth.

Summary of Employer Reporting

Regardless of whether an employer government is trustee for a given pension plan, certain accounting, financial reporting, note disclosure, and required supplementary schedules are required. The nature and extent of GASB requirements for employer reporting depend upon whether plans are single employer, agent multiple-employer, cost-sharing multiple-employer, or defined contribution.

Governments that contribute to single employer and agent multiple-employer plans compute annual pension cost as the **annual required contributions (ARC)**, which are actuarially determined as the employer's **normal cost** plus a provision for amortizing the **unfunded actuarial liability**. If the government has a **net pen-**

ILLUSTRATION 7–5

VILLAGE OF ELIZABETH
Public Employee Retirement Fund
Schedule of Funding Progress
Six Years Ending November 30, 2004
($000 Omitted)

Actuarial Valuation Date	Actuarial Value of Assets	Actuarial Accrued Liability— Entry Age	Unfunded Accrued Liability	Funded Ratio	Covered Payroll	Unfunded Accrued Liability as a Percentage of Covered Payroll
11/30/99	4,500	7,200	2,700	62.5%	2,000	135.0%
11/30/00	4,700	7,500	2,800	62.7	2,150	130.2
11/30/01	4,900	7,900	3,000	62.0	2,300	130.4
11/30/02	5,400	8,200	2,800	65.9	2,500	112.0
11/30/03	5,800	8,400	2,600	69.0	2,800	92.9
11/30/04	6,500	8,900	2,400	73.0	3,000	80.0

ILLUSTRATION 7–6

VILLAGE OF ELIZABETH
Public Employee Retirement Fund
Schedule of Employer Contributions
Six Years Ended December 31, 2004

Year Ended December 31	Annual Required Contribution	Percentage Contributed
1999	$160,000	100%
2000	168,000	100
2001	173,000	100
2002	182,000	100
2003	196,000	100
2004	210,000	100

sion obligation (NPO) (the cumulative difference between the employers' required and actual contributions), the annual pension cost will include the ARC, interest on the NPO, and an adjustment to the ARC. The computations are beyond the scope of this book; any one of several generally accepted actuarial methods may be used as long as it meets certain parameters defined by the GASB. Contributions by governmental funds are recorded as expenditures using modified accrual accounting—the amount that will be liquidated by available resources. Unfunded amounts (the NPO) are recorded in the government-wide statements. All contributions by proprietary funds are recorded as expenses on the full accrual basis in the proprietary fund, and the NPO is recorded as a fund liability.

Governments that contribute to cost-sharing multiple-employer plans should record expenditures (for governmental funds) and expenses (for proprietary funds) equal to the annual contractually required contributions to the plans. By definition, individual amounts cannot be computed for each employer, for cost sharing plans.

Note disclosures for all defined benefit plans include plan descriptions and funding policies. In addition, note disclosures for single-employer and agent multiple-employer plans include the annual pension cost compared with the actual contributions made. Three-year schedules list the annual pension cost, the percentage of annual pension cost contributed, and the NPO at the end of the year. Contributors to single-employer and agent multiple-employer plans are also required to provide supplementary schedules listing additional three-year information. Keep in mind that these disclosures are required of all employers, even when they are not trustees of the pension plans.

Pension contributions to defined contribution plans should be measured as an expenditure or expense equal to the amount required in accordance with the terms of the plan. Assets and liabilities arise only if the required and actual contributions differ.

A Note about IRS 457 Deferred Compensation Plans

Many governments have established **IRS 457 Deferred Compensation Plans** for their employees. If legal requirements are met, these represent tax deferred compensation plans in which employees are not required to pay taxes on the amounts withheld until distributed to them after retirement. If the plans are administered by an entity outside a government, which is the most common case, then no accounting is required by the government, other than to account for funds withheld and distributed. If a government administers the plan, the resources are held in trust and accounted for as a pension (and other employee benefit) trust fund.

A Note about Other Postemployment Benefits

Currently, GASB standards do not require accrual of other postemployment benefits, such as health plan payments for retirees. As this text is written, GASB is involved in several projects that will likely require accrual of these benefits. As most governments have not been setting aside funds for these payments, it is likely that these new requirements will have a significant effect on the financial statements in the future.

INTERFUND TRANSACTIONS

Chapter 4 introduces the concept of interfund transactions, and provides examples for the General Fund of the Village of Elizabeth. Other chapters provide examples of the effect those transactions have on other funds. This section reviews and illustrates interfund transactions

GASB provides for two major types of interfund activity, each with two subtypes:
1. Reciprocal interfund activity (the internal counterpart to exchange transactions).
    a. Interfund loans.

    b. Interfund services provided and used.
2. Nonreciprocal interfund activity (the internal counterpart to nonexchange transactions).
    a. Interfund transfers.
    b. Interfund reimbursements.

Reciprocal Interfund Activity—Interfund Loans

Interfund loans are amounts provided with requirements for repayment. These might be either short-term or long-term. Assuming the General Fund loaned $300,000 to an internal service fund (a short-term loan), the following entries would be made:

	Debits	Credits
General Fund		
Due from Internal Service Fund	300,000	
Cash		300,000
Internal Service Fund		
Cash	300,000	
Due to General Fund		300,000

Now, assume a long-term loan in the same amount is made from the General Fund to an enterprise fund. The term *Advance* or *Long-Term Advance* is used. Note also, that when making a long-term loan, a governmental fund is required to reserve fund balance in the same amount, as the amount is no longer available for expenditure:

	Debits	Credits
General Fund		
Long-Term Advance to Enterprise Fund	300,000	
Cash		300,000
Fund Balance—Unreserved	300,000	
Fund Balance—Reserved for Long-Term Advances to Other Funds		300,000
Enterprise Fund		
Cash	300,000	
Long-Term Advance from General Fund		300,000

If the borrowing fund does not repay the loan in a reasonable period of time, it should be treated as a transfer (see below).

Reciprocal Interfund Activity—Interfund Services Provided and Used

This type of interfund transaction provides for sales and purchases of goods and services for a price approximating the external exchange price. One fund reports a revenue; the other fund reports an expenditure or expense. Examples include services provided by internal service funds to other funds, sales of water from an enterprise fund to the General Fund, and contributions from the General Fund to a pension trust fund (where an addition would be recorded). An example of the first type of transaction would be if a print shop fund (an internal service fund) provided $10,000 in services to a General Fund Department:

	Debits	Credits
Print Shop (Internal Service) Fund		
Due from General Fund	10,000	
Operating Revenues—Charges for Sales and Services		10,000
General Fund		
Expenditures Control	10,000	
Due to Print Shop Fund		10,000

Nonreciprocal Interfund Activity—Interfund Transfers

This type of transaction represents the flow of assets without equivalent flow of assets in return and without requirement for repayment. Examples would be the annual transfer of funds from the General Fund to a debt service fund, the one-time transfer of unused funds from a capital projects fund to a debt service fund, a subsidy from an enterprise fund to the General Fund (or the other way), and a one-time transfer from the General Fund to establish an internal service fund. An example of a transfer from the General Fund to a debt service fund would be as follows:

	Debits	Credits
General Fund		
Other Financing Uses—Transfers Out	200,000	
Cash		200,000
Debt Service Fund		
Cash	200,000	
Other Financing Sources—Transfers In		200,000

Nonreciprocal Interfund Activity—Interfund Reimbursements

These are "repayments from the funds responsible for particular expenditures or expenses to the funds that initially paid for them." (GASB *Statement 34,* Paragraph 112) Generally, in interfund reimbursements, one fund debits an expense or expenditure and another fund credits an expenditure or expense. Assume that, initially, the General Fund paid for supplies in the amount of $30,000 that should have been paid for by a special revenue fund. At the time of payment, the General Fund had debited Expenditures Control. To correct the transaction, an adjustment, an interfund reimbursement, would be made:

	Debits	Credits
Special Revenue Fund		
Expenditures Control	30,000	
Cash		30,000
General Fund		
Cash	30,000	
Expenditures Control		30,000

A FINAL COMMENT ON FUND ACCOUNTING AND REPORTING

Chapters 4–7 presented accounting and financial reporting requirements for governmental, proprietary, and fiduciary fund types. Governmental fund reports for the General and major governmental funds include the Balance Sheet (Illustration 5–1) and the Statement of Revenues, Expenditures, and Changes in Fund Balances (Illustration 5–2). Finally, a Budgetary Comparison Schedule is required as an RSI schedule and is presented in Illustration 3–3. Proprietary fund reports for major enterprise funds and the internal service fund type include the Statement of Net Assets (Illustration 6–1) and the Statement of Revenues, Expenses, and Changes in Fund Net Assets (Illustration 6–2), and the Statement of Cash Flows (Illustration 6–3).

Fiduciary fund reporting, by fund type, includes the Statement of Fiduciary Net Assets (Illustration 7–3) and the Statement of Changes in Fiduciary Net Assets (Illustration 7–4). In addition, GAAP require two RSI schedules for governments with pension trust funds: a Schedule of Funding Progress (Illustration 7–5) and a Schedule of Employer Contributions (Illustration 7–6).

As indicated in Chapter 2, GAAP require the presentation of government-wide financial statements: a Statement of Net Assets and a Statement of Activities. These are *consolidated* statements, presented using the economic resources measurement focus and accrual basis of accounting. Most governments will use fund accounting for internal record-keeping, as described in Chapters 3–7. Those governments will prepare worksheet adjustments necessary to present the government-wide statements. Chapter 8 will present the major necessary adjustments and the government-wide statements, using the Village of Elizabeth as an example.

Questions and Exercises

7–1. Using the annual report obtained for Exercise 1–1, answer the following questions:

    a. Look at the Statement of Fiduciary Net Assets. Which fund types are included? Is the Statement prepared in a format in which Assets − Liabilities = Net assets? Are net assets shown as being held in trust for employee benefits and other purposes? Look at the Statement of Changes in Fiduciary Net Assets. Has the government refrained from including agency funds in that statement? Are increases shown as additions and deductions, rather than revenues and expenses? What are the main additions? What are the main deductions?

b. Are agency funds included in the Statement of Fiduciary Net Assets? If so, look to the notes or combining schedules and list the individual agency funds. Has the government limited itself to agency funds that are held for individuals, organizations, or other governments—not for other government funds? Do agency funds report only assets and liabilities, not net assets? Does the government report a Statement or Schedule of Changes in Assets and Liabilities for agency funds?

c. Does the government have private-purpose funds? If so, list them. Describe the purposes for which they exist. Can you tell if any of those funds are endowments, and have resources permanently restricted? How much income was generated by each of the private-purpose funds, and how much was released for use? Does the government report escheat property as private-purpose funds? If so, indicate the nature of the process by which property is released and for what purposes.

d. Does the government report investment trust funds? If so, describe the nature of the external investment pool. Which other governments are included? Has your government refrained from including its own investments in the investment trust funds?

e. List the pension funds included in the financial statements. From the notes, list the other pension plans that are available to employees of your governmental unit. Are those plans agent plans or cost-sharing plans? Defined contribution or defined benefit? Are required disclosures made in the notes for all pension plans, whether or not the plans are included as trust funds? Are the two RSI Schedules included in your report (when pension trust funds are reported)? Look at the actuarial status of the plans and comment about the potential impact of pensions on the financial condition of the government. Does the report have special revenue funds through which the government sends funds to statewide plans?

f. Look at the note disclosures regarding investments. Are investments reported at fair value? Do the notes disclose the realized gains or losses on investments? Do the notes categorize investments based on risk? When the government creates internal investment pools for management purposes, does the government report the individual investments and income from those investments in the funds which provided the resources?

7–2. For each of the following, select the letter with the best answer:
1. The County of Clarke collects property taxes from each of the governmental jurisdictions within its borders. Clarke would account for these collections and payments in:

a. The General Fund.
b. A private-purpose trust fund.
c. An agency fund.   p. 194
d. An internal service fund.

2. Agency funds should use which basis of accounting?
   a. Cash.
   b. Modified accrual.   p.192
   c. Accrual.
   d. Either modified accrual or accrual, depending on the circumstances.

3. DeKalb County collects property taxes within its boundaries and receives from the other governments a 3 percent fee for administering those collections. For the fiscal year ended June 30, 2004, the county collected $300,000 for the City of DeKalb, $1,000,000 for the DeKalb School District, and $400,000 for the County General Fund. The total amount received by the County General Fund would be:
   a. $400,000.
   b. $412,000.
   c. $451,000.
   d. $439,000.

4. Fiduciary funds include which of the following?
   a. Agency, expendable trust, nonexpendable trust, pension trust.
   b. Agency, private-purpose trust, investment trust, pension trust.
   c. Agency, permanent, private-purpose trust, pension trust.
   d. Agency, permanent, private-purpose trust, investment trust, pension trust.

5. Which of the following is true regarding fiduciary funds?
   a. Fiduciary funds use the economic resources measurement focus and the accrual basis of accounting.
   b. All fiduciary funds report, in the Statement of Net Assets, assets, liabilities, and net assets.   p.200
   c. Both of the above.
   d. Neither of the above.

6. The City of Eastern Shores is trustee for a multi-government investment pool and has established an investment trust fund. Included in the investment trust fund, for management purposes, are investments in the amount of $13 million from the City's General Fund, $4 million from the City's private-purpose funds, and $58 million from other governments. Which of the following statements would be true?
   a. The City would report all investments in the investment trust fund.
   b. The City would report the $58 million in the investment trust fund, and $17 million in a permanent fund.

c. The City would report the $58 million in the investment trust fund, the $13 million in the General Fund, and the $4 million in private-purpose funds.

d. None of the above are true.

7. The City of X has investments in bonds. These bonds have an amortized cost of $1,010,000 and a market value of $1,012,000. The market value is quoted and available in the financial press. The original cost of the bonds was $1,015,000. The amount at which the investments would be reported is:

   a. $1,010,000.
   b. $1,012,000.
   c. $1,015,000.
   d. Either $1,010,000 or $1,012,000, depending on the policy of the government.

8. Which of the following is true regarding pension accounting and reporting?

   a. Pension trust funds are reported in a government's CAFR in all cases where the government makes contributions.
   b. The Statement of Fiduciary Net Assets reports all assets, liabilities, and net assets of pension plans, including the actuarial liability.
   c. Both of the above.
   d. Neither of the above.

9. A statewide pension plan exists for all local governments in a certain state. The provisions of the plan indicate that each qualifying retiree receive 2 percent multiplied by the number of years active employment multiplied by the average of the last four years service. A separate actuarial liability is calculated for each local government, which must make up its own deficit over a period of 40 years. This plan would be known as a:

   a. Multiemployer, defined benefit, agent plan.
   b. Multiemployer, defined contribution, cost-sharing plan.
   c. Multiemployer, defined benefit, cost-sharing plan.
   d. Multiemployer, defined contribution, agent plan.

10. The Western Falls School District received a $100,000 gift from a wealthy alumnus, and an agreement was reached that $10,000 per year would be paid to the valedictorian of the high school class as a freshman scholarship to college, until the funds were depleted. The $100,000 would be accounted for as:

    a. An expendable trust fund.
    b. An investment trust fund.
    c. An agency fund.
    d. A private-purpose trust fund.

7–3. For each of the following, select the letter with the *best* answer.
   1. For which of the following activities, does GASB require agency fund reporting by a county?
      a. Tax collections for the county.
      b. Working cash funds for all government departments.
      c. Special assessment collections for which the government is not responsible for the debt.
      d. Payroll deductions.
   2. The County of Y collects property taxes levied within its boundaries and receives from the other governments a 2 percent fee for administering those collections. For the fiscal year ended June 30, 2004, the county collected $300,000 for the City of Y, $1,200,000 for the Y School District, and $400,000 for the County General Fund. For the initial recording of the fee, the Tax Agency Fund should record a credit to:
      a. Revenues Control in the amount of $30,000.
      b. Tax Agency Fund Balance in the amount of $30,000.
      c. Tax Agency Net Assets in the amount of $30,000.
      d. Due to Y County General Fund in the amount of $30,000.
   3. Which of the following is *not* true regarding the accounting for investments?
      a. Investments in stocks with determinable fair value should be reported at fair value.
      b. Investments in debt securities with determinable fair values should be reported at fair value.
      c. When a government has both realized and unrealized gains from securities reported at fair value, it is not permissible to report, in the statements, separate amounts for the realized and unrealized amounts.
      d. None of the above; all are true.
   4. The City of X received $1,000,000 in securities from a donor with the agreement that the $1,000,000 be invested permanently and that the income be used for the purchase of books for the city library. The donation of the $1,000,000 would be recorded in:
      a. A permanent fund.
      b. A private-purpose trust fund.
      c. A nonexpendable trust fund.
      d. None of the above.
   5. Which of the following would use modified accrual accounting?
      a. Private-purpose trust funds.
      b. Agency funds.
      c. Permanent funds.
      d. None of the above.

6. Which of the following is true regarding pension accounting and reporting?
   a. When the government is trustee for the pension plan, the government is required to include the pension trust fund in the Statement of Fiduciary Net Assets and Statement of Changes in Fiduciary Net Assets.
   b. Whether or not the government is trustee for the pension plan, it is required to record expenditures (or expenses) for required contributions in the appropriate funds (for example, General, enterprise) for those contributions.
   c. Both of the above.
   d. Neither of the above.
7. Agency funds would be included in the CAFR in:
   a. The government-wide statements.
   b. The Statement of Fiduciary Net Assets.
   c. The Statement of Changes in Fiduciary Net Assets.
   d. All of the above.
8. Where, in the CAFR for a local government unit, would one find the actuarial liability for pension funds for which a government is trustee?
   a. In the government-wide Statement of Net Assets.
   b. In the Statement of Fiduciary Net Assets.
   c. In the RSI Schedule of Funding Progress.
   d. In all of the above.
9. A defined-benefit pension plan, administered by the state, that does not keep an individual balance for the obligations of each government, is known as:
   a. A cost-sharing multiemployer plan.
   b. An agency multiemployer plan.
   c. A statewide employer plan.
   d. A statewide, general plan.
10. Which of the following is true regarding fiduciary funds?
    a. Fiduciary funds are not reported in government-wide statements.
    b. Agency funds and private-purpose trust funds use modified accrual accounting; investment and pension trust funds use accrual accounting.
    c. Both of the above are true.
    d. Neither of the above is true.

7–4. Benton County maintains a tax agency fund for use by the County Treasurer to record receivables, collections, and disbursements of all property tax collections to all other units of government in the county. For FY 2003–2004, the following taxes were assessed:

Benton County General Fund	$10,500,000
City of Thomas	7,400,000
City of Hart	3,200,000
Benton County School District	23,900,000
Various Special Districts	6,300,000
Total	$51,300,000

During the first six months of the fiscal year, the following transactions took place:

1. The tax levy became effective. All units of government provided for an estimated 3 percent in uncollectible taxes.
2. Cash collections of the first installment of taxes amounted to $5,080,000 for the County General Fund and $19,544,000 for the other governments.
3. It was determined that the cash collections pertained to the funds and governmental units in the following amounts. Record the liability to the county General Fund and to the other governmental units, assuming that the county General Fund charges other governments 1 percent of all tax collected because the county General Fund incurs all costs of billing, recording, and collecting taxes.

Benton County General Fund	$ 5,080,000
City of Thomas	4,070,000
City of Hart	1,018,000
Benton County School District	11,472,000
Various Special Districts	2,984,000
Total	$24,624,000

4. Cash was transferred to the various governmental units.

Required:

Record the transactions on the books of the:
   a. Benton County Tax Agency Fund.
   b. Benton County General Fund.
   c. Benton County School District.

7–5. On July 1, 2003, the City of Belvedere accepted a gift of cash in the amount of $3,000,000 from a number of individuals and foundations and signed an agreement to establish a private-purpose trust. The $3,000,000 and any additional gifts are to be invested and retained as principal. Income from the trust is to be distributed to community nonprofit groups as directed by a Board consisting of city officials and other community leaders. The agreement provides that any increases in the market value of the principal investments are to be held in trust; if the investments fall below the gift amounts, then earnings are to be withheld until the principal amount is reestablished.

   a. The following events and transactions occurred during the fiscal year ended June 30, 2004. Record them in the Belvedere Community Trust Fund.

(1) On July 1, the original gift of cash was received.
(2) On July 1, $2,000,000 in XYZ Company bonds were purchased at par plus accrued interest. The bonds pay an annual rate of 6 percent interest semiannually on April 1 and October 1.
(3) On July 2, $950,000 in ABC Company common stock was purchased. ABC normally declares and pays dividends semiannually, on January 31 and July 31.
(4) On October 1, 2003, the first semiannual interest payment was received from XYZ Company. Note that part of this is for accrued interest due at the time of purchase; the remaining part is an addition that may be used for distribution.
(5) On January 31, 2004, a cash dividend was received from ABC Company in the amount of $19,000.
(6) On March 1, the ABC stock was sold for $960,000. On the same day, DEF Company stock was purchased for $965,000.
(7) On April 1, the second semiannual interest payment was received from XYZ Company.
(8) During the month of June, distributions were approved by the Board and paid in cash in the amount of $95,000.
(9) Administrative expenses were recorded and paid in the amount of $12,000.
(10) An accrual for interest on the XYZ bonds was made as of June 30, 2002.
(11) As of June 30, 2004, the fair value of the XYZ bonds, exclusive of accrued interest, was determined to be $1,998,000. The fair value of the DEF stock was determined to be $968,000.
(12) Closing entries were prepared.

b. Prepare, in good form, (1) a Statement of Fiduciary Net Assets and (2) a Statement of Changes in Fiduciary Net Assets for the Belvedere Community Trust Fund.

7–6. On July 1, 2003, the Morgan County School District received a $10,000 gift from a local civic organization with the stipulation that, on June 30 of each year, $2,000 plus any interest earnings on the unspent principal be awarded as a college scholarship to the high school graduate with the highest four-year academic average. A private-purpose trust fund, the Civic Scholarship Fund, was created.

a. Record the following transactions on the books of the Civic Scholarship Fund:
(1) On July 1, 2003, the gift was received and immediately invested.
(2) On June 30, 2004, $2,000 of the principal plus $600 interest was converted into cash.
(3) On June 30, 2004, the $2,600 was awarded to Ann Korner, who had maintained a 4.0 grade point average throughout each of her four years.

(4) The nominal accounts were closed.

b. Prepare a Statement of Changes in Fiduciary Net Assets for the Civic Scholarship Fund for the Year Ended June 30, 2004.

7–7. Describe GASB requirements for accounting for Investment Trust Funds. Include (a) a discussion of when the use of investment trust funds is appropriate; (b) the investments to be included and excluded; (c) the basis at which investments are to be reported; (d) reporting of realized and unrealized gains and losses on investments; and (e) financial reporting.

7–8. With regard to current GASB standards for pension reporting do the following:

  a. Distinguish between (1) defined contribution plans and (2) defined benefit plans.
  b. Distinguish between (1) agent and (2) cost-sharing multiemployer plans.
  c. Define the following terms: (1) annual required contribution and (2) net pension obligation.
  d. Distinguish between expenditure/expense reporting for (1) agent multiemployer plans and (2) cost-sharing multiemployer plans.
  e. Distinguish between reporting for employers for (1) general government employees, and for (2) enterprise fund employees.

7–9. The City of Sweetwater maintains an Employees' Retirement Fund, a single-employer, defined benefit plan that provides annuity and disability benefits. The fund is financed by actuarially determined contributions from the city's General Fund and by contributions from employees. Administration of the retirement fund is handled by General Fund employees, and the retirement fund does not bear any administrative expenses. The Statement of Net Assets for the Employees' Retirement Fund as of July 1, 2003, is shown here:

CITY OF SWEETWATER
Employees' Retirement Fund
Statement of Net Assets
As of July 1, 2003

Assets	
Cash	$ 50,000
Accrued Interest Receivable	135,000
Investments, at Fair Value:	
Bonds	4,500,000
Common Stocks	1,300,000
Total Assets	5,985,000
Liabilities	
Accounts Payable and Accrued Expenses	350,000
Net Assets Held in Trust for Pension for Benefits	$5,635,000

During the year ended June 30, 2004, the following transactions occurred:
1. The interest receivable on investments was collected in cash.
2. Member contributions in the amount of $600,000 were received in cash. The city's General Fund also contributed $600,000 in cash.
3. Annuity benefits of $700,000 and disability benefits of $150,000 were recorded as liabilities.
4. Accounts payable and accrued expenses in the amount of $900,000 were paid in cash.
5. Interest income of $240,000 and dividends in the amount of $40,000 were received in cash. In addition, bond interest income of $140,000 was accrued at year-end.
6. Refunds of $130,000 were made in cash to terminated, nonvested participants.
7. Common stocks, carried at a fair value of $500,000, were sold for $520,000. That $520,000, plus an additional $500,000, was invested in stocks.
8. At year-end, it was determined that the fair value of stocks held by the pension plan had increased by $50,000; the fair value of bonds had decreased by $30,000.
9. Nominal accounts for the year were closed.
    a. Record the transactions on the books of the Employees' Retirement Fund.
    b. Prepare a Statement of Net Assets for the Employees' Retirement Fund as of June 30, 2004.
    c. Prepare a Statement of Changes in Net Assets for the Employees' Retirement Fund for the Year Ended June 30, 2004.

7–10. Assume that a local government unit is the trustee for the pension assets for its police and fire department employees and participates in a statewide plan for all of its other employees. Individual accounts are maintained for all local governments in the statewide plan. Discuss the financial reporting requirements related to pensions for (*a*) police and fire department employees and (*b*) all other employees.

7–11. The Village of Sharpeville had all of the fund types authorized by GASB standards. Journalize each of the following transactions, and indicate the name of the fund in which each entry is made. Assume all transactions are cash transactions.
    a. The General Fund purchased water from the Water Utility (enterprise) Fund. The amount was $50,000.
    b. The General Fund made an annual transfer of $300,000 to a debt service fund for the payment of principal and interest on general obligation bonds.
    c. The General Fund loaned, on a long-term basis, $100,000 to help establish a Motor Pool (internal service) Fund.

d. The Motor Pool Fund provided $60,000 in services to General Fund departments.
e. The General Fund had purchased supplies, costing $25,000. Upon further investigation, it was determined that the supplies should have been charged to the Summer Youth Employment Fund, a special revenue fund.
f. The General Fund made a required contribution of $230,000 to the Police Officers Pension Trust Fund.
g. The City Hall Annex Construction Fund made a transfer of residual funds to the City Hall Annex Debt Service Fund. The amount was $36,500.
h. An enterprise fund loaned $300,000 to an internal service fund, on a long-term basis.
i. Upon further reflection, it was determined that the internal service fund would never be able to repay the $300,000 mentioned in *(h)*, and it was decided that the funds would stay with the internal service fund.

Continuous Problem

7–C. *Part 1.* The City of Everlasting Sunshine Community Foundation private-purpose trust fund had the following account balances on January 1, 2004:

	Debits	Credits
Cash	$ 35,000	
Accrued Interest Receivable	13,333	
Investments in MNO Company Bonds	1,000,000	
Net Assets Held in Trust for Distribution		$1,048,333
Totals	$1,048,333	$1,048,333

Open a general journal for the City of Everlasting Sunshine Community Foundation Trust Fund and record the following transactions for the year ending December 31, 2004:

(1) On May 1, the first semiannual interest payment was received on the MNO Company bonds. The bonds pay 8 percent annual interest, semiannually on May 1 and November 1.

(2) During the first half of the year, additional contributions from individuals and foundations amounted to $300,000, in cash. These funds were invested in RST Corporation stock on June 15.

(3) On November 1, the second semiannual interest payment was received from MNO Company.

(4) On November 15, a dividend was declared by RST Corporation in the amount of $6,000 and was received in cash.

(5) On December 1, RST Corporation stock was sold for $297,000 cash. Those funds were immediately invested in UVW Corporation stock.

(6) On December 15, cash distributions in the amount of $80,000 were made to various nonprofit organizations.
(7) On December 31, an accrual was made for year-end interest on MNO Company bonds.
(8) Also, on December 31, it was determined that the market value of MNO Company bonds, exclusive of accrued interest, was $1,002,000 and that the market value of UVW Company stock was $301,000.
(9) Closing entries were prepared.

Part 2. The City of Everlasting Sunshine Police Department pension plan, a single-employer, defined-benefit plan, reported the following account balances as of January 1, 2004:

	Debits	Credits
Cash	$ 55,000	
Accrued Interest Receivable	85,000	
Investments: Bonds	5,100,000	
Investments: Common Stock	1,700,000	
Accounts Payable		$ 235,000
Net Assets Held in Trust for Employee Benefits		6,705,000
Totals	$6,940,000	$6,940,000

Open a general journal for the City of Everlasting Sunshine Police Department Pension Trust Fund and record the following transactions for the year ending December 31, 2004:

(1) Member contributions were received in the amount of $400,000. The City General Fund contributed the same amount.
(2) Interest was received in the amount of $310,000, including the accrued interest receivable at the beginning of the year. The interest accrual at year-end amounted to $110,000.
(3) During the year, common stock dividends amounted to $180,000.
(4) Investments were made during the year in common stock in the amount of $700,000.
(5) Annuity benefits in the amount of $390,000, disability benefits of $110,000, and refunds to nonvested terminated employees of $50,000 were recorded as liabilities.
(6) Accounts payable, in the amount of $620,000, were paid in cash.
(7) During the year, common stock valued at $600,000 was sold for $613,000. The $613,000 was reinvested in common stock of a different company.
(8) At year-end, the market value of investments in bonds increased by $16,000; the market value of investments in stocks decreased by $3,000.

(9) The books were closed.

Part 3. Open a ledger and enter the balances for (*a*) the Sunshine Community Foundation Trust Fund and (*b*) the Police Department Pension Trust Fund. Allow five lines for each account, except where indicated. Post the entries made for Parts 1 and 2.

(*a*) For the Sunshine Community Foundation Trust Fund, use the following accounts:

>   Cash (9 lines) (31–101)
>   Accrued Interest Receivable (31–105)
>   Investment in MNO Company Bonds (31–106)
>   Investment in RST Corporation Stock (31–107)
>   Investment in UVW Corporation Stock (31–108)
>   Net Assets Held in Trust for Distribution (31–361)
>   Additions—Contributions—Individuals (31–420)
>   Additions—Investment Earnings—Interest (31–431)
>   Additions—Investment Earnings—Dividends (31–432)
>   Additions—Investment Earnings—Net Increase (Decrease) in Fair Value of Investments (31–433)
>   Deductions—Distribution to Nonprofit Organizations (31–550)

(*b*) For the Police Department Pension Trust Fund, use the following accounts:

>   Cash (8 lines) (32–101)
>   Accrued Interest Receivable (32–103)
>   Investments in Bonds (32–104)
>   Investments in Common Stock (32–105)
>   Accounts Payable (32–201)
>   Net Assets Held in Trust for Employee Benefits (32–362)
>   Additions—Contributions—Plan Members (32–421)
>   Additions—Contributions—Employer (32–422)
>   Additions—Investment Earnings—Interest (32–431)
>   Additions—Investment Earnings—Dividends (32–432)
>   Additions—Investment Earnings—Net Increase in Fair Value of Investments (32–433)
>   Deductions—Annuity Benefits (32–551)
>   Deductions—Disability Benefits (32–552)
>   Deductions—Refunds to Terminated Employees (32–553)

Part 4. Using the balances from Part 3, prepare for the City of Everlasting Sunshine (*a*) a Statement of Fiduciary Net Assets and (*b*) a Statement of Changes in Fiduciary Net Assets. Use the format illustrated in the text.

Chapter Eight

Government-Wide Statements, Fixed Assets, Long-Term Debt

Chapters 3 through 7 of this text illustrate fund accounting and the fund financial statements that are required for state and local governments. As the reporting requirements of GASB *Statement 34* are implemented, it is likely that most governments will maintain their records on the basis of funds, as illustrated in the previous chapters. GASB *Statement 34* also requires the preparation of two government-wide statements: the Statement of Net Assets and the Statement of Activities. Remember that GASB illustrated statements, both fund and government-wide, are presented in Chapter 2. Many governments will prepare adjusting and consolidating entries, on a worksheet basis only, to convert from the fund financial statements to the government-wide financial statements.

The purpose of this chapter is to illustrate how to adjust fund accounting records to prepare government-wide statements. The Village of Elizabeth example, used in Chapters 3–7, is extended in this chapter through the use of adjusting entries and the preparation of the government-wide statements. This chapter has four major sections. First, adjustments will be made and explained, both in narrative and worksheet form. Second, the government-wide Statement of Net Assets and Statement of Activities will be illustrated. This will include the reconciliation schedules, required by GASB, to convert from governmental fund statements to government-wide statements. Third, general fixed assets (including infrastructure), not accounted for in fund financial statements, will be discussed. Finally, a discussion will be presented regarding general long-term debt, also not accounted for in fund financial statements.

CONVERSION FROM FUND FINANCIAL RECORDS TO GOVERNMENT-WIDE FINANCIAL STATEMENTS

To prepare government-wide financial statements in accordance with GASB *Statement 34*, a number of changes are necessary. First, because the governmental fund statements are prepared using the current financial resources measurement focus and modified accrual basis of accounting, adjustments must be made to prepare statements using the economic resources measurement focus and accrual basis of accounting. This includes adjustments to bring in general capital assets and general long-term debt. Enterprise fund statements require few (or no) adjustments, as accrual accounting is used, and fixed assets and long-term debt are included. Second, the governmental fund and proprietary fund statements must be consolidated and brought into two categories: governmental activities and business-type activities. This second adjustment requires, in most cases, that governmental fund statements be consolidated, eliminating interfund entries. Also, internal service fund accounts, presented as proprietary funds, should be included with governmental activities, as GASB has concluded that most internal service funds service governmental activities. Third, fiduciary funds are not included in the government-wide statements. Finally, component unit financial statements, not included with the fund statements, must be added.

This section of the text discusses and presents, for the Village of Elizabeth, example adjustments necessary to convert from fund financial statements to government-wide statements. These examples are not exhaustive but contain the major changes and include:

1. Recording capital assets, removing expenditures for capital outlays, and recording depreciation.
2. Changing "proceeds of bonds" to debt liabilities, changing expenditures for debt service principal to reduction of liabilities, and adjusting for interest accruals.
3. Adjusting to convert revenue recognition to the accrual basis.
4. Adjusting to record expenses on the accrual basis.
5. Changing a special item: proceeds on sale of fixed assets to the gain on the sale of fixed assets.
6. Adding internal service funds to governmental activities.
7. Eliminating interfund activities and balances within governmental activities.
8. Eliminating fiduciary funds.

Each of these is discussed and illustrated in turn, using the information in the governmental funds Balance Sheet (Illustration 5–1) and Statement of Revenues, Expenditures, and Changes in Fund Balances (Illustration 5–2) as the starting point.

Recording Capital Assets, Removing Expenditures for Capital Outlays, and Recording Depreciation

GASB requires that general fixed assets be included in the government-wide financial statements. General fixed assets include fixed assets other than those used by proprietary or fiduciary funds and are usually acquired through General, special revenue, or capital projects funds. Fixed assets acquired through proprietary and fiduciary funds are reported in the Statement of Net Assets of those funds. Assume that the Village of Elizabeth maintains memorandum fixed asset records for general fixed assets, including the original cost and accumulated depreciation. Categories include land, buildings, improvements other than buildings (infrastructure), and equipment. The first memorandum adjustment is needed to record the capital assets and related depreciation as of the beginning of the year:

	Debits	Credits
1. Land	3,100,000	
Buildings	38,300,000	
Improvements Other Than Buildings	15,400,000	
Equipment	5,600,000	
Accumulated Depreciation—Buildings		15,100,000
Accumulated Depreciation—Improvements Other Than Buildings		6,300,000
Accumulated Depreciation—Equipment		3,700,000
Net Assets		37,300,000

Because worksheet entries are not posted to the fund general ledger, this entry, to record beginning balances, will be required each year. Note that the account, Net Assets, is credited for the difference. The difference between assets and liabilities in the government-wide statements is called net assets.

A second adjustment is required to eliminate the charge to expenditures for capital outlay and to record those expenditures as capital assets, as is required for accrual accounting. In practice, this would require a review of all governmental fund expenditures, including the General and special revenue funds, to determine which should be capitalized. In the Village of Elizabeth example, it is assumed that the only capital assets acquired this year were reflected in the capital projects fund example in Chapter 5. Note that the amount of expenditures, including interest, closed out in entry 17 of the capital projects fund example in Chapter 5, is $1,963,500.

GASB *Statement 37* specifically prohibits interest during construction in governmental funds from being capitalized in the government-wide statements. As a result, the $2,500 in interest is charged to interest expense, and the $1,961,000 is capitalized. The following adjustment is required.

	Debits	Credits
2. Buildings	1,961,000	
Interest Expense	2,500	
Expenditures—Capital Outlay		1,963,500

Remember that these entries are only memorandum adjusting entries used to prepare the government-wide statements and would not be posted to the general ledgers of the governmental funds.

A third adjustment is necessary to record depreciation expense. Assume that the Village of Elizabeth uses straight-line depreciation with no salvage value and that buildings have a 40-year life, improvements other than buildings have a 20-year life, and equipment has a 10-year life. Also assume the building capitalized this year was acquired late in the year, and that no depreciation is charged. The adjustment would be:

		Debits	Credits
3.	Depreciation Expense	2,287,500	
	Accumulated Depreciation—Buildings ($38,300,000/40)		957,500
	Accumulated Depreciation—Improvements Other Than Buildings ($15,400,000/20)		770,000
	Accumulated Depreciation—Equipment ($5,600,000/10)		560,000

Additional information regarding fixed asset accounting and reporting is discussed in the third section of this chapter.

Changing "Proceeds of Bonds" to Debt Liabilities, Changing Expenditures for Debt Service Principal to Reduction of Liabilities, and Adjusting for Interest Accruals

Another set of requirements for accrual accounting is related to debt. Under accrual accounting, debt principal is recorded as a liability, interest expense is accrued at year-end, and premiums and discounts are amortized over the life of bonds. In the Village of Elizabeth example, 10-year serial bonds, with a principal amount of $1,200,000 were sold on January 2, 2004, for $1,212,000. Annual interest of 8 percent was paid semiannually on June 30 and December 31, and the first principal payment of $120,000 was paid on December 31. The $1,212,000 was recorded as an other financing source in the capital projects fund (entries 8a and 8b in Chapter 5). To convert to accrual accounting, the following entry would be required:

		Debits	Credits
4.	Other Financing Sources—Proceeds of Bonds	1,200,000	
	Other Financing Sources—Premium on Bonds	12,000	
	Bonds Payable		1,200,000
	Premium on Bonds Payable		12,000

The account, Premium on Bonds Payable, is an addition to the liability, as would be the case in business accounting. In subsequent years the debit in this entry to offset the recording of the liability will be to Net Assets. To adjust the principal payment (entry 22b, debt service funds, Chapter 5), the following would be required:

		Debits	Credits
5.	Bonds Payable	120,000	
	Expenditures—Bond Principal		120,000

Normally, an adjustment would be required to accrue interest at year-end. In the Village of Elizabeth example, the last interest payment is the last day of the fiscal year, so an accrual is not necessary. However, the bond premium must be amortized. Assume, for simplicity, that the straight-line method of amortization is considered not materially different from the effective interest method. As a result, the amortization would be $1,200. An adjusting entry to convert interest expenditures to interest expense and to provide for the amortization would be as follows:

		Debits	Credits
6.	Interest Expense	94,800	
	Premium on Bonds Payable ($12,000/10)	1,200	
	Expenditures—Interest		96,000

No entries would be required for debt issued by proprietary funds, which already report on the accrual basis.

Adjusting to Convert Revenue Recognition to the Accrual Basis

Chapter 4 provides a discussion of revenue recognition under the requirements of GASB Statement 33, *Accounting and Financial Reporting for Nonexchange Transactions*. Governmental fund accounting and reporting, as illustrated in Chapter 4, follows modified accrual accounting in which revenues are recognized only when measurable and available. When converting to government-wide statements, governments need to examine all revenue sources to see which should be accrued. Assume, for the Village of Elizabeth, the only revenue that needs adjustment is property taxes. Chapter 4 reflected property tax revenue of $3,178,800 (See Illustration 4–2). Entry 27 of the General Fund example in Chapter 4 indicated that the Village deferred $40,000 in property tax revenues because that amount was not considered "measurable and available." Assume it is determined that the entire property tax levy is for 2004. An adjustment would be required to convert to the accrual basis:

7a.	Deferred Revenues—Property Taxes	40,000	
	Revenues—Property Taxes		40,000

Because the deferred revenue at 12/31/03 is recognized in the fund basis statements (see entry 3 in Chapter 4), an additional worksheet entry is required. That entry debits property tax revenues and credits net assets for the $20,000 recognized as revenue under modified accrual accounting.

7b.	Revenues—Property Taxes	20,000	
	Net Assets		20,000

Remember that interest on property taxes was accrued at year-end, using modified accrual accounting, in Chapter 4 (entry 26), so no adjustment is required for that interest.

Adjusting to Record Expenses on Accrual Basis

Under modified accrual, most expenditures are recorded as goods and services are received, similar to the accrual basis. A major exception is interest on long-term debt, which is recorded when due. As indicated above, interest payments on the general obligation long-term debt for the Village of Elizabeth was paid on the last day of the fiscal year; as a result, no accrual is necessary. Another exception, to recording expenditures on the accrual basis, is that expenditures for compensated absences are not recorded in excess of the amount to be liquidated with available resources. Assume the Village of Elizabeth had memorandum records indicating accumulated compensated absences payable at the first of the year in the amount of $300,000 and that an additional accrual of $25,000 is necessary in 2004. The following memorandum adjusting entries would be necessary to convert to government-wide statements:

		Debits	Credits
8.	Net Assets	300,000	
	Compensated Absences Payable		300,000
9.	Compensated Absences Expense	25,000	
	Compensated Absences Payable		25,000

A worksheet entry similar to entry 8 would be used to record any long-term liabilities outstanding at the beginning of the year, including bonds payable.

Changing Proceeds on Sale of Fixed Assets to Gain on Sale of Fixed Assets

Entry 28 in the General Fund example in Chapter 4 reflects proceeds in the amount of $300,000 on the sale of land. That amount was properly reported as another financing source in the Governmental Fund Statement of Revenues, Expenditures, and Changes in Fund Balances (Illustration 5–2). Assume now that the cost of that land was $225,000, which is included in the land amount reported in transaction 1 of this chapter. It is necessary to convert this to an accrual basis so that the gain on the sale is reflected in the Statement of Activities and land removed from the Statement of Net Assets.

10. Special Item—Proceeds from the Sale of Land	300,000	
Land		225,000
Special Item—Gain on Sale of Land		75,000

Adding Internal Service Funds to Governmental Activities

Internal service funds are not included in the governmental fund statements as they are considered to be proprietary funds. However, most internal service funds serve primarily governmental departments. Three steps are necessary to incorporate internal service funds into the governmental fund category, keeping in mind that the starting point is the governmental fund statements illustrated in Chapter 4. The first step is to bring in the balance sheet accounts from the Statement of Net Assets. For the Village of Elizabeth, these are found in the Internal Service Fund column of the proprietary funds Statement of Net Assets (Illustration 6–1). To be consistent with entry 1 in this section, the same detail of the capital assets is posted:

	Debits	Credits
11. Cash	3,500	
Investments	50,000	
Due from Other Funds	55,000	
Inventory of Materials and Supplies	233,500	
Land	80,000	
Buildings	270,000	
Equipment	140,000	
Accumulated Depreciation—Capital Assets		27,500
Accounts Payable		11,000
Advance from Water Utility Fund		190,000
Net Assets		603,500

The remaining steps relate to the Statement of Activities. In the second step, any transactions of the Internal Service Fund that are with entities external to the government would be added to the governmental activities. In this case, the only activity would be the investment income of $3,000, shown on the proprietary funds Statement of Revenues, Expenses, and Changes in Net Assets (Illustration 6–2). In order to add this to the investment earnings of the governmental funds, the following adjustment would be made:

12. Net Assets	3,000	
Investment Income		3,000

This worksheet debit to Net Assets is due to the fact that the $3,000 earnings contributed to the $603,500 net assets shown in entry 11; when the change in net assets is computed for governmental activities later in this exercise, then it will be added back.

A third and major step is to eliminate the effect of all the transactions of the internal service fund with governmental activities, or funds in this case. GASB has provided instructions on how to accomplish this. Note that the income before contributions and transfers for the internal service fund in Illustration 6–2 is $7,500. Of that, $3,000 is to remain, as explained above. This leaves $4,500. The $4,500 is to be deducted (since it is profit) from the appropriate expense function categories of the governmental activities. If the profit to be deducted were large, an effort would be made to determine which functions contributed to that profit and deduct the profit on a pro rata basis. As the number is small in this case, $4,500, a decision is made to credit Expenditures—General Government:

	Debits	Credits
13. Net Assets	4,500	
Expenditures—General Government		4,500

The account, Net Assets, is debited (reduced) in this worksheet entry using the same logic as in entry 12; that account will be credited (increased) by this much more when the accounts are closed.

Finally, to incorporate the internal service funds completely, it is necessary to bring in the Transfer In from the General Fund in the amount of $596,000 (See Illustration 6–2, entry 22 of the General Fund example in Chapter 4, and entry 1 of the internal service fund example in Chapter 6.) This transfer will be eliminated in the next section:

14. Net Assets	596,000	
Transfers In		596,000

Eliminating Interfund Activities and Balances within Governmental Activities

First, examine the governmental funds Statement of Revenues, Expenditures, and Changes in Fund Balances (Illustration 5–2). Note the Transfers In and Transfers Out and consider the effect of entry 14 to bring in the internal service fund Transfers In of $596,000. After entry 14, the governmental funds report a total of $1,048,500 Transfers In and $848,500 Transfers Out. The $1,048,500 Transfers In include $204,000 from the General Fund to the Fire Station Debt Service Fund, $200,000 from an enterprise fund to the Fire Station Addition Capital Projects Fund, $48,500 from the capital projects fund to the debt service fund, and the $596,000 from the General Fund to the internal service fund. The $848,500 Transfers Out includes the $800,000 from the General Fund ($204,500 + $596,000) and the $48,500 from the Capital Projects Fund. To present a consolidated governmental activities column, now including internal service funds, it is necessary to eliminate $848,500 from the Transfers In and Transfers Out accounts:

15. Transfers In	848,500	
Transfers Out		848,500

This leaves a $200,000 transfer in from the enterprise fund to the Fire Station Capital Projects Fund, which should be reported as a transfer between governmental activities and business-type activities.

When looking at the governmental funds Balance Sheet (Illustration 5–1), note the liability account, Due to Other Funds in the amount of $75,000. This consists of $55,000 due to internal service funds, which is now incorporated into the governmental funds through entry 11 above and $20,000 due to the Water Utility Fund, an enterprise fund (see Illustration 6–1 for the detail). The $55,000 must be eliminated; the $20,000 should remain, as it is a liability from governmental activities to business-type activities and will be reported as internal balances in the Statement of Net Assets:

	Debits	Credits
16. Due to Other Funds	55,000	
Due from Other Funds		55,000

Eliminating Fiduciary Funds

GASB standards do not incorporate fiduciary funds into the government-wide statements. Remember that fiduciary funds account for trust and agency activities conducted for individuals and organizations outside the government as well as other governments. As we have been working with the governmental funds as a starting point, no adjustments are necessary to produce the government-wide financial statements.

Worksheet to Illustrate the Adjustments

Illustration 8–1 presents a worksheet incorporating the adjustments listed above. The worksheet begins by reproducing the accounts from the governmental funds Balance Sheet (Illustration 5–1) and Statement of Revenues, Expenditures, and Changes in Fund Balances (Illustration 5–2). The worksheet uses a trial balance format with accounts classified as to whether they are debits or credits. The fund balance accounts have been grouped into one Net Assets account as a starting point. (Remember that all this is in memorandum form to produce the government-wide statements.) The memorandum adjusting and consolidating entries are then incorporated into the worksheet, and ending account balances are produced. The ending balances are measured on the economic resources measurement focus and accrual basis of accounting. Items previously labeled as expenditures are now expenses. These ending account balances would be, in effect, a preclosing trial balance for the governmental activities section of the government-wide statements.

In order to save some space, certain accounts have been consolidated in the worksheet. For example, the capital assets are shown as one number. Expenditures for current purposes are grouped together; expenditures for debt service principal and capital outlay are separated out as those costs are eliminated in the worksheet entries. The same is true for revenues; those that are affected by the worksheet are shown separately. In addition, revenues that are to be shown as program revenues in the Statement of Activities are shown separately.

To take full advantage of the presentation in this chapter, trace the beginning balances from the governmental funds statements (Illustrations 5–1 and 5–2) to the worksheet. Then, trace the entries discussed earlier in this chapter to the worksheet by number. Finally, trace the ending balances in the worksheet to the statements presented in the next section.

GOVERNMENT-WIDE FINANCIAL STATEMENTS

The GASB requires two government-wide financial statements: the Statement of Net Assets and the Statement of Activities. These two statements are presented in this section, using the Village of Elizabeth example presented in Chapters 4–7 and continued in the first section of this chapter.

Statement of Net Assets

The Statement of Net Assets for the Village of Elizabeth is presented as Illustration 8–2. Note the similarity in format to the GASB illustrative Statement of Net Assets in Illustration 2–1. Assets, liabilities, and net assets are broken down between governmental activities and business-type activities. In the case of the Village of Elizabeth, governmental activities include those activities accounted for by the governmental funds (General, special revenue, debt service, capital projects, and permanent) and internal service funds. Business-type activities include activities of enterprise funds. The Village of Elizabeth has no component units; if it had component units, they would be displayed separately as shown in Illustration 2–1. Previous sections of this chapter reflected how the governmental funds statements were adjusted to prepare this Statement.

Assets and liabilities are reported generally in order of liquidity; the GASB does allow reporting a classified statement. It is also permissible to use a balance sheet format, where Assets = Liabilities + Net assets. Net assets are classified as: (1) invested in capital assets, net of related debt, (2) restricted, and (3) unrestricted. For governmental activities, the net assets invested in capital assets, net of related debt ($35,930,200) is computed by taking the net assets, net of depreciation ($37,211,000) less the general obligation bonds payable ($1,090,800), and the long-term advance ($190,000). For business-type activities the net assets invested in capital assets, net of depreciation ($1,088,265) is computed by subtracting the revenue bonds payable ($2,700,000) from the capital assets, net of depreciation ($3,788,265).

As described in Chapter 2, the restricted net assets would be (a) externally imposed by creditors (such as through debt covenants), and (b) imposed by law through constitutional provisions or enabling legislation. In the case of the Village of Elizabeth, restricted net assets in the amount of $583,000 for governmental activities include (a) $237,500 motor fuel tax resources restricted by legislation for road maintenance, (b) $36,500 set aside for debt service, and (c) $309,000 permanent funds restricted by agreement for the maintenance of the city cemetery. See Chapters 4 and 5 for details of these restrictions in the discussions concerning special revenue, debt service, and permanent funds. The $110,000 restricted in the business-type activities include the $144,200 restricted assets discussed in Chapter 6, less the customer deposit of $34,200. The remaining net assets for both types of activities are unrestricted.

ILLUSTRATION 8–1

VILLAGE OF ELIZABETH
Worksheet to Convert Governmental Fund Statements to Government-Wide Statements
As of and for the Year Ending December 31, 2004

	Governmental Fund Balances	Adjustments and Eliminations Debits	Adjustments and Eliminations Credits	Internal Service Funds Debits	Internal Service Funds Credits	Revised Balances
Debits:						
Cash	$ 728,000			(11) 3,500		$ 731,500
Investments	302,000			(11) 50,000		352,000
Due from other funds			(16) 55,000			—
Interest receivable, net	40,490					40,490
Taxes receivable, net	528,800					528,800
Due from state govt.	125,000					125,000
Inventories				(11) 233,500		233,500
Capital assets		(1) 62,400,000	(10) 225,000	(11) 490,000		64,626,000
		(2) 1,961,000				
Expenditures (expenses)—current	6,016,300				(13) 4,500	6,011,800
Expenditures (expenses)—debt service:						
Principal	120,000		(5) 120,000			—
Interest	96,000		(6) 96,000			—
Expenditures—capital outlay	1,963,500		(2) 1,963,500			—
Expenses—compensated absences		(9) 25,000				25,000
Expenses—interest		(21) 2,500				—
Expenses—depreciation		(6) 94,800				97,300
OFS—transfers out	848,500	(3) 2,287,500	(15) 848,500			2,287,500
Total debits	$10,768,590					$75,058,890

234

Credits:						
Accounts payable	$ 185,300				(11) 11,000	196,300
Due to other funds	75,000	(16)	55,000			20,000
Deferred revenues	40,000	(7a)	40,000			—
Bonds payable		(5)	120,000	(4) 1,200,000		1,080,000
Premium on bonds payable		(6)	1,200	(4) 12,000		10,800
Comp. absences payable				(8) 300,000		325,000
				(9) 25,000		190,000
Advances from water utility fund					(11) 190,000	
Accumulated depreciation				(1) 25,100,000	(11) 27,500	27,415,000
				(3) 2,287,500		
Net assets	502,500	(8)	300,000	(1) 37,300,000	(11) 603,500	37,522,500
				(7b) 20,000		
Revenues—property taxes	3,178,800	(7b)	20,000	(7a) 40,000		3,198,800
Revenues—inv. income	20,000				(12) 3,000	23,000
Revenues—charges for services	100,000					100,000
Revenues—SRF—state grant for road repairs	350,000					350,000
Revenues—CPF—capital grant for police station	600,000					600,000
Revenues—capital contribution	300,000					300,000
Revenues—GF-grant for law enf.	350,000					350,000
Revenues—other	3,102,490					3,102,490
OFS—proceeds of bonds	1,200,000	(4)	1,200,000			—
OFS—premium on bonds	12,000	(4)	12,000			—
OFS—transfers in	452,500	(15)	848,500		(14) 596,000	200,000
Special item—proceeds of sale of land	300,000	(10)	300,000			—
Special Item: Gain on sale of land				(10) 75,000		75,000
Total credits	$10,768,590					
Totals			$69,667,500	$69,667,500	$1,435,500 $1,435,500	$75,058,890

235

ILLUSTRATION 8-2

VILLAGE OF ELIZABETH
Statement of Net Assets
December 31, 2004

	Governmental Activities	Business-Type Activities	Total
Assets:			
Cash	$ 731,500	$ 78,230	$ 809,730
Investments	352,000	—	352,000
Interest receivable	40,490	—	40,490
Taxes receivable, net	528,800	—	528,800
Accounts receivable	—	60,895	60,895
Due from state government	125,000	—	125,000
Due from governmental activities	—	20,000	20,000
Inventories	233,500	31,000	264,500
Restricted cash and cash equivalents	—	144,200	144,200
Long-term advance to governmental activities	—	190,000	190,000
Capital assets, net of depreciation	37,211,000	3,788,265	40,999,265
Total assets	39,222,290	4,312,590	43,534,880
Liabilities:			
Accounts payable	196,300	29,600	225,900
Due to business-type activities	20,000	—	20,000
Customer deposits	—	34,200	34,200
Taxes payable	—	9,000	9,000
Long-term advance from business-type activities	190,000	—	190,000
Revenue bonds payable	—	2,700,000	2,700,000
General obligation bonds payable	1,090,800	—	1,090,800
Compensated absences payable	325,000	—	325,000
Total liabilities	1,822,100	2,772,800	4,594,900
Net assets:			
Invested in capital assets, net of related debt	35,930,200	1,088,265	37,018,465
Restricted	583,000	110,000	693,000
Unrestricted	886,990	341,525	1,228,515
Total net assets	$37,400,190	$ 1,539,790	$38,939,980

Statement of Activities

Illustration 8–3 reflects the Statement of Activities for the Village of Elizabeth. This is the same format as Illustration 2–2, although GASB does permit different formats. The general concept is that expenses less program revenues equal net expenses; general revenues are subtracted from net expenses to get the change in net assets. Information is available separately for governmental and business-type activities. Information would also be presented for component units if the Village of Elizabeth had component units.

Expenses for governmental activities are taken from the governmental funds Statement of Revenues, Expenditures, and Changes in Fund Balances (Illustration 5–2) as modified by the worksheet developed in this chapter (Illustration 8–1). The program revenues were identified as follows:

- $350,000 of General Fund intergovernmental revenues were considered a grant for law enforcement.
- $600,000 was received, through capital projects funds, as a grant for the construction of the police station addition.
- $350,000 was received, through a special revenue fund, as a state reimbursement grant for road repairs.
- $300,000 was received as a gift for establishment of permanent fund for the maintenance of the city cemetery.
- $100,000 in charges for services were assumed to be for charges for city parks and recreation.

These revenues were deducted directly from related expenses to arrive at net expenses. All other revenues were considered to be general. GASB has determined that all taxes, including motor fuel taxes, are general revenues.

Transfers, special items, and extraordinary items are to be reported separately. In the case of the Village of Elizabeth a transfer is shown in the amount of $200,000 from business-type activities to governmental activities. This represents a transfer from the Water Utility Enterprise Fund to the Fire Station Addition Capital Projects Fund (see entry 2 in the capital projects section of Chapter 5 and entry 17 in the enterprise fund section of Chapter 6). All other transfers were eliminated as those transfers were between funds that are reported as governmental activities.

Required Reconciliation to Government-Wide Statements

GASB requires a reconciliation from the fund financial statements to the government-wide financial statements. Normally no reconciliation is required when going from the proprietary fund financial statements to the government-wide statements' business-activities columns because enterprise funds use accrual accounting. On the other hand, reconciliations are required from the governmental fund Balance Sheet to the Statement of Net Assets and from the governmental fund Statement of Revenues, Expenditures, and Changes in Fund Balances to the Statement of Activities. These reconciliations are required to be presented on the face of the governmental fund financial statements or in separate schedules immediately after the fund financial statements.

Illustration 8–4 reflects a reconciliation between the governmental fund Balance Sheet (Illustration 5–1) and the governmental activities column in the Statement of Net Assets (Illustration 8–2) for the Village of Elizabeth. The elements in this reconciliation can be traced through earlier sections of this chapter.

ILLUSTRATION 8–3

VILLAGE OF ELIZABETH
Statement of Activities
For the Year Ended December 31, 2004

Functions/Programs	Expenses	Program Revenues			Net (Expense) Revenue and Changes in Net Assets		
		Charges for Services	Operating Grants and Contributions	Capital Grants and Contributions	Governmental Activities	Business-Type Activities	Total
Governmental activities:							
General government	$ 805,500	—	—	—	$ (805,500)	—	$ (805,500)
Public safety	2,139,500	—	$350,000	$600,000	(1,189,500)	—	(1,189,500)
Public works	1,605,000	—	350,000	—	(1,255,000)	—	(1,255,000)
Health and welfare	480,100	—	—	—	(480,100)	—	(480,100)
Cemetery	11,000	—	—	300,000	289,000	—	289,000
Parks and recreation	527,400	$ 100,000	—	—	(427,400)	—	(427,400)
Contribution to retirement funds	423,000	—	—	—	(423,000)	—	(423,000)
Compensated absences	25,000	—	—	—	(25,000)	—	(25,000)
Depreciation expense	2,287,500	—	—	—	(2,287,500)	—	(2,287,500)
Interest expense	97,300	—	—	—	(97,300)	—	(97,300)
Miscellaneous	20,300	—	—	—	(20,300)	—	(20,300)
Total governmental activities	8,421,600	100,000	700,000	900,000	(6,721,600)	—	(6,721,600)
Business-type activities:							
Water utility	828,100	1,053,100	—	12,500	—	$ 237,500	237,500
Total government	$9,249,700	1,153,100	700,000	912,500	(6,721,600)	237,500	(6,484,100)

238

General revenues:			
Taxes:			
Property taxes	3,198,800	—	3,198,800
Motor fuel taxes	650,000	—	650,000
Sales taxes	1,410,000	—	1,410,000
Interest and penalties on taxes	42,490	—	42,490
Licenses and permits	540,000	—	540,000
Fines and forfeits	430,000	—	430,000
Investment income	23,000	—	23,000
Miscellaneous	30,000	—	30,000
Special item—gain on sale of park land	75,000	—	75,000
Transfers	200,000	(200,000)	—
Total general revenues, special items, and transfers	6,599,290	(200,000)	6,399,290
Change in net assets	(122,310)	37,500	(84,810)
Net assets—beginning	37,522,500	1,502,290	39,024,790
Net assets—ending	$37,400,190	$1,539,790	$38,939,980

ILLUSTRATION 8–4

VILLAGE OF ELIZABETH
Reconciliation of the Balance Sheet of Governmental Funds
to the Statement of Net Assets
As of December 31, 2004

Fund balances reported in governmental funds Balance Sheet (Illustration 5–1)	$ 1,423,990
Amounts reported for *governmental activities* in the Statement of Net Assets (Illustration 8–1) are different because:	
Capital assets used in governmental activities are not financial resources and, therefore, are not reported in the funds.	36,748,500*
Internal service funds are used by management to charge the costs of certain activities (stores and services) to individual funds. The assets and liabilities of internal service funds are included in governmental funds in the Statement of Net Assets.	603,500
Deferred revenue for property taxes are reported in the funds but accrued as revenue in the government-wide statements and added to net assets.	40,000
Long-term liabilities, including bonds payable, are not due and payable in the current period and, therefore, are not reported in the funds.	(1,415,800)
Net assets of governmental activities (Illustration 8–2).	$37,400,190

*This number does not include the capital assets of internal service funds, which are included in the $603,500.

Illustration 8–5 presents a reconciliation between the changes in fund balances in the governmental fund Statement of Revenues, Expenditures, and Changes in Fund Balances (Illustration 5–2) and the governmental activities change in net assets in the Statement of Activities (Illustration 8–3). Again, the elements in the reconciliation are generated in earlier sections of this chapter.

ACCOUNTING FOR FIXED ASSETS, INCLUDING INFRASTRUCTURE

GASB *Statement 34*, paragraph 80 states:

> General capital assets are capital assets of the government that are not specifically related to activities reported in proprietary or fiduciary funds. General capital assets are associated with and generally arise from governmental activities. Most often, they result from the expenditure of governmental fund financial resources. They should not be reported as assets in governmental funds but should be reported in the governmental activities column of the government-wide statement of net assets.

As a result, the fund financial statements for proprietary and fiduciary funds report fixed assets used in operations; those of governmental funds do not. However, both are included and depreciated in the government-wide statements. In this text, the term **general fixed assets** describes those fixed assets used in governmental fund operations that are not reported in the fund financial statements.

ILLUSTRATION 8–5

VILLAGE OF ELIZABETH
Reconciliation of the Statement of Revenues, Expenditures, and Changes in Fund Balances of Governmental Funds to the Statement of Activities
For the Year Ended December 31, 2004

Net change in fund balances—total governmental funds. (Illustration 5–2)	$ 921,490
Amounts reported for *governmental activities* in the Statement of Activities (Illustration 8–2) are different because:	
Governmental funds report capital outlays as expenditures. However, in the Statement of Activities, the cost of those assets is allocated over their estimated useful lives as depreciation expense. This is the amount by which depreciation exceeded capital outlays in the current period. (See entries 2 and 3.)	(326,500)
In the Statement of Activities, only the *gain* on the sale of land is reported, whereas in the governmental funds, the proceeds from the sale increase financial resources. Thus, the change in net assets differs from the change in fund balance by the cost of the land sold. (See entry 10.)	(225,000)
Revenues in the Statement of Activities that do not provide current financial resources are not reported as revenues in the funds. (See entries 7a and 7b.)	20,000
Bond proceeds provide current financial resources to governmental funds, but issuing debt increases long-term liabilities in the Statement of Net Assets. Repayment of bond principal is an expenditure in the governmental funds, but the repayment reduces long-term liabilities in the Statement of Net Assets. This is the amount by which proceeds exceeded repayments. (See entries 4 and 5.)	(1,080,000)
Some expenses reported in the Statement of Activities do not require the use of current financial resources and therefore are not reported as expenditures in governmental funds. (See entry 9.)	(25,000)
Internal service funds are used by management to charge the costs of certain activities, such as stores and services. The net revenue of the internal service funds is reported with governmental activities.	7,500
A transfer was made from the General Fund to an Internal Service Fund; that transfer reduced the changes in fund balance of governmental funds but not the change in net assets of governmental activities. (See entry 14.)	596,000
Bond premium was reported as another financing source in the governmental funds. The amortization of bond premium was reported as an expense reduction in the Statement of Activities. This is the amount by which the bond premium exceeded the amortization for the period. (See entries 4 and 6.)	(10,800)
Change in net assets of governmental activities (Illustration 8–3)	$ (122,310)

Accounting for General Fixed Assets

Even though general fixed assets are not reported in fund financial statements, it is necessary to maintain fixed asset records to support the reporting that is done in the government-wide statements. Accounting principles required prior to the adoption of *Statement 34* required the use and reporting of a General Fixed Asset Account Group that reflected fixed assets by category (land, buildings, improvements other than buildings, equipment, etc.) and by source of funding. The equity account

Invested in General Fixed Assets was broken down by source, including the fund. For example, if a computer were acquired through general fund resources, an entry would have been made in the account group as follows:

	Debits	Credits
Equipment	5,000	
Investment in General Fixed Assets—General Fund Revenues		5,000

Records were maintained to support the amounts shown in the General Fixed Asset Account Group. In the past, depreciation of general fixed assets was not required. As a result, governments are now required to estimate the amount of depreciation that would have been charged on currently existing assets.

Governments must maintain memorandum records of the cost and accumulated depreciation of general fixed assets. This can be done through entries such as the previous one to prepare government-wide financial statements and the adjusting entries such as worksheet entry 1. As this is not a reporting issue, GASB does not provide guidance regarding how those records might be kept.

GASB *Statement 34* does contain guidance regarding depreciation. Any of the generally recognized methods might be used, such as straight-line, sum-of-the-years digits, or declining-balance methods. It is likely that most governments use the straight-line method. GASB indicates that useful lives for fixed assets may be estimated from (1) general guidelines obtained from professional or industry organizations, (2) information for comparable assets of other governments, or (3) internal information. In the case of the Village of Elizabeth, buildings, improvements other than buildings, and equipment were assumed to have 40-year, 20-year, and 10-year lives, respectively. GASB also permits the use of composite methods.

GASB *Statement 34* requires significant disclosures in the notes to financial statements regarding capital assets. These disclosures should be by major classes of capital assets (land, buildings, improvements other than buildings, equipment, etc.) and separated between capital assets associated with governmental activities and business-type activities. Disclosure must be made of the beginning balances, capital acquisitions, sales and other dispositions, ending balances, and current period depreciation expense. Disclosure must be made of the amounts charged to each of the functions in the statement of activities. In addition to note disclosures, GASB requires that summary information be presented in the Management's Discussion and Analysis.

Accounting for Infrastructure

According to GASB, infrastructure assets are "long-lived capital assets that normally are stationary in nature and normally can be preserved for a significantly greater number of years than most capital assets. Examples of infrastructure assets include roads, bridges, tunnels, drainage systems, water and sewer systems, dams, and lighting systems" (GASB *Statement 34,* paragraph 19).

Prior to the adoption of *Statement 34,* few governments reported general government infrastructure assets, as that reporting was optional. Upon adoption of *Statement 34,* governments must capitalize and report infrastructure prospectively; that is, report all infrastructure obtained on or after adoption. GASB also requires that infrastructure be recorded retroactively (for infrastructure acquired or significantly improved after June 30, 1980) according to the following schedule:

- For Phase 1 governments (total annual revenues of $100 million or more), for fiscal years beginning after June 15, 2005.
- For Phase 2 governments (total annual revenues of $10 million but less than $100 million), for fiscal years beginning after June 15, 2006.
- For Phase 3 governments (total annual revenues of less than $10 million), those governments are encouraged but not required to adopt infrastructure retroactively.

When recording infrastructure, governments are permitted to group assets according to major systems. Retroactive recording will require estimates; prospective recording will involve reporting at historical cost, as is the case with all other fixed assets.

Governments are permitted a choice regarding depreciation of infrastructure. First, governments may record depreciation, in the same manner as for other depreciable fixed assets. This is the method assumed in the Village of Elizabeth example, where a 20-year life was assumed. Second, governments may use the modified approach.

The Modified Approach for Reporting Infrastructure

Governments may choose not to depreciate infrastructure but instead use the modified approach, if these two conditions exist: First, the government must have an asset management system that (1) keeps an up-to-date inventory of eligible infrastructure assets, (2) performs condition assessments of those eligible infrastructure assets at least every three years, using a consistent measurement scale, and (3) estimates each year the annual amount to maintain and preserve those assets at the condition level established and disclosed by the government. Second, the government must document that the eligible infrastructure assets are being maintained at a level at or above the condition level established and disclosed by the government.

These requirements are documented by a government in two RSI schedules reflecting (1) the assessed condition of eligible infrastructure assets and (2) the estimated annual amount to maintain and preserve eligible infrastructure assets compared with the amount actually expended for each of the preceding five fiscal periods. These schedules are listed in Illustration 2–11. Certain note disclosures are also required.

When using the modified approach, expenditures *to extend the life* of infrastructure assets are charged to expense; if governments choose to depreciate infrastructure assets rather than use the modified approach, expenditures to extend the life of infrastructure assets would be capitalized in the government-wide statements. In either case, expenditures to add to or improve infrastructure assets would be capitalized.

For example, assume a government expends the following for infrastructure: $2,000,000 for general repairs; $2,500,000 for improvements that extend the life (but not the quality) of existing infrastructure; and $3,000,000 to add to and improve existing infrastructure. Assume that, if depreciation is charged, the amount would be $2,750,000. If the depreciation approach were used, $4,750,000 would be charged to expense ($2,000,000 + $2,750,000) and $5,500,000 would be added to capital assets ($2,500,000 + 3,000,000). If the modified approach were used, $4,500,000 would be charged to expense ($2,000,000 + $2,500,000), and $3,000,000 would be added to capital assets.

Collections

Governments are encouraged, but not required, to capitalize collections. To qualify as a **collection,** a donated or purchased item must meet all of the following conditions (from Paragraph 27 of *Statement 34*):

- Held for public exhibition, education, or research in furtherance of public service, rather than for financial gain.
- Protected, kept unencumbered, cared for, and preserved.
- Subject to an organizational policy that requires the proceeds from sales of collection items to be used to acquire other items for collections.

Disclosures are required for collections. Donated collections would be reported as revenues; if donated collections are not capitalized, the amount would be charged to the proper expense category; the revenue and expense would be equal. Collections are especially important for public colleges and universities and for governmental museums reported as special entities, discussed in Chapter 9. It should be noted that the same criteria exist for private sector not-for-profit organizations to choose not to capitalize collections (Chapter 10).

ACCOUNTING FOR LONG-TERM DEBT

As is the case for capital assets, long-term liabilities associated with proprietary funds and fiduciary funds are reported with those funds. However, long-term liabilities associated with governmental funds are not reported in the governmental fund financial statements. These long-term liabilities are referred to as **general long-term debt** and are reported in the government-wide statements only. General long-term debt includes all debt that is to be paid with general governmental resources. Sometimes this is called **general obligation debt.** General obligation debt has as backing the **full faith and credit** of the governmental unit, including its taxing power. However, it should be noted that in some cases, general obligation debt will be paid with enterprise fund resources and would properly be reported in the enterprise funds. The term, general long-term debt, represents debt that is to be paid out of general government resources.

Types of General Long-Term Debt

General long-term debt includes the principal of unmatured bonds, the noncurrent portion of capital lease agreements, compensated absences, claims and judgments, pensions (the net pension obligation, not the actuarial liability), special termination benefits, operating leases with scheduled rent increases, and landfill closure and postclosure care liabilities (when to be paid out of general government resources).

As is the case with general fixed assets, detailed records must be kept on all long-term debt. Historically, this was accomplished through the General Long-Term Debt Account group. Extensive disclosures and schedules are required that are very important to users of governmental financial reports, especially financial analysts. Some of these disclosures and schedules are illustrated in this chapter.

Debt Disclosures and Schedules

GASB *Statement 34* requires a number of note disclosures for general long-term debt. This includes, by class of debt, the beginning balances, increases, decreases, and ending balances. An example of this disclosure, shown as a Schedule of Changes in Long-Term Debt, is shown in Illustration 8–6. GASB also requires a schedule of Principal and Interest Due in Future Years, shown in Illustration 8–7.

Another matter of importance in relation to long-term indebtedness is the legal limitation upon the amount of long-term indebtedness that may be outstanding at a given time, in proportion to the assessed value of property within the jurisdiction represented. **Debt limit** means the total amount of indebtedness of specified kinds that is allowed by law to be outstanding at any time. **Debt margin,** sometimes referred to as *borrowing power,* is the difference between the amount of debt limit calculated as prescribed by law and the net amount of outstanding indebtedness subject to limitation. A schedule showing the Computation of Legal Debt Margin is shown in Illustration 8–8. This schedule is often shown in the statistical section of the Comprehensive Annual Financial Report. Financial analysts are concerned if the legal debt margin is small, indicating that the government will not be able to issue additional debt in times of need.

Finally, property owners of a given government are subject to not only the debt of the government but also to the debt of other governments. For example, a resident of a city may also be a resident of a county, a school district, a community college district, and a park district. A statistical schedule, designed to show the impact on one government's citizens of the debt of other governments, is the Schedule of Direct and Overlapping Debt, shown in Illustration 8–9. In this schedule, note that city residents provide 56.23 percent of the assessed valuation of the county, school board, and hospital board. A different basis is used to allocate the state gasoline tax. Financial analysts are interested to see the total debt burden placed on residents of a government, as well as the burden imposed by the government only.

ILLUSTRATION 8-6

CITY OF ANYWHERE, USA
Schedule of Changes in Long-Term Debt
Year Ended September 30, 2004

	Balances 10/01/03	Additions	Deductions	Balances 09/30/04
General Obligation Bonds	$ 770,000	$ —	$ 125,000	$ 645,000
Public Improvement Revenue Certificates 1987	650,000	—	200,000	450,000
Public Improvement Revenue and Refunding Bonds 1989	10,485,000	—	275,000	10,210,000
First State Financing Commission Loan 1989	1,610,000	—	530,000	1,080,000
First State Financing Commission Loan 1990	1,165,000	—	370,000	795,000
Promissory Note	240,217	—	11,345	228,872
Capital Leases	150,172	—	45,916	104,256
Compensated Absences	1,245,486	90,534	—	1,336,020
Total General Long-Term Debt	16,315,875	90,534	1,557,261	14,849,148
Enterprise Long-Term Debt:				
Utility Revenue Bonds	361,233,692	—	1,725,000	359,508,692
Utility Notes	74,803,000	—	1,542,000	73,261,000
	436,036,692	—	3,267,000	432,769,692
Less unamortized discount	(7,652,304)	—	314,105	(7,338,199)
	428,384,388	—	2,952,895	425,431,493
Total Long-Term Debt	$444,700,263	$ 90,534	$4,510,156	$440,280,641

ILLUSTRATION 8-7

CITY OF ANYWHERE, USA
Notes to Financial Statements
September 30, 2004

Aggregate annual debt service requirements (excluding the Commercial Paper Notes) including maturities of principal and payment of current interest are as follows:

	Debt Service Requirements		
Fiscal Year(s)	General	Enterprise*	Total
2005	$ 2,150,674	$ 28,722,221	$ 30,872,895
2006	1,964,189	30,120,932	32,085,121
2007	1,239,723	31,569,681	32,809,404
2008	1,261,976	34,434,528	35,696,504
2009	1,178,451	34,625,497	35,803,948
2010–2014	5,460,907	172,692,497	178,153,404
2015–2019	5,105,000	173,124,868	178,229,868
2020–2024	5,131,247	209,735,291	214,866,538
2025–2034	5,125,971	166,647,351	171,773,322

ILLUSTRATION 8–7 (continued)

Fiscal Year(s)	Debt Service Requirements		
	General	Enterprise*	Total
2035–2039	1,036,160	13,525,062	14,561,222
	29,654,298	895,197,928*	924,852,226
Less interest	(16,141,170)	(535,689,236)*	(551,830,406)
Total principal	$ 13,513,128	$ 359,508,692	$ 373,021,820

*Excludes principal of $73,261,000 and undeterminable amount of interest. See prior description of the Utility System Commercial Paper Notes.
Included in the tabulation are debt service requirements for the city's capital lease obligations as follows:
Fiscal year-end September 30:

2005	$ 58,340
2006	58,341
Net minimum lease payments	116,681
Less amount representing interest	(12,425)
Present value of net minimum lease payments	$104,256

ILLUSTRATION 8–8

CITY OF ANYWHERE, USA
Computation of Legal Debt Margin
September 30, 2004
(Not Reported on by Certified Public Accountants)

Assessed Value of Real Property, September 30, 2004			$694,147,340
Assessed Value of Personal Property, September 30, 2004			53,012,260
Total Assessed Value of Real and Personal Property			$747,159,600
Debt Limit, 20 percent of Assessed Value			$149,431,920
Amount of Debt Applicable to Debt Limit:			
General Obligation Bonds and Warrants		$121,695,000	
Notes and Mortgages Payable		125,256	
Other		4,618,363	
		126,438,619	
Less:			
Net Assets in Debt Service Funds			
Applicable to Bonds and Warrants			
Included in Legal Debt Limit	$ 9,446,524		
Items Excluded from Legal Debt Limit:			
General Obligation Warrants Applicable to Sewer Improvements	31,190,000		
General Obligation Lease with Public Building Authority	5,200,000	45,836,524	
Total Amount of Debt Applicable to Debt Limit			80,602,095
Legal Debt Margin			$ 68,829,825

ILLUSTRATION 8–9

CITY OF ANYWHERE, USA
Schedule of Direct and Overlapping Debt
September 30, 2004
(Not Reported on by Certified Public Accountants)

	Gross Debt Less Debt Service Assets	Percentage of Debt Applicable to City of Anywhere	Amount of Debt Applicable to City of Anywhere
City of Anywhere:			
Gross Debt	$121,695,000		
Less Debt Service Assets	13,665,319		
Direct Net Debt	108,029,681	100.00%	$108,029,681*
Overlapping Debt			
Anywhere County:			
Special Highway Fund	20,553,000	56.23	11,556,952
Road and Bridge Fund:			
General Obligation	57,000	56.23	32,051
State Gasoline	60,000	33.41	20,046
Medical School	2,200,000	56.23	1,237,060
Total Anywhere County	22,870,000	56.17	12,846,109
Board of School Commissioners	25,285,000	56.23	14,217,755
Anywhere Hospital Board	2,665,000	56.23	1,498,529
Total Overlapping Debt	50,820,000	56.20	28,562,393†
Total Direct and Overlapping Debt	$158,849,681	85.99%	$136,592,074‡

*Direct net debt, 15.56 percent of assessed value of real property; $541.64 per capita.
†Overlapping debt, 4.11 percent of assessed value of real property; $143.23 per capita.
‡Direct and overlapping debt, 19.67 percent of assessed value of real property; $684.87 per capita.

Questions and Exercises

8–1. Using the annual financial report obtained for Exercise 1–1, answer the following questions:

 a. Find the reconciliation between the governmental fund balances and the governmental-type activities net assets. This might be on the governmental fund Balance Sheet or in a separate schedule in the basic financial statements. List the major differences. What is the amount shown for capital assets? How much is due to the incorporation of internal service funds? Was an adjustment made for deferred property taxes or any other revenue? What is the adjustment due to the inclusion of long-term liabilities? What other adjustments are made?

 b. Find the reconciliation between the governmental fund changes in fund balances and the governmental type activities changes in net assets. This might be on the governmental Statement of Revenues, Expenditures, and Changes in Fund Balances or in a separate schedule. List the major differences. How much is due to the difference between depreciation reported on the Statement of Activities and the reported expenditures for capital outlays on the Statement of Revenues, Expenditures, and Changes in Fund Balances? How much is due to differences in reporting expenditures versus expenses for debt service? How much is due to the incorporation of internal service funds? How much is due to differences in reporting proceeds versus gains on sale of capital assets? How much is due to additional revenue accruals? How much is due to additional expense accruals? What other items are listed?

c. Look at the Statement of Net Assets, especially the net asset section. Attempt to prove the Net Assets Invested in Capital Assets, Net of Related Debt figure from the information in the statement or the notes. List the individual items of net assets that are restricted; this might require examination of the notes to the financial statements.

d. Look at the Statement of Activities. List the net expenses (revenues) for governmental activities, business-type activities, and component units. List the change in net assets for governmental activities, business-type activities, and component units. Attempt to find from the notes the component units that are discretely presented.

e. Look throughout the annual report for disclosures related to capital assets. This would include the notes to the financial statements, any schedules, and information in the Management's Discussion and Analysis (MD&A). Summarize what is included. What depreciation method is used? Are lives of major classes of capital assets disclosed?

f. Look throughout the annual report for disclosures related to long-term debt. This would include the notes to the financial statements, any schedules in the financial and statistical sections, and the MD&A. Summarize what is included. Are the schedules listed in this chapter included? What is the debt limit and margin? What is the direct debt per capita? The direct and overlapping debt per capita?

8–2. For each of the following, select the letter with the *best* answer:

1. Which of the following adjustments would be made when moving from the governmental fund financial statements to the governmental activities in the government-wide financial statements?
   a. Eliminate expenditures for debt principal.
   b. Eliminate expenditures for capital outlay and charge depreciation.
   c. Both of the above.
   d. Neither of the above.

2. Which of the following is true regarding government-wide financial statements?
   a. Internal service funds are normally included with governmental-type activities.

b. Component units and fiduciary funds are not included.
c. Both of the above.
d. Neither of the above.

3. A governmental funds Statement of Revenues, Expenditures, and Changes in Fund Balances reported expenditures of $33,500,000, including capital outlay expenditures of $3,200,000. Capital assets for that government cost $56,000,000, including land of $3,000,000. Depreciable assets are amortized over 20 years, on average. The reconciliation from governmental fund changes in fund balances to governmental activities changes in net assets would reflect a(n):

a. Increase of $22,500,000.
b. Increase of $550,000.
c. Decrease of $550,000.
d. Increase of $400,000.

4. A governmental funds Statement of Revenues, Expenditures, and Changes in Fund Balances reported property tax revenues of $3,900,000. That same government reported a liability for deferred revenues, related to property taxes, in the amount of $120,000 and zero in the previous year. The property taxes in question related to the fiscal year of the report. The amount that would be reported for property tax revenues for the year in the Statement of Activities would be:

a. $3,900,000.
b. $3,780,000.
c. $4,020,000.
d. $0.

5. Which of the following would be considered a program revenue in the Statement of Activities for a governmental unit?

a. Motor fuel taxes restricted for road repairs.
b. A grant from the state restricted for road repairs.
c. Both of the above.
d. Neither of the above.

6. A government's Statement of Revenues, Expenditures, and Changes in Fund Balances reflected expenditures for interest in the amount of $60,000 and expenditures for principal in the amount of $100,000. That statement also reflected proceeds of bonds in the amount of $300,000. Assuming no other changes, the effect, when moving from the changes in fund balances in the governmental funds Statement of Revenues, Expenditures, and Changes in Fund Balances to the changes in net assets for governmental activities in the Statement of Activities would be a:

a. $200,000 decrease.
b. $200,000 increase.
c. $140,000 decrease.
d. $140,000 increase.

7. Which of the following is true regarding the incorporation of internal service funds into the government-wide financial statements?
   a. Internal service funds are not included in the government-wide financial statements.
   b. Internal service funds are incorporated into the business-type activities sections of the government-wide financial statements.
   c. Both of the above.
   d. Neither of the above.

8. Which of the following would likely need an adjustment when moving from the governmental funds Statement of Revenues, Expenditures, and Changes in Fund Balances to the government-wide Statement of Activities?
   a. Recording an additional expense for compensated absences.
   b. Recording an additional expense related to salaries earned at year-end.
   c. Both of the above.
   d. Neither of the above.

9. Which of the following must exist in order for a government to use the modified approach to record infrastructure?
   a. An up-to-date inventory of eligible infrastructure assets must be maintained.
   b. A condition assessment must be performed at least every three years.
   c. Both of the above.
   d. Neither of the above.

10. A city government is located entirely within the boundaries of the county. The city had debt of $3,000,000, assessed property value of $100,000,000, and a population of 10,000. The county had debt of $2,000,000, assessed property value of $200,000,000, and a population of 15,000. The direct and overlapping debt per capita for the city would be:
    a. $300.00.
    b. $500.00.
    c. $400.00.
    d. $450.00.

8–3. For each of the following, select the *best* answer:
   1. In its Statement of Net Assets, a government reported assets of $100 million, including $30 million in capital assets (net), and liabilities of $60 million, including long-term debt of $15 million, all related to capital asset acquisition. In addition, $1 million of cash was restricted for payment of debt service. The government's unrestricted net assets would be reported as:
      a. $14 million.

b. $25 million.
c. $24 million.
d. $15 million.

2. A government reported an other financing source in the amount of $600,000 related to the sale of land in its governmental funds Statement of Revenues, Expenditures, and Changes in Fund Balances. The land had a cost of $430,000. The adjustment in the reconciliation when moving from the changes in fund balances in the Statement of Revenues, Expenditures, and Changes in Fund Balances to the change in net assets in the Statement of Activities would be:
   a. $170,000.
   b. $430,000.
   c. $600,000.
   d. $0.

3. A government had the following transfers reported in its governmental funds Statement of Revenues, Expenditures, and Changes in Fund Balances: (1) a transfer from the General Fund to a debt service fund in the amount of $600,000; (2) a transfer from the General Fund to an internal service fund in the amount of $500,000, and (3) a transfer from the General Fund to an enterprise fund in the amount of $400,000. The amount that would be shown as a transfer out in the governmental activities column in the Statement of Activities would be:
   a. $1,500,000.
   b. $900,000.
   c. $400,000.
   d. $0.

4. An internal service fund reported net income of $300,000 in the proprietary fund Statement of Revenues, Expenses, and Changes in Fund Net Assets, including interest income of $40,000. All transactions were with governmental funds. The net impact of incorporating the internal service fund in the Statement of Activities would be to:
   a. Increase the governmental funds change in net assets by $300,000.
   b. Increase the governmental funds change in net assets by $260,000.
   c. Increase the governmental funds change in net assets by $40,000.
   d. Cause no impact.

5. A small city had revenues of $5,000,000. Which of the following would be true regarding requirements to record infrastructure, at some date in the future?
   a. The city would not be required to record infrastructure, either prospectively or retroactively.
   b. The city would be required to record infrastructure prospectively, but not retroactively.

c. The city would be required to record infrastructure retroactively, but not prospectively.

d. The city would be required to record infrastructure, both prospectively and retroactively.

6. A governmental funds Statement of Revenues, Expenditures, and Changes in Fund Balances reported expenditures of $40,000,000, including capital outlay expenditures of $8,300,000. Capital assets for that government cost $112,000,000, including land of $6,300,000. Depreciable assets are amortized over 20 years, on average. The reconciliation from governmental fund changes in fund balances to governmental activities changes in net assets would reflect a(n):

a. Increase of $3,015,000.
b. Decrease of $3,015,000.
c. Increase of $72,000,000.
d. Decrease of $2,000,000.

7. Which of the following would be considered a program revenue in the Statement of Activities of a local government?

a. Charges for services for a city park.
b. A gift of $200,000 by a resident to establish a permanent fund to maintain the city cemetery.
c. Both of the above.
d. Neither of the above.

8. Reconciliations are required to be presented, showing the change from the fund balances shown in the governmental funds Balance Sheet to the net assets shown in the governmental activities column of the Statement of Net Assets in:

a. A separate schedule in the basic financial statements.
b. The face of the Statement of Net Assets.
c. The face of the governmental funds Balance Sheet.
d. Either (a) or (c).

9. A government incurred expenses for its infrastructure as follows: $12 million for general repairs; $13 million to extend the life of existing infrastructure; and $14 million for improvements other than extending the life. The government chooses to use the modified approach to record infrastructure, thus avoiding depreciation. The amount that would be shown as expense would be:

a. $39 million.
b. $26 million.
c. $25 million.
d. $12 million.

10. A city had general obligation debt outstanding of $30,000,000 and had available resources in the amount of $8,000,000 to pay that debt. The

assessed valuation of property in the city is $600,000,000. The state applies an 8 percent debt limit, based on assessed valuation. The debt margin to be reported in the city's statistical section of the CAFR would be:

a. $18 million.
b. $48 million.
c. $24 million.
d. $26 million.

8-4. Under the reporting model required by GASB *Statement 34*, fund statements are required for governmental, proprietary, and fiduciary funds. Government-wide statements include the Statement of Net Assets and Statement of Activities. Answer the following questions related to the reporting model:

1. What is the measurement focus and basis of accounting for: *(a)* governmental fund statements, *(b)* proprietary fund statements, *(c)* fiduciary fund statements, and *(d)* government-wide statements?
2. Indicate differences between fund financial statements and government-wide statements with regard to: *(a)* component units, *(b)* fiduciary funds, and *(c)* location of internal service funds.
3. Indicate what should be included in the Statement of Net Assets categories: *(a)* Invested in Capital Assets, Net of Related Debt, *(b)* Restricted, and *(c)* Unrestricted.

8-5. List some of the major adjustments required when converting from fund financial statements to government-wide statements.

8-6. The City of Grinders Switch maintains its books so as to prepare fund accounting statements and prepares worksheet adjustments in order to prepare government-wide statements. You are to prepare, in journal form, worksheet adjustments for each of the following situations.

1. General fixed assets as of the beginning of the year, which had not been recorded, were as follows:

Land	$ 3,125,000
Buildings	32,355,000
Improvements Other Than Buildings	16,111,000
Equipment	11,554,000
Accumulated Depreciation, Capital Assets	14,167,000

2. During the year, expenditures for capital outlays amounted to $6,113,000. Of that amount, $4,321,000 was for buildings; the remainder was for improvements other than buildings.

3. The capital outlay expenditures outlined in (2) were completed at the end of the year. For purposes of financial statement presentation, all capital assets are depreciated using the straight-line method, with no estimated salvage value. Estimated lives are as follows: buildings, 40

years; improvements other than buildings, 20 years; and equipment, 10 years.

4. At the beginning of the year, general obligation bonds were outstanding in the amount of $4,000,000. Unamortized bond premium amounted to $40,000. Note: this entry is not covered in the text. Debit Net Assets to offset the other accounts.

5. During the year, debt service expenditures for the year amounted to: interest, $580,000; principal, $400,000. For purposes of government-wide statements, the premium listed in (4) should be amortized in the amount of $4,000. No adjustment is necessary for interest accrual.

6. At year-end, additional general obligation bonds were issued in the amount of $1,200,000, at par.

8–7. The City of South Pittsburgh maintains its books so as to prepare fund accounting statements and prepares worksheet adjustments in order to prepare government-wide statements. You are to prepare, in journal form, worksheet adjustments for each of the following situations:

1. The City levied property taxes for the current fiscal year in the amount of $10,000,000. When making the entries, it was estimated that 2 percent of the taxes would not be collected. At year-end, $600,000 of the taxes had not been collected. It was estimated that $300,000 of that amount would be collected during the 60-day period after the end of the fiscal year and that $100,000 would be collected after that time. The City had recognized the maximum of property taxes allowable under modified accrual accounting.

2. In addition to the expenditures recognized under modified accrual accounting, the City computed that $250,000 should be accrued for compensated absences.

3. In the governmental funds Statement of Revenues, Expenditures, and Changes in Fund Balances, the City reported proceeds from the sale of land in the amount of $600,000. The land had a cost basis of $235,000.

4. In the Statement of Revenues, Expenditures, and Changes in Fund Balances, General Fund transfers out included $500,000 to a debt service fund, $600,000 to a special revenue fund, and $900,000 to an enterprise fund.

8–8. The City of Southern Pines maintains its books so as to prepare fund accounting statements and prepares worksheet adjustments in order to prepare government-wide statements. As such, the City's internal service fund, a motor pool fund, is included in the proprietary funds statements. Prepare necessary adjustments in order to incorporate the internal service fund in the government-wide statements as a part of governmental activities.

1. Balance sheet asset accounts include: Cash, $150,000; Investments; $125,000; Inventories, $325,000; and Capital Assets (net), $1,355,000. Liability accounts include: Accounts Payable, $50,000; Long-Term Advance from Enterprise Fund, $800,000.

2. The only transaction in the internal service fund that is external to the government is interest revenue in the amount of $5,300.
3. Exclusive of the interest revenue, the internal service fund reported net income in the amount of $36,000. An examination of the records indicates that services were provided as follows: one-third to general government, one-third to public safety, and one-third to public works.

8–9. With regard to recording infrastructure, answer the following questions:
1. What is infrastructure according to GASB?
2. What are the rules for recording infrastructure, both prospectively and retroactively? When are those rules effective?
3. What are the two methods that might be used to record infrastructure from year-to-year? How is the accounting different under those two methods?
4. What conditions must exist in order to use the modified approach to record and report infrastructure?
5. What are the disclosure requirements, if the modified approach is used?

8–10. Prepare a solution to Exercise 2–6.

8–11. Prepare a solution to Exercise 2–7.

8–12. You are asked to prepare a Statement of Legal Debt Margin for the Village of Bog Hollow as of December 31, 2004. You ascertain that the following bond issues are outstanding:

General obligation serial bonds	$12,000,000
Water utility bonds	33,000,000
Special assessment bonds	3,500,000
Village auditorium bonds	3,500,000
Street improvement bonds	8,400,000
Electric utility bonds	14,200,000
Golf course clubhouse bonds	750,000

Other information you obtain includes the following items:
1. Assessed valuation of real and taxable property in the village totaled $700,000,000.
2. The rate of debt limitation applicable to the Village of Bog Hollow, was 10 percent of total real and taxable personal property valuation.
3. No general liability existed in connection with the special assessment bonds.
4. Electric utility, water utility, and golf clubhouse bonds were all serviced by enterprise revenues, but each carried a full faith and credit contingency provision and by law was subject to debt limitation.
5. The village auditorium bonds and street improvement bonds were general obligation issues.
6. The amount of assets segregated for debt retirement at December 31 of the current year is $6,650,000.

7. None of the bonds matured during the following year.

8–13. At December 31, 2004, all property inside the limits of the City of Dunlap was situated within four governmental units, each authorized to incur long-term debt. At that date, net long-term debt of the four units was as follows:

Dunlap County	$23,555,000
City of Dunlap	9,444,000
Consolidated School District	14,998,000
Dunlap Library District	1,200,000

Assessed values of property at the same date were as follows: county and library districts, $900,560,000; city, $360,224,000; and school district, $450,280,000.

a. Prepare a Schedule of Direct and Overlapping Debt for the City of Dunlap. (Round the percentages to the nearest whole percent.)

b. Compute the actual ratio (round percentages to the nearest tenth of a percent) of total debt to assessed valuation applicable to the property within the City of Dunlap.

c. Compute the share of the City's direct and overlapping debt that pertained to your home, which had an assessed valuation of $36,000 at December 31, 2004.

Continuous Problem

8–C. Assemble the following from previous continuous problems: (1) the governmental funds Balance Sheet from Problem 5–C (4) (a); (2) the governmental funds Statement of Revenues, Expenditures, and Changes in Fund Balances from Problem 5–C (4) (b); (3) the proprietary funds Statement of Net Assets from Problem 6–C (3) (1); and the proprietary funds Statement of Revenues, Expenses, and Changes in Fund Net Assets from Problem 6–C (3) (2).

1. Start a worksheet for adjustments, using the format in the text, by listing all the accounts in the statements, except to use one account for net assets (which will include all fund balance accounts and all net asset accounts). Use the following order: assets, liabilities, net assets, revenues, expenditures (expenses), transfers, gains and losses, special items. Use all accounts. Use $1,230,990 as the beginning net assets figure. (Do not enter fund balance accounts; use beginning net assets instead. Confirm that the total debits and credits equal $19,202,240.

2. Record adjustments on the worksheet (or in journal format if your instructor indicates) for the following items. Identify each adjustment by the letter used in the problem:

    a. Record general fixed assets and related accumulated depreciation accounts. The City of Everlasting Sunshine had the following balances:

Land	$ 5,125,000
Buildings	30,200,000
Accumulated Depreciation—Buildings	(12,100,000)
Improvements Other Than Buildings	20,000,000
Accumulated Depreciation—Improvements Other Than Buildings	(8,200,000)
Equipment	8,375,000
Accumulated Depreciation—Equipment	(4,800,000)

b. Eliminate the construction expenditures shown in the governmental funds Statement of Revenues, Expenditures, and Changes in Fund Balances. Assume that $4,468,550 was for buildings and $445,600 was for equipment.

c. Depreciation expense is as follows: buildings, $755,000; improvements other than buildings, $1,000,000; equipment, $837,500.

d. Eliminate the proceeds from sales of bonds by recording bonds payable. Adjust the premium on bonds from another financing source to a liability.

e. As of January 1, 2002, the City of Everlasting Sunshine had $6,000,000 in general obligation bonds outstanding. Debit Net Assets and credit Bonds Payable for that amount.

f. Eliminate the expenditures for bond principal.

g. Convert interest expenditures in the amount of $508,000 to interest expense.

h. Accrue interest in the amount of $328,000. See Exercise 5–C. Two bond issues were outstanding; interest payments for both were last made on July 1, 2003. The computation is as follows: ($5,600,000 × .06 × ½) + ($4,000,000 × .08 × ½) = $328,000.

i. Adjust for the interest accrued in the prior year ($6,000,000 × .06 × ½) = $180.000. Debit Net Assets and credit Interest Expense.

j. Amortize bond premium in the amount of $2,500. See Exercise 5–C (1)(a)(1).

k. Make adjustments for additional revenue accrual. The only adjustment is for property taxes to eliminate the deferral. Debit Deferred Revenues and credit Revenues—Property Taxes for the amount (see entry 21 in Chapter 4).

l. At the beginning of the year, an adjustment was made to reverse the property tax deferral in the General Fund (see entry 1 in Chapter 4). The amount was $20,000. Debit Revenues—Property Taxes and credit Net Assets for that amount.

m. Make an adjustment for expense accrual. Assume the charge for compensated absences is $316,000. Charge compensated absences expense.

n. Bring in the balances of the internal service fund balance sheet accounts. When doing this, record the detail of capital assets. Assume the detail was as follows:

Land	$ 15,000
Buildings	44,000
Accumulated Depreciation—Buildings	(13,200)
Equipment	21,000
Accumulated Depreciation—Equipment	(12,600)

Credit Net Assets for the difference between assets and liabilities.

o. No revenues from internal service funds were with external parties. Assume $13,200 of the $21,200 "Due from Other Funds" in the internal service accounts represents a receivable from the General Fund and the remaining $8,000 is due from the enterprise fund. Eliminate the $13,200 interfund receivables.

p. Reduce governmental fund expenses by the net profit ($1,000) of internal service funds. As the amount is small, reduce general government expenditures for the entire amount. Debit Net Assets.

q. Eliminate transfers that are within governmental activities. See the governmental fund Statement of Revenues, Expenditures, and Changes in Fund Balances.

3. Prepare, in good form, a Statement of Activities for the City of Everlasting Sunshine for the Year Ended December 31, 2004. Looking at the solution to Exercise 5–C (4) (b), make the following three assumptions. (1) Assume the $288,000 state grant in the General Fund is an operating grant specifically for law enforcement programs. (2) Assume the $975,000 in the Street and Highway Fund is an operating grant specifically for certain highway and street expenses. (3) Assume the $500,000 grant in the City Hall Construction Fund is a capital grant that applies one-half to general government and one-half to public safety.

Use the solution to P6–C (3) (2) to prepare the business activities portion. Assume the beginning net asset balances are governmental, $33,778,990; business-type, $1,624,840.

4. Prepare, in good form, a Statement of Net Assets for the City of Everlasting Sunshine as of December 31, 2004. Include a breakdown in the Net Assets section for (a) capital assets, net of related debt, (b) restricted, and (c) unrestricted. Group all capital assets, net of depreciation, as shown in Illustration 8–2. For the governmental activities capital assets, net of related debt, the related debt includes the bonds payable, the premium on bonds payable, and the $20,000 advance from the water utility fund. Prove that the total net assets equal the ending net assets shown in Part 3 above. Assume that the debt service fund balances are restricted for debt service in governmental activities and that

the restricted assets in business activities should be restricted in the net asset section.
5. Prepare the reconciliation necessary to convert from the change in fund balances in the governmental funds Statement of Revenues, Expenditures, and Changes in Fund Balances to the change in net assets in the government-wide Statement of Activities.
6. Prepare the reconciliation necessary to convert from the fund balance reported in the governmental funds Balance Sheet to the net assets in the government-wide Statement of Net Assets.

Chapter Nine

Analysis of Governmental Financial Statements, GASB Accounting for Special-Purpose Entities, Accounting for Public Institutions of Higher Education

This chapter begins with a discussion of the analysis of state and local government financial statements. Next, GASB accounting guidance for special-purpose entities is described. Finally, public college accounting and financial reporting are discussed and illustrated.

ANALYSIS OF STATE AND LOCAL GOVERNMENT FINANCIAL STATEMENTS

In a study for the Governmental Accounting Standards Board, Jones and others listed three primary groups of users of governmental financial reports: (1) citizen groups, (2) legislative and oversight officials, and (3) investors and creditors.[1] They suggest that citizen groups use financial reports to:
1. Evaluate efficiency and effectiveness.
2. Compare results of the current year with previous years.

---

[1] See Jones et al., *The Needs of Users of Governmental Financial Reports* (Norwalk, CT: Governmental Accounting Standards Board, 1985), 26–31.

3. Assess financial operations and financial condition.
4. Determine compliance with the budget.
5. Advocate certain programs or actions.

The study indicated that legislative and oversight officials use governmental financial reports to:

1. Evaluate executive branch funding and spending proposals.
2. Determine compliance with the budget and other finance-related requirements.
3. Monitor fund activity and financial position and analyze fund balances.

Finally, investors and creditors use reports to ascertain the ability of government to repay its debt. The study considered investors and creditors to be investors, bond raters, bond insurers, and underwriters.

This section of the chapter provides suggestions as to how readers might use governmental financial statements to gather information that would meet the needs just described.

Public Finance Market

The public finance market includes many types of bonds, short-term notes, and other financing arrangements. Often described as the municipal bond market, participants include issuers, investors, underwriters, and financial advisors, rating agencies, bond attorneys, and debt insurers. This text previously differentiated **general obligation bonds,** which carry the full faith and credit of the governmental unit and its taxing power, from **limited obligation** and **revenue bonds,** which are serviced from the revenues of particular facilities.

Debt-rating services, such as Moody's, Standard & Poor's, and Fitch's Investors Service, assist investors by rating bonds and other forms of debt. Ranging from highest to lowest, Moody's rates bonds as Aaa, Aa, A, Baa, Ba, B, Caa, Ca, and C.[2] Bonds insured with certain insurance companies are automatically Aaa, as payments of interest and principal are guaranteed.

While rating agencies, underwriters, and large institutional investors in the public finance market can obtain information directly from issuers, other investors depend upon publicly available information. When bonds are initially issued an "official statement" is prepared. The Government Finance Officers Association and the National Federation of Municipal Analysts have prepared disclosure guidelines for these official statements. After initial issuance, many in the investment community depend on the Comprehensive Annual Financial Report for information related to municipal governments, especially in the secondary market (the market for bonds after initial issuance).

Analysis of the Comprehensive Annual Financial Report

This section presents financial statement analysis using the Village of Elizabeth financial statements contained in this book. Of course, a final decision regarding the financial viability of a government involves many factors, only some of which are

---

[2] Moody's Public Finance Department, 1997 Medians: Selected Indicators of Municipal Performance, New York.

available from the financial statements. An analyst has many sources available which list ratios that might be useful. This text uses information from GASB,[3] Standard & Poor's,[4] Moody's Investors Service,[5] and Chaney, Mead, and Schermann.[6] In this example, the population of the Village of Elizabeth is assumed to be 10,000, and the market value of property in the government is assumed to be $100 million.

Some of the 10 ratios calculated for the Village of Elizabeth have been in use for a number of years. Others are new, based on the GASB *Statement 34* reporting model. When possible, the ratios are evaluated, either from information from one of the sources or from a sample of 88 CAFRs from Illinois municipalities and computed by students in the spring of 2000. Remember that sophisticated analysis would include many more factors and a trend analysis of governments over time.

Net debt per capita is a measure of the ability of the citizens to pay general government debt; a high figure indicates that citizens of a government bear an above-average burden. The government-wide Statement of Net Assets (Illustration 8–2) indicates that the Village of Elizabeth has $1,090,800 in general obligation bonds outstanding. The Village of Elizabeth governmental funds Balance Sheet (Illustration 5–1) indicates that $36,500 is on hand for payment of debt; thus the net debt is $1,054,300. The net debt per capita, then is

$$\$1,054,300/10,000 = \$105.43$$

The sample median for 88 Illinois municipalities was $435.23, and Standard & Poor's indicates that anything below $1,000 would indicate low fiscal stress (p. 29). As a result, it is clear that the Village of Elizabeth has low fiscal stress from this factor. When analyzing debt, analysts also consider other long-term liabilities, such as capital leases, compensated absences, and unfunded pension obligations. They also consider overlapping debt (see Chapter 8) to determine the overall impact of debt on the citizens of a municipality.

Net debt to fair value of property measures the ability of the government to pay its long-term debt based on the fair value of its property subject to tax. As is the case for net debt per capita, a high ratio indicates the possibility of stress. Using the same net debt factor as for net debt per capita, the net debt to fair value of property would be:

$$\$1,054,300/\$100,000,000 = 1.054\%$$

The class median for Illinois municipalities was 1.71 percent. Standard & Poor's indicated that anything below 3 percent indicates low fiscal stress (see note 4, p. 29), 3–6 percent indicates medium stress, and more than 6 percent indicates high stress.

---

[3] Dean Michael Mead, "An Analyst's Guide to Government Financial Statements" (Norwalk, CT: GASB, 2001).
[4] Standard & Poor's, "Public Finance Criteria" (New York: Standard & Poor's, 2000).
[5] See Footnote 2.
[6] Barbara A. Chaney, Dean Michael Mead, and Kenneth R. Schermann, "The New Governmental Financial Reporting Model: What It Means for Analyzing Government Financial Condition," *Journal of Government Financial Management* (Spring 2002), pp. 26–31.

Net debt to assets is a measure of solvency that is included in both the GASB and the Chaney, Mead, and Schermann materials. This can be obtained from the government-wide Statement of Net Assets and can be computed separately for governmental activites, business-type activities, and the total primary government. Following the sources, the amount available (used in previous computations) is ignored. The computations for the Village of Elizabeth, taken from Illustration 8–2 are

Governmental Activities: $1,090,800/$39,222,290 = 2.78%
Business-type Activities: $2,700,000/$4,312,590 = 62.6%
Primary Government: $3,790,800/$43,534,880 = 8.71%

Chaney, Mead, and Schermann reported these numbers for the City of Alexandria, Virginia, as 22.37 percent, 0 percent, and 22.30 percent and for the City of Corona, California, as 15.59 percent, 26.82 percent, and 18.68 percent.

Debt service to total expenditures—General and debt service funds measures the degree to which expenditures are tied up in debt service charges. Governments that have low ratios have more flexibility for operations and ability to incur more debt. Standard & Poor's indicates that 5 percent or below represents a low carrying charge, 10 percent represents a moderate carrying charge, and 15 percent or greater represents a high carrying charge. This information is obtained from the Statement of Revenues, Expenditures, and Changes in Fund Balances for the governmental funds for the Village of Elizabeth (Illustration 5–2):

($120,000 + $96,000)/($5,030,300 + $216,000) = 4.12%

The Village of Elizabeth, then, is carrying a relatively low debt burden, in terms of governmental operating expenditures.

Net assets/expenses is a measure of overall financial position, according to GASB and Chaney, Mead, and Schermann. This can be computed for governmental activities, business-type activities, and the total primary government. For the Village of Elizabeth, this information would be found in the government-wide Statement of Net Assets (Illustration 8–2) and Statement of Activities (Illustration 8–1):

Governmental Activities: $37,400,190/$8,421,600 = 4.44
Business-type Activities: $1,539,790/$828,100 = 1.859
Primary Government: $38,939,980/9,249,700 = 4.21

Unrestricted net assets/expenses provides a more conservative measure of the availability of resources to meet expenses. This information comes from the same financial statements as the previous measure. For the Village of Elizabeth, the factors are

Governmental Activities: = $886,990/$8,421,600 = 0.1053
Business-type Activities: = $341,525/$828,100 = 0.4124
Primary Government: = $1,228,515/$9,249,700 = 0.1328

Chaney, Mead, and Schermann report factors of 0.1621, 2.3053, and 0.1661 for Alexandria, Virginia, and 0.7642, 0.9837, and 0.8288 for Corona, California. Compared with these two cities, the Village of Elizabeth has relatively low unrestricted resources available to meet expenses.

Unreserved fund balance/revenues—General Fund is a liquidity measure long used in financial statement analysis. For the Village of Elizabeth, the information would be found in the General Fund column of the governmental funds Balance Sheet (Illustration 5–1) and the governmental funds Statement of Revenues, Expenditures, and Changes in Fund Balances (Illustration 5–2):

$$\$790,990/\$6,081,290 = 13.01\%$$

Standard & Poor's indicate that a figure above 8 percent is strong. Many governments establish a policy regarding this figure; for example, the City of DeKalb, Illinois, aims for 25 percent. The median for the 88 Illinois municipalities was a very high 89 percent.

Governmental revenues per capita measures the demand for services for a particular jurisdiction. The total governmental revenues for the Village of Elizabeth can be obtained from Illustration 5–2:

$$\$8,001,290/10,000 = \$800.13$$

This was very close to the median for Illinois municipalities.

Interest coverage—revenue bonds is a measure of an enterprise's ability to pay the interest on its enterprise debt. In many cases, a government may have several enterprises; in some cases, revenue bonds are payable specifically out of the revenues of each individual enterprise. In that case, this and the following ratio should be computed separately for each enterprise. The Village of Elizabeth has a single enterprise, reported as a Water Utility Fund. This ratio divides the net revenues (total revenues minus operating expenses) by the interest charges. For the Village of Elizabeth, both of these figures can be found in the proprietary funds Statement of Revenues, Expenses, and Changes in Fund Net Assets (Illustration 6–2). Total operating revenues (the Village of Elizabeth reports no nonoperating revenues) amount to $1,053,100, operating expenses amount to $659,900, and interest charges are $171,200:

$$(\$1,053,100 - \$656,900)/\$171,200 = 2.31 \text{ times}$$

The sample median for the Illinois municipalities was 3.28, so the Village of Elizabeth is not covering its interest as often as the average. Some enterprises may not cover interest at all; this is often the case for public transportation systems. Some enterprises do not have debt, and analysts will not be able to calculate this ratio. Note that some governments may issue general obligation bonds to be paid by enterprise revenues; in this case, the bonds (and the interest) would be reported in the enterprise funds.

Operating ratio—enterprise funds provides a measure of the expense coverage of an enterprise, based on operations. This ratio can be calculated, whether or not an enterprise has debt. A high ratio indicates stress. This ratio divides the operating expenses, excluding depreciation, by the operating revenues. Both figures can be obtained from Illustration 6–2.

$$(\$656,900 - \$122,800)/\$1,053,100 = 50.72\%$$

The sample median was 71.9 percent. The Village of Elizabeth, then, has a lower percentage, indicating that a lot of margin exists to handle debt. The apparent inconsistency between the results of this ratio and the interest coverage ratio is caused by the fact that the Village of Elizabeth Water Utility Fund has a relatively high interest payment. Note in the government-wide Statement of Net Assets (Illustration 8–2) or the proprietary funds Statement of Net Assets (Illustration 6–1) that $2,700,000 in revenue bonds are outstanding.

Additional Analysis

Citizen groups, legislative and oversight officials, and investors and creditors would want to examine financial statements in much greater depth than is suggested by listing only 10 ratios. Population trends, trends in assessed and market value of property, economic indicators, budget to actual figures, analysis of individual enterprise funds related to separate revenue bond issues, tax rate limitations and margins, debt limitations and margins, growth or contraction of employee numbers, management of pension liabilities, analysis of infrastructure and other capital facility maintenance, and examination of the notes to uncover any contingent liabilities are examples of additional analysis. The analyst must be aware of how financial statements are prepared and of the limitations in the numbers when making judgments. Nevertheless, the Comprehensive Annual Financial Report contains much that is useful to those who make political and financial decisions affecting governmental units.

GASB *STATEMENT 34* REPORTING RULES FOR SPECIAL-PURPOSE ENTITIES

Chapters 2 through 8 provide accounting and financial reporting guidance for **general-purpose** state and local governments. General-purpose local governments include states, counties, cities, towns, and villages. Other governments are called **special-purpose** local governments and include governments such as fire protection districts, park districts, library districts, tollway authorities, and transit authorities. Special-purpose governments may be stand-alone local governments or may be component units of other governments that are issuing separate reports. GASB does not give a clear definition of either general purpose or special-purpose governments. The distinction is not always between types of governments, as one government (say, a township) may be either a general purpose or special-purpose government, for purposes of financial reporting.

However, the *Implementation Guide for GASB Statement 34* provides a distinction by indicating that, "General-purpose governments are thought to be those that offer more than one type of *basic governmental services*—for example, general government, public safety, transportation, health and welfare. Special-purpose governments generally provide a limited (or sometimes a single) set of services or programs—for example, fire protection, library services, mosquito abatement, and drainage" (Question 257). Governmental health care entities, public school systems, other not-for-profit entities (e.g., museums), and public colleges and universities may be considered special-purpose entities for financial reporting purposes.

Chapter 2 of this text provides an introduction to financial reporting for special-purpose local governments. This chapter provides more detail and a few examples. Financial reporting for a special-purpose local government depends upon whether that government is engaged in governmental-type activities, business-type activities only, or fiduciary-type activities only.

Reporting by Special-Purpose Local Governments Engaged in Governmental Activities

According to paragraph 15 of GASB *Statement 34,* governmental activities "generally are financed through taxes, intergovernmental revenues, and other nonexchange revenues. These activities are usually reported in governmental funds and internal service funds." This would include general government, public safety, general public works, and other activities such as public health, culture and recreation, and community development when paid for through general governmental revenues. A special-purpose local government may be engaged in (1) both governmental activities and business-type activities, (2) more than one governmental activity, or (3) a single governmental activity.

Special-purpose governments that are engaged in both governmental and business-type activities or in more than one governmental activity are required to follow the reporting outlined in Chapters 2 through 8 of this text. That is, the full reporting model is required, including MD&A, government-wide and fund basic financial statements, notes to the financial statements, and Required Supplementary Information (RSI).

Some special-purpose governments are engaged in only one governmental-type activity. Examples might include fire protection, sanitation, or cemetery districts. Special-purpose governments that are engaged in only one governmental-type activity are permitted to combine the fund and government-wide financial statements. This could be done by showing reconciliations between governmental-fund accounting policies (modified accrual) and government-wide statements (accrual) on the face of the statements. Thus, a government might present only one Balance Sheet and one Statement of Revenues, Expenditures, and Changes in Fund Balances. Other information, including Management's Discussion & Analysis, notes, and RSI would also be included.

Illustration 9–1 reflects the GASB illustrative Balance Sheet/Statement of Net Assets for a Sample County Fire Protection District, a single-program entity. Note that the left-hand columns provide fund information and that adjustments are entered to provide the government-wide Statement of Net Assets. The adjustments, which would be detailed in note disclosure, include capital assets ($5,519,206), long-term debt ($4,033,161), a reduction in deferred revenues, presumably for property taxes ($1,303,366), accrual of interest ($217), and the elimination of internal receivables and payables ($12,293). Alternatively, separate statements could be presented for the Balance Sheet and the Statement of Net Assets.

Illustration 9–2 reflects one of the GASB illustrative Statements of Governmental Fund Revenues, Expenditures, and Changes in Fund Balances/Statement of Activities for the same Sample County Fire Protection District. Again, the fund information is shown to the left with adjustments leading to the Statement of

ILLUSTRATION 9–1

SAMPLE COUNTY FIRE PROTECTION DISTRICT
Governmental Funds Balance Sheet/Statement of Net Assets
June 30, 2004

	General Fund	Other Funds	Total	Adjustments (Note C)*	Statement of Net Assets
Assets					
Cash and investments	$6,505,557	$1,211,192	$7,716,749	$ —	$ 7,716,749
Taxes receivable	1,427,885	52,651	1,480,536	—	1,480,536
Other receivables	567,607	6,874	574,481	—	574,481
Internal receivables	—	12,293	12,293	(12,293)	—
Prepayments	7,763	—	7,763	—	7,763
Inventories	197,308	—	197,308	—	197,308
Capital assets, net of accumulated depreciation	—	—	—	5,519,206	5,519,206
Total assets	$8,706,120	$1,283,010	$9,989,130	5,506,913	15,496,043
Liabilities					
Accounts payable	$ 73,828	$ 33,171	$ 106,999	—	106,999
Salaries and benefits payable	273,367	—	273,367	—	273,367
Accrued interest payable	—	1,294	1,294	217	1,511
Internal payables	12,293	—	12,293	(12,293)	—
Deferred revenues	1,534,321	42,791	1,577,112	(1,303,366)	273,746
Long-term liabilities:					
Due within one year	—	—	—	636,655	636,655
Due after one year	—	—	—	3,396,506	3,396,506
Total liabilities	1,893,809	77,256	1,971,065	2,717,719	4,688,784
Fund Balances/Net Assets					
Fund balances:					
Reserved for inventories	197,308	—	197,308	(197,308)	—
Unreserved, reported in:					
General fund	6,615,003	—	6,615,003	(6,615,003)	—
Debt service funds	—	468,167	468,167	(468,167)	—
Capital projects funds	—	737,587	737,587	(737,587)	—
Total fund balances	6,812,311	1,205,754	8,018,065	(8,018,065)	—
Total liabilities and fund balances	$8,706,120	$1,283,010	$9,989,130		
Net assets:					
Invested in capital assets, net of related debt				2,087,848	2,087,848
Restricted for debt service				468,167	468,167
Unrestricted				8,251,244	8,251,244
Total net assets				$10,807,259	$10,807,259

*Source: GASB *Statement 34*, p. 204.

ILLUSTRATION 9-2

SAMPLE COUNTY FIRE PROTECTION DISTRICT
Statement of Governmental Fund Revenues, Expenditures,
and Changes in Fund Balances/Statement of Activities
For the Year Ended June 30, 2004

	General Fund	Other Funds	Total	Adjustments (Note Y)*	Statement of Activities
Revenues:					
Property taxes	$10,750,111	$ 391,442	$11,141,553	$ 270,601	$11,412,154
Investment earnings	526,079	71,582	597,661	—	597,661
Charges for services	622,590	—	622,590	—	622,590
Miscellaneous	29,245	—	29,245	—	29,245
Total revenues	11,928,025	463,024	12,391,049	270,601	12,661,650
Expenditures/expenses:					
Current:					
Personal services	9,434,005	—	9,434,005	6,018	9,440,023
Materials and services	1,250,788	—	1,250,788	—	1,250,788
Depreciation	—	—	—	306,623	306,623
Capital outlay	76,090	219,175	295,265	(295,265)	—
Debt service:					
Principal	5,452	220,000	225,452	(225,452)	—
Interest	1,534	204,028	205,562	217	205,779
Total expenditures/ expenses	10,767,869	643,203	11,411,072	(207,859)	11,203,213
Excess (deficiency) of revenues over expenditures	1,160,156	(180,179)	979,977	478,460	—
Other financing sources/uses:					
Transfers— internal activities	(500,000)	500,000	—	—	—
Excess (deficiency) of revenues and transfers in over expenditures and transfers out	660,156	319,821	979,977	(979,977)	—
Change in net assets	—	—	—	1,458,437	1,458,437
Fund balances/net assets:					
Beginning of the year	6,152,155	885,933	7,038,088	—	9,348,822
End of the year	$ 6,812,311	$1,205,754	$ 8,018,065	$ 0	$10,807,259

*Source: GASB *Statement 34*, p. 217.

Activities. The Statement of Revenues, Expenditures, and Changes in Fund Balances format is used in this illustrative statement. GASB also has an illustrative statement that shows expenses by program, a deduction from program revenues, and then deductions from general revenues. Note adjustments in this statement for property tax revenues ($270,601), accrued salaries ($6,018), depreciation ($306,623), elimination of capital outlay expenditures ($295,265), elimination of expenditures for debt service principal ($225, 452), and additional accrued interest ($217). Note that the ending fund balances and net assets agree with the totals in Illustration 9–1.

GASB stresses that only governments that have a single-program should use this format. Governments that budget and account for activities as separate programs should be considered as having multiple programs and are not eligible for this type of reporting.

Reporting by Special-Purpose Local Governments Engaged Only in Business-Type Activities

Paragraph 15 of GASB *Statement 34* indicates that "Business-type activities are financed in whole or in part by fees charged to external parties for goods or services. These activities are usually reported in enterprise funds." This would include water and sewer utilities, airports, transit systems, and other authorities. GASB *Statement 35* indicates that public higher education institutions may choose to report as business-type activities, as will be described later. It should be noted that these entities may have more than one program but must be involved only in business-type activities.

Special-purpose local governments engaged only in business-type activities are required to include the following in their financial statements:

- Management's Discussion and Analysis (MD&A)
- Enterprise Fund Financial Statements, including:
    Statement of Net Assets or Balance Sheet
    Statement of Revenues, Expenses, and Changes in Net Assets
    Statement of Cash Flows
- Notes to the Financial Statements
- Required Supplementary Information (RSI), other than MD&A, if applicable

These financial statements are illustrated in Chapter 6, related to enterprise funds. All of the requirements for enterprise financial statements described in Chapter 6, such as using an operating income figure, are required for the separate financial statements for single-purpose governments engaged only in business-type activities. In other words, the basic financial statements for a stand-alone utility would appear the same as the enterprise fund columns of Illustrations 6–1, 6–2, and 6–3.

Reporting by Special-Purpose Local Governments Engaged Only in Fiduciary-Type Activities

Public Employee Retirement Systems (PERS) are special-purpose governments that manage one or more retirement plans. Some of these are defined benefit plans; others include defined contribution plans, deferred compensation, and health care plans.

Many states have special-purpose local governments that exist solely to manage retirement systems for state and/or local government employees. These are often statewide systems. An example is the Illinois Municipal Retirement System, a stand-alone government that provides retirement benefits for nonuniformed local government employees in the State of Illinois. This is an agency, defined benefit plan with contributions from employees and employer local governments. Another example is the Illinois State University Retirement System, a statewide component unit of the State of Illinois that manages a defined benefit plan for university employees. Contributions come from the State and from employees. Both prepare separate financial statements and would qualify as special-purpose local governments that are engaged only in fiduciary-type activities.

These governments are required to prepare the following financial reports:

- MD&A.
- Statement of Fiduciary Net Assets.
- Statement of Changes in Fiduciary Net Assets.
- Notes to the Financial Statements.

These statements are illustrated in Chapter 7 in the discussion of pension trust funds and would be similar to the public employee retirement fund column of Illustrations 7–3 and 7–4. GASB *Statement 34* indicates that, if a PERS has more than one defined benefit plan, each plan should be reported in a separate column of the basic statements or that combining statements be included in the basic statements. This is to ensure that each plan is reported separately.

ACCOUNTING AND FINANCIAL REPORTING FOR PUBLIC COLLEGES AND UNIVERSITIES

In November 1999, GASB issued Statement 35, *Basic Financial Statements—and Management's Discussion and Analysis—for Public Colleges and Universities*. GASB *Statement 35* was an amendment to *Statement 34* in that it incorporated public institutions of higher education into the basic governmental reporting model. Public colleges and universities are allowed to choose, as special-purpose entities, to report as entities: (1) engaged in only business-type activities; (2) engaged in both governmental and business-type activities; or (3) engaged in only governmental-type activities. It is likely that most institutions will choose to report as engaged in only business-type activities, although some community colleges may choose to report as engaged in both governmental and business-type activities if they are significantly supported by a property tax.

The Environment of Public Higher Education

According to the *Chronicle of Higher Education*, during 1998–1999, the United States had 1,681 public institutions of higher education, compared with 1,695 private not-for-profit institutions and 672 private for-profit institutions.[7] The public institutions included 612 four-year colleges and 1,069 two-year colleges. More

---

[7] *Chronicle of Higher Education.* 2001/2002 Almanac Issue. Vol XLVII, No. 1, August 31, 2001, p. 9.

students attend public colleges than private colleges. In the fall of 1999, 11,309,399 students attended public colleges (76 percent), and 3,481,825 attended private colleges (24 percent).

Each state has established unique arrangements for the governance of public higher education. Public four-year higher education institutions are often (but not always) in systems of higher education, with several institutions under the same governing board. Governing board members are often appointed by state officials, often the governor. Institutions have varying degrees of autonomy from their state government officials and regulations, from state to state. Often, a coordinating council (say, a Board of Higher Education) exists to provide oversight and to coordinate budget requests. Sometimes, but not always, public colleges and universities are included as component units in the state CAFR. However, nearly all issue separate financial reports.

Community colleges, in some states, are distinct governmental entities, with independently elected board members, with the power to tax, to prepare budgets, and to hire administrators. In other states, community colleges are more like four-year colleges, in effect, state agencies.

Revenue sources include tuition and fees, state appropriations, specific state and federal grants, revenues from auxiliary enterprise activities (dormitories, etc.), alumni and other donations, and endowment income. Public higher education institutions often create separate foundations, legally separate not-for-profit organizations, to receive and administer some or all of the following: contributions, research, and athletics. These foundations are sometimes, but not always, included as component units in the institutions' annual reports. Many public higher education institutions have the power to issue debt; however, that debt is often for revenue-producing activities only, such as dormitories, student centers, food service activities, and athletics. Debt for academic facilities may be issued by the institution but is often issued as state general obligation debt.

Accounting and Financial Reporting for Public Institutions of Higher Education

Institutions that choose to report as special-purpose entities engaged in governmental and business-type activities prepare reports similar to those of general government, as described in Chapters 2 through 8. It is likely that few, if any, institutions will choose to report as special-purpose entities engaged only in governmental activities. This text focuses on institutions that choose to report as special-purpose entities engaged only in business-type activities. These institutions will be required to prepare the following:

- Management's Discussion and Analysis (MD&A).
- Statement of Net Assets (or Balance Sheet).
- Statement of Revenues, Expenses, and Changes in Net Assets.
- Statement of Cash Flows.
- Notes to the Financial Statements.
- Required Supplementary Information Other Than MD&A.

The basic requirements for the statements are the same as outlined for proprietary funds in Chapter 6 of this text. However, due to the scope and importance of public higher education, separate coverage is given.

Higher education institutions were required to adopt the reporting requirements for fiscal years beginning after June 15, 2001 (for institutions with revenues of $100 million or more), June 15, 2002 (for institutions with revenues of $10 million or more but less than $100 million), and June 15, 2003 (for institutions with revenues of less than $10 million). However, institutions that are component units of their states are required to adopt the reporting requirements at the same time as their states, which in most cases was for fiscal years beginning after June 15, 2001.

Prior to the adoption of *Statement 35*, public higher education institutions used a form of fund accounting. Fund groups included: current unrestricted, current restricted, loan, endowment and similar, annuity and life income, plant, and agency. Many institutions will likely continue to use some form of fund accounting to manage their operations. However, fund accounting is not illustrated in this text, which is concerned primarily with external reporting.

Public colleges and universities receive many grants and contributions. The net assets for these grants and contributions are often, but not always, restricted. The business-type activity model provides for a separation of net assets that are restricted. As indicated earlier, many institutions have most of their restricted resources sent to and managed by related entities, called *foundations*. In addition, net assets may be restricted by external parties for debt reserves and for resources restricted by state legislation and regulation.

With respect to public college foundations, GASB Statement 39: *Determining Whether Certain Organizations Are Component Units* was issued in May 2002. The effect of *Statement 39* is to require that most public college foundations be reported as discretely presented component units in the college financial reports. Specifically, foundations are to be reported if they meet all three of the following criteria:

- The economic resources received or held by the separate organization are entirely or almost entirely for the direct benefit of the primary government, its component units, or its constituents.
- The primary government, or its component units, is entitled to, or has the ability to otherwise access, a majority of the economic resources received or held by the separate organization.
- The economic resources received or held by an individual organization that the specific primary government is entitled to, or has the ability to otherwise access, are significant to that primary government.

GASB *Statement 39* applies to foundations of all types of governments, including general governments, public colleges, public schools, museums, and health care entities. The last criterion effectively rules out organizations that are insignificant financially, such as most PTA organizations and booster clubs.

Public colleges and universities often have extensive plant, including infrastructure. Included are land, buildings for academic and auxiliary enterprise purposes, research and other equipment, improvements other than buildings (infrastructure), library books, and collections and other works of art. GASB standards require that plant be recorded and depreciated. As indicated in Chapter 8, infrastructure may be reported using the modified approach. Institutions reporting as business-type activities must record infrastructure prospectively and retroactively when adopting the reporting requirements of *Statement 35*. Other institutions may report retroactively in accord with the dates shown in Chapter 8.

As indicated earlier, many educational institutions have the power to issue debt. This debt is often revenue bonds that are backed by revenue-producing facilities such as dormitories, bookstores, and food service operations. GASB requirements for business-type activities call for full accrual accounting for debt, including accrual of interest and amortization of debt discount and premium.

Institutions of higher education often issue tuition discounts and other forms of financial aid. Some of this financial aid comes from institutional funds, and some comes from the outside, including the federal government, specific state appropriations, and grants from individuals and businesses. Recently, responding to GASB *Statement 35,* the National Association of College and Business Officers issued Advisory Report 00–5, *Accounting and Reporting Scholarship Discounts and Allowances to Tuition and Other Fee Revenues by Public Higher Education.* Public institutions are to report all tuition and fee revenue net of any scholarship discounts and allowances. Only amounts that are to be paid by students and third-party payers can be shown as tuition fee income. The amounts paid by institutional funds and other sources must be deducted from student fee income (normally using contra-revenue accounts, which are reflected parenthetically or deducted directly, as illustrated in this chapter example). On the other hand, fees waived by the institution in return for services provided by institutional employees and graduate assistants are shown as expenses, and tuition and fee revenue is reported at the gross amount.

Illustrative Case—Northern State University—Beginning Trial Balance

This section presents a beginning trial balance, journal entries, and financial statements for Northern State University, a hypothetical state four-year institution choosing to report as a special-purpose entity engaged only in business-type activities. The fiscal year is the year ended June 30, 2004.

Assume the following trial balance as of July 1, 2003, the first day of the new fiscal year (in thousands):

	Debits	Credits
Cash and cash equivalents	$ 2,500	
Accounts receivable—net	1,250	
Short-term investments	12,520	
Interest receivable—unrestricted	25	
Inventories	1,560	
Deposits with bond trustee	2,100	
Restricted cash and cash equivalents	135	
Endowment investments	11,300	
Interest receivable—restricted	185	
Land	6,300	

	Debits	Credits
Buildings	56,100	
Accumulated depreciation—buildings		$ 22,000
Equipment	31,400	
Accumulated depreciation—equipment		16,200
Improvements other than buildings	8,900	
Accumulated depreciation—improvements other than buildings		4,800
Accounts payable and accrued liabilities		1,725
Deferred revenue		830
Long-term liabilities—current portion		1,525
Revenue bonds payable		25,000
Compensated absences payable		3,200
Net assets—invested in capital assets, net of related debt		33,175
Net assets—restricted, nonexpendable—scholarships and fellowships		9,000
Net assets—restricted, nonexpendable—research		2,300
Net assets—restricted, expendable—scholarships and fellowships		6,300
Net assets—restricted, expendable—research		5,040
Net assets—restricted, expendable—capital projects		1,500
Net assets—restricted, expendable—debt service		2,100
Net assets—unrestricted	420	
Totals	$134,695	$134,695

Illustrative Case—Journal Entries

Student tuition and fees, exclusive of summer session, were assessed in the amount of $21,500,000. Scholarship allowances were made, for which no services were required, in the amount of $800,000. Graduate and other assistantships awarded, for which services were required, amounted to $1,500,000 of unrestricted resources. Collections were made on student fees in the amount of $19,100,000. All amounts are reported in thousands:

		Debits	Credits
1.	Accounts Receivable	21,500	
	Operating Revenue—Student Tuition and Fees		21,500
2.	Operating Revenue Deduction—Scholarship Allowances	800	
	Accounts Receivable		800
3.	Scholarships and Fellowships Expense	1,500	
	Accounts Receivable		1,500
4.	Cash and Cash Equivalents	19,100	
	Accounts Receivable		19,100

Note that the $800,000 is recorded as a revenue reduction and the $1,500,000 is recorded as an expense. This is due to the requirement that scholarships for which no services are required are to be recorded as a revenue deduction, and scholarships for which services are required are to be recorded as an expense.

The $830,000 Deferred Revenue in the beginning trial balance represents tuition and fees that applied to the summer school term running from June to August 2003. As of June 30, 2003, services had not been provided for much of that summer school session. The $830,000 is recognized as a revenue for the year ended June 30, 2004. In June 2004, $1,150,000 was assessed for the summer term that takes place June through August 2004. Of that amount, $300,000 applied to the year ending June 30, 2004; the remainder is deferred until the following year. No scholarships or fellowships were involved.

		Debits	Credits
5.	Deferred Revenues	830	
	Operating Revenues—Student Tuition and Fees		830
6.	Cash and Cash Equivalents	1,150	
	Operating Revenues—Student Tuition and Fees		300
	Deferred Revenues		850

State appropriations were received in cash as follows: $22,500,000 for unrestricted general purposes and $1,300,000 for capital outlay, set aside for specific projects.

7.	Cash and Cash Equivalents	22,500	
	Restricted Cash and Cash Equivalents	1,300	
	Nonoperating Revenues—State Appropriations		22,500
	Capital Appropriations		1,300

It should be noted that GASB made a deliberate decision to categorize the general state appropriation as a nonoperating revenue of public colleges and universities, even though similar items, such as those shown in the next entry are considered operating revenues.

Federal grants and contracts were awarded and received in cash in the amount of $4,250,000. State grants and contracts were awarded and also received in cash in the amount of $1,690,000. All of these grants and contracts were restricted for specific purposes, as the following entries show:

8.	Restricted Cash and Cash Equivalents	5,940	
	Operating Revenues—Restricted—Federal Grants and Contracts—Research		2,250
	Operating Revenues—Restricted—Federal Grants and Contracts—Scholarships and Fellowships		2,000

	Debits	Credits
Operating Revenues—Restricted—State Grants and Contracts—Research		890
Operating Revenues—Restricted—State Grants and Contracts—Scholarships and Fellowships		800

In practice, many grants are reimbursement grants, which are reimbursed after expenditures take place. If this were the case, GASB *Statement 33* requires that revenues be recognized only after the expenditure takes place. Assume that expenditures for these grants are included in entry 18.

Revenues from bookstore, dormitory, food service, and other auxiliary enterprise operations are received in cash in the amount of $15,200,000.

	Debits	Credits
9. Cash and Cash Equivalents	15,200	
Operating Revenues—Auxiliary Enterprises		15,200

Contributions were received as follows, all in cash: unrestricted, $870,000; restricted for scholarships and fellowships, $500,000; restricted for research, $620,000; restricted for building projects, $600,000:

	Debits	Credits
10. Cash and Cash Equivalents	870	
Restricted Cash and Cash Equivalents	1,720	
Nonoperating Revenues—Gifts		870
Nonoperating Revenues—Restricted—Gifts—Scholarships and Fellowships		500
Nonoperating Revenues—Restricted—Gifts—Research		620
Capital grants and gifts		600

GASB *Statement 33* contains provisions regarding the recognition of voluntary nonexchange transactions, including contributions. Generally speaking, pledges or contributions receivable are recognized as assets and revenues when eligibility requirements are met. In order to be recognized in advance of collection, the contribution must be unconditional and must not contain a provision that funds may not be expended until future years. Chapter 4 contains more detail on GASB *Statement 33* provisions.

Donors contributed $1,200,000 for endowments, the principal of which may not be expended. Income from principal amounting to $700,000 was for scholarships and fellowships; the remainder was for research. The cash was immediately invested.

	Debits	Credits
11. Restricted Cash and Cash Equivalents	1,200	
Additions to Permanent Endowments— Income Restricted for Scholarships and Fellowships		700
Additions to Permanent Endowments— Income Restricted for Research		500
12. Endowment Investments	1,200	
Restricted Cash and Cash Equivalents		1,200

Interest receivable at the beginning of the year was collected in the amount of $210,000. Note that, of that amount, $185,000 was restricted:

	Debits	Credits
13. Cash and Cash Equivalents	25	
Restricted Cash and Cash Equivalents	185	
Interest Receivable—Unrestricted		25
Interest Receivable—Restricted		185

During the year, investment income was earned on investments whose income is unrestricted in the amount of $430,000, of which $30,000 was accrued interest at year-end. Investment income was earned on investments for which income is restricted amounted to $1,970,000, of which $200,000 was accrued interest at year-end. Of the $1,970,000, $1,260,000 is for scholarships and fellowships and $710,000 is for research:

	Debits	Credits
14. Cash and Cash Equivalents	400	
Interest Receivable—Unrestricted	30	
Nonoperating Revenues—Investment Income		430
15. Restricted Cash and Cash Equivalents	1,770	
Interest Receivable—Restricted	200	
Nonoperating Revenues—Restricted— Investment Income—Scholarships and Fellowships		1,260
Nonoperating Revenues—Restricted—Investment Income— Research		710

All accounts payable and accrued liabilities existing at the beginning of the year were paid. Of the $1,725,000, $1,234,000 was paid with unrestricted cash and $491,000 was paid with restricted cash:

	Debits	Credits
16. Accounts Payable and Accrued Liabilities	1,725	
Cash and Cash Equivalents		1,234
Restricted Cash and Cash Equivalents		491

Unrestricted expenses amounted to: salaries—faculty, $17,432,000; salaries—exempt staff, $14,143,000; wages—nonexempt employees, $6,212,000; benefits, $4,567,000; utilities, $5,515,000; supplies and other services, $4,753,000. All beginning inventories ($1,560,000) were consumed in the process of incurring those expenses, cash was paid in the amount of $50,000,000; accounts payable and accrued liabilities increased by $1,062,000:

	Debits	Credits
17. Operating Expenses—Salaries—Faculty	17,432	
Operating Expenses—Salaries—Exempt Staff	14,143	
Operating Expenses—Wages—Nonexempt	6,212	
Operating Expenses—Benefits	4,567	
Operating Expenses—Utilities	5,515	
Operating Expenses—Supplies and Other Services	4,753	
Inventories		1,560
Cash and Cash Equivalents		50,000
Accounts Payable and Accrued Liabilities		1,062

Note that the expenses are reported by object classification rather than by functions such as instruction and research. Past accounting principles required the reporting of expenditures by function; public colleges and universities normally budget by departments, which can be combined into functions. Colleges may wish to report by function in lieu of (or in addition to) reporting by object classification; however, the GASB *Statement 35* illustrative statements reflect reporting by object classification.

Restricted operating expenses included salaries—faculty, $1,899,000; salaries—exempt staff, $644,000; wages—nonexempt staff, $499,000; benefits, $634,000; utilities, $253,000; supplies and other services, $142,000; scholarships and fellowships, $4,000,000. Restricted cash was paid in the amount of $7,872,000; accounts payable and accrued liabilities increased by $199,000:

18. Operating Expenses—Restricted—Salaries—Faculty	1,899	
Operating Expenses—Restricted—Salaries—Exempt Staff	644	
Operating Expenses—Restricted—Wages—Nonexempt	499	
Operating Expenses—Restricted—Benefits	634	
Operating Expenses—Restricted—Utilities	253	
Operating Expenses—Restricted—Supplies and Other Services	142	
Operating Expenses—Restricted—Scholarships and Fellowships	4,000	
Restricted Cash and Cash Equivalents		7,872
Accounts Payable and Accrued Liabilities		199

During the year, depreciation was recorded in the following amounts: buildings, $1,402,000; equipment, $3,140,000; improvements other than buildings, $600,000.

Northern State depreciates infrastructure (improvements other than buildings) rather than using the modified approach:

	Debits	Credits
19. Operating Expenses—Depreciation	5,142	
Accumulated Depreciation—Buildings		1,402
Accumulated Depreciation—Equipment		3,140
Accumulated Depreciation—Improvements Other Than Buildings		600

During the year, the following capital expenditures were made: land, $2,125,000; buildings, $1,600,000; equipment, $2,400,000; improvements other than buildings, $400,000. Restricted cash was decreased in the amount of $2,600,000; unrestricted cash was decreased in the amount of $3,825,000; accounts payable and accrued liabilities increased by $100,000:

	Debits	Credits
20. Land	2,125	
Buildings	1,600	
Equipment	2,400	
Improvements Other Than Buildings	400	
Restricted Cash and Cash Equivalents		2,600
Cash and Cash Equivalents		3,825
Accounts Payable and Accrued Liabilities		100

Inventories were purchased and on hand in the amount of $1,355,000; unrestricted cash was paid:

	Debits	Credits
21. Inventories	1,355	
Cash and Cash Equivalents		1,355

Interest on revenue bonds, all related to capital outlay purchases, amounted to $1,500,000; all but $120,000 was paid in cash. In addition, revenue bonds were paid in the amount of $1,525,000; no new revenue bonds were issued. Next year, revenue bonds in the amount of $1,475,000 will be payable. Additional cash was sent to the bond trustee, as required by the bond indenture, in the amount of $200,000. Unrestricted cash was used for all these transactions:

	Debits	Credits
22. Nonoperating Expenses—Interest on Capital-Asset-Related Debt	1,500	
Cash and Cash Equivalents		1,380
Accounts Payable and Accrued Liabilities		120
23. Long-Term Liabilities—Current Portion	1,525	
Cash and Cash Equivalents		1,525

	Debits	Credits
24. Revenue Bonds Payable	1,475	
Long-Term Liabilities—Current Portion		1,475
25. Deposits with Bond Trustee	200	
Cash and Cash Equivalents		200
Net Assets—Unrestricted	200	
Net Assets—Restricted—Debt Service		200

It was determined that the accrued liability for compensated absences increased by $412,000 during the year:

	Debits	Credits
26. Operating Expenses—Benefits	412	
Compensated Absences Payable		412

All short-term investments existing at the beginning of the year, in the amount of $12,520,000, were sold for $12,770,000. New short-term investments were purchased in the amount of $13,550,000. Unrealized gains on short-term investments at year-end amounted to $166,000. The value of endowment investments remained unchanged.

	Debits	Credits
27. Cash and Cash Equivalents	12,770	
Short-Term Investments		12,520
Investment Income		250
28. Short-Term Investments	13,550	
Cash and Cash Equivalents		13,550
29. Short-Term Investments	166	
Investment Income		166

The same account, Investment Income, is credited in entries 27 and 29, as GASB *Statement 31* does not allow realized and unrealized gains to be reported separately.

Illustrative Case—Closing Entries

A number of closing entries are required to place the correct amounts in the appropriate net asset classifications. The first is to close all unrestricted revenues and expenses to Net Assets—Unrestricted:

	Debits	Credits
30. Operating Revenues—Student Tuition and Fees	22,630	
Nonoperating Revenues—State Appropriations	22,500	
Operating Revenues—Auxiliary Enterprises	15,200	
Nonoperating Revenues—Gifts	870	
Nonoperating Revenues—Investment Income	846	
Operating Revenue Deduction—Scholarship Allowances		800

	Debits	Credits
Operating Expenses—Scholarships and Fellowships		1,500
Operating Expenses—Salaries—Faculty		17,432
Operating Expenses—Salaries—Exempt Staff		14,143
Operating Expenses—Wages—Nonexempt		6,212
Operating Expenses—Benefits		4,979
Operating Expenses—Utilities		5,515
Operating Expenses—Supplies and Other Services		4,753
Operating Expenses—Depreciation		5,142
Nonoperating Expenses—Interest on Capital-Related Debt		1,500
Net Assets—Unrestricted		70

The restricted revenues and expenses are closed out to the related restricted net asset accounts. First, the nonexpendable additions are closed out:

31. Addition to Permanent Endowment—		
Scholarships and Fellowships	700	
Addition to Permanent Endowment—Research	500	
Net Assets—Restricted—Nonexpendable—		
Scholarships and Fellowships		700
Net Assets—Restricted—Nonexpendable—Research		500

Next, the grants for scholarships and fellowships are closed out against the restricted expenses:

32. Operating Revenues—Restricted—Federal Grants		
and Contracts—Scholarships and Fellowships	2,000	
Operating Revenues—Restricted—State Grants		
and Contracts—Scholarships and Fellowships	800	
Nonoperating Revenues—Restricted—Gifts—		
Scholarships and Fellowships	500	
Nonoperating Revenues—Restricted—Investment Income—		
Scholarships and Fellowships	1,260	
Operating Expenses—Scholarships and Fellowships		4,000
Net Assets—Restricted—Expendable—		
Scholarships and Fellowships		560

The grants for research are closed out against the related expenses, with the difference going to the appropriate net asset category:

33. Operating Revenues—Restricted—Federal Grants		
and Contracts—Research	2,250	

	Debits	Credits
Operating Revenues—Restricted—State Grants and Contracts—Research	890	
Nonoperating Revenues—Restricted—Gifts—Research	620	
Nonoperating Revenues—Restricted—Investment Income—Research	710	
Operating Expenses—Restricted—Salaries—Faculty		1,899
Operating Expenses—Restricted—Salaries—Exempt Staff		644
Operating Expenses—Restricted—Wages—Nonexempt		499
Operating Expenses—Restricted—Benefits		634
Operating Expenses—Restricted—Utilities		253
Operating Expenses—Restricted—Supplies and Other Services		142
Net Assets—Restricted—Expendable—Research		399

The capital appropriations and gifts restricted for capital acquisition are closed to the Net Assets—Restricted—Expendable—Capital Projects:

34. Capital Appropriations	1,300	
Capital Gifts and Grants	600	
Net Assets—Restricted—Expendable—Capital Projects		1,900

An examination of entry 20 reveals that $2,600,000 of restricted resources were used to acquire plant; this amount should be taken from the account Net Assets—Expendable—Capital Projects classification and transferred to the Net Assets—Invested in Capital Assets, Net of Related Debt classification:

35. Net Assets—Restricted—Expendable—Capital Projects	2,600	
Net Assets—Invested in Capital Assets, Net of Related Debt		2,600

Finally, it is necessary to adjust the Net Assets—Invested in Capital Assets, Net of Related Debt to reflect the balance of the fixed assets, less depreciation, less debt. The balance of the capital assets accounts (land, buildings, equipment, improvements other than buildings) is $109,225,000. The balance of the accumulated depreciation accounts is $48,142,000. The accounts for capital related debt (Revenue Bonds Payable plus Long-Term Liabilities—Current Portion) is $25,000,000. The balance in the Net Assets—Invested in Capital Assets, Net of Related Debt, should be $36,083,000. As the balance reflects $35,775,000 (after entry 35), an adjusting entry is needed to increase the account by $308,000:

36. Net Assets—Unrestricted	308	
Net Assets—Invested in Capital Assets, Net of Related Debt		308

An examination of related journal entries explains the $308,000:

Entry 20, purchase of capital assets	$ 6,525,000
Entry 19, depreciation	(5,142,000)
Entry 23, debt payment	1,525,000
Less adjustment for entry 35	(2,600,000)
Entry 35	$ 308,000

Illustrative Case—Financial Statements

As indicated earlier in the chapter, colleges reporting as special-purpose entities engaged only in business-type activities are required to prepare three statements. These are (1) the Statement of Net Assets, (2) the Statement of Revenues, Expenses, and Changes in Net Assets, and (3) the Statement of Cash Flows. Illustrations 9–3, 9–4, and 9–5 present these statements for Northern State University. These statements incorporate the beginning trial balance and journal entries shown above and follow the illustrative statements in GASB *Statement 35*.

Illustration 9–3 reports the Statement of Net Assets for Northern State University. Northern State does not have a discretely presented component unit: if it did, then a column would be prepared for this and the other two statements for the component unit. As mentioned earlier, many public universities have related foundations that hold resources, some of which are nonexpendable (endowments) and some of which are expendable for restricted and unrestricted purposes. Such foundations normally meet the requirements for presentation as component units.

Note the unrestricted net asset balance is a deficit $858,000, which increased from a deficit of $420,000 at the beginning of the year. This deficit is not unusual for public universities; note that a liability of $3,612,000 exists for compensated absences; legislatures are not likely to appropriate funds in advance for compensated absences. Keeping that in mind, Northern State University is in reasonable financial condition. Note that a reader can observe the restricted balances. Some are nonexpendable; note that the nonexpendable investments of $12,500,000 equal the balances of the two nonexpendable net asset balances. Others are expendable, in this case for scholarships and fellowships, research, capital outlay, and debt service.

Illustration 9–4 reports the Statement of Revenues, Expenses, and Changes in Net Assets for Northern State University. This is in the same general format as presented for the enterprise fund for the Village of Elizabeth in Chapter 6 (Illustration 6–2) and follows the GASB illustrative statement in *Statement 35*. Note that an operating income figure is presented; this is required. GASB specifically requires that state appropriations for operating purposes be shown as nonoperating revenue. As is true with all GASB operating statements, an "all-inclusive" format is used, reconciling to the ending net asset balance. The net asset balance in this statement is the same as the total net assets in Illustration 9–3.

Illustration 9–5 presents the Statement of Cash Flows for Northern State University. This statement follows the rules outlined in Chapter 6 for cash flows for enterprise funds. GASB specifically requires that cash received for the state appropriation for operations be reported under cash flows from noncapital financing

ILLUSTRATION 9-3

NORTHERN STATE UNIVERSITY
Statement of Net Assets
June 30, 2004
(in thousands)

Assets	
Current assets:	
Cash and cash equivalents	$ 1,446
Short-term investments	13,716
Accounts receivable, net	1,350
Interest receivable, unrestricted	30
Inventories	1,355
Deposits with bond trustee	2,300
Total current assets	20,197
Noncurrent assets:	
Restricted cash and cash equivalents	87
Endowment investments	12,500
Interest receivable, restricted	200
Capital assets, net	61,083
Total noncurrent assets	73,870
Total assets	94,067
Liabilities	
Current liabilities:	
Accounts payable and accrued liabilities	1,481
Deferred revenues	850
Long-term liabilities—current portion	1,475
Total current liabilities	3,806
Noncurrent liabilities:	
Revenue bonds payable	23,525
Compensated absences payable	3,612
Total noncurrent liabilities	27,137
Total liabilities	30,943
Net Assets	
Invested in capital assets, net of related debt	36,083
Restricted for:	
Nonexpendable:	
Scholarships and fellowships	9,700
Research	2,800
Expendable:	
Scholarships and fellowships	6,860
Research	5,439
Capital projects	800
Debt service	2,300
Unrestricted	(858)
Total net assets	$63,124

ILLUSTRATION 9–4

NORTHERN STATE UNIVERSITY
Statement of Revenues, Expenses, and Changes in Net Assets
For the Year Ended June 30, 2004
(in thousands)

Revenues	
Operating revenues:	
Student tuition and fees (net of scholarship allowances of $800)	$21,830
Federal grants and contracts	4,250
State grants and contracts	1,690
Auxiliary enterprises	15,200
Total operating revenues	42,970
Expenses	
Operating expenses:	
Salaries:	
Faculty	19,331
Exempt staff	14,787
Nonexempt wages	6,711
Benefits	5,613
Scholarships and fellowships	5,500
Utilities	5,768
Supplies and other services	4,895
Depreciation	5,142
Total operating expenses	67,747
Operating income (loss)	(24,777)
Nonoperating Revenues (Expenses)	
State appropriations	22,500
Gifts	1,990
Investment income	2,816
Interest on capital-related debt	(1,500)
Total nonoperating revenues (expenses)	25,806
Income before other revenues expenses, gains, or losses	1,029
Capital appropriations	1,300
Capital gifts and grants	600
Additions to permanent endowments	1,200
Increase in net assets	4,129
Net Assets	
Net assets—beginning of year	58,995
Net assets—end of year	$63,124

activities rather than cash flows for operating activities. The direct method is required by GASB, and a reconciliation is provided between the operating income (loss) in Illustration 9–4 and the cash flow from operations in this illustration. Note, as was the case in Chapter 6, that cash received for interest is shown as cash flows received from investing activities, cash paid for interest is shown as cash used for financing activities, and capital asset acquisitions are shown as financing activities.

ILLUSTRATION 9–5

NORTHERN STATE UNIVERSITY
Statement of Cash Flows
For the Year Ended June 30, 2004
(in thousands)

Cash Flows from Operating Activities	
Tuition and fees	$ 20,250
Federal grants and contracts	4,250
State grants and contracts	1,690
Auxiliary enterprises	15,200
Payments to employees, including benefits	(46,030)
Payment to suppliers	(10,922)
Payment of scholarships to students	(4,000)
Net cash provided (used) by operating activities	(19,562)
Cash Flows from Noncapital Financing Activities	
State appropriations	22,500
Gifts, other than for endowment purposes	1,990
Gifts for endowment purposes	1,200
Net cash flows provided by noncapital financing activities	25,690
Cash Flows from Capital and Related Financing Activities	
Capital appropriations	1,300
Capital grants and gifts	600
Purchases of capital assets	(6,425)
Interest on capital-related debt	(1,380)
Principal on capital-related debt	(1,525)
Cash deposited with bond trustee	(200)
Net cash provided (used) by capital and related financing activities	(7,630)
Cash Flows from Investing Activities	
Purchase of endowment investments	(1,200)
Interest on investments	2,380
Proceeds from sales of investments	12,770
Purchase of investments other than endowments	(13,550)
Net cash provided by investing activities	400
Net increase (decrease) in cash	(1,102)
Cash—beginning of year	2,635
Cash—end of year	$ 1,533
Reconciliation of net operating revenues (expenses) to net cash provided (used) by operating activities:	
Operating income (loss)	$(24,777)
Adjustments to reconcile operating income (loss) to net cash provided (used) by operating activities:	
Depreciation expense	5,142
Changes in assets and liabilities:	
Receivables, net	(100)
Inventories	205
Deposit with bond trustee	(200)
Accounts payable and accrued liabilities	(264)
Deferred revenue	20
Compensated absences	412
Net cash provided (used) by operating activities	$(19,562)

The numbers in the Statement of Cash Flows can be traced from the trial balance, journal entries, and other statements. With one exception, in the reconciliation section, Accounts Payable and Accrued Liabilities includes liabilities for accrued interest payable and for plant acquisition, both of which are not related to cash flows from operations. If $180,000 of the $1,725,000 balance in the beginning trial balance is related to debt service and plant acquisition and $220,000 of the ending balance of $1,481,000 in the Statement of Net Assets (Illustration 9–3) is related to debt service and plant acquisition (see entries 20 and 22), then the decrease in cash caused by a decrease in accounts payable and accrued liabilities from operations would be $244,000 ($1,525,000 − $1,281,000).

Summary

This chapter presents three topics: (1) analysis of governmental financial statements, (2) reporting by special-purpose entities, and (3) accounting and financial reporting by public colleges and universities.

Governmental financial statements are used especially by those engaged in the secondary market for tax exempt municipal bonds. Municipal financial analysts calculate ratios, establish trends in those ratios, and use many other factors in evaluating a government's ability to make principal and interest payments in a timely fashion.

Financial reporting by a special-purpose governmental entity depends upon whether that entity is engaged in governmental and business-type activities, multiple governmental activities, a single governmental activity, business-type activities only, or fiduciary activities only. Special-purpose entities that are engaged only in one governmental activity are allowed to combine fund and government-wide statements. Special-purpose governments that are engaged in business-type or fiduciary activities only are permitted to report only fund information.

Accounting and financial reporting by public colleges and universities follows GASB *Statement 35*, which incorporated public educational institutions into GASB *Statement 34* as special-purpose entities. Many public colleges and universities follow the provisions outlined in *Statement 34* for reporting as special-purpose entities engaged in business-type activities only. GASB *Statement 35* included nonauthoritative financial statement presentations which serve as the basis for the presentation in this text.

Questions and Exercises

9–1. Using the annual financial report obtained for Exercise 1–1, answer the following questions:
   a. Report the following ratios, using the text material for the Village of Elizabeth as a guide:
      (1) Net debt per capita.

(2) Net debt to fair value of property.
(3) Net debt to assets.
(4) Debt service to total expenditures—General and debt service funds.
(5) Net assets/expenses.
(6) Unrestricted net assets/expenses.
(7) Unreserved fund balance/revenues—General Fund.
(8) Governmental revenues per capita.
(9) Interest coverage—revenue bonds.
(10) Operating ratio—enterprise funds.

b. Write a memorandum, based on the ratios you calculated in part (*a*) of this problem, giving a recommendation as to whether to purchase (1) general obligation or (2) revenue bonds of your governmental unit.

9–2. Obtain an annual report from a public college or university and answer the following questions:

a. Does the institution report as a special-purpose entity engaged in (1) governmental and business-type activities or (2) business-type activities only? Are the financial statements appropriate, based on the choice made by the institution? (The remaining questions assume the institution reports as a special-purpose entity engaged only in business-type activities.)

b. Does the institution report a Statement of Net Assets? Are net assets separated between (1) invested in capital assets, net of related debt, (2) restricted, and (3) unrestricted? List the major restrictions. Is the statement reported in a classified format? Does the institution report component units? What are they? Note the balance of unrestricted net assets. Is the number negative? Look at the number shown for compensated absences. Would that change your opinion of the financial status of the institution?

c. Does the institution report a Statement of Revenues, Expenses, and Changes in Net Assets? If so, is a measure of operations (such as operating income) reported? Are scholarships and fellowships, for which no service is provided, deducted from student tuition and fees? Is the state appropriation for operations shown as a nonoperating revenue? Are operating expenses reported by object classification or by function? Are capital appropriations, capital gifts and grants, additions to permanent endowments, and any special or extraordinary items shown after nonoperating revenues (expenses)? Does the statement reconcile to the ending net assets figure?

d. Does the institution report a Statement of Cash Flows? Is the direct method used, as required by GASB? Are the four categories required by GASB shown? If not, which is not shown? Are interest receipts shown as cash provided by investing activities and interest payments shown as cash used for financing activities? Are capital assets acquired shown as cash used for financing activities? Is a reconciliation schedule prepared, reconciling operating income to cash provided (used) for operations? Is the state appropriation for operations shown as cash provided by financing activities?

e. Look at the college from the point of view of a financial analyst. Compute (1) the interest coverage—revenue bonds (assume all bonds are revenue) and (2) the operating ratio from the Statement of Revenues, Expenses, and Changes in Net Assets. Comment on the availability of unrestricted resources and other relevant items from the Statement of Net Assets. Comment on operating income and other relevant items from the Statement of Revenues, Expenses, and Changes in Net Assets. Do any items in the Statement of Cash Flows seem relevant? If a foundation is reported as a component unit, comment on the availability of resources from the component unit.

9–3. For each of the following, select the letter with the *best* answer:
1. Which of the following is (are) considered by the GASB to be primary users of governmental financial reports?
   a. Investors and creditors.
   b. Citizen groups.
   c. Legislative and oversight officials.
   d. All of the above.
2. Which of the following is true regarding GASB requirements for reporting by special-purpose entities?
   a. All special-purpose entities reporting as governmental activities must prepare both government-wide and fund financial statements.
   b. Special-purpose entities reporting as fiduciary activities may prepare only the statements and (when relevant) RSI schedules required for fiduciary funds.
   c. Both of the above.
   d. Neither of the above.
3. Public colleges and universities may report as:
   a. Special-purpose entities that report as entities engaged in governmental and business-type activities.
   b. Special-purpose entities that report as entities engaged in business-type activities only.
   c. Either of the above.
   d. Neither of the above.
4. Which of the following financial statements would be required for public colleges reporting as special-purpose entities engaged only in business-type activities?
   a. Statement of Net Assets.

b. Statement of Activities.
  c. Statement of Revenues, Expenditures, and Changes in Fund Balances.
  d. Budgetary Comparison Statement.
5. A college had tuition and fees of $33,500,000. Scholarships, for which no services were required, amounted to $1,200,000. Graduate assistantships, for which services were required, amounted to $1,300,000. The amount to be reported by the college as net tuition and fees would be:
  a. $33,500,000
  b. $32,300,000
  c. $32,200,000
  d. $31,000,000
6. A college had total assets of $120,000,000, including $65,000,000 in capital assets, which had accumulated depreciation of $15,000,000. The same college had total liabilities of $75,000,000, including $40,000,000 in debt related to acquisition of capital assets. Restricted resources existed in the amount of $15,000,000. The amount to be reported as unrestricted net assets would be:
  a. $30,000,000
  b. $10,000,000
  c. $20,000,000
  d. $15,000,000
7. Many public colleges and universities report infrastructure assets. When the infrastructure provisions of the reporting standards take effect, public colleges will be required to:
  a. Record and depreciate infrastructure.
  b. Record infrastructure but not depreciate infrastructure.
  c. Record infrastructure and either depreciate or use the modified approach for infrastructure.
  d. Omit any mention of infrastructure.
8. Which of the following is true regarding the Statement of Revenues, Expenses, and Changes in Net Assets for public colleges and universities?
  a. A measure of operations, such as operating income, is required.
  b. The state appropriation for operations is displayed as nonoperating revenue.
  c. Both of the above.
  d. Neither of the above.
9. Which of the following is true regarding the Statement of Cash Flows for a public college or university?
  a. Either the direct or indirect method may be used.
  b. A reconciliation is required, when the direct method is used, reconciling net income to the cash flows provided by operations.

c. Both of the above.
d. Neither of the above.
10. Which of the following is true regarding accounting and reporting standards for public colleges and universities?
    a. GASB *Statement 35* amends GASB *Statement 34* by requiring that public colleges and universities follow *Statement 34* provisions.
    b. GASB *Statement 35* requires those public colleges and universities that are component units of state governments to adopt the provisions of *Statement 34* at the same time the state adopts those requirements.
    c. Both of the above.
    d. Neither of the above.

9–4. For each of the following, select the *best* answer:
1. Which of the following is true regarding the municipal bond market?
    a. Municipal market participants include bond buyers, rating agencies, insurers, underwriters, and bond attorneys.
    b. The Comprehensive Annual Financial Report (CAFR) is especially useful in the secondary market.
    c. Both of the above.
    d. Neither of the above.
2. Which of the following is true regarding reporting by special-purpose entities?
    a. Special-purpose entities that engage only in governmental activities might include fire protection districts, cemetery districts, and sanitation districts.
    b. Special-purpose entities that engage only in one governmental activity are permitted to combine the government-wide and fund financial statements.
    c. Both of the above.
    d. Neither of the above.
3. Which of the following is *not* one of the basic financial statements of a public college or university that engages only in business-type activities?
    a. Statement of Net Assets.
    b. Statement of Cash Flows.
    c. Statement of Revenues, Expenses, and Changes in Fund Balances.
    d. Statement of Revenues, Expenses, and Changes in Net Assets.
4. A public college reported deferred revenues related to its student tuition and fees as of July 1, 2003, in the amount of $650,000. This amount was for the deferred portion of cash collections of summer school revenues for the term ending August 15, 2003. During the fiscal year ended June 30, 2004, $4,350,000 was collected in student tuition and fees, including $700,000 for the deferred portion related to the summer

term ending August 15, 2004. The amount to be reported as student tuition and fee revenue for the year ended June 30, 2004 would be:
 a. $4,300,000
 b. $4,350,000
 c. $5,000,000
 d. $5,050,000

5. A college had tuition and fees for the year ended June 30, 2004, in the amount of $16,400,000. Scholarships, for which no services were required, amounted to $1,300,000. Graduate assistantships, for which services were required, amounted to $1,200,000. The amount to be reported by the college as net tuition and fee revenue would be:
 a. $16,400,000
 b. $15,200,000
 c. $15,100,000
 d. $13,900,000

6. A college had total assets of $110,000,000, including $64,000,000 in capital assets, net of accumulated depreciation. The same college had total liabilities of $50,000,000, including $30,000,000 in debt related to the acquisition of capital assets. Restricted resources amounted to $20,000,000. The amount of net assets—invested in capital assets, net of related debt, would be:
 a. $6,000,000
 b. $14,000,000
 c. $34,000,000
 d. $40,000,000

7. Which of the following is true regarding the Statement of Net Assets of a public college or university reporting as a special-purpose entity engaging in only business-type activities?
 a. A classified approach is required, with current- and long-term assets and liabilities reported separately.
 b. Unrestricted net assets include resources that are expendable at the discretion of the governing board.
 c. Both of the above.
 d. Neither of the above.

8. Which of the following is true regarding the Statement of Revenues, Expenses, and Changes in Net Assets of a public college or university reporting as a special-purpose entity engaging in only business-type activities?
 a. Expenses may be reported by object of expenditure (salaries, supplies, etc.) or on a functional basis (instruction, research, etc.).
 b. Student tuition and fees are to be reported as an operating revenue.
 c. Both of the above.

d. Neither of the above.
9. Which of the following is true regarding the Statement of Cash Flows of a public college or university reporting as a special-purpose entity engaging in only business-type activities?
   a. Interest received on investments is to be reported as an increase in cash flows from operations.
   b. In all cases, capital acquisitions are to be shown as decreases in cash flows from investing activities.
   c. Both of the above.
   d. Neither of the above.
10. Which of the following is true regarding the reporting of state appropriations for operations?
    a. The state appropriation for operations should be reported as a nonoperating revenue in the Statement of Revenues, Expenses, and Changes in Net Assets.
    b. The state appropriation for operations should be reported as an increase in cash flows from noncapital financing activities in the Statement of Cash Flows.
    c. Both of the above.
    d. Neither of the above.

9–5. Assume you are an analyst charged with the responsibility of advising investors regarding the general obligation and revenue bonds of 10 cities. You have Comprehensive Annual Financial Reports for the 10 cities, and each report has received a Certificate of Achievement for Excellence in Financial Reporting from the Government Finance Officers Association. You have decided to investigate the following ratios:
   (1) Net debt per capita
   (2) Net debt to fair value of property
   (3) Net debt to assets
   (4) Debt service to total expenditures—General and debt service funds
   (5) Net assets/expenses
   (6) Unrestricted net assets/expenses
   (7) Unreserved fund balance/revenues—General Fund
   (8) Governmental revenues per capita
   (9) Interest coverage—revenue bonds
   (10) Operating ratio—enterprise funds

Required:
   a. Indicate precisely where in the CAFR you would find data needed to compute each of the ratios. Be specific.
   b. Indicate briefly the purpose of each of the ratios. What would you learn from the numbers calculated?

9–6. Indicate the information you would extract and some ratios you might calculate from the Comprehensive Annual Financial Report for each of the following major areas. Do not limit your answer to the 10 ratios listed in the text.
   a. Analysis of the ability to repay revenue bonds for the Water and Sewer Fund.
   b. Analysis of the ability to repay general obligation debt of a government.
   c. Analysis of the ability to repay a short-term loan to a local bank.
   d. Analysis of the ability to increase services next year without raising taxes.
   e. Analysis of the ability to provide raises to employees next year without raising taxes.
   f. Analysis of the ability to raise taxes next year.
   g. Analysis to see if the budget is under control.

9–7. GASB Statement 34, *Basic Financial Statements—and Management's Discussion and Analysis—for State and Local Governments,* provides guidance for reporting by special-purpose entities. That guidance depends upon whether special-purpose entities are engaged in activities that are governmental-type, business-type only, or fiduciary-type only. Discuss the guidance and list required basic financial statements for:
   a. Governments engaged in governmental-type activities. Include those that are engaged in governmental- and business-type activities, more than one governmental activity, and only one governmental activity.
   b. Governments engaged in business-type activities only.
   c. Governments engaged in fiduciary-type activities only.

9–8. Southern State University had the following account balances as of June 30, 2004. Debits are not distinguished from credits, so assume all accounts have a "normal" balance:

Accounts receivable	$ 325,000
Accounts payable	265,000
Net assets—invested in capital assets, net of related debt	?
Cash and cash equivalents	144,000
Deferred revenue—current	220,000
Endowment investments	6,123,000
General obligation bonds payable (related to capital acquisition)	1,250,000
Inventories	333,000
Short-term investments—unrestricted	1,444,000
Net assets—restricted—nonexpendable	6,123,000
Restricted cash and cash equivalents	92,000
Capital assets, net of depreciation	7,236,000
Revenue bonds payable (related to capital acquisition)	2,500,000
Long-term investments	1,683,000
Long-term liabilities—current portion (related to capital acquisition)	200,000
Net assets—restricted—expendable	1,775,000
Net assets—unrestricted	?

Required:

Prepare, in good form, a Statement of Net Assets for Southern State University as of June 30, 2004.

9–9. Western State University had the following account balances for the year ended and as of June 30, 2004. Debits are not distinguished from credits, so assume all accounts have a "normal" balance.

Student tuition and fee revenue	$ 9,345,000
Scholarship tuition and fee contra revenue	1,210,000
Scholarships and fellowships expense	988,000
State appropriation for operations	10,000,000
Auxiliary enterprise revenue	9,321,000
Salaries—faculty	8,312,000
Capital appropriations	2,100,000
Depreciation expense	3,276,000
Salaries—exempt staff	5,432,000
Capital grants and gifts	1,110,000
Benefits	3,582,000
Federal grants and contracts revenue	1,221,000
Nonexempt wages	4,729,000
State and local grants and contracts revenue	888,000
Gifts	1,345,000
Additions to permanent endowments	900,000
Investment income	873,000
Other operating expenses	2,982,000
Interest on capital-related debt	1,984,000
Net assets, beginning of year	35,217,000

Required:

Prepare, in good form, a Statement of Revenues, Expenses, and Changes in Net Assets for Western State University for the year ended June 30, 2004.

9–10. The New City College reported deferred revenues of $600,000 as of July 1, 2003, the first day of its fiscal year. Record the following transactions related to student tuition and fees and related scholarship allowances for New City College for the year ended June 30, 2004.

   a. The deferred revenues related to unearned revenues for the summer session, which ended in August 2003.

   b. During the fiscal year ended June 30, 2004, student tuition and fees were assessed in the amount of $12,000,000. Of that amount $9,600,000 was collected in cash. Also of that amount, $650,000 pertained to that portion of the 2004 summer session that took place after June 30.

   c. Student scholarships, for which no services were required, amounted to $1,010,000. Students applied these scholarships to their tuition bills at the beginning of each semester.

   d. Student scholarships and fellowships, for which services were required, such as graduate assistantships, amounted to $760,000. These students also applied their scholarship and fellowship awards to their tuition bills at the beginning of each semester.

9–11. Eastern State College had the following trial balance as of July 1, 2003, the first day of its fiscal year (in thousands):

	Debits	Credits
Cash and cash equivalents	$ 330	
Accounts receivable—net	1,100	
Short-term investments	2,400	
Interest receivable—unrestricted	50	
Deposits with bond trustee	1,800	
Restricted cash and cash equivalents	210	
Endowment investments	9,100	
Long-term investments	8,400	
Interest receivable—restricted	200	
Capital assets	22,300	
Accumulated depreciation—capital assets		$ 9,210
Accounts payable and accrued liabilities		800
Deferred revenues		500
Long-term liabilities—current portion		800
Bonds payable (related to capital outlay)		5,000
Compensated absences payable		900
Net assets—invested in capital assets, net of related debt		7,290
Net assets—restricted—nonexpendable		9,100
Net assets—restricted—expendable—debt service		1,800
Net assets—restricted—expendable—capital outlay		500
Net assets—restricted—expendable—other		8,100
Net assets—unrestricted		1,890
Totals	$45,890	$45,890

During the fiscal year ended June 30, 2004, the following transactions occurred (amounts are in thousands):

1. Student tuition and fees were assessed in the amount of $18,300. Scholarship allowances were made, for which no services were required, in the amount of $1,210. Graduate and other assistantships were awarded, for which services were required, in the amount of $1,420. All scholarship and assistantship allowances were credited against student's bills. Collections were made on account in the amount of $15,700.

2. The $500 in deferred revenues relates to cash collected prior to June 30, 2003, and relates to tuition revenue that should be recognized in the current year. $550 of the $18,300 assumed in (1) above applies to fees that should be recognized as revenue in the year ended June 30, 2005.

3. State appropriations were received in cash as follows: $13,020 for general operations and $800 for capital outlay, set aside for specific projects.

4. Federal grants and contracts, for restricted purposes, were received in cash in the amount of $2,310. State and local grants and contracts, also for restricted purposes, were received in cash in the amount of $930.

5. Revenues from auxiliary enterprise operations amounted to $12,300, of which $12,100 was received in cash.
6. Contributions were received in cash as follows: unrestricted, $650; restricted for capital projects, $300; restricted for other purposes, $500.
7. Donors contributed $600 for endowments, the principal of which may not be expended. The income from these endowments is all restricted for operating purposes. The cash was immediately invested.
8. Interest receivable at the beginning of the year was collected.
9. During the year, investment income was earned on investments whose income is unrestricted in the amount of $200, of which $175 was received in cash. Investment income was earned on investments whose income is restricted in the amount of $1,500, of which $1,250 was received in cash.
10. All accounts payable and accrued liabilities as of the end of the previous year were paid in cash at year-end, using unrestricted cash.
11. Unrestricted expenses amounted to: salaries—faculty, $14,123; salaries—exempt staff, $10,111; nonexempt wages, $6,532; benefits, $6,112; other operating expenses, $1,100. Cash was paid in the amount of $36,878; the remainder was payable at year-end.
12. Restricted expenses amounted to: salaries—faculty, $2,256; salaries—exempt staff, $745; nonexempt wages, $213; benefits, $656; other operations, $1,100. Cash was paid in the amount of $4,612; the remainder was payable at year-end.
13. Depreciation was recorded in the amount of $1,410, all charged as unrestricted expense.
14. During the year, expenditures were made for property, plant, and equipment in the amount of $3,265, of which $1,050 was from resources restricted for capital outlay and the remainder was from unrestricted cash.
15. Interest on bonds payable, all related to capital outlay purchases, amounted to $348; all but $22 was paid in cash. Bonds were paid in the amount of $800; next year, $300 will be payable. No new revenue bonds were issued during the year. Unrestricted cash was used for all these transactions.
16. An additional $100 was deposited with the bond trustee, in accord with legal requirements.
17. The accrued liability for compensated absences increased by $100 during the year.
18. All short-term investments existing at the beginning of the year were sold for $2,450. New short-term investments were purchased for $2,650. Unrealized gains were recorded at year-end as follows: short-term investments (unrestricted), $40; long-term investments (restricted) $120; endowment investments, $61.

19. Closing entries were prepared, separately, for each net asset class.

Required:

a. Prepare journal entries for each of the above transactions.
b. (Optional) Prepare a ledger. Enter beginning balances from the trial balance and all transactions.
c. Prepare, in good form, a Statement of Net Assets for Eastern State College as of June 30, 2004.
d. Prepare, in good form, a Statement of Revenues, Expenses, and Changes in Net Assets for Eastern State College for the year ended June 30, 2004.
e. Prepare, in good form, a Statement of Cash Flows for Eastern State College for the year ended June 30, 2004. (Note to instructor: assign this only when detailed coverage is required.) Assume, in entries 11 and 12, that all accounts payable and accrued liabilities apply to suppliers, not employees. Also, in the reconciliation, show an increase in accounts payable and accrued liabilities in the amount of $758,000; this is necessary due to the fact that the account applies to nonoperating as well as operating activities.

Continuous Problem

9–C. Assemble the financial statements prepared for the City of Everlasting Sunshine. These financial statements will be in the solutions to Exercises 5–C, 6–C, 7–C, and 8–C. Assume a population of 20,000 and fair value of property in the amount of $300 million. Compute the following ratios, following the guidance used for the Village of Elizabeth in this chapter:

(1) Net debt per capita.
(2) Net debt to fair value of property.
(3) Net debt to assets.
(4) Debt service to total expenditures—General and debt service funds.
(5) Net assets/expenses.
(6) Unrestricted net assets/expenses.
(7) Unreserved fund balance/revenues—General Fund.
(8) Governmental revenues per capita.
(9) Interest coverage—revenue bonds.
(10) Operating ratio—enterprise funds.

Chapter Ten

Accounting for Not-for-Profit Organizations

Governmental and not-for-profit organizations are distinguished from commercial businesses by the absence of an identifiable individual or group of individuals who hold a legally enforceable residual claim to the excess of revenues over expenses. Generally, governments and not-for-profit organizations offer goods or services that cannot be priced in a way that naturally encourages commercial entrepreneurs to enter the marketplace. Commonly this is because the good or service is subject to free-riding. A public radio broadcast is an example of a service that cannot effectively be restricted to only those individuals choosing to support the public radio station.

This chapter describes the accounting and reporting practices of nongovernmental (private) not-for-profit organizations. A distinguishing characteristic of these organizations is that they are not owned or controlled by a government. The existence of not-for-profit organizations can be explained by heterogeneous demand for the goods or services they provide. The political process works to ensure that governments provide activities supported by a majority of the population. However, when the demand for an activity is not supported by a large proportion of the population, private not-for-profits are created to obtain resources to support the activity. Examples include historic preservation, religious institutions, and humanitarian organizations. The activities of nongovernmental not-for-profits are financed through voluntary contributions and their financial statements are intended primarily for use by present and potential donors.

Chapter 1 indicated that the authority to set GAAP is split between the Financial Accounting Standards Board (FASB), the Governmental Accounting Standards Board (GASB), and the Federal Accounting Standards Advisory Board (FASAB). The FASB has standards-setting authority over business organizations and nongovernmental not-for-profit organizations. The GASB has standards-setting authority over state and local governments, including governmentally related not-for-profit organizations such as hospitals and colleges and universities. Chapters 2 through 8 described accounting for state and local governmental units as outlined by the GASB. Chapter 9 outlined accounting for special-purpose entities and public colleges and universities.

Prior to 1993, accounting for not-for-profit organizations was separated into four categories, and accounting principles were established primarily by the American Institute of Certified Public Accountants (AICPA) in separate audit guides for each.

In 1993 the FASB issued Statement 116: *Accounting for Contributions Received and Contributions Made* and Statement 117: *Financial Statements of Not-for-Profit Organizations.* These statements made drastic changes in measurement and reporting for nongovernmental not-for-profits and are currently effective. These standards apply to all types of nongovernmental, not-for-profit organizations.

The FASB, in Appendix D of *Statement 116,* distinguished a not-for-profit organization from a business as follows:

> an entity that possesses the following characteristics that distinguish it from a business enterprise: (a) contributions of significant amounts of resources from resource providers who do not expect commensurate or proportionate pecuniary return, (b) operating purposes other than to provide goods or services at a profit, and (c) absence of ownership interests like those of business enterprises.

As a result, private-sector not-for-profit organizations are to be distinguished both from business organizations, as indicated, and from governmental units, as defined by the AICPA and reflected in Chapter 1. The AICPA revised two audit and accounting guides, *Not-for-Profit Organizations* (Not-for-Profit Guide)[1] and *Health Care Organizations* (Health-Care Guide).[2] The Health-Care Guide is discussed extensively in Chapter 12. The Not-for-Profit Guide applies only to nongovernmental not-for-profits and includes the following types of organizations:

- Cemetery organizations
- Civic and community organizations
- Colleges and universities (covered in Chapter 11)
- Federated fund-raising organizations
- Fraternal organizations
- Labor unions
- Museums
- Other cultural organizations
- Performing arts organizations
- Political action committees
- Political parties
- Private and community foundations
- Private elementary and secondary schools
- Private libraries
- Professional associations
- Public broadcasting stations
- Religious organizations

---

[1] American Institute of Certified Public Accountants, *AICPA Audit and Accounting Guide: Not-for-Profit Organizations.* (New York: AICPA, 2002).
[2] *AICPA Audit and Accounting Guide: Health Care Organizations.* (New York: AICPA, 2002).

- Research and scientific organizations
- Social and country clubs
- Trade associations
- Voluntary health and welfare organizations
- Zoological and botanical societies

This chapter introduces the FASB and AICPA standards as applied to voluntary health and welfare organizations and other not-for-profit organizations. Chapters 11 and 12 cover nongovernmental colleges and universities and health-care entities, respectively.

ORGANIZATIONS COVERED IN THIS CHAPTER

A **voluntary health and welfare** organization receives most of its support from voluntary contributions and is engaged in activities that promote the general health and well-being of the public. Typically, these organizations generate some revenues through user charges but receive most of their support from others who do not receive direct benefits. For example, a community mental health center may charge patients a fee based on their ability to pay, receive allocations from a United Way drive and direct gifts, get federal and state grants, and receive donated services and materials. Other examples of voluntary health and welfare organizations are family-planning agencies, charities such as the American Heart Association and the American Cancer Society, Meals on Wheels, senior citizen centers, Girl and Boy Scouts, and Big Brothers/Big Sisters.

Other not-for-profit organizations include cemetery associations, civic organizations, fraternal organizations, labor unions, libraries, museums, other cultural institutions, performing arts organizations, political parties, private schools, professional and trade associations, social and country clubs, research and scientific organizations, and religious organizations. Not-for-profit entities that operate essentially as commercial businesses for the direct economic benefit of members or stockholders (such as employee benefit and pension plans, mutual insurance companies, mutual banks, trusts, and farm cooperatives) are specifically excluded, as are governmental units.

OVERVIEW OF NOT-FOR-PROFIT ACCOUNTING

Three Classes of Net Assets

The FASB has identified three classes of net assets: unrestricted, temporarily restricted, and permanently restricted. To be restricted, resources must be restricted by donors or grantors; internally (Board) designated resources are considered unrestricted.

Permanently restricted net assets include permanent endowments (resources that must be invested permanently) and certain assets such as land or artwork that must be maintained or used in a certain way. As the term indicates, these resources are expected to be restricted as long as the organization has custody.

Temporarily restricted net assets include unexpended resources that are to be used for a particular purpose or at a time in the future and resources that are to be invested for a period of time (under a term endowment). Temporarily restricted resources might also be used for the acquisition of a fixed asset. Temporarily restricted net assets come from contributions with donor imposed restrictions and are released from restriction at some point in the future either through the passage of time or as a result of the organization using the resources according to the donor's wishes.

Unrestricted net assets include all other resources such as unrestricted contributions, revenues from providing services, and unrestricted income from investments. Resources are presumed to be unrestricted unless there is evidence of donor-imposed restrictions. Donor-restricted contributions whose restrictions are satisfied in the same accounting period that the contribution is received may also be reported as unrestricted.

Financial Reporting

Statements required are (1) Statement of Financial Position, (2) Statement of Activities, and (3) Statement of Cash Flows. Certain note disclosures are also required and others are recommended. In addition, voluntary health and welfare organizations are required to report a Statement of Functional Expenses that shows expenses by both function and natural classification. A great deal of flexibility is permitted in statement preparation, as long as certain requirements are met.

The **Statement of Financial Position** reports assets, liabilities, and net assets. Assets and liabilities are reported in order of liquidity, or a classified statement may be prepared. Net assets must be broken down into unrestricted, temporarily restricted, and permanently restricted classes. It is not necessary to identify which assets and liabilities are restricted.

The **Statement of Activities** reports revenues, expenses, gains, losses, and reclassifications (between classes of net assets). Organizationwide totals must be provided. Separate revenues, expenses, gains, losses, and reclassifications are also provided for each class of net assets. (Expenses are only reported for unrestricted net assets.)

The **Statement of Cash Flows** uses the standard FASB categories (operating, investing, and financing). Either the indirect or the direct method may be used. The indirect method or the reconciliation schedule for the direct method reconciles the change in *total* net assets to the net cash used or provided by operating activities. Restricted contributions or restricted investment proceeds that will be used for long-term purposes (endowments or plant) are reported as financing activities.

A **Statement of Functional Expenses** is required for voluntary health and welfare organizations. It presents a matrix of expenses classified, on the one hand, by function (various programs, fund-raising, etc.) and, on the other hand, by object or natural classification (salaries, supplies, travel, etc.).

Note Disclosures

Note disclosures are required for all the standard FASB items that are relevant to nonprofit organizations. Additional specific requirements are: (1) policy disclosures related to choices made regarding whether temporarily restricted gifts received and expended in the same period and donated plant are reported first as temporarily restricted or unrestricted; (2) detailed information regarding the nature of temporarily and permanently restricted resources; (3) the amount of unconditional promises receivable in less than one year, one to five years, and more than five years; (4) the amount of the allowance for uncollectible promises receivable; (5) the total of conditional amounts promised; and (6) a description and amount for each group of conditional promises having similar characteristics.

Note disclosures are encouraged for (1) detail of reclassifications, (2) detail of investments, and (3) breakdown of expenses by function and natural classifications.

Accounting, Including Reclassifications of Net Assets

Revenues, expenses, gains, and losses are to be recorded on the full accrual basis. Revenues and expenses should be reported at gross amounts; gains and losses may be reported net. Realized and unrealized investment gains and losses may be reported net.

FASB *Statement 116* requires unconditional promises to give to be recorded as contribution revenues when the promise is made. Conditional promises to give are not recognized as revenues until the conditions are met. If a condition is not met, the potential donor is not bound by the promise. However, conditions are carefully distinguished from restrictions. Conditions require some action on the part of the donee before the gift is given. Restrictions are created when the donor indicates that contributions are to be expended for a particular purpose or in a certain time period. Specifically, contributions may be restricted as to purpose or time or for plant acquisition.

Revenues, including contributions, are considered to be unrestricted unless donor-imposed restrictions apply, either for purpose, time, or plant acquisition. In the case of contributions restricted for purpose or plant acquisition, a presumption is made that subsequent disbursements are made first from restricted resources and any additional disbursements are made from unrestricted resources.

All contributions are to be recorded at fair market value at the date of receipt. Multiyear promises to give are recorded as revenues at the present value of the future collections net of an allowance for estimated uncollectibles. The difference between the previously recorded temporarily restricted revenue at present value amounts and the current value is recorded as contribution revenue, not interest.

If temporarily restricted resources are used, a reclassification is made from temporarily restricted net assets to unrestricted net assets. Reclassifications are made for (1) satisfaction of program restrictions (a purpose restriction by a donor), (2) satisfaction of equipment acquisition restrictions (depreciation of assets classified as temporarily restricted and/or use of temporarily restricted assets to purchase plant), and (3) satisfaction of time restrictions (donor actual or implied restrictions as to when funds should be used).

Expenses are reported only in the unrestricted net asset class. Expenses are to be reported by function. The FASB does not prescribe functional classifications but does describe functions as *program* and *supporting*. Major program classifications should be shown. Supporting activities include management and general, fundraising, and membership development. Other classifications, such as operating income, may be included, but they are not required.

Collections, such as artwork in a museum, may or may not be recorded. To be classified as collections, the items must be held for public display and be protected and preserved. In the event of sale, the proceeds must be reinvested in other collections. If recorded, collections are recorded as permanently restricted assets. If not recorded, extensive note disclosures are required.

With the exception of collections, fixed assets may be recorded as either temporarily restricted or unrestricted, depending on the policy of the organization. This is true both when an asset is acquired with temporarily restricted resources and when it is acquired with unrestricted resources. All fixed assets other than land and museum collections are depreciated. If plant is recorded as temporarily restricted assets, then a reclassification is made each accounting period to unrestricted resources in an amount equal to the depreciation or an allocation of the time the asset is restricted, whichever is shorter.

FASB Statement 124, *Accounting for Certain Investments of Not-for-Profit Organizations* requires that investments in equity securities with determinable fair values and investments in debt securities be carried at fair value. Income from these investments is recorded as increases in unrestricted, temporarily restricted, or permanently restricted net assets, depending upon the presence or absence of donor restrictions or legal requirements. Unrealized gains and losses and realized gains and losses on investments are reported together in the Statement of Activities as unrestricted, temporarily restricted, or permanently restricted gains or losses, again depending on the presence or absence of donor instructions or legal requirements.

Statement 124 does not apply to investments that are accounted for under the equity method or investments in consolidated subsidiaries (in which a not-for-profit owns the majority of the voting stock of a corporation).

FASB Statement 133, *Accounting for Derivative Instruments and Hedging Activities*, requires that investments in derivative instruments be recorded as either assets or liabilities and be measured at fair value. Additionally, Statement of Position 94–3, *Reporting of Related Entities by Not-for-Profit Organizations,* requires consolidation of entities controlled through majority stock ownership or if there is an economic interest or control and the not-for-profit appoints a majority of the related entity's governing board. At the time of this printing, the FASB also had a project to develop further guidelines for combinations of private not-for-profit entities. Some investments (interest in trusts, oil and gas properties, real estate ventures, and closely held companies and partnerships) are not covered by *Statement 124*. In such case, not-for-profits would follow the reporting rules in effect for commercial businesses with similar investments.

Special Topics: Accounting for Contributions

Contributed Services Contributed services are recognized as revenue only when the service (1) creates or enhances nonfinancial assets or (2) requires specialized skills, is provided by someone possessing those skills, and typically would be purchased if not provided by donation. The journal entry to record donated services would debit a fixed asset if the service created or enhanced a nonfinancial asset (e.g., carpenter) or an expense if the service required specialized skills and would have been purchased if not donated (e.g., lawyer). In both cases the credit would be to Contribution Revenue —Unrestricted (donated services), and the amount would be the fair value of the services contributed.

Exchange Transaction It is sometimes difficult to determine whether a transaction is a nonreciprocal gift (i.e., contribution) or an exchange of goods and services. Exchange transactions do not meet the definition of a contribution. Therefore they should be accounted for following accrual basis accounting where revenues are recognized when earned. In contrast to contributions, payments received in advance of exchange transactions are recorded as deferred revenue, a liability, rather than as a revenue. Some payments may be partially exchange transactions and partially contributions. If significant, the two parts should be separately accounted for.

This sometimes becomes an issue in evaluating how to record dues or memberships. Assume that an organization with a June 30 year-end collects annual dues in January. At fiscal year-end, six months remain on these memberships. How these amounts are recorded depends on whether the memberships are deemed to be contributions or exchange transactions.

Assume that the organization is a public radio station, there are no gifts exchanged at the time of membership, and membership provides little more direct benefit than a monthly schedule of programming. Since the benefits of public radio are not restricted to members, the dues have the characteristic of a contribution and would be recorded as follows:

		Debits	Credits
Jan. 1	Cash	5,000	
	Contribution Revenue—Unrestricted		5,000

Assume instead that the organization is a YMCA and that members have access to a gym, pool, and other facilities that nonmembers do not enjoy. In this case the dues have the characteristic of an exchange transaction and would be recorded as follows:

Jan. 1	Cash	5,000	
	Deferred Revenue		5,000
June 30	Deferred Revenue	2,500	
	Membership Revenue Unrestricted		2,500

Intentions to Give Assume that a parishioner informs her church that she has named the church in her will and provides a written copy of the will to the church. At what point should the church record this as a contribution? FASB *Statement 116* explains that an intention to give is not the same thing as an unconditional promise to give. Therefore, the church would make no entry to record a contribution until the individual dies and the probate court declares the will valid.

Transfers to a Not-for-Profit Organization That Holds Contributions for Others

It is common for a not-for-profit organization to accept cash or other assets that are intended to be redirected to other organizations or individuals. For example, an individual transfers cash to a seminary and instructs the seminary to grant a scholarship to a specified student. Under most circumstances, the recipient organization (i.e., the seminary) records the asset. The central issue is whether the recipient organization should record a liability or a contribution as the other half of the journal entry.

FASB Statement 136 *Transfer of Assets to a Not-for-Profit Organization or Charitable Trust That Raises or Holds Contributions for Others* provides guidance on how the original donor, intermediary recipient organization, and final beneficiary should record the transaction. Generally, if the recipient organization agrees to transfer the assets to a specified beneficiary, the recipient organization is deemed to merely be an agent; therefore, a liability, rather than a contribution, is recorded. If the recipient organization has the ability to redirect the assets to another beneficiary, or if the recipient organization and beneficiary are financially interrelated, the transfer is recorded as a contribution.

ILLUSTRATIVE TRANSACTIONS AND FINANCIAL STATEMENTS

In the following section, a beginning trial balance, journal entries, and financial statements for a performing arts organization are provided as an example.

Beginning Trial Balance

Assume that the Performing Arts Organization has the following balances as of June 30, 2004.

PERFORMING ARTS ORGANIZATION Post Closing Trial Balance June 30, 2004		
	Debits	**Credits**
Cash	$ 1,128	
Accounts receivable	240	
Interest receivable	744	
Contributions receivable	996	
Supplies inventories	264	
Investments: current	4,344	
Investments: endowment	42,000	
Land	6,000	
Buildings	14,400	
Accumulated depreciation: buildings		$ 4,800
Equipment	15,000	
Accumulated depreciation: equipment		3,600
		(continued)

(concluded)	Debits	Credits
Accounts payable		64
Grants payable		360
Notes payable		2,400
Deferred revenue		2,400
Long-term debt		9,600
Net assets unrestricted		11,900
Net assets temporarily restricted		7,992
Net assets permanently restricted		42,000
Totals	$85,116	$85,116

Assume that the $7,992 in temporarily restricted net assets is restricted for the following: (1) restricted as to providing continuing professional education for instructors in particular programs, $3,480; (2) restricted for future time periods, $4,272; and (3) restricted for future musical instrument acquisitions, $240. The organization maintains an endowment. Income from this endowment is unrestricted. Also assume Performing Arts Organization reports expenses by function and has Program (performance, ballet school, neighborhood productions, and grants), Management and General, Fund-Raising, and Membership Development as functional categories. Fixed assets are recorded as unrestricted when acquired.

Transactions

During the fiscal year ended June 30, 2005, unrestricted cash receipts included: $240 accounts receivable at the beginning of the year (for tuition); $2,640 in contributions, $1,440 single ticket admission charges, $600 tuition, $480 concessions, and $960 interest revenue.

1.	Cash	6,360	
	Accounts Receivable		240
	Contributions—Unrestricted		2,640
	Admission Revenue—Unrestricted		1,440
	Tuition Revenue—Unrestricted		600
	Concession Revenue—Unrestricted		480
	Interest Revenue—Unrestricted		960

Note that revenue accounts are identified as unrestricted, temporarily restricted, or permanently restricted. It is not necessary to label asset and liability accounts in this manner.

A receivable of $360 was recorded for tuition related to the current fiscal year:

2.	Accounts Receivable	360	
	Tuition Revenue—Unrestricted		360

The deferred revenue liability at the end of the previous year represented the unexpired portion of season tickets. The related performances were completed in the current fiscal year.

	Debits	Credits
3. Deferred Revenue	2,400	
Admission Revenue—Unrestricted		2,400

Season tickets totaling $6,240 were sold in the current year. In addition, 60 memberships were sold at $200 each. Members receive a season ticket ($80 value), but no other direct benefit.

4. Cash	6,240	
Deferred Revenue		6,240
5. Cash	12,000	
Deferred Revenue ($80 × 60)		4,800
Contributions—Unrestricted ($120 × 60)		7,200

Half of the performances were completed by year-end. (($6,240 + 4,800) /2).

6. Deferred Revenue	5,520	
Admission Revenue—Unrestricted		5,520

Interest received on the endowment investments amounted to $2,280. This included $744 accrued at the end of the previous year. Accrued interest at the end of the current year was $240. By agreement with donors, endowment income is unrestricted.

7. Cash	2,280	
Interest Receivable	240	
Interest Receivable		744
Interest Revenue—Unrestricted		1,776

Note: in some instances the trust agreement governing permanently restricted resources may specify that the principal must grow by a certain percentage or by the excess of earnings over a specified annual draw. In such cases, the income that is required to remain in the endowment would be credited to Interest Revenue—Permanently Restricted.

Pledges are received for the following: $1,080 promise to give for unrestricted purposes; $2,280 to support specific programs, and a promise to provide $600 in each of the next five years to support an educational program in those years (the present value of five payments discounted at 6 percent is $2,527). Assume the five-year pledge was made on January 1, 2005. Entry 8b records interest from January 1 to June 30 ($2,527 × 6% × $\frac{6}{12}$ = $76).

	Debits	Credits
8a. Contributions Receivable	5,887	
Contributions—Temporarily Restricted		4,807
Contributions—Unrestricted		1,080
8b. Contributions Receivable	76	
Contributions—Temporarily Restricted		76

No additional contribution revenue is recorded upon collection of the pledge. The journal entry would debit Cash and credit Contributions Receivable.

Cash of $996 pledged in the prior year for unrestricted use in the current year was received.

9. Cash	996	
Contributions Receivable		996

Cash of $3,360 was received on the pledges recorded in journal entry 8a.

10. Cash	3,360	
Contributions Receivable		3,360

Continuing professional education expenses for instructors were incurred and paid. These were supported by restricted gifts as follows: $1,920 performance assistance, $600 ballet school, and $960 neighborhood productions.

11a. Performance Expense—CPE	1,920	
Ballet School Expense—CPE	600	
Neighborhood Productions Expenses—CPE	960	
Cash		3,480
11b. Reclassification from temporarily restricted net assets—		
Satisfaction of Program Restrictions	3,480	
Reclassification to Unrestricted Net Assets—		
Satisfaction of Program Restrictions		3,480
(To record expiration of program restrictions)		

A new organ was donated to the organization. It had a fair value of $22,500.

	Debits	Credits
12. Equipment	22,500	
Contributions—Unrestricted		22,500

The $240 received in a prior year for musical instrument acquisitions, together with an additional $90, was used to acquire percussion instruments.

	Debits	Credits
13a. Equipment	330	
Cash		330
13b. Reclassification from Temporarily Restricted Net Assets—Satisfaction of Plant Acquisition Restrictions	240	
Reclassification to Unrestricted Net Assets—Satisfaction of Plant Acquisition Restrictions		240
(To record expiration of plant acquisition restrictions)		

At the beginning of this year, Temporarily Restricted Net Assets included $4,272 restricted for future time periods. Of this total, $2,100 collected in the prior year plus the $996 received in entry 9 relates to the current year. The time restriction has now expired and these assets are released from restriction.

	Debits	Credits
14. Reclassification from Temporarily Restricted Net Assets—Expiration of Time Restrictions	3,096	
Reclassification to Unrestricted Net Assets—Expiration of Time Restrictions		3,096
(To record expiration of time restrictions)		

A gift of securities with a fair market value of $12,000 is received for the endowment. The principal of the gift is to be maintained indefinitely with interest to be used for unrestricted purposes.

	Debits	Credits
15. Investments—Endowment	12,000	
Contributions—Permanently Restricted		12,000

At year-end, all of the investments had determinable market values. FASB Statement 124: *Accounting for Certain Investments Held by Not-for-Profit Organizations* requires that investments in equity securities with readily determinable values and all debt investments be reported at fair market value. The resulting gains or losses are recorded as increases or decreases in unrestricted net assets, unless unrealized gains or losses are explicitly restricted by donor or by law. It was determined that the endowment investments had a fair value of $2,100 in excess of recorded amounts.

	Debits	Credits
16. Investments—Endowment	2,100	
Gains on Investments—Unrestricted		2,100

Salaries were paid in the following amounts: $2,400 performance, $4,800 ballet school, $600 neighborhood productions, $4,200 management and general, $500 fund raising, and $700 membership development.

	Debits	Credits
17. Performance Expense—Salaries	2,400	
Ballet School Expense—Salaries	4,800	
Neighborhood Productions Expense—Salaries	600	
Management and General Expense—Salaries	4,200	
Fund-Raising Expense—Salaries	500	
Membership Development Expense—Salaries	700	
Cash		13,200

During the year, depreciation is recorded as follows: $720 buildings and $3,330 equipment. The depreciation was allocated to functional categories in the following amounts: $1,610 performance, $840 ballet school, $60 neighborhood productions, $720 management and general, and $520 fund raising, and $300 membership development.

	Debits	Credits
18. Performance Expense—Depreciation	1,610	
Ballet School Expense—Depreciation	840	
Neighborhood Productions Expense—Depreciation	60	
Management and General Expense—Depreciation	720	
Fund-Raising Expense—Depreciation	520	
Membership Development Expense—Depreciation	300	
Accumulated Depreciation—Buildings		720
Accumulated Depreciation—Equipment		3,330

To assist in school productions, $960 in grants were awarded to local schools. Of that amount, $840 was paid in addition to the $360 recorded as a payable in the beginning trial balance.

	Debits	Credits
19. Grant Expense	960	
Grants Payable	360	
Cash		1,200
Grants Payable		120

Supplies were purchased for the following activities: $720 performance, $600 ballet school, $120 neighborhood productions, $480 management and general, $240 fund raising, and $120 membership development. $2,316 was paid during the year, including $64 of the beginning accounts payable.

	Debits	Credits
20. Performance Expense—Supplies	720	
Ballet School Expense—Supplies	600	
Neighborhood Productions Expense—Supplies	120	
Management and General Expense—Supplies	480	
Fund Raising Expense—Supplies	240	
Membership Development Expense—Supplies	120	
Accounts Payable	64	
Cash		2,316
Accounts Payable		28

The only supplies on hand at the beginning of the year ($264) were office supplies used for management and general administration. Supply inventories (also for management and general purposes) at year-end were zero except for office supplies ($180).

	Debits	Credits
21. Management and General Expense—Supplies	84	
Supplies Inventories		84

Interest expense in the amount of $720 was paid during the year, along with $500 of the principal of the notes payable and $400 of the long-term debt. Interest expense was allocated to functional categories in the following amounts: $256 performance, $180 ballet school, $20 neighborhood productions, $200 management and general, $32 fund raising, and $32 membership development.

	Debits	Credits
22. Performance Expense—Interest	256	
Ballet School Expense—Interest	180	
Neighborhood Productions Expense—Interest	20	

	Debits	Credits
Management and General Expense—Interest	200	
Fund Raising Expense—Interest	32	
Membership Development Expense—Interest	32	
Notes Payable	500	
Long-Term Debt	400	
Cash		1,620

Note that revenues are identified as unrestricted, temporarily restricted, or permanently restricted. All expenses appear in the financial statements as unrestricted and entries 11b, 13b, and 14 have been made in response to temporarily restricted net assets being released from restriction due to the expiration of time restrictions or the satisfaction of program restrictions.

Closing entries for the three categories of net assets are as follows:

		Debits	Credits
23.	Contributions—Unrestricted	33,420	
	Admission Revenue—Unrestricted	9,360	
	Interest Revenue—Unrestricted	2,736	
	Concession Revenue—Unrestricted	480	
	Tuition Revenue—Unrestricted	960	
	Gains on Investments—Unrestricted	2,100	
	Reclassification to Unrestricted Net Assets— Expiration of Time Restrictions	3,096	
	Reclassification to Unrestricted Net Assets— Satisfaction of Plant Acquisition Restrictions	240	
	Reclassification to Unrestricted Net Assets— Satisfaction of Program Restrictions	3,480	
	Performance Expense—Total		6,906
	Ballet School Expense—Total		7,020
	Neighborhood Productions Expense—Total		1,760
	Management and General Expense—Total		5,684
	Grant Expense		960
	Fund Raising Expense—Total		1,292
	Membership Development Expense—Total		1,152
	Net Assets—Unrestricted		31,098
24.	Contributions—Temporarily Restricted	4,883	
	Net Assets—Temporarily Restricted	1,933	
	Reclassification from Temporarily Restricted Net Assets— Expiration of Time Restrictions		3,096
	Reclassification from Temporarily Restricted Net Assets— Satisfaction of Plant Acquisition Restrictions		240
	Reclassification from Temporarily Restricted Net Assets— Satisfaction of Program Restrictions		3,480

	Debits	Credits
25. Contributions—Permanently Restricted	12,000	
Net Assets—Permanently Restricted		12,000

Financial Statements

FASB *Statement 117* requires three basic statements for nonprofit organizations: (1) Statement of Activities, (2) Statement of Financial Position, and (3) Statement of Cash Flows. Voluntary health and welfare organizations are required also to present a Statement of Functional Expenses, and other not-for-profits are encouraged to provide the information included in that statement.

Statement of Activities   FASB *Statement 117* provides flexibility in this statement and illustrates a variety of formats. Requirements are to provide totals for revenues, expenses, gains, losses, the amounts of assets released from restriction, and the change in net assets for each of the three classes (unrestricted, temporarily restricted, and permanently restricted). Generally, revenues and expenses are reported gross, and gains and losses may be reported net. Expenses must be reported by functional classifications, either in the statements or the notes. The functional expense categories are not dictated, but the illustrative examples include Programs, Management and General, Fund-Raising, and Membership Development.

Illustration 10–1 presents a Statement of Activities for the Performing Arts Organization. Note that all expenses appear in the unrestricted category and that the net assets released from restrictions (i.e., the effects of entries 11b, 13b, and 14) appear at the bottom of the revenue section as increases in unrestricted net assets and decreases in temporarily restricted net assets. Because permanently restricted net assets result from permanent donor imposed restrictions, no such reclassification should occur for these resources.

Statement of Financial Position   Again, more than one format is possible for this statement. However, *Statement 117* illustrates a comparative statement showing organizationwide totals, with assets organized according to liquidity and liabilities according to term. In place of an equity section, the statement presents separate totals for unrestricted, temporarily restricted, and permanently restricted net assets. Some organizations present additional details of unrestricted net assets, such as net assets internally designated for some purpose or unrestricted assets invested in property, plant, and equipment net of related debt. Illustration 10–2 presents the Statement of Financial Position for the Performing Arts Organization.

Statement of Cash Flows   The third required statement is the Statement of Cash Flows. Either the direct or indirect method may be used. The indirect method is presented in Illustration 10–3. Illustration 11–4 presents a cash flow statement using the direct method for a private not-for-profit college. Either method is permitted

ILLUSTRATION 10–1

Income Statement

PERFORMING ARTS ORGANIZATION
Statement of Activities
For the Year Ended June 30, 2005

	Unrestricted	Temporarily Restricted	Permanently Restricted	Total
Revenues, gains, and other support:				
Contributions	$33,420	$4,883	$12,000	$ 50,303
Admission revenues	9,360			9,360
Tuition	960			960
Concessions	480			480
Interest	2,736			2,736
Net gains on endowment investments	2,100			2,100
Net assets released from restrictions:				
Satisfaction of program/use restrictions	3,480	(3,480)		
Satisfaction of plant acquisition restrictions	240	(240)		
Expiration of time restrictions	3,096	(3,096)		
Total revenues, gains, and other support	55,872	(1,933)	12,000	65,939
Expenses				
Performance	6,906			6,906
Ballet school	7,020			7,020
Neighborhood productions	1,760			1,760
Grant expense	960			960
Management and general	5,684			5,684
Fund raising	1,292			1,292
Membership development	1,152			1,152
Total expenses	24,774			24,774
Change in net assets	31,098	(1,933)	12,000	41,165
Net assets 7/1/04	11,900	7,992	42,000	61,892
Net assets 6/30/05	$42,998	$6,059	$54,000	$103,057

under *Statement 117*. Generally, classification of cash flows follows the format for business entities (operating, investing, and financing activities). However, *Statement 117* requires that donor restricted cash that must be used for long-term purposes is classified as cash flows from financing activities.

Statement of Functional Expenses Voluntary health and welfare organizations are required to prepare a Statement of Functional Expenses that shows expenses detailed by both function (program, management and general, etc.) and object (salaries, supplies, etc.). The FASB also recommends that other not-for-profit organizations disclose this information. Illustration 10–4 presents a Statement of Functional Expenses for the Performing Arts Organization.

ILLUSTRATION 10–2

PERFORMING ARTS ORGANIZATION
Statement of Financial Position
June 30, 2005 and 2004

	2005	2004
Assets:		
Cash	$ 10,218	$ 1,128
Short-term investments	4,344	4,344
Accounts receivable	360	240
Interest receivable	240	744
Supplies inventories	180	264
Contributions receivable	2,603	996
Land, buildings and equipment, net of accumulated depreciation of 12,450 and 8,400	45,780	27,000
Long-term investments	56,100	42,000
Total assets	119,825	76,716
Liabilities:		
Accounts payable	28	64
Grants payable	120	360
Deferred revenues	5,520	2,400
Notes payable	1,900	2,400
Long-term debt	9,200	9,600
Total liabilities	16,768	14,824
Net Assets:		
Unrestricted	42,998	11,900
Temporarily restricted	6,059	7,992
Permanently restricted	54,000	42,000
Total net assets	103,057	61,892
Total liabilities and net assets	$119,825	$76,716

Alternative Procedure for Recording Fixed Assets

As indicated earlier in this chapter, the FASB gives not-for-profit organizations the option of (1) recording all fixed assets as unrestricted and reclassifying resources donated to purchase fixed assets to unrestricted net assets (entries 13a and 13b) or (2) recording fixed assets as temporarily restricted and reclassifying net assets to unrestricted as the asset is depreciated or over the term of the restriction, if shorter. If the latter method were followed, entries 13a and 13b would be as follows:

(Alternative entries)	Debits	Credits
13a. Equipment	330	
Cash		330

ILLUSTRATION 10–3

PERFORMING ARTS ORGANIZATION
Statement of Cash Flows
For the Year Ended June 30, 2005

Cash flows from operating activities:		
Change in net assets	$ 41,165	
Depreciation expense	4,050	
Noncash contributions	(34,500)	
Gains on endowment investments	(2,100)	
Increase in accounts receivable	(120)	
Decrease in interest receivable	504	
Decrease in supplies inventories	84	
Increase in contributions receivable	(1,607)	
Decrease in accounts payable	(36)	
Decrease in grants payable	(240)	
Increase in deferred revenues	3,120	
Net cash provided by operating activities		$10,320
Cash flows from investing activities:		
Purchase of equipment	(330)	
Net cash provided by investing activities		(330)
Cash flows from financing activities:		
Payment of notes payable	(500)	
Payment of long-term debt	(400)	
Net cash provided by financing activities		(900)
Net increase in cash		9,090
Cash July 1, 2004		1,128
Cash June 30, 2005		$10,218
Noncash investing and financing activities:		
Gift of investments	$ 12,000	
Gift of equipment	22,500	
Supplemental disclosure of cash flow information:		
Cash paid during the year for interest	$ 720	

(Alternative entries)	Debits	Credits
13b. Reclassification from Unrestricted Net Assets— Use of Unrestricted Assets to Acquire Fixed Assets	90	
Reclassification to Temporarily Restricted Net Assets— Use of Unrestricted Assets to Acquire Fixed Assets		90

Similar entries would be made for all acquisitions of fixed assets using unrestricted resources (e.g., entry 12). Entry 18, to record depreciation, would be followed by an additional entry to reclassify the depreciated portion of the assets:

ILLUSTRATION 10–4

PERFORMING ARTS ORGANIZATION
Statement of Functional Expenses
For the Year Ended June 30, 2005

	Program Services					Supporting Services				Total Expenses
	Performance	Ballet School	Neighborhood Productions	Grants	Total	Management	Fund Raising	Membership	Total	
Salaries	$2,400	$4,800	$ 600		$ 7,800	$4,200	$ 500	$ 700	$5,400	$13,200
Continuing education	1,920	600	960		3,480					3,480
Supplies	720	600	120		1,440	564	240	120	924	2,364
Grants				$960	960					960
Interest	256	180	20		456	200	32	32	264	720
Depreciation	1,610	840	60		2,510	720	520	300	1,540	4,050
Total expenses	$6,906	$7,020	$1,760	$960	$16,646	$5,684	$1,292	$1,152	$8,128	$24,774

(Alternative entry)	Debits	Credits
18b. Reclassification from Temporarily Restricted Net Assets—Satisfaction of Fixed Asset Restrictions	4,050	
Reclassification to Unrestricted Net Assets—Satisfaction of Fixed Asset Restrictions		4,050

PERFORMANCE EVALUATION

The not-for-profit organizations described in this chapter apply accrual accounting concepts and measure revenues and expenses in much the same manner as business enterprises. In the Statement of Activities, change in net assets is computationally equivalent to net income reported on the financial statements of business enterprises (i.e., revenues − expenses). However, change in net assets is not as effective a performance measure for not-for-profits as net income is for businesses. This is not surprising since not-for-profit organizations are established for purposes other than generating net income.

It is commonly perceived that not-for-profit organizations should not generate surpluses at all. However, there are a number of reasons why a not-for-profit organization would need to generate a surplus (positive change in net assets). These include:

- Establishing working capital.
- Expanding or replacing physical facilities.
- Retiring debt.
- Continuing a program beyond the period that initial funding is provided.

If these needs are satisfied, a not-for-profit organization may also find it desirable to draw upon earlier surpluses and operate at a deficit for a period of time. For these reasons, a positive change in net assets is not inherently either a good or a bad condition.

The financial measure of greatest interest in evaluating not-for-profit organizations is the ratio of program service expenses to total expenses. The ratio is readily calculated from the financial statements. For example, Illustration 10–4 reports program expenses totaling $16,646 and total expenses of $24,774 for a ratio of approximately 67 percent. The ratio is a measure of the efficiency of a not-for-profit organization in utilizing resources to fulfill its mission, rather than for fund raising and administration. The ratio is commonly reported in rankings of charitable organizations. For example, *Money* magazine does an annual ranking of charitable organizations. The Better Business Bureau recommends a minimum ratio of 60 percent.

Because of the importance of this ratio, care is taken in the allocation of costs between program and supporting expense categories. Not-for-profits frequently require employees to keep detailed records of their time for purposes of allocating salary and benefit costs. Additionally, depreciation is commonly allocated on the basis of square feet dedicated to program versus administrative functions.

The American Institute of CPAs issued Statement of Position 98–02 which establishes guidance for allocation of costs that involve fund raising. Examples of the activities covered by the statement are mass mailings, annual dinners, and TV or radio commercials. The statement indicates that it is appropriate to allocate costs from fund raising to another function when the activity meets three conditions:

1. Purpose: The purpose of the joint activity includes accomplishing program functions. (Merely asking the audience to make contributions is not an activity that fulfills the organization's mission.)
2. Audience: The audience is selected based on characteristics other than ability or likelihood to make contributions.
3. Content: The activity calls for specific action by the recipient that will help accomplish the organization's mission.

If any of the conditions are not met, all costs of the joint activity should be reported as fund raising.

SUMMARY OF ACADEMIC RESEARCH

Increasingly, not-for-profit organizations are the subject of academic studies. Most of these studies focus on the ratio of program service expenses to total expenses (i.e., the program services ratio). Tinkleman examines the relationship between charities' program services ratios and subsequent donations.[3] Using financial information filed with the State of New York, he finds that more efficient charities are rewarded with greater donations. This suggests that donors consider the efficiency of charitable organizations, as reflected in their financial ratios. Another study finds that governing boards consider the program expense ratio in determining executive compensation paid to managers of charitable organizations.[4]

Although these studies demonstrate that not-for-profit financial reports are useful, another study suggests that nonfinancial performance measures are of greater importance to individuals making donation decisions. Using an experimental setting, Khumawala and Gordon find that individuals who were asked to make donation decisions were most interested in nonfinancial disclosures about the purpose of the organization and its accomplishments.[5] Presently these disclosures are voluntary and not uniform across not-for-profit organizations.

SUMMARY OF NOT-FOR-PROFIT ACCOUNTING AND REPORTING

Not-for-profit organizations in the private sector are required to follow the standards of reporting outlined in this chapter. The FASB requires three statements:

---

[3] D. Tinkleman, "Factors Affecting the Relation Between Donations to Not-for-profit Organizations and an Efficiency Ratio," *Research in Governmental and Nonprofit Accounting* 10 (1999), pp. 135–62.
[4] W. Baber, P. Daniel, and A. Roberts, "Compensation Paid to Executives of Charitable Organizations: An Empirical Study of the Role of Accounting Performance," *Accounting Review* 77 (2002).
[5] S. Khumawala and T. Gordon, "Bridging the Credibility of GAAP: Individual Donors and the New Accounting Standards for Nonprofit Organizations," *Accounting Horizons* 11, no. 3 (1997) pp. 45–68.

(1) Statement of Financial Position, (2) Statement of Activities, and (3) Statement of Cash Flows. A Statement of Functional Expenses is required for voluntary health and welfare organizations and encouraged for all not-for-profit organizations. The FASB allows flexibility in the preparation of financial statements.

Full accrual accounting is required, and depreciation is recorded on fixed assets. Net assets are classified as (1) unrestricted, (2) temporarily restricted, or (3) permanently restricted. Contributions are recorded as revenue in the appropriate net asset class when unconditional. This means that unconditional pledges, even multiyear pledges, are recorded as revenue when pledged. Temporarily restricted net assets are restricted as to (1) purpose, (2) time period, or (3) plant acquisition. All expenses are recorded and reported as unrestricted expenses. As temporarily restricted resources are released from restrictions, reclassification entries are made, increasing unrestricted net assets.

QUESTIONS AND EXERCISES

10–1. Write the letter corresponding with the *best* answer to each of the following questions:

1. Which of the following organizations would *not* be required to follow the accounting and financial reporting pronouncements of FASB *Statements 116* and *117?*
    a. The Boy Scouts of America
    b. Western State University
    c. St. Francis Catholic Hospital
    d. American Institute of Certified Public Accountants

2. The three classes of net assets required by the FASB are:
    a. Current, endowment, and plant.
    b. Restricted, unrestricted, and plant.
    c. Unrestricted, temporarily restricted, and permanently restricted.
    d. Unrestricted, temporarily restricted, and endowment.

3. The three statements required by the FASB for all nonprofit organizations are:
    a. Statement of Financial Position, Statement of Activities, and Statement of Cash Flows.
    b. Statement of Financial Position, Statement of Activities, and Statement of Functional Expenses.
    c. Statement of Financial Position; Statement of Revenues, Expenditures, and Changes in Fund Balances; and Statement of Changes in Financial Position.
    d. Statement of Financial Position; Statement of Activities; and Statement of Revenues, Expenditures, and Changes in Fund Balances.

4. A donor made a pledge in December 2004 to a nonprofit organization with the intent to give the cash in 2005 for unrestricted use in 2005. The nonprofit organization should:
   a. Record the pledge as deferred revenue in 2004 and as unrestricted revenue in 2005.
   b. Record the pledge as deferred revenue in 2004 and as temporarily restricted revenue in 2005.
   c. Record the pledge as temporarily restricted revenue in 2004 and reclassify the amount to unrestricted in 2005.
   d. Record the pledge as unrestricted revenue in 2004.

5. A donor gave $10,000 to a nonprofit organization in 2004 with an expressed purpose restriction. In 2004, the nonprofit organization expended $10,000 for that purpose but using cash held as a part of unrestricted resources. In 2004, the nonprofit organization should:
   a. Report that the funds came from restricted resources.
   b. Report that the funds came from unrestricted resources.
   c. Report that the funds came from either restricted or unrestricted resources, depending on institutional policy.
   d. Consider the $10,000 as deferred revenues until expended.

6. Which of the following is *not* true regarding the reporting of expenses by nonprofit organizations?
   a. All expenses are considered to be unrestricted.
   b. Expenses must be reported by function, either in the Statement of Activities or in the notes.
   c. The FASB has dictated that expenses be reported in the categories of Program and Supporting.
   d. Expenses should be reported on the full accrual basis.

7. With regard to accounting for plant, the nonprofit accounting and reporting standards:
   a. Require that all plant be recorded as unrestricted assets when acquired, and then depreciated.
   b. Require that all plant be recorded in a plant fund.
   c. Allow plant acquired with restricted resources to be recorded as either unrestricted or temporarily restricted.
   d. Do not provide for depreciation.

8. A nonprofit is seeking a donation of services it would normally purchase if not provided by donation. What additional characteristics must the service have to recognize the contribution as revenue?
   a. The service creates or enhances a nonfinancial asset.
   b. The service requires specialized skills and is provided by individuals possessing those skills.

324 Chapter 10

  c. Both *a* and *b* above.
  d. Either *a* or *b* above.
 9. A donor contributed cash to a nonprofit organization and stated in writing that it was to be expended in the following fiscal year for any purpose approved by the board of the nonprofit organization. When the cash was contributed, it was placed in the temporarily restricted net asset class. The amount would be released from restrictions:
  a. When the nonprofit organization expended the funds.
  b. In the following fiscal year, regardless of whether or not the organization had expended the funds.
  c. In the year of the donation or in the following fiscal year, depending on the decision of the nonprofit organization.
  d. As one-half in the year of donation and one-half in the following fiscal year.
 10. A donor made a conditional promise to give $10 million in unrestricted resources to a nonprofit organization if it could raise the same amount from other donors. The nonprofit organization should:
  a. Not record the $10 million as revenue until the condition is met.
  b. Record the $10 million as a temporarily restricted revenue, and then reclassify it to unrestricted when the condition is met.
  c. Record the $10 million as unrestricted income when the promise is made.
  d. Record the $10 million as temporarily restricted revenue and record expenses from temporarily restricted resources when incurred.

10–2. Write the letter corresponding with the *best* answer to each of the following questions:
 1. In January 2004 a donor pledges $1,000 per year for each of the next five years beginning in 2004 supporting operations of a charitable organization in those years. How should the pledge be reported?
  a. The pledge should be recorded at its present value and unrestricted contribution revenue recognized in 2004.
  b. The pledge should be recorded at its present value and unrestricted contribution revenue recognized for the amount to be received in 2004. The present value of amounts to be received in other years is recorded as temporarily restricted contribution revenue in 2004.
  c. Unrestricted contribution revenue should be recognized each year in the amount of $1,000.
  d. Unrestricted contribution revenue of $5,000 should be recognized in 2004.
 2. In 2004 a charity purchased securities for $500,000 with funds given to it by a donor for permanent investment in an endowment. The earnings of the endowment are to support ongoing program expenses. At December 31, the securities had accrued $3,000 in investment income. At

December 31, 2004, what amount of the securities and accrued interest should be included as current assets in the classified balance sheet?
a. $0.
b. $3,000.
c. $500,000.
d. $503,000.

3. On December 31, 2004, Hyers Museum received an $8,000,000 donation of stock with donor stipulations as follows:
   - Shares valued at $5,000,000 are to be sold with the proceeds used to erect a new building. *Temporarily*
   - Shares valued at $3,000,000 are to be maintained in endowment with the earnings to be used to support ongoing programs.

   As a consequence of the donation of stock, how much should Hyers report as permanently restricted net assets?
   a. $0.
   b. $3,000,000.
   c. $5,000,000.
   d. $8,000,000.

4. In 2004 a private college received $50,000 designated by the donor for scholarships. The college selected the students and awarded the scholarships in 2004. How should the transactions be reported on the Statement of Activities for the year ended 2004?
   a. As both an increase and decrease of $50,000 in net assets.
   b. As a decrease only in net assets.
   c. By footnote disclosure only.
   d. The $50,000 was initially recorded as a liability and would not affect the Statement of Activities.

5. On December 28, 2004, a church member donated $5,000 to his church to pay the medical bills of a specified needy family. The medical bills were paid by the church in 2005. In its 2004 financial statements, how should the church report the $5,000? *Agency*
   a. As an unrestricted contribution.
   b. As a temporarily restricted contribution.
   c. As a liability.
   d. In the footnotes only.

6. In an audit of a not-for-profit organization, you discover costs related to a mailing. The costs included $10,000 in postage, $18,000 in return envelopes and postage, printing costs of $3,000, and consultant's fees of $5,000. Your investigation revealed that 80 percent of the lines in the promotional material described the organization and what it accomplished and 20 percent was devoted to a fund-raising appeal. The

mailing was sent to previous donors. The amount that would be reported as fund-raising expense would be:
a. $0.
b. $18,000.
c. $28,800.
d. $36,000.

7. A not-for-profit organization has investments in equity securities with determinable fair values. At year-end the fair value of the securities had increased by $5,000. How should the resulting gain be reported in the organization's financial statements?
   a. Not-for-profits use the lower of cost or market. Since the securities increased in value, no gain is recognized.
   b. As an increase in permanently restricted net assets.
   c. As an increase in unrestricted net assets unless donor restrictions or legal restrictions stipulate how the income could be used.
   d. Since no cash was received or expended, it would not be reported.

8. A storm damaged the roof of a new building owned by a not-for-profit organization. A supporter of the organization, a professional roofer, repaired the roof at no charge. How should the repair be reported in the organization's financial statements?
   a. Be reported by footnote disclosure only.
   b. Be reported as both an increase in contributions and expenses for the fair value of any materials donated.
   c. Be reported as both an increase in contributions and expenses for the fair value of any materials donated, as well as the fair value of the roofing labor.
   d. Since no cash was received or expended, it would not be reported.

9. A not-for-profit organization expanded their current building, providing a storage facility. A supporter of the organization, a professional carpenter, built cabinets necessary for the storage of specialized supplies and equipment. How should the donated cabinets be reported in the organization's financial statements?
   a. Be reported by footnote disclosure only.
   b. Be reported as both an increase in contributions and expenses for the fair value of any materials and labor donated.
   c. Be reported as both an increase in contributions and fixed assets for the fair value of any materials and labor donated.
   d. Since no cash was received or expended, it would not be reported.

10. A not-for-profit museum receives a contribution of art. Assuming the donated art is to be sold, the museum need not recognize the contribution if the proceeds are to be used to:

a. Support general museum activities.
b. Acquire other items for the art collection.
c. Purchase a building to house collections.
d. None of the above.

10–3. For the following transactions and events, indicate what effect each will have on the three classes of net assets using this format. Put an X in the appropriate column. If the net assets are unaffected, leave the column blank.

	Unrestricted Net Assets		Temporarily Restricted Net Assets		Permanently Restricted Net Assets	
	Increase	Decrease	Increase	Decrease	Increase	Decrease
Ex1			X			
Ex2	X			X		

Ex1: Received a pledge from a donor to provide $1,000 a year to support summer educational programs to be held each July for five years.

Ex2: A time restriction on cash received in a prior year expired in the current period.

1. A capital campaign in support of a new building brought in pledges of $150,000.
2. Cash collections on the pledges described in (1) totaled $97,000 in the current year.
3. $25,000 was expended from the capital campaign on architects' fees. The organization records all fixed assets in the unrestricted class of net assets.
4. Interest income on the unexpended capital campaign funds amounted to $560. No restriction exists as to how the income may be used.
5. Operating revenues (admission fees and gift shop sales) amounted to $80,000.
6. Salaries, utilities, and operating supplies totaled $76,000.
7. Depreciation on plant and equipment amounted to $25,000.
8. Volunteers staffing the gift shop contributed 500 hours. The services did not require specialized skills but are estimated at a value of $8.50 per hour.
9. Securities valued at $100,000 are received for permanent endowment. Income earned on the endowment is to be used to sponsor visiting speakers.
10. Interest and dividends received on the endowment totaled $2,000.

10–4. With regard to FASB standards of accounting and reporting for nonprofit organizations, do the following:

a. List the financial reports required of all nonprofit organizations. What additional report is required for voluntary health and welfare organizations?

    b. List the three classes of net assets.
    c. Outline revenue recognition criteria for resources restricted for (1) time and (2) purpose.
    d. Describe the differences, in accounting for contributions, between a condition and a restriction.
    e. Outline the accounting required for property, plant, and equipment. Include accounting for plant acquired with both unrestricted and restricted resources.
    f. Outline requirements for recognizing contributed services as revenues.
    g. Outline accounting and reporting for multiyear pledges.
    h. Outline accounting and reporting for investments.

10–5. Obtain a copy of the annual report of a private not-for-profit organization. Answer the following questions from the report. (Use the site search button or site index to locate the annual report.)

Note: Many organizations are now putting their annual reports on their websites. For examples try:

The American Accounting Association	www.aaa-edu.org
American Institute of CPAs	www.aicpa.org
Habitat for Humanity	www.habitat.org
American Diabetes Association	www.diabetes.org
Save the Children	www.savethechildren.org

    1. What financial statements are presented?
    2. How are contribution revenues recognized?
    3. Does the organization have temporarily restricted net assets? What is the nature of the restrictions?
    4. Does the organization have permanently restricted net assets?
    5. Compute the ratio of program service expenses to total expenses.

10–6. Hope Haven, a voluntary health and welfare nonprofit organization, follows FASB standards of accounting and reporting. Record in journal form the following transactions, indicating in which net asset classification each entry is made. Hope Haven has a calendar fiscal year. Closing entries are not required.
    1. A pledge of $25,000 was made on December 28, 2004, indicating that the funds would be available for unrestricted purposes in 2005.
    2. A pledge of $18,000 was made on December 29, 2004, indicating that the funds should be expended for free counseling services in 2005.
    3. The books were opened for 2005. Reclassify the resources that were temporarily restricted by donors for unrestricted use in 2005.
    4. Cash was received for both pledges on January 2, 2005.
    5. Cash outlays of $9,000 were made for the free counseling services (mentioned in transaction 2) during 2005. None of the unrestricted resources (mentioned in transaction 1) were expended in 2005.

Chapter Eleven

College and University Accounting—Private Institutions

As indicated in Chapters 1 and 10, authority to establish accounting and financial reporting principles for certain organizations is split between the Financial Accounting Standards Board (FASB) and the Governmental Accounting Standards Board (GASB). This split is especially significant for colleges and universities. Private institutions, such as Northwestern University and Notre Dame, are subject to the standards issued by the FASB, and public institutions, such as the University of Georgia and Northern Illinois University, are subject to the standards issued by the GASB. This chapter illustrates FASB principles for private institutions, and Chapter 9 illustrates GASB standards for public institutions.

Accounting standards for colleges and universities evolved through the efforts of the **National Association of College and University Business Officers (NACUBO)**, an industry group composed of university financial vice presidents, comptrollers, and other finance officers. In 1973, the American Institute of Certified Public Accountants (AICPA) issued *Audits of Colleges and Universities,* which incorporated and modified the principles issued by NACUBO. With respect to private colleges and universities, the 1973 *Audit Guide* is now superceded by *Accounting and Audit Guide: Not-for-Profit Organizations*, issued in 2002 for all private not-for-profit organizations.

As mentioned in Chapter 10, the FASB has issued a number of pronouncements that relate to all private sector not-for-profit organizations, including colleges and universities. These include *SFAS 93,* which requires depreciation, *SFAS 116,* which provides regulations for accounting for contributions, *SFAS 117,* which provides guidelines for display in financial statements of not-for-profit organizations, and *SFAS 124,* which requires that investments in equity securities with determinable fair values and all investments in debt securities be reported at fair value and that unrealized gains and losses be reported with realized gains and losses in the Statement of Activities. Additionally, FASB issued *Statement 136, Transfers of Assets to a Not-for-Profit Organization That Raises or Holds Contributions for Others.* This statement was described in Chapter 10.

This chapter describes and illustrates FASB and AICPA requirements for private-sector not-for-profit colleges and universities. In addition, this chapter introduces the concept of split-interest agreements which also apply to the organizations covered in Chapters 10 and 12. The chapter does not illustrate accounting for commercial proprietary (for profit) schools. Those organizations follow FASB standards applicable to other commercial businesses.

OVERVIEW OF PRIVATE COLLEGE AND UNIVERSITY ACCOUNTING

Net Asset Classification

Private colleges and universities are required to report net assets in the same manner as other not-for-profits within three categories: **unrestricted**, **temporarily restricted**, and **permanently restricted**. As is the case for other not-for-profit organizations, donors or grantors must establish the restrictions; resources subject to designations by the governing board would be considered unrestricted.

Unrestricted inflows include tuition and fees, governmental appropriations (some states provide per student grants to private institutions), unrestricted contributions, unrestricted income on endowments and other investments, gains on investments, and sales and services of **auxiliary enterprises**. Auxiliary enterprises are college operations that are generally intended to be self-supporting, such as bookstores, dormitories, food service operations, and (for some institutions) college athletics. Unrestricted outflows are generally reported in categories of Educational and General, Auxiliary Enterprises, and Other Gains and Losses. Educational and General is often classified functionally as instruction, research, public service, academic support, student services, institutional support, operation and maintenance of physical plant, and scholarships and fellowships.

Temporarily restricted inflows include contributions temporarily restricted for time, purpose, plant acquisition, and term endowments. Temporarily restricted inflows include split interest agreements such as annuity agreements, in which donors contribute funds that are to be invested, with a certain portion going to the donors or other outside parties and the rest going to the institution. Life income agreements, also temporarily restricted, pay investment income in total to the donor during the donor's lifetime, with the institution receiving the proceeds upon the death of the donor. Also in this category are temporarily restricted investment income and gains and losses on investments. All expenses are reported in the unrestricted net asset section of the Statement of Activities. However, temporarily restricted net assets may decrease as the result of net assets released from restrictions and payments to annuity and life income beneficiaries.

Permanently restricted inflows include permanently restricted contributions for endowments and for plant and museum collections that are intended to be maintained permanently. It should be noted that funds held as endowments might be classified in any of the three net asset types. If a donor were to give $1,000,000 to an institution with instructions to invest the money permanently (with income either restricted or unrestricted), then this would be a permanent **endowment** and would be classified as permanently restricted. If a donor were to contribute $1,000,000 with instructions that the funds be invested for 10 years and then released, this would be a **term endowment**, and the assets would be classified as temporarily restricted. If a donor gave $1,000,000 as an unrestricted gift, but the institution's governing board decided to create an endowment, this would be called a **quasi-endowment** and would be unrestricted.

Expenses are to be reported as unrestricted. As was the case in Chapter 10, reclassifications are made from the temporarily restricted class to the unrestricted class as the assets are released from restrictions for time, purpose, or plant acquisition (or depreciation charges) and for the expiration of a term endowment.

Financial Statements

As is true for all not-for-profit organizations under the jurisdiction of the FASB, private colleges and universities are to prepare a Statement of Financial Position, a Statement of Activities, and a Statement of Cash Flows. Considerable flexibility is allowed for colleges and universities as well as for other not-for-profit organizations. For example, the NACUBO *Financial Accounting and Reporting Manual for Higher Education* (Section 500) illustrates Statements of Financial Position using (1) single-column, "corporate" style, (2) FASB Net Asset Class Disaggregation, (3) Operating/Capital Disaggregation, (4) Managed Asset Group Disaggregation, and (5) AICPA Audit Guide Fund Groups Disaggregation. All are acceptable, and similar flexibility is allowed for the Statement of Activities and Statement of Cash Flows. This text uses the single-column "corporate" model for the Statement of Financial Position and for the Statement of Cash Flows and presents an illustrative Statement of Unrestricted Revenues, Expenses, and Changes in Unrestricted Net Assets and an illustrative Statement of Changes in Net Assets. These latter two statements are acceptable alternatives to the Statement of Activities illustrated in Chapter 10.

Revenue Reduction versus Expenses

An issue particularly relevant to colleges and universities is the distinction between discounts and expenses. In general, revenues and expenses are to be reported separately, rather than netting expenses from revenues. However, if a transaction is deemed to be a discount rather than an expense, the revenue is reported net of the discount.

The most frequent situation where this issue arises is for student financial aid. Scholarship allowances are the difference between the stated charges for tuition and fees and the amount actually billed to the student. Some of these allowances represent discounts and others expenses. The National Association of College and University Business Officers (NACUBO) has issued a position paper titled, "Accounting and Reporting Scholarship Allowances to Tuition and Other Revenues by Higher Education" to address this issue. The paper advises that if the tuition or fee reduction is an employee benefit, the reduction is to be treated as compensation expense, rather than a discount. As a result, tuition waivers associated with graduate assistantships and work-study programs are expenses. However, academic or athletic scholarships that do not require service to the college or university are considered scholarship allowances and treated as reductions in revenue. Interestingly, the NACUBO *Financial Accounting and Reporting Manual* treats estimates of uncollectible accounts as reductions in tuition and fee revenue, rather than bad debt expense.

Academic Terms Encompassing More than One Fiscal Year

Because colleges and universities commonly use June 30 as fiscal year-end, tuition and other revenues for summer school frequently cover parts of two fiscal years. Under the 1973 *Audits of Colleges and Universities* audit guide, the accepted practice was to recognize revenues and expenses associated with these split sessions in the academic year in which the term was predominantly conducted. Neither *SFAS 116* nor the 2001 audit guide, *Not-for-Profit Organizations,* provides any support for this practice. Accordingly, NACUBO requires both revenues and expenses for split sessions to be apportioned to the two fiscal years, following accrual accounting practices similar to those employed by commercial organizations.

Other Accounting Guidance

Some additional features of accounting for colleges and universities under the jurisdiction of the FASB follow:

- Full accrual accounting is used. Revenues and expenses are reported at gross amounts; gains and losses are reported net.
- Depreciation is recorded. When reporting by function, depreciation is allocated to functional categories such as Instruction, Research, and Auxiliary Enterprises.
- If both unrestricted and restricted resources are available for a restricted purpose, the FASB requires that the institution recognize the use of restricted resources first.
- A contribution is recorded as a revenue when the promise to give is unconditional. Multiyear pledges are recorded at the present value of the scheduled receipts.
- As is true for other not-for-profits, plant acquired with either unrestricted or restricted resources may be (1) recorded initially as unrestricted or (2) recorded initially as temporarily restricted and then reclassified in accordance with the depreciation schedule.
- Expenses are reported by function, either in the statements or in the notes. This text illustrates entries and statements leading to functional reporting.
- The FASB requires that investments in stocks with determinable fair values and all debt securities be reported at market value. Unrealized as well as realized gains are reported as a part of the change in net assets.
- Contributed services should be recognized only when the services create or enhance nonfinancial assets or require specialized skills, are provided by individuals possessing those skills, and would typically be purchased if not provided by donation.
- Museum and other inexhaustible collections may or may not be capitalized and recorded in the accounts. If a college or university decides to capitalize, it may do so retroactively or prospectively. If an institution decides not to capitalize these items, extensive note disclosures are required regarding the collections.
- Student aid, for which no services are required, is recorded as a discount and reported as a reduction of student tuition and fee revenue. If services are required,

such as for graduate assistantships, the revenue account is shown at the gross amount, and an expense is charged.
- When a private college or university has a foundation, and that foundation receives contributions specifically directed for the benefit of the college or university, the college or university must recognize its interest in the contribution as an asset and as a revenue. The same is true when the college and foundation are financially interrelated.
- As indicated in Chapter 10, if a private college solicits funds, the cost of that solicitation must be considered fund-raising expenses, unless the solicitation meets criteria of purpose, audience, and content. When all of those criteria are met, joint costs can be allocated between fund-raising and other functions.

ILLUSTRATIVE TRANSACTIONS AND FINANCIAL STATEMENTS

A beginning trial balance, entries for typical transactions, and financial statements for a hypothetical private college, the College of St. Michael, are illustrated next. Entries for revenues, expenses, gains, losses, and net assets are identified by net asset class, but individual assets and liabilities are not. All amounts are in thousands of dollars. The fiscal year is the year ending June 30, 2004. Assume the following trial balance for the College of St. Michael as of July 1, 2003 (in thousands of dollars):

	Debits	Credits
Cash	$ 1,950	
Accounts Receivable	4,200	
Allowance for Uncollectible Accounts		$ 400
Accrued Interest Receivable	300	
Contributions Receivable	5,400	
Allowance for Uncollectible Contributions		1,000
Loans to Students and Faculty	900	
Long-Term Investments	19,550	
Property, Plant, and Equipment	18,100	
Accumulated Depreciation—Property, Plant, and Equipment		7,500
Accounts Payable		700
Long-Term Debt—Current Installment		100
Long-Term Debt		1,900
Net Assets: Unrestricted—Board Designated		2,000
Net Assets: Unrestricted—Undesignated		15,200
Net Assets: Temporarily Restricted		10,400
Net Assets: Permanently Restricted		11,200
Totals	$50,400	$50,400

Assume it is the policy of St. Michael's to record fixed assets initially as an increase in unrestricted net assets. St. Michael's does not record museum collections, as permitted by the FASB.

Illustrative Transactions

Cash receipts, related to assets at the beginning of the year, include accounts receivable, $3,700; accrued interest receivable, $300; contributions receivable, $4,200; and loans to students and faculty, $500:

	Debits	Credits
1. Cash	8,700	
Accounts Receivable		3,700
Accrued Interest Receivable		300
Contributions Receivable		4,200
Loans to Students and Faculty		500

Cash payments, related to liabilities existing at the beginning of the year, include $700 for accounts payable and $100 for the current installment of long-term debt:

	Debits	Credits
2. Accounts Payable	700	
Long-Term Debt—Current Installment	100	
Cash		800

Unrestricted revenues include tuition and fees of $15,500. Of this amount, $400 is expected to be uncollectible and $10,500 was collected during registration for classes. Student scholarships for which no service was required amounted to $1,500 and tuition waivers for work-study students (institutional support) amounted to $1,000.

	Debits	Credits
3a. Cash	10,500	
Accounts Receivable	5,000	
Allowance for Uncollectible Accounts		400
Revenues: Unrestricted—Tuition and Fees		15,100
3b. Tuition Discount: Unrestricted—Student Aid	1,500	
Institutional Support Expense	1,000	
Accounts Receivable		2,500

Other unrestricted cash receipts included: $1,500 state appropriations, $5,600 contributions (not previously recorded as receivables), $500 investment income on endowment investments, $100 other investment income, and $11,600 sales of services by auxiliary enterprises. An additional $100 of accrued interest is receivable at year-end.

	Debits	Credits
4. Cash	19,300	
Accrued Interest Receivable	100	
Revenues: Unrestricted—State Appropriations		1,500
Revenues: Unrestricted—Contributions		5,600
Revenues: Unrestricted—Unrestricted Income on Endowment Investments		500
Revenues: Unrestricted—Other Investment Income		200
Revenues: Unrestricted—Sales of Services by Auxiliary Enterprises		11,600

Accounts receivable are written off in the amount of $400; uncollectible contributions are written off in the amount of $300.

	Debits	Credits
5. Allowance for Uncollectible Accounts	400	
Allowance for Uncollectible Contributions	300	
Accounts Receivable		400
Contributions Receivable		300

Temporarily restricted pledges for time, purpose, and plant acquisition were received in the amount of $2,250. In addition, $4,000 was received in cash contributions for temporarily restricted purposes; $1,000 of the resources was restricted for plant acquisition.

	Debits	Credits
6. Contributions Receivable	2,250	
Cash	4,000	
Revenues: Contributions—Temporarily Restricted		6,250

Cash in the amount of $1,000 and pledges in the amount of $350 were received, establishing endowments, and are recorded as revenue-increasing permanently restricted net assets:

	Debits	Credits
7. Cash	1,000	
Contributions Receivable	350	
Contributions—Permanently Restricted		1,350

Interest income that is temporarily restricted amounts to $760. Of that amount, $570 is received in cash and $190 is accrued at year-end:

	Debits	Credits
8. Cash	570	
Accrued Interest Receivable	190	
Revenues: Temporarily Restricted—Investment Income		760

Expenses, exclusive of depreciation, are as follows: instruction, $17,400; research, $2,300; public service, $1,900; academic support, $600; student services, $1,000; institutional support, $1,100; and auxiliary enterprises, $8,500. In addition, the college experiences an uninsured fire loss in the amount of $300. Cash is paid in the amount of $32,100, and accounts payable is increased by $1,000:

	Debits	Credits
9. Instruction Expense	17,400	
Research Expense	2,300	
Public Service Expense	1,900	
Academic Support Expense	600	
Student Services Expense	1,000	
Institutional Support Expense	1,100	
Auxiliary Enterprise Expense	8,500	
Fire Loss	300	
Cash		32,100
Accounts Payable		1,000

Depreciation is charged in the amount of $1,500 and is allocated to functions as shown:

	Debits	Credits
10. Instruction Expense	800	
Research Expense	80	
Public Service Expense	60	
Academic Support Expense	30	
Student Services Expense	70	
Institutional Support Expense	90	
Auxiliary Enterprise Expense	370	
Accumulated Depreciation—Property, Plant, and Equipment		1,500

Reclassifications are made in the total amount of $7,000 from temporarily restricted to unrestricted net assets. The $7,000 includes $2,000 reclassified on the basis of expiration of time restrictions, $3,000 reclassified for program restrictions (research), $1,200 for plant acquisition, and $800 for the expiration of time endowments:

	Debits	Credits
11. Reclassification from Temporarily Restricted Net Assets—Expiration of Time Restrictions	2,000	
Reclassification from Temporarily Restricted Net Assets—Satisfaction of Program Restrictions	3,000	
Reclassification from Temporarily Restricted Net Assets—Satisfaction of Plant Acquisition Restrictions	1,200	
Reclassification from Temporarily Restricted Net Assets—Expiration of Term Endowments	800	
Reclassification to Unrestricted Net Assets—Expiration of Time Restrictions		2,000
Reclassification to Unrestricted Net Assets—Satisfaction of Program Restrictions		3,000
Reclassification to Unrestricted Net Assets—Satisfaction of Plant Acquisition Restrictions		1,200
Reclassification to Unrestricted Net Assets—Expiration of Term Endowments		800

Research expenses are incurred and plant is acquired. As indicated earlier, it is the policy of St. Michael's to record plant as increases in unrestricted net assets, one of the options permitted by the FASB. These two entries cause the reclassifications for program and plant purposes above in entry 11:

12. Research Expense	3,000	
Property, Plant, and Equipment	1,200	
Cash		4,200

Long-term investments, costing $3,500, are sold for $3,750. Of the $250 gain, $200 was required by gift agreement to be added to temporarily restricted net assets, and $50 was required by the endowment agreement to be added to endowments.

13. Cash	3,750	
Long-Term Investments		3,500
Gains on Long-Term Investments—Temporarily Restricted		200
Gains on Long-Term Investments—Permanently Restricted		50

Loans to students and faculty are made in the amount of $750:

14. Loans to Students and Faculty	750	
Cash		750

Long-term investments are purchased in the amount of $5,800:

	Debits	Credits
15. Long-Term Investments	5,800	
Cash		5,800

The Board of Trustees of St. Michael's College decides to invest an additional $1,000 of unrestricted resources. These investments are designated by the board for permanent endowment, technically known as a *quasi-endowment*. Two entries are necessary:

16a. Long-Term Investments	1,000	
Cash		1,000
16b. Net Assets: Unrestricted—Undesignated	1,000	
Net Assets: Unrestricted—Designated		1,000

At year-end, it is determined that the fair value of long-term investments has increased by $1,900. Of that amount, $800 is restricted temporarily by donor agreements and $1,100 is restricted for future endowment purposes:

17. Long-Term Investments	1,900	
Gains on Long-Term Investments—Temporarily Restricted		800
Gains on Long-Term Investments—Permanently Restricted		1,100

The current portion of long-term debt is recognized:

18. Long-Term Debt	100	
Long-Term Debt: Current Installment		100

The closing entry is made for the unrestricted net asset class. Note that revenues and reclassifications have been recorded by net asset class; all expenses are considered unrestricted.

19. Revenues: Unrestricted—Tuition and Fees	15,100	
Revenues: Unrestricted—State Appropriation	1,500	
Revenues: Unrestricted—Contributions	5,600	
Revenues: Unrestricted—Investment Income on Endowment Investments	500	

	Debits	Credits
Revenues: Unrestricted—Other Investment Income	200	
Revenues: Unrestricted—Sales and Services of Auxiliary Enterprises	11,600	
Reclassification to Unrestricted Net Assets—Expiration of Time Restrictions	2,000	
Reclassification to Unrestricted Net Assets—Satisfaction of Program Restrictions	3,000	
Reclassification to Unrestricted Net Assets—Satisfaction of Plant Acquisition Restrictions	1,200	
Reclassification to Unrestricted Net Assets—Expiration of Term Endowments	800	
Tuition Discount—Student Aid		1,500
Instruction Expense		18,200
Research Expense		5,380
Public Service Expense		1,960
Academic Support Expense		630
Student Services Expense		1,070
Institutional Support Expense		2,190
Auxiliary Enterprise Expense		8,870
Fire Loss		300
Net Assets: Unrestricted: Undesignated		1,400

The entry to close accounts for temporarily restricted net assets was made:

20. Revenues: Temporarily Restricted—Contributions	6,250	
Revenues: Temporarily Restricted—Other Investment Income	760	
Gains on Long-Term Investments	1,000	
Reclassifications from Temporarily Restricted Net Assets—Expiration of Time Restrictions		2,000
Reclassifications from Temporarily Restricted Net Assets—Satisfaction of Program Restrictions		3,000
Reclassifications from Temporarily Restricted Net Assets—Satisfaction of Plant Acquisition Restrictions		1,200
Reclassifications from Temporarily Restricted Net Assets—Expiration of Term Endowments		800
Net Assets: Temporarily Restricted		1,010

Finally, the closing entry is made for the permanently restricted net asset class:

21. Revenues: Permanently Restricted Contributions	1,350	
Gains on Long-Term Investments	1,150	
Net Assets: Permanently Restricted		2,500

Illustrative Financial Statements for Private Colleges and Universities

Financial statements required for private-sector nonprofit colleges and universities include a Statement of Financial Position, Statement of Activities, and Statement of Cash Flows. An acceptable alternative to the Statement of Activities is to present two statements: (1) Statement of Unrestricted Revenues, Expenses, and Other Changes in Unrestricted Net Assets and (2) Statement of Changes in Net Assets. Illustrative financial statements for the College of St. Michael are shown in this section.

Statement of Unrestricted Revenues, Expenses, and Other Changes in Unrestricted Net Assets   As mentioned in Chapter 10, several different alternatives are acceptable for the Statement of Activities as long as revenues, expenses, and reclassifications are clearly shown and as long as the changes in net assets are shown separately for each of the three net asset classes and in total. Illustration 10–1 presented a four-column Statement of Activities for a performing arts organization with separate columns for each net asset class and a total. Illustration 11–1 presents a Statement of Unrestricted Revenues, Expenses, and Other Changes in Unrestricted Net Assets.

Statement of Changes in Net Assets   If an organization prepares a Statement of Unrestricted Revenues, Expenses, and Other Changes in Unrestricted Net Assets in lieu of a complete Statement of Activities, the FASB requires that a Statement of Changes in Net Assets be prepared. One way of preparing it is shown as the Statement of Changes in Net Assets for the College of St. Michael in Illustration 11–2.

Statement of Financial Position   The Statement of Financial Position for the College of St. Michael is presented as Illustration 11–3. Note that the statement is not classified, but assets are generally shown in the order of liquidity, and liabilities are generally shown in the order of payment dates.

Statement of Cash Flows   Illustration 11–4 presents a Statement of Cash Flows for the College of St. Michael. The indirect method is used.

SPLIT-INTEREST AGREEMENTS

The *Not-for-Profit Guide* provides guidance to not-for-profit organizations, including those covered in Chapter 10 and this chapter, regarding split-interest agreements. **Split-interest agreements** represent trust or other arrangements with donors in which not-for-profit organizations receive benefits that are shared with other beneficiaries. Annuity and life income agreements, discussed earlier in this chapter, are examples. The *Not-for-Profit Guide* categorizes these split-interest agreements into five types: (1) charitable lead trusts, (2) perpetual trusts held by third parties, (3) charitable remainder trusts, (4) charitable gift annuities, and (5) pooled (life) income funds. Each of these is discussed in the following paragraphs.

ILLUSTRATION 11–1

COLLEGE OF ST. MICHAEL
Statement of Unrestricted Revenues, Expenses,
and Other Changes in Unrestricted Net Assets
For the Year Ended June 30, 2004
(in thousands of dollars)

Unrestricted Revenues:	
Net Tuition and Fees	$13,600
State Appropriation	1,500
Contributions	5,600
Investment Income on Endowment	500
Other Investment Income	200
Sales and Services of Auxiliary Enterprises	11,600
Total Revenues	33,000
Net Assets Released from Restrictions:	
Expiration of Time Restrictions	2,000
Satisfaction of Program Restrictions	3,000
Satisfaction of Plant Acquisition Restrictions	1,200
Expiration of Term Endowment	800
Total Net Assets Released from Restrictions	7,000
Total Unrestricted Revenues and Other Support	40,000
Expenses and Losses:	
Educational and General:	
Instruction	18,200
Research	5,380
Public Service	1,960
Academic Support	630
Student Services	1,070
Institutional Support	2,190
Total Educational and General Expenses	29,430
Auxiliary Enterprises	8,870
Total Expenses	38,300
Fire Loss	300
Total Expenses and Losses	38,600
Increase in Unrestricted Net Assets	$ 1,400

A **charitable lead trust** is an arrangement whereby a donor establishes a trust in which a fixed amount (charitable lead annuity trust) or a percentage of the fair value of the trust (charitable lead unitrust) is distributed to a not-for-profit organization for a certain term. At the end of the term, the remainder of the trust assets is paid to the donor or other beneficiary. The not-for-profit organization may or may not hold the trust assets. When the trust is created and is irrevocable, the not-for-profit organization recognizes a receivable for the fair value of the assets received and a temporarily restricted revenue at the present value of the anticipated receipts that will be retained by the not-for-profit. If the not-for-profit is the trustee of the

ILLUSTRATION 11–2

COLLEGE OF ST. MICHAEL
Statement of Changes in Net Assets
For the Year Ended June 30, 2004
(in thousands of dollars)

Total Unrestricted Revenues	$33,000
Net Assets Released from Restrictions	7,000
Total Unrestricted Expenses and Losses	(38,600)
Increase in Unrestricted Net Assets	1,400
Temporarily Restricted Net Assets:	
Contributions	6,250
Gains on Long-Term Investments	1,000
Other Investment Income	760
Net Assets Released from Restrictions	(7,000)
Increase in Temporarily Restricted Net Assets	1,010
Permanently Restricted Net Assets:	
Contributions	1,350
Gains on Long-Term Investments	1,150
Increase in Permanently Restricted Net Assets	2,500
Increase in Net Assets	4,910
Net Assets, July 1, 2003	38,800
Net Assets, June 30, 2004	$43,710

trust assets, the difference between the trust assets and the present value of anticipated receipts is recognized as a liability. Year-to-year changes are recognized as Changes in the Value of Split-Interest Agreements, which are recognized as additions to or deductions from the temporarily restricted net asset class in the Statement of Activities.

A **perpetual trust held by a third party** is not exactly a split-interest agreement but is accounted for in a similar fashion. Assume that a person establishes a permanent trust at a bank with the income to go to a not-for-profit organization in perpetuity. The present value of anticipated receipts (usually the fair value of the assets contributed) is recorded as an asset and as contribution revenue in the permanently restricted net asset class. Income received each year is recorded as either unrestricted or temporarily restricted investment income, depending on the trust agreement. Changes in the value of trust principal are recorded as additions to or deductions from the permanently restricted net asset class.

A **charitable remainder trust** is a trust established by a donor to ensure that a specified dollar amount (charitable remainder annuity trust) or a specified percentage of the trust's fair market value (charitable remainder unitrust) is paid to a beneficiary. At the end of the term of the trust, the trust principal is paid to the institution for unrestricted or temporarily restricted purposes or as an endowment (permanently restricted). The trust assets are recorded at fair market value, the present

ILLUSTRATION 11-3

COLLEGE OF ST. MICHAEL
Statements of Financial Position
For the Years Ended June 30, 2004 and 2003
(in thousands of dollars)

	2004	2003
Assets		
Cash and Cash Equivalents	$ 5,120	$ 1,950
Accounts Receivable (Net of Allowance for Uncollectibles of $400 and $400)	2,200	3,800
Accrued Interest Receivable	290	300
Contributions Receivable (Net of Allowance for Uncollectibles of $700 and $1,000)	2,800	4,400
Loans to Students and Faculty	1,150	900
Long-Term Investments	24,750	19,550
Property, Plant, and Equipment (Net of Accumulated Depreciation of $9,000 and $7,500)	10,300	10,600
Total Assets	$46,610	$41,500
Liabilities and Net Assets		
Accounts Payable	$ 1,000	$ 700
Long-Term Debt: Current Installment	100	100
Long-Term Debt: Noncurrent	1,800	1,900
Total Liabilities	2,900	2,700
Net Assets:		
Board Designated	3,000	2,000
Other Unrestricted	15,600	15,200
Total Unrestricted	18,600	17,200
Temporarily Restricted	11,410	10,400
Permanently Restricted	13,700	11,200
Total Net Assets	$43,710	$38,800
Total Liabilities and Net Assets	$46,610	$41,500

value of the amounts to be paid to the beneficiary are recorded as a liability, and the difference is recorded as contribution revenue in the appropriate net asset class. Adjustments in the present value of the liability are recorded each year as a change in the value of split-interest agreements in the Statement of Activities.

A **charitable gift annuity** is the same as a charitable remainder trust except that no formal trust agreement exists; normally a contract is signed. The accounting is the same as for a charitable remainder trust.

A **pooled (life) income fund** represents a situation in which the assets of several life income agreements are pooled together. A life income fund represents a situation in which all of the income is paid to a donor or a beneficiary during his or her lifetime. At the end of the donor's or beneficiary's life, the assets go to the not-for-profit organization for unrestricted or restricted purposes. In a pooled (life) income

ILLUSTRATION 11–4

COLLEGE OF ST. MICHAEL
Statement of Cash Flows
For the Year Ended December 31, 2004
(in thousands of dollars)

Cash Flows from Operating Activities:	
Cash Received from Service Recipients	$ 25,800
Cash Received from State Appropriations	1,500
Cash Received from Contributors	12,800
Interest and Dividends Received	1,470
Cash Paid to Employees and Suppliers	(35,800)
Cash Flows from Operating Activities	5,770
Cash Flows from Investing Activities:	
Acquisition of Property, Plant, and Equipment	(1,200)
Purchase of Investments	(6,800)
Sale of Investments	3,750
Disbursement of Loans to Students and Faculty	(750)
Repayment of Loans to Students and Faculty	500
Cash Flows from Investing Activities	(4,500)
Cash Flows from Financing Activities:	
Proceeds from Contributions Restricted for:	
Investment in Property, Plant, and Equipment	1,000
Investment in Endowments	1,000
Other Financing Activities:	
Payments on Long-Term Debt	(100)
Cash Flows from Financing Activities	1,900
Net Increase in Cash and Cash Equivalents	3,170
Cash and Cash Equivalents, July 1, 2003	1,950
Cash and Cash Equivalents, June 30, 2004	$ 5,120
Reconciliation of change in net assets to cash flows from operating activities:	
Change in Net Assets	$ 4,910
Adjustments to Reconcile Change in Net Assets to Net Cash	
Provided by Operating Activities:	
Depreciation	1,500
Decrease in Accounts Receivable	1,600
Decrease in Accrued Interest Receivable	10
Decrease in Contributions Receivable	1,600
Increase in Accounts Payable	300
Gains on Long-Term Investments	(2,150)
Contribution Restricted to Investment in Property,	
Plant, and Equipment	(1,000)
Contribution Restricted to Long-Term Investment in Endowments	(1,000)
Cash Flows from Operating Activities	5,770

fund, the assets are recorded and entered into the pool based on the fair value of all assets at the time of entry. Each life income agreement is assigned a certain number of units. A revenue is recognized in the temporarily restricted net asset class, discounted for the time period until the donor's or beneficiary's death. The difference between the fair value of the assets received and the revenue is recorded as deferred revenue, representing the amount of the discount for future interest.

Illustrative journal entries (without numbers) are presented in the *Not-for-Profit Guide*, and illustrative journal entries (with numbers) are presented in the NACUBO *Financial Accounting and Reporting Manual*.

ACADEMIC RESEARCH

Most of the academic research relating to either private or public sector colleges and universities was conducted prior to the issuance of GASB *Statement 35* and FASB *Statement 117*. Brown (1993) presents a history of financial reporting for American colleges and universities from 1910 to 1990.[1] Prior to the issuance of GASB *35* and FASB *117*, the reporting practices of public institutions varied significantly from those of private. Much of the early research focused on these differences and raised the question of whether two very different sets of practices within a single industry were justified. See for example, Fischer 1997[2] and Engstrom and Fountain 1989.[3]

More recently, Gordon, Fischer, Malone, and Tower (2002) examined the financial reports of a sample of both public and private colleges and universities.[4] The purpose of this study was to determine what institutional characteristics are associated with increased levels of disclosure. One objective of studies of this type is to identify factors which create demand for accounting information. Particularly interesting are the findings related to service efforts and accomplishments reporting. They found that public institutions disclose more nonfinancial performance information than private colleges and universities. They also found that many reports lacked information, such as enrollment levels useful in computing ratios necessary for comparisons between institutions.

SUMMARY OF ACCOUNTING AND REPORTING

Private colleges and universities are required to follow the accounting principles promulgated by the FASB and in the AICPA *Not-for-Profit Guide*. These pronouncements include FASB statements on display, contributions, depreciation, and investments. The *Not-for-Profit Guide*, unlike the *Health Care Guide* (described in Chapter 12), does not prescribe or illustrate reporting format. However, significant guidance is given for split-interest agreements. The NACUBO *Financial*

---

[1] K. W. Brown, "History of Financial Reporting Models for American Colleges and Universities: 1910 to the Present," *The Accounting Historians Journal* 20, no. 2 (1993), pp. 1–29.
[2] M. Fischer, "Two Accounting Standard Setters: One Industry," *Journal of Public Budgeting Accounting and Financial Management* 9, no. 2 (1997), pp. 251–84.
[3] J. Engstrom and J. Fountain, "College and University Financial Reporting: A Survey of Important Decision Makers," *Government Accountants Journal* 38, no. 2 (1989), pp. 39–49.
[4] T. Gordon, M. Fischer, D. Malone, and G. Tower, "A Comparative Empirical Examination of Extent of Disclosure by Private and Public Colleges and Universities in the United States," *Journal of Accounting and Public Policy*, 2002.

Accounting and Reporting Manual for Higher Education provides more detailed guidance and illustrative entries for both private and public institutions.

Governmental colleges and universities are under the jurisdiction of the GASB, for purposes of financial reporting. GASB *Statement 35* requires governmental colleges and universities to follow GASB *Statement 34* guidance for special-purpose entities. Most choose to report as special-purpose entities engaged in business-type activities only. That accounting is described and illustrated in Chapter 9.

QUESTIONS AND EXERCISES

11–1. Select the letter corresponding with the *best* answer to each of the following questions:

1. Accounting and financial reporting principles for colleges and universities are now established by the:
   a. Financial Accounting Standards Board.
   b. American Institute of Certified Board Accountants.
   c. National Association of College and University Business Officers.
   d. The Financial Accounting Standards Board or the Governmental Accounting Standards Board, depending upon whether the institution is private or governmental.

2. A donor gave $1,000,000 to a private college. The college's governing board decided to establish an endowment, with the intent to keep the principal intact forever. The income would be used, by action of the board, for a chaired faculty position in accountancy. The $1,000,000 would be classified as:
   a. Unrestricted.
   b. Temporarily restricted.
   c. Permanently restricted.
   d. Either unrestricted or permanently restricted, at the option of the institution.

3. A private university received $15,000,000 in tuition and fees during an academic year. Scholarships, for which no services were required, were awarded in the amount of $1,200,000, and graduate assistantships, for which services were required, were awarded in the amount of $200,000. The net tuition and fees that would be reported in the Statement of Activities would be:
   a. $15,000,000.
   b. $13,800,000.
   c. $13,600,000.
   d. $14,800,000.

4. A split-interest agreement (a trust) in which the donor or a beneficiary receives payments for a specified period of time and in which, at the

end of that term, a not-for-profit organization will receive the trust principal is known as a:
- a. Charitable remainder trust.
- b. Charitable lead trust.
- c. Pooled (life) income agreement.
- d. Charitable gift annuity.

5. If a private college receives contributed services, in order for those services to be recognized, the services:
   - a. Must create or enhance nonfinancial assets.
   - b. Must require specialized skills, be provided by individuals possessing those skills, and typically be purchased if not provided by donation.
   - c. Either *a* or *b* must exist.
   - d. Both *a* and *b* must exist.

6. Under the provisions of FASB *Statement 124*, private colleges should report investments in equity securities with determinable fair values and investments in debt securities at:
   - a. Cost.
   - b. The lower of cost or market.
   - c. Fair value.
   - d. None of the above

7. A donor gave a gift of $10,000 to a private college on June 15, 2003, with the expressed intent that the college expend the funds in the year ending June 30, 2004. The gift was not restricted as to purpose. The college expended the funds, as required, in the year ending June 30, 2004. The college should recognize:
   - a. The revenue in the year ended June 30, 2003, and recognize the expense in the year ended June 30, 2004.
   - b. Both the revenue and expense in the year ended June 30, 2003.
   - c. Both the revenue and expense in the year ended June 30, 2004.
   - d. Both the revenue and expense in either fiscal year, as long as both are recognized in the same year.

8. A donor gave a gift of $5,000 to a private college on June 15, 2003, with the expressed restriction that the funds be used for a certain kind of cancer research. The college conducted the research during the month of August 2003. The fiscal year ends June 30. The college should recognize:
   - a. The revenue in the year ended June 30, 2003, and recognize the expense in the year ended June 30, 2004.
   - b. Both the revenue and expense in the year ended June 30, 2003.
   - c. Both the revenue and expense in the year ended June 30, 2004.
   - d. Both the revenue and expense in either fiscal year, as long as both are recognized in the same year.

9. If a private college has museum collections, the college:
    a. Must capitalize all collections retroactively to include all collections.
    b. Must capitalize all collections, either retroactively or prospectively, to include only those collections that have been acquired since *FAS 116* became effective.
    c. May or may not capitalize collections.
    d. Is not permitted to capitalize collections.
10. Which of the following is *not* true regarding cash flow statements of private colleges?
    a. Either the direct or indirect method may be used.
    b. Disbursement of loans to students and faculty is considered a financing activity.
    c. The purchase of equipment is considered an investing activity.
    d. The same categories of activities (operating, investing, financing) used by business organizations are used for private colleges.

11–2. Select the letter corresponding with the *best* answer to each of the following questions:

1. "Net Assets Invested in Capital Assets, Net of Related Debt" is an account title that may appear in the statement of net assets for:

	Public Colleges & Universities	Private Colleges & Universities
a.	Yes	No
b.	No	Yes
c.	Yes	Yes
d.	No	No

2. A Statement of Cash Flows is a required financial statement of:

	Public Colleges & Universities	Private Colleges & Universities
a.	Yes	No
b.	No	Yes
c.	Yes	Yes
d.	No	No

3. The Current Financial Resource measurement focus and Modified Accrual Basis of Accounting is used by:

	Public Colleges & Universities	Private Colleges & Universities
a.	Yes	No
b.	No	Yes
c.	Yes	Yes
d.	No	No

4. Assume summer school runs from June 15 to August 1 and that the institution's fiscal year-end is June 30. How should summer school tuition revenue be recognized when the institution's fiscal year-end falls during the summer term?
   a. Recognize the revenue in the period most of the cash is collected.
   b. Recognize the revenue in the period containing most of the instructional days.
   c. Recognize a proportion of the revenue in both fiscal periods on a systematic basis, such as the number of instructional days.
   d. Recognize the revenue in the period in which most of the expenses are incurred.

5. A private university received a grant of $50,000 to conduct medical research. In addition, the university budgeted an additional $50,000 to the project from unrestricted resources. Assume research expenses during the current year totaled $80,000. How much should the university reclassify as "net assets released from restriction" as a result of the research program?
   a. $30,000.
   b. $40,000.
   c. $50,000.
   d. $80,000.

6. A private college billed students $560,000 for the current semester. The college expects the amount ultimately collected to be $440,000. The $120,000 difference is comprised of the following items: scholarships for which no services required, $60,000; tuition waivers resulting from work-study programs, $40,000; estimated uncollectible accounts, $20,000. How much tuition, net of discounts, should be reported for the current semester?
   a. $560,000.
   b. $500,000.
   c. $480,000.
   d. $440,000.

7. How does financial reporting for private colleges and universities differ from public (government-owned) colleges and universities?
   a. Different sets of account classifications appear in the net assets section of the Statement of Net Assets.
   b. Private colleges and universities are required to report changes in net assets within the categories of unrestricted, temporarily restricted, and permanently restricted.
   c. Public colleges and universities are required to report cash flows on the direct method but private institutions may use the indirect method.
   d. All of the above.

8. Which of the following is done in recording creation of a charitable lead trust in which the not-for-profit serves as trustee?
   a. The not-for-profit recognizes an asset for the fair value of the assets received.
   b. The not-for-profit recognizes temporarily restricted revenue at the present value of any anticipated receipts that will be retained by the not-for-profit.
   c. The not-for-profit records a liability for the difference between the fair value of the assets received and the present value of the anticipated receipts to be retained by the not-for-profit.
   d. All of the above.
9. A university grants a tuition waiver to a student under a graduate assistantship. Under the assistantship, the student works 14 hours per week under the direction of a faculty member. What effect will the assistantship have on the revenues and expenses of the university?

	Revenues	Expenses
a.	Decrease	No Effect
b.	No Effect	Increase
c.	Decrease	Increase
d.	No Effect	No Effect

10. In which net asset classification is income earned on an endowment recorded?
    a. Unrestricted Net Assets
    b. Temporarily Restricted Net Assets
    c. Permanently Restricted Net Assets
    d. All of the above are possible, depending on the terms of the endowment trust agreement.

11–3. With regard to private sector colleges and universities:
   a. List the three net asset classes required under FASB *Statement 117*.
   b. List the financial reports required under FASB *Statement 117*.
   c. Distinguish between an endowment, a term endowment, and a quasi-endowment. Indicate the accounting required for each.
   d. Outline the accounting required by the FASB for
      (1) an endowment gift received in cash.
      (2) a pledge received in 2003, unrestricted as to purpose but restricted for use in 2004.
      (3) a pledge received in 2003, restricted as to purpose other than plant. The purpose was fulfilled in 2004.
   e. Discuss the requirements necessary before contributed services are recorded as revenues.

11-4. Define and outline the accounting required for each of the following types of agreements:
   a. charitable lead trusts.
   b. charitable remainder trusts.
   c. perpetual trust held by a third party.

11-5. During the year ended June 30, 2004, the following transactions were recorded by St. Ann's College, a private institution:
   1. Tuition and fees amounted to $6,600,000, of which $4,300,000 was received in cash. A state appropriation was received in cash in the amount of $600,000. Sales and services of auxiliary enterprises amounted to $3,500,000, all of which was received in cash.
   2. Student scholarships were awarded in the amount of $800,000. Recipient students were not required to provide services for this financial aid.
   3. The provision for doubtful accounts for the year ended June 30, 2004, amounted to $25,000. During the year, doubtful accounts related to student fees were written off in the amount of $20,000.
   4. During the year, contributions received, all in cash, amounted to: unrestricted, $600,000; temporarily restricted for use in the year ended June 30, 2005, $1,100,000 (unrestricted as to purpose); temporarily restricted for certain purposes, $900,000; and restricted for endowments, $1,000,000.
   5. During the year, $500,000 was released from restrictions based on time, and $800,000 was released from restrictions for program purposes (research). The applicable research expense of $800,000 was paid in cash.
   6. Investment income amounted to: unrestricted income from endowments, $150,000; income from endowments for purposes restricted by program, $200,000; and income from endowments required to be added to the endowment, $15,000.
   7. During the year, St. Ann's received a gift of $500,000, which was to be used for the future construction of an addition to the library.
   8. During the year, $1,300,000 was released from restriction for the construction of a new wing to the student services building. The building was constructed using the cash. St. Ann's records all fixed assets in the unrestricted net asset class.
   9. Endowment long-term investments, carried at a basis of $2,000,000, were sold for $2,150,000. The total proceeds were reinvested. Income is to remain as permanently restricted.
   10. Expenses for the year (in addition to expenses provided for in other parts of the problem) were instruction, $5,050,000; research, $1,200,000; public service, $300,000; academic support, $200,000; student services, $600,000; institutional support, $700,000; and auxiliary enterprises, $3,400,000. All but $600,000 was paid in cash.

11. Depreciation recorded for the year amounted to $540,000. One-third of that amount was charged to instruction, one-third to institutional support, and one-third to auxiliary enterprises.
12. The institution sustained an uninsured fire loss of $130,000. Repairs were paid in cash and charged to the fire loss account.
13. Closing entries were prepared.
    a. Record the transactions on the books of St. Ann's College. Indicate the net asset class for revenues and reclassification.
    b. Prepare, in good form, a Statement of Unrestricted Revenues, Expenses, and Other Changes in Unrestricted Net Assets for St. Ann's College for the year ended June 30, 2004.
    c. Prepare, in good form, a Statement of Changes in Net Assets for St. Ann's College for the year ended June 30, 2004. The net assets at the beginning of the year amounted to $10,580,000.

11-6. Record the following transactions on the books of Calvin College, which follows FASB standards, for Calvin's fiscal year, which ends on June 30, 2004.
   1. During the year ended June 30, 2004, a donor made a cash contribution in the amount of $1,000,000 with the stipulation that the principal be invested permanently and that the income be used for research in biology. The cash was invested.
   2. Also during the year ended June 30, 2004, a donor made an unrestricted cash contribution of $500,000. Calvin's governing board decided to establish this gift as a permanent investment and invested the funds.
   3. By the end of the year, the investments mentioned in transaction 1 received $40,000 and the investments mentioned in transaction 2 received $20,000 in cash.
   4. The fair value of investments in transaction 1 increased by $5,000 at year-end.
   5. During the year ended June 30, 2005, the biology research was completed, using the income mentioned in transaction 3.

11-7. Record the following transactions on the books of Carnegie College, a private institution that follows FASB standards. The year is 2004.
   1. During 2004, Carnegie received a pledge in the amount of $200,000, unrestricted as to purpose, indicating that the amount was to be paid to and used by the college in 2005.
   2. Carnegie received $80,000 in cash from a donor who specified that the funds were to be used for research in voting behavior. The university did not conduct the research in 2004.
   3. Carnegie conducted certain research in the behavior of cats during 2004, costing $50,000. A grant had been given in 2002 for just that purpose, but Carnegie hoped to use unrestricted resources for the 2004 research and keep the $50,000 for future use in cat behavior research. (Hint: Follow the required procedure in this case.)

4. During 2004, Carnegie reclassified funds that had been given in 2003 but unrestricted as to purpose. The amount was $70,000, which remained unspent by the end of 2004.

5. During 2003, Carnegie received $800,000 to renovate a dormitory. During 2004, the funds were spent. Carnegie records all plant in the unrestricted net asset class.

11-8. **Comprehensive Problem.** As of July 1, 2003, the trial balance for Korner College was as follows:

	Debits	Credits
Cash	$ 618,000	
Accounts Receivable	1,350,000	
Allowance for Uncollectible Accounts		$ 60,000
Accrued Interest Receivable	49,000	
Contributions Receivable	5,425,000	
Allowance for Uncollectible Contributions		125,000
Loans to Students and Faculty	350,000	
Long-Term Investments	15,500,000	
Property, Plant, and Equipment	15,450,000	
Accumulated Depreciation—Property, Plant, and Equipment		7,530,000
Accounts Payable		520,000
Long-Term Debt: Current Installment		150,000
Long-Term Debt: Noncurrent		8,500,000
Net Assets—Unrestricted—Board Designated		2,400,000
Net Assets—Unrestricted—Undesignated		4,815,000
Net Assets—Temporarily Restricted		5,555,000
Net Assets—Permanently Restricted		9,087,000
Totals	$38,742,000	$38,742,000

During the year ended June 30, 2004, the following transactions occurred:

1. Cash collections included: accounts receivable, $1,200,000; accrued interest receivable, $49,000; contributions receivable, $5,345,000; and for loans to students and faculty, $155,000. Of the contributions, $1,900,000 was for plant acquisition (use for cash flow statement).

2. Cash payments included accounts payable, $520,000; and the current portion of long-term debt, $150,000.

3. Unrestricted revenues included tuition and fees, $21,800,000; unrestricted income on endowment investments, $400,000; other investment income, $300,000; and sales and services of auxiliary enterprises, $14,440,000. $33,390,000 in cash was received, and the following receivables were increased: accounts receivable, $3,500,000; accrued interest receivable, $50,000.

4. Scholarships, for which no services were required, were applied to student accounts in the amount of $2,000,000.

5. Contributions were received in the following amounts: unrestricted, $4,900,000; temporarily restricted, $5,400,000; permanently restricted,

$2,000,000. Of that amount, $7,020,000 was received in cash; contributions receivable increased $5,280,000. None of these contributions were restricted to plant acquisition.

6. Accounts receivable were written off in the amount of $50,000, and contributions receivable were written off in the amount of $20,000. Provisions for bad debts were increased by $125,000 for accounts receivable (tuition and fees) and by $30,000 for unrestricted contributions receivable.

7. Expenses, exclusive of depreciation and uncollectible accounts, were as follows: instruction, $18,460,000; research, $1,980,000; public service, $1,910,000; academic support, $990,000; student services, $1,310,000; institutional support, $1,050,000; and auxiliary enterprises, $13,500,000. The college had an uninsured fire loss in the amount of $600,000. Cash was paid in the amount of $39,200,000, and accounts payable increased by $600,000.

8. Depreciation was charged in the amount of $900,000. One-third of that amount was charged each to instruction, institutional support, and auxiliary enterprises.

9. Interest income was received as follows: addition to temporarily restricted net assets, $30,000; addition to permanently restricted net assets, $35,000. Of those amounts, $55,000 was received in cash and $10,000 was accrued at year-end.

10. Research expense was incurred in the amount of $1,800,000; and property, plant, and equipment were acquired in the amount of $1,400,000. Both were paid in cash.

11. Reclassifications were made from temporarily restricted to unrestricted net assets as follows: on the basis of time restrictions, $2,100,000; for program restrictions (research), $1,800,000; and for plant acquisition restrictions, $1,400,000. Korner records plant as increases in unrestricted net assets.

12. Long-term investments, with a carrying value of $1,700,000, were sold for $1,770,000. Of the $70,000 gain, $50,000 was temporarily restricted by donor agreement and $20,000 is required to be added to permanently restricted net assets.

13. Additional investments were purchased in the amount of $3,970,000. Loans were made to students and faculty in the amount of $200,000.

14. In addition to 13 above, the board of trustees decided to purchase $2,000,000 in long-term investments, from unrestricted net assets, to create a quasi-endowment.

15. At year-end, the fair value of investments increased by $530,000. Of that amount, $300,000 increased unrestricted net assets, $30,000 increased temporarily restricted net assets, and $200,000 increased permanently restricted net assets.

16. $150,000 of the long-term debt was reclassified as a current liability.
17. Closing entries were prepared for *(a)* unrestricted net assets, *(b)* temporarily restricted net assets, and *(c)* permanently restricted net assets.

Required:

a. Prepare journal entries for each of the above transactions.
b. Prepare a Statement of Unrestricted Revenues, Expenses, and Other Changes in Unrestricted Net Assets for Korner College for the fiscal year ended June 30, 2004.
c. Prepare a Statement of Changes in Net Assets for Korner College for the fiscal year ended June 30, 2004.
d. Prepare a Statement of Financial Position for Korner College as of June 30, 2004.
e. Prepare a Statement of Cash Flows for Korner College for the year ended June 30, 2004. Use the indirect method.

Chapter Twelve

Accounting for Hospitals and Other Health Care Providers

Health care expenditures now exceed $1.3 trillion or 13 percent of the gross national product of the United States, and this percentage is expected to grow in the future. A major national debate continues over how health care should be provided and paid for. Health care entities are subject to a complex set of regulatory requirements established by federal and state governments as well as by third-party payors, such as insurance companies. The relationships among physicians, patients, health care entities, insurance companies, and regulators have been changing, and many mergers have taken place, resulting in complex organizations that may include several participants in the health care process. Occupancy rates for inpatient care are dropping, more procedures are being conducted on an outpatient basis, and primary care physicians are becoming more important through health maintenance organizations and other organizations in providing access to specialized care. Health care accounting and auditing can provide an exciting and profitable career to individuals who are willing and able to deal with complexity and change.

Health care providers may be private not-for-profits, governmentally owned, or owned by private investors. Like charities and private colleges, private not-for-profit health care organizations follow FASB standards. In particular, several standards are written specifically for not-for-profits, including *Statements 116, 117, 124, and 136*. If a health care organization is owned or controlled by a government, it is typically considered a special-purpose entity engaged only in business-type activities (GASB *Statement 34*) and would use proprietary fund accounting, similar to government-owned colleges and universities described in Chapter 9. Other health care organizations are privately owned and operated to provide a return to investors. For example, Hospital Corporation of America (HCA) owns or operates hundreds of hospitals in the United States and internationally; its stock is traded on the New York Stock Exchange. HCA and other private for profit health care organizations follow FASB standards *excluding* those written specifically for not-for-profits.

While the three types of health care organizations follow different sets of generally accepted accounting standards, the differences lie mainly in presentation. All three types of organizations measure assets and liabilities similarly, recognize revenue and expenses under the accrual basis, and all three present comparable performance (i.e., income) measures. Helping to assure comparability across health care organizations with varying ownership structures, the *AICPA Audit and Accounting Guide: Health Care Organizations* applies equally to private not-for-profit, governmentally owned, and investor owned health care organizations.[1]

This chapter concentrates on reporting by private not-for-profit health care organizations, the most numerous of the three types. However, unique features of governmental health care reporting are also described in a separate section. For accounting purposes, health care organizations include the following:

- Clinics, medical group practices, individual practice associations, individual practitioners, emergency care facilities, laboratories, surgery centers, and other ambulatory care organizations.
- Continuing care retirement communities.
- Health Maintenance Organizations (HMOs) and similar prepaid health care plans.
- Home health agencies.
- Hospitals.
- Nursing homes that provide skilled, intermediate, and less intensive levels of health care.
- Drug and alcohol rehabilitation centers and other rehabilitation facilities (*AICPA Audit and Accounting Guide: Health Care Organizations*).

Payments for these health care organizations come from many sources, including Medicare, Medicaid, commercial insurance companies, nonprofit insurance companies, state and local assistance programs, and directly from patients.

The *Health Care Guide* makes a distinction between health care organizations and voluntary health and welfare organizations, a distinction that is sometimes difficult in practice. The organizations just listed that are legally nonprofit but raise essentially all revenues from services produced are health care organizations and are subject to the *Health Care Guide*. The *Health Care Guide* calls these organizations Not-for-Profit, Business-Oriented Organizations. If similar organizations raise a significant amount or nearly all their resources from voluntary contributions or grants, then they are subject to the guidance in the *Not-for-Profit Guide* as illustrated in Chapter 10 of this text. The *Health Care Guide* calls these organizations Not-for-Profit Nonbusiness-Oriented Organizations.

ACCOUNTING AND REPORTING REQUIREMENTS OF THE *HEALTH CARE GUIDE*

The AICPA *Health Care Guide* provides certain additional accounting and reporting requirements beyond those required by the FASB (Chapter 10) and the GASB

---

[1] American Institute of Certified Public Accountants, *AICPA Audit and Accounting Guide: Health Care Organizations* (New York: AICPA, 2002).

(Chapter 6) standards. As both the FASB and the GASB approved the *Health Care Guide,* its requirements constitute Category B GAAP and must be followed by all health care organizations. Some of the more important requirements follow:

Financial Statements
- Financial statements include a Balance Sheet, a Statement of Operations, a Statement of Changes in Equity (or Net Assets/Fund Balance), a Statement of Cash Flows, and the Notes. FASB and GASB requirements determine much of the format; for example, different rules apply to cash flow statements. The Statement of Operations may be combined with the Statement of Changes in Equity, especially for governmental health care entities.
- Private sector not-for-profit hospitals must provide a performance indicator, such as Excess of Revenues over Expenses, as well as all other changes in unrestricted net assets for the period. The same is true for governmental health care entities. The following items *must* be shown below the performance indicator:
  - Transactions with owners acting in that capacity.
  - Equity transfers involving other entities that control the reporting entity, are controlled by the reporting entity, or are under the common control of the reporting entity.
  - Receipt of restricted contributions.
  - Contributions of (and assets released from donor restrictions related to) long-lived assets.
  - Unrealized gains and losses on investments not restricted by donors or by law, except for those investments classified as trading securities.
  - Investment returns restricted by donors or by law.
  - Other items that are required by GAAP to be reported separately (such as extraordinary items, the effect of discontinued operations, and accounting changes).
- Health care organizations, other than continuing care communities, are required to provide a classified balance sheet.

Revenues
- Patient service revenues are to be reported net of adjustments for contractual and other adjustments in the operating statement. Significant revenue under capitation agreements (revenues from third-party payors based on number of employees to be covered, for example, instead of services performed) is to be reported separately. Note disclosure is to indicate the methods of revenue recognition and description of the types and amounts of contractual adjustments.
- Patient service revenue does not include charity care. Management's policy for providing charity care and the level of charity care provided should be disclosed in the notes.

- Operating revenues are often classified as net patient service revenue, premium revenue (from capitation agreements—agreements whereby the entity is to provide service to a group or individual for a fixed fee), and other revenue from activities such as parking lot, gift shop, cafeteria, and tuition. If significant, tuition revenue may be reported separately. Unrestricted gifts and bequests and investment income for current unrestricted purposes may be reported as either operating or nonoperating revenue, depending on the policy of the entity.

Classifications
- Expenses may be reported by either their natural classifications (salaries, supplies, and so on) or their functional classifications (professional care of patients, general services, and so on). Private sector not-for-profit health care entities must disclose expenses by their functional classifications if not provided in the Statement of Operations. Functional classifications should be based on full cost allocations. The *Health Care Guide* suggests that functions may be as abbreviated as (1) health services and (2) general and administrative or given more detailed descriptions such as *physician services, research,* and *teaching.*
- As is true for other not-for-profits, plant acquired with either unrestricted or restricted resources may be (1) recorded initially as unrestricted or (2) recorded initially as temporarily restricted and then reclassified in accordance with the depreciation schedule.
- "Assets whose use is limited" is an unrestricted balance sheet category used in health care reporting to show limitations on the use of assets due to bond covenant restrictions and governing board plans for future use. This category is especially important for private sector, not-for-profit health care entities as the restricted category is limited to restrictions placed by contributors.
- FASB *Statement 117* reports net assets as permanently restricted, temporarily restricted, or unrestricted. It also requires that the changes in each of the three net asset classifications be shown. As will be described later, GASB standards present net assets of governmental health care organizations using different categories than those of private organizations.

ILLUSTRATIVE TRANSACTIONS AND FINANCIAL STATEMENTS

Entries for typical transactions are listed next as they are assumed to occur in a hypothetical nongovernmental, nonprofit hospital. The entries are directly traceable to the financial statements (Illustrations 12–2 through 12–4). All amounts are in thousands.

Beginning Trial Balance
Assume the beginning trial balance for the Nonprofit Hospital, as of January 1, 2003, is as follows (in thousands):

	Debits	Credits
Cash	$ 2,450	
Patient Accounts Receivable	14,100	
Allowance for Uncollectible Patient Accounts Receivable		$ 1,500
Contributions Receivable	5,250	
Allowance for Uncollectible Contributions		800
Supplies	400	
Investments—Assets Whose Use Is Limited	1,500	
Investments—Other	17,100	
Property, Plant, and Equipment	22,300	
Accumulated Depreciation— Property, Plant, and Equipment		11,300
Accounts Payable		800
Accrued Expenses		900
Long-Term Debt—Current Installment		1,000
Long-Term Debt—Noncurrent		10,800
Net Assets—Unrestricted—Board Designated		1,500
Net Assets—Unrestricted—Undesignated		13,100
Net Assets—Temporarily Restricted		10,100
Net Assets—Permanently Restricted		11,300
Totals	$63,100	$63,100

Assume that the $10,100 of temporarily restricted net assets are restricted as follows: program, $4,000; time, $4,500; plant acquisition, $1,600. Assume that the board designations are all for capital improvements. Note that all property, plant, and equipment are recorded in the unrestricted net asset class—it is the policy of the Nonprofit Hospital to record acquisitions of plant with either unrestricted or restricted resources in the unrestricted net asset class, as permitted by the FASB. Also note that it is the policy to record all gifts, bequests, and investment income as Nonoperating Income.

During the year, gross patient service revenue amounted to $82,656, of which $71,650 was received in cash. Contractual adjustments to third-party payors, such as insurance companies and health maintenance organizations, amounted to $10,000. These amounts do not include charity care, which is not formally recorded in the accounts. In the Statement of Operations, Contractual Adjustments (a contra-revenue account) is offset against Patient Service Revenue, and Net Patient Service Revenue is reported in the amount of $72,656 in accord with *Health Care Guide* pronouncements.

	Debits	Credits
1a. Cash	71,650	
Patient Accounts Receivable	11,006	
Operating Revenues—Unrestricted—Patient Service Revenue		82,656

	Debits	Credits
1b. Contractual Adjustments—Unrestricted	10,000	
Patient Accounts Receivable		10,000

Patient accounts receivable in the amount of $1,300 were written off. The estimated bad debts for 2003 amounted to $1,500 and are classified as General Services:

	Debits	Credits
2a. Allowance for Patient Accounts Receivable	1,300	
Patient Accounts Receivable		1,300
2b. General Services Expense	1,500	
Allowance for Patient Accounts Receivable		1,500

During the year, premium revenue from capitation agreements amounted to $20,000, all of which was received in cash. Other operating revenues were also received in cash in the amount of $5,460; these included revenues from the gift shop, parking lot, and cafeteria operations and from tuition from nursing students:

	Debits	Credits
3. Cash	25,460	
Operating Revenues—Unrestricted—Premium Revenue		20,000
Operating Revenues—Unrestricted—Other Revenue		5,460

Nonoperating revenues related to undesignated resources amounted to $1,856, all of which was received in cash. This included $822 in unrestricted gifts and bequests, $750 in unrestricted income on investments of endowment funds, and $284 in investment income from other investments:

	Debits	Credits
4. Cash	1,856	
Nonoperating Income—Unrestricted—Gifts and Bequests		822
Nonoperating Income—Unrestricted—Income on Investments of Endowment Funds		750
Nonoperating Income—Unrestricted—Investment Income		284

Investment income related to Assets Whose Use Is Limited amounted to $120, all of which is board designated for future capital improvements:

	Debits	Credits
5. Cash—Assets Whose Use Is Limited	120	
Nonoperating Income—Unrestricted—		
Assets Whose Use Is Limited for Capital Improvements—		
Investment Income		120

Supplies were purchased in the amount of $500; accounts payable and accrued expenses at the beginning of the year were paid:

	Debits	Credits
6. Supplies	500	
Accounts Payable	800	
Accrued Expenses	900	
Cash		2,200

Expenses for the year included: professional care of patients, $75,656; general services, $14,105; administrative services, $15,245. Of that amount, $3,500 was from resources restricted by the donors for program purposes. The expenses included depreciation and amortization of $4,800, and the use of supplies amounting to $400. Cash was paid in the amount of $97,906, accounts payable increased $900, and accrued expenses increased $1,000:

	Debits	Credits
7a. Operating Expenses—Professional Care of Patients	75,656	
Operating Expenses—General Services	14,105	
Operating Expenses—Administrative Services	15,245	
Accumulated Depreciation—		
Property, Plant, and Equipment		4,800
Supplies		400
Accounts Payable		900
Accrued Expenses		1,000
Cash		97,906
7b. Reclassifications from Temporarily Restricted Net Assets—		
Satisfaction of Program Restrictions	3,500	
Reclassifications to Unrestricted Net Assets—		
Satisfaction of Program Restrictions		3,500

Cash was received for pledges made in 2002 in the amount of $4,200. That amount had been reflected as temporarily restricted net assets, based on time restrictions:

	Debits	Credits
8a. Cash	4,200	
Contributions Receivable		4,200

	Debits	Credits
8b. Reclassifications from Temporarily Restricted Net Assets— Expiration of Time Restrictions	4,200	
Reclassifications to Unrestricted Net Assets— Expiration of Time Restrictions		4,200

Property, plant, and equipment was acquired at a cost of $5,200. Of that amount, $1,200 was from resources temporarily restricted for plant acquisition. Since the policy of the Nonprofit Hospital is to record all plant as unrestricted, the $1,200 is reclassified.

9a. Property, Plant, and Equipment	5,200	
Cash		5,200
9b. Reclassifications from Temporarily Restricted Net Assets— Satisfaction of Plant Acquisition Restrictions	1,200	
Reclassification to Unrestricted Net Assets— Satisfaction of Plant Acquisition Restrictions		1,200

Contributions were received as follows: for unrestricted purposes in 2004 and beyond (time restrictions), $4,400; for restricted purposes other than plant, $3,800; $4,300 for the construction of a new maternity wing (scheduled for 2004); $800 for endowment purposes. $5,600 was received in cash, and $7,700 was pledged:

10. Cash	5,600	
Contributions Receivable	7,700	
Revenues—Temporarily Restricted—Contributions		12,500
Revenues—Permanently Restricted—Contributions		800

Endowment pledges receivable at the beginning of the year in the amount of $800 were received. Remaining pledges of $300 were written off:

11. Cash	800	
Allowance for Uncollectible Contributions	300	
Contributions Receivable		1,100

Principal on long-term debt was paid in the amount of $1,000; an additional $1,000 was classified as current; and $600 of interest was paid on the last day of the year. Interest is classified as an operating expense in the statement of operations.

	Debits	Credits
12a. Long-Term Debt—Current Installment	1,000	
Cash		1,000
12b. Long-Term Debt—Noncurrent	1,000	
Long-Term Debt—Current Installment		1,000
12c. Operating Expenses—Interest	600	
Cash		600

Investment income, restricted as to purpose, amounted to $200:

	Debits	Credits
13. Cash	200	
Investment Income—Temporarily Restricted		200

Investments, carried at a value of $4,000, were sold for $4,100. The gain was an increase in temporarily restricted net assets:

	Debits	Credits
14. Cash	4,100	
Investments—Other		4,000
Net Realized and Unrealized Gains on Investments— Temporarily Restricted		100

$6,600 in investments were purchased during the year. This included the $120 set aside for capital improvements in transaction 5:

	Debits	Credits
15. Investments—Assets Whose Use Is Limited	120	
Investments—Other	6,480	
Cash—Assets Whose Use Is Limited		120
Cash		6,480

At year-end, it was determined that the market value of investments (other than board designated) increased in value by $100. However, this is a combination of a gain of $650 in resources held for temporarily restricted purposes and a loss of $550 in resources held for permanently restricted resources.

	Debits	Credits
16. Investments—Other	100	
Net Realized and Unrealized Losses on Investments— Permanently Restricted	550	
Net Realized and Unrealized Gains on Investments— Temporarily Restricted		650

Closing entries are made for the unrestricted net asset class. Two entries are necessary:

	Debits	Credits
17. Operating Revenues—Unrestricted—Patient Service Revenue	82,656	
Operating Revenues—Unrestricted—Premium Revenue	20,000	
Operating Revenues—Unrestricted—Other Revenue	5,460	
Nonoperating Income—Unrestricted—Gifts and Bequests	822	
Nonoperating Income—Unrestricted—Income on Investments of Endowment Funds	750	
Nonoperating Income—Unrestricted—Investment Income	284	
Reclassifications to Unrestricted Net Assets—Satisfaction of Program Restrictions	3,500	
Reclassifications to Unrestricted Net Assets—Expiration of Time Restrictions	4,200	
Reclassifications to Unrestricted Net Assets—Satisfaction of Plant Acquisition Restrictions	1,200	
Contractual Adjustments—Unrestricted		10,000
Operating Expenses—Professional Care of Patients		75,656
Operating Expenses—General Services		15,605
Operating Expenses—Administrative Services		15,245
Operating Expenses—Interest		600
Operating Expenses—Net Assets—Unrestricted—Undesignated		1,766
18. Nonoperating Income—Unrestricted—Assets Whose Use Is Limited for Capital Improvements—Investment Income	120	
Net Assets—Unrestricted—Board Designated		120

The closing entry is made for temporarily restricted net assets:

	Debits	Credits
19. Revenues—Temporarily Restricted—Contributions	12,500	
Investment Income—Temporarily Restricted	200	
Net Realized and Unrealized Gains on Investments—Temporarily Restricted	750	
Reclassifications from Temporarily Restricted Net Assets—Satisfaction of Program Restrictions		3,500
Reclassifications from Temporarily Restricted Net Assets—Expiration of Time Restrictions		4,200
Reclassifications from Temporarily Restricted Net Assets—Satisfaction of Plant Acquisition Restrictions		1,200
Net Assets—Temporarily Restricted		4,550

Finally, the closing entry is made for permanently restricted net assets:

	Debits	Credits
20. Revenues—Permanently Restricted—Contributions	800	
Net Realized and Unrealized Losses on Investments— Permanently Restricted		550
Net Assets—Permanently Restricted		250

Illustrative Statements for Private Sector Not-for-Profit Health Care Entities

Financial statements required for private sector not-for-profit hospitals include the Statement of Operations, Statement of Changes in Net Assets, Statement of Financial Position, and a Statement of Cash Flows. Illustrative statements for the Nonprofit Hospital are shown as Illustrations 12–1 through 12–4 in this chapter.

ILLUSTRATION 12–1

NONPROFIT HOSPITAL
Statement of Operations
For the Year Ended December 31, 2003
(in thousands of dollars)

Operating Revenues:			
Net Patient Service Revenue			$ 72,656
Premium Revenue			20,000
Other Revenue			5,460
Net Assets Released from Restrictions Used for Operations:			
Expiration of Time Restrictions			4,200
Satisfaction of Program Restrictions			3,500
Total Operating Revenues			$105,816
Operating Expenses:			
Professional Care of Patients	$75,656		
General Services	15,605		
Administrative Services	15,245		
Interest	600		
Total Operating Expenses			107,106
Operating Loss			(1,290)
Other Income:			
Unrestricted Gifts and Bequests		$ 822	
Income on Investments of Endowment Funds		750	
Investment Income		284	
Investment Income Limited by Board Action for Capital Improvements		120	1,976
Excess of Revenues over Expenses			686
Net Assets Released from Restrictions Used for Plant Acquisition			1,200
Increase in Unrestricted Net Assets			$ 1,886

Statement of Operations As the FASB permits considerable flexibility for the Statement of Activities, the *Health Care Guide* has prescribed a Statement of Operations and a Statement of Changes in Net Assets, although the two may be combined. Illustration 12–1 reflects a Statement of Operations that meets the requirements of FASB *Statement 117* and the AICPA *Health Care Guide*.

Statement of Changes in Net Assets The Statement of Changes in Net Assets shown in Illustration 12–2 fulfills the FASB requirement to show the changes in net assets by net asset class and in total. As indicated earlier, the information presented in Illustration 12–2 might have been combined with the information in Illustration 12–1.

Statement of Financial Position Several format possibilities also exist for the Statement of Financial Position, or Balance Sheet, as long as total assets, liabilities, and net assets as well as the unrestricted, temporarily restricted, and permanently restricted net assets are shown. Illustration 12–3 presents one possibility.

ILLUSTRATION 12–2

NONPROFIT HOSPITAL
Statement of Changes in Net Assets
For the Year Ended December 31, 2003
(in thousands of dollars)

Unrestricted Net Assets:	
Excess of Revenues over Expenses	$ 686
Net Assets Released from Restrictions Used for Plant Acquisition	1,200
Increase in Unrestricted Net Assets	1,886
Temporarily Restricted Net Assets:	
Contribution for Future Years	4,400
Contributions for Restricted Purposes Other Than Plant	3,800
Contributions for New Maternity Wing	4,300
Net Realized and Unrealized Gains and Losses on Investments	750
Investment Income	200
Net Assets Released from Restrictions:	
Expiration of Time Restrictions	(4,200)
Satisfaction of Program Restrictions	(3,500)
Satisfaction of Plant Acquisition Restrictions	(1,200)
Increase in Temporarily Restricted Net Assets	4,550
Permanently Restricted Net Assets:	
Endowment Contributions	800
Net Realized and Unrealized Gains and Losses on Investments	(550)
Increase in Permanently Restricted Net Assets	250
Increase in Net Assets	6,686
Net Assets, Beginning of Year	36,000
Net Assets, End of Year	$42,686

ILLUSTRATION 12-3

NONPROFIT HOSPITAL
Statements of Financial Position
For the Years Ended December 31, 2003 and 2002
(in thousands of dollars)

	2003	2002
Assets:		
Current Assets:		
Cash and Cash Equivalents	$ 2,930	$ 2,450
Patient Accounts Receivable (Net of Allowance for Uncollectibles of $1,700 and $1,500)	12,106	12,600
Contributions Receivable (Net of Allowance for Uncollectibles of $500 and $800)	7,150	4,450
Supplies	500	400
Total Current Assets	22,686	19,900
Noncurrent Assets:		
Investments—Assets Whose Use Is Limited	1,620	1,500
Investments—Other	19,680	17,100
Property, Plant, and Equipment (Net of Accumulated Depreciation of $16,100 and $11,300)	11,400	11,000
Total Assets	$55,386	$49,500
Liabilities and Net Assets:		
Current Liabilities:		
Accounts Payable	$ 900	$ 800
Accrued Expenses	1,000	900
Current Installment of Long-Term Debt	1,000	1,000
Total Current Liabilities	2,900	2,700
Long-Term Debt	9,800	10,800
Total Liabilities	12,700	13,500
Net Assets:		
Board Designated	1,620	1,500
Other Unrestricted	14,866	13,100
Total Unrestricted	16,486	14,600
Temporarily Restricted	14,650	10,100
Permanently Restricted	11,550	11,300
Total Net Assets	42,686	36,000
Total Liabilities and Net Assets	$55,386	$49,500

The Statement of Financial Position might be modified in several ways. For example, some of the assets that are set aside for restricted purposes might be reported on separate lines. The restricted net assets might be labeled as to the nature of the restrictions. Alternatively, much of that information could be presented in the notes to the financial statements.

ILLUSTRATION 12–4

NONPROFIT HOSPITAL
Statement of Cash Flows
For the Year Ended December 31, 2003
(in thousands of dollars)

Cash Flows from Operating Activities:	
Change in Net Assets	$ 6,686
Adjustments to Reconcile Change in Net Assets to	
Net Cash Provided by Operating Activities:	
Depreciation	4,800
Net Unrealized Gains on Investments	(100)
Decrease in Patient Accounts Receivable	494
Increase in Contributions Receivable	(2,700)
Increase in Supplies	(100)
Increase in Accounts Payable	100
Increase in Accrued Expenses	100
Gain on Sale of Investments	(100)
Contribution Restricted to Investment in	
Property, Plant, and Equipment	(1,300)
Contribution Restricted to Long-Term Investment	(1,300)
Cash Flows from Operating Activities	6,580
Cash Flows from Investing Activities:	
Acquisition of Property, Plant, and Equipment	(5,200)
Purchase of Investments	(6,600)
Sale of Investments	4,100
Cash Flows from Investing Activities	(7,700)
Cash Flows from Financing Activities:	
Proceeds from Contributions Restricted for:	
Investment in Endowment	1,300
Investment in Property, Plant, and Equipment	1,300
Other Financing Activities:	
Payments on Long-Term Debt	(1,000)
Cash Flows from Financing Activities	1,600
Net Increase in Cash and Cash Equivalents	480
Cash and Cash Equivalents, January 1, 2003	2,450
Cash and Cash Equivalents, December 31, 2003	$ 2,930
Supplemental disclosure of cash flow information:	
Cash paid during the year for interest	600

Statement of Cash Flows Illustration 12–4 presents a Statement of Cash Flows for the Nonprofit Hospital using the indirect method. The direct method is also acceptable (see Illustration 11–4) for private not-for-profit organizations and is required for governmental health care organizations (see Illustration 6–3).

FINANCIAL REPORTING FOR GOVERNMENTAL HEALTH CARE ENTITIES

Because health care organizations may be private not-for-profits or governmental, it is important to identify the appropriate set of standards that govern financial reporting. The first and second columns of Illustration 1–1 of this text describe the various levels of GAAP for private-not-for-profit and governmental health care organizations, respectively. As mentioned earlier, health care entities that are determined to be state and local governments, such as county hospitals, follow the accounting and reporting standards of GASB *Statement 34* (category A GAAP) and the AICPA *Health Care Guide* (category B GAAP). Governmental health care entities that choose to report as special-purpose entities that are engaged only in business-type activities will prepare a Statement of Net Assets; a Statement of Revenues, Expenses, and Changes in Net Assets; and a Statement of Cash Flows. The Statement of Revenues, Expenses, and Changes in Net Assets may be separated into two statements, as shown for private health care entities; however, the reporting framework does not encourage such a presentation.

Governmental health care entities reporting as enterprise activities use full accrual accounting. The statements are similar to those presented in Chapter 6 (Illustrations 6–1, 6–2, and 6–3) with modifications as required by the AICPA *Health Care Guide*.

The **Statement of Net Assets** (not illustrated) is similar to that presented in Illustration 6–1 or in Illustration 9–3 for public colleges and universities. It is permissible to use a balance sheet format, where assets equal liabilities plus net assets. Net assets are to be categorized as (1) invested in capital assets, net of related debt, (2) restricted, and (3) unrestricted.

The **Statement of Revenues, Expenses, and Changes in Net Assets** (not illustrated) is similar to Illustrations 6–2 and 9–4. Both GASB and the AICPA require presentation of a performance indicator, such as Excess of Revenues over Expenses. In addition, the requirement of the AICPA to place certain items below the performance indicator (such as receipt of restricted contributions) applies.

The **Statement of Cash Flows** (not illustrated) follows GASB standards, as reflected in Illustrations 6–3 and 9–5. The direct method must be used. Four categories of cash flows must be presented. A reconciliation is made between operating income and the cash flows from operating activities.

FINANCIAL REPORTING FOR COMMERCIAL (FOR-PROFIT) HEALTH CARE ENTITIES

Health care entities that are investor-owned and are for-profit enterprises are subject to the FASB (category A GAAP) and the AICPA *Health Care Guide* (category B

GAAP). However, none of the FASB pronouncements related to not-for-profit organizations, such as *Statements 116* and *117,* apply. Full accrual accounting applies in the same manner as it would for other commercial enterprises. Equity accounts consist of paid in capital and retained earnings. Consult intermediate and advanced accounting texts for accounting and financial reporting for commercial health care entities.

ACADEMIC RESEARCH

Despite the significance of health care costs and the continuing debate regarding the role of the federal government in regulating the industry, relatively little academic research has been done on financial reporting by health care organizations. Forgione (1999) provides a review of the existing academic studies and describes sources of financial information that might lead to new studies.[2] Important issues in early studies are measuring hospital performance, determining optimal capital structure, and predicting business failure. However, all of the accounting studies reviewed by Forgione predate the issuance of FASB *Statement 117* and GASB *Statement 34* and we do not know how well current financial reports are meeting the needs of users. Forgione concludes "the opportunities for future research are manifold, high-quality data is available, and the topic carries a timeliness, and economic and social relevance that is unparalleled by many other lines of inquiry."

Summary and Conclusions regarding Health Care Accounting and Reporting

Health care entities may be nongovernmental, not-for-profit, governmental, or commercial (for-profit). Nongovernmental, not-for-profit, and commercial health care entities have Category A GAAP established by the Financial Accounting Standards Board. State and local governmental health care entities follow the principles of the GASB. All, however, are subject to the AICPA *Health Care Guide,* which is accepted by both FASB and GASB as being Category B GAAP.

This chapter has concentrated on accounting and financial reporting required for nongovernmental, not-for-profit health care entities, as these are the most numerous. General FASB requirements regarding financial reporting, the use of net asset classes, and so on are supplanted by requirements of the *Health Care Guide.* The financial statements reported as Illustrations 12–1 through 12–4 meet the requirements of both the FASB and the AICPA.

---

[2] D. Forgione, "Healthcare Accouting Research: A Review of the Professional Literature, Models, Data, and Research Opportunities," *Research in Governmental and Nonprofit Accouting,* 10, pp. 163–200.

Questions and Exercises

12–1. Write the letter corresponding with the *best* answer to each of the following questions:

1. Which of the following health care entities is to follow the requirements listed in the AICPA *Health Care Guide?*
    a. Governmental health care entities.
    b. Nongovernmental, not-for-profit health care entities.
    c. Nongovernmental, for-profit health care entities.
    d. All of the above

2. Which of the following health care entities would *not* be subject to the standards issued by the Financial Accounting Standards Board?
    a. Nongovernmental, not-for-profit health care entities.
    b. Nongovernmental, for-profit health care entities.
    c. Governmental health care entities.
    d. None of the above.

3. The fund types required under the FASB standards include:
    a. Unrestricted, specific purpose, plant replacement and expansion, and endowment.
    b. Unrestricted and restricted.
    c. Permanently restricted, temporarily restricted, and unrestricted.
    d. None of the above.

4. Financial statements required for nongovernmental, not-for-profit health care entities include:
    a. Statement of Operations, Statement of Changes in Net Assets, Balance Sheet, Statement of Cash Flows.
    b. Statement of Activities, Statement of Financial Position, and Statement of Cash Flows.
    c. Statement of Operations, Statement of Changes in Fund Balances, Balance Sheet, Statement of Cash Flows.
    d. Statement of Revenues, Expenses, and Changes in Retained Earnings, Statement of Financial Position, and Statement of Cash Flows.

5. The Hope Hospital, a private-sector nonprofit entity, received $1,000,000 in unrestricted cash from a donor. The board decided to place that money in an endowment and never expend the principal. The $1,000,000 would be classified, in the Statement of Financial Position, as:
    a. Unrestricted, undesignated.
    b. Permanently restricted.
    c. Temporarily restricted.
    d. Unrestricted Assets Whose Use Is Limited.

6. In 2003, a nonprofit hospital received a pledge of $100,000 restricted to cancer research. The cash was received and the research expenditures took place in 2004. The hospital would record a(n):
   a. Temporarily restricted revenue in 2003 and an unrestricted expense in 2004.
   b. Temporarily restricted revenue in 2003 and a temporarily restricted expense in 2004.
   c. Unrestricted revenue and expense in 2004.
   d. Temporarily restricted revenue in 2003 and an unrestricted expenditure in 2004.
7. A donor gave $100,000 to a nonprofit hospital in 2003 with the restriction that it be used for the purchase of equipment. While the cash was received in 2003, the equipment was purchased in 2004. The hospital would record the $100,000 as:
   a. A temporarily restricted revenue in 2003 and the equipment as an unrestricted fixed asset in 2004.
   b. A temporarily restricted revenue in 2003 and the equipment as a temporarily restricted fixed asset in 2004.
   c. A temporarily restricted revenue in 2004 and the equipment as an unrestricted fixed asset in 2004.
   d. Either *a* or *b*, depending on the choice of the hospital.
8. A donor gave $100,000 to a nonprofit hospital in 2003 with the restriction that it be used for the purchase of equipment. While the cash was received in 2003, the equipment was purchased in 2004. In its Statement of Cash Flows, the hospital would report the $100,000 as:
   a. Cash provided by operating activities in 2003 and as cash used for investing activities in 2004.
   b. A noncash transaction.
   c. Cash provided by financing activities in 2003 and as cash used for investing activities in 2004.
   d. Cash provided by investing activities in 2003 and as cash used for financing activities in 2004.
9. A donor made a pledge, unrestricted as to purpose, in late 2003 with the intent that the funds be used in 2004. The cash was transferred in 2004. The health care organization would record the amount as:
   a. Unrestricted revenue when cash is received in 2004.
   b. Temporarily restricted revenue in 2003 and as a reclassification when expended in 2004 or later years.
   c. Temporarily restricted revenue in 2003 and as a reclassification in 2004, whether or not expended.
   d. Unrestricted revenue in 2003.

10. Which of the following is *not* true regarding the accounting and reporting requirements for private sector not-for-profit health care entities?
    a. An intermediate measure of operations, such as operating income, is required, except for continuing care retirement communities.
    b. Requirements apply to health maintenance organizations, private practice associations, and home health agencies as well as hospitals.
    c. Patient service revenue does not include charity care.
    d. None of the above; all are true.

12–2. Select the letter corresponding with the *best* answer to each of the following questions:

1. Net Assets Invested in Capital Assets, Net of Related Debt is an account title that may appear in the statement of net assets for a:

	Government Owned Hospital	Private Not-for-Profit Hospital
a.	Yes	No
b.	No	Yes
c.	Yes	Yes
d.	No	No

2. Retained Earnings is an account title that may appear in the statement of net assets for a (an):

	Investor Owned Hospital	Private Not-for-Profit Hospital
a.	Yes	No
b.	No	Yes
c.	Yes	Yes
d.	No	No

3. Which of the following organizations would typically raise a significant portion of their resources from voluntary contributions or grants:

	Health Care Organizations	Voluntary Health and Welfare Organizations
a.	Yes	No
b.	No	Yes
c.	Yes	Yes
d.	No	No

4. Health care organizations are required to present a performance measure such as Excess of Revenues over Expenses. Which of the following items may be taken into account in the determination of this measure?
   a. Unrestricted contributions.
   b. Contributions restricted for cancer research.
   c. Contributions restricted for plant acquisition.
   d. All of the above.

5. A private not-for-profit health care organization provides services to an individual that it knows has no ability to pay. How should the organization report this activity?
   a. Record revenue for the amount of the care provided.
   b. Record bad debt expense for the amount of the care provided.
   c. Both *a* and *b* above.
   d. None of the above, record neither a revenue nor bad debt expense.

6. A private hospital billed patients $560,000 for the current month. The hospital expects the amount ultimately collected to be $440,000. The $120,000 difference is comprised of the following items: contractual adjustments with third-party payors $70,000, estimated uncollectible accounts $50,000. There is no charity care in the amount billed. How much net patient service revenue should be reported for the current month?
   a. $560,000.
   b. $510,000.
   c. $490,000.
   d. $440,000.

7. A private not-for-profit hospital billed patients $660,000 for the current month. The hospital expects the amount ultimately collected to be $460,000. The $200,000 difference is comprised of the following items: contractual adjustments with third-party payors $110,000, estimated uncollectible accounts $60,000, charity care $30,000. What is the amount of bad debt expense to be reported for the current month?
   a. $200,000.
   b. $170,000.
   c. $90,000.
   d. $60,000.

8. Which of the following are health care organizations according to the *AICPA Audit and Accounting Guide: Health Care Organizations* and must follow the reporting requirements of the guide? (Assume most revenues are received from patient service charges, rather than contributions.)

a. Individual doctors' practices.
b. Nursing homes.
c. Alcohol rehabilitation centers.
d. All of the above.

9. Government owned health care organizations differ from private not-for-profit heath care organizations in which of the following ways?

   a. Government owned organizations use the modified accrual basis of accounting and current financial resources measurement focus.
   b. Government owned organizations do not have to follow the requirements of the *AICPA Audit and Accounting Guide: Health Care Organizations*.
   c. Private not-for-profit organizations must distinguish between unrestricted, temporarily restricted, and permanently restricted net assets.
   d. All of the above.

10. Which of the following are applicable to a private investor owned health care facility?

    a. FASB *Statement 117*.
    b. The *AICPA Audit and Accounting Guide: Health Care Organizations*.
    c. Both *a* and *b* above.
    d. Neither *a* nor *b* above.

12–3. For each of the following transactions and events, indicate the effect it will have on each of the three categories appearing in the Statement of Operations for a not-for-profit health care organization.

Put an X in the appropriate column. If the net assets are unaffected, leave the column blank.

	Operating Revenues		Operating Expenses		Other Income	
	Increase	Decrease	Increase	Decrease	Increase	Decrease
Ex1			X			
Ex2						

Ex1: Recorded nursing salaries of $16,000.

Ex2: Collected $10,000 on patient accounts receivable.

1. A capital campaign in support of a new building brought in pledges of $50,000.
2. $5,000 was expended from the capital campaign on architects' fees. The organization records all fixed assets in the unrestricted class of net assets.
3. Estimate that the amounts collected from third-party payors will be $22,000 less than the amount billed, due to contractual adjustment.

4. Estimate that the amounts collected from individual patients will be $10,000 less than the amount billed.
5. Performed charity care of $6,000, (at normal billing rates).
6. Unrestricted income on endowments amounted to $5,000.
7. Interest expense totaled $850.
8. Investment income limited by board action for capital improvement amounted to $240.
9. Determined depreciation on plant and equipment to be $12,000.
10. Received $500 in unrestricted contributions.

12–4. Outline some of the similarities and differences in accounting and reporting among (a) nongovernmental, not-for-profit health care organizations, (b) governmental health care organizations, and (c) nongovernmental, for-profit health care organizations. Include the sources of GAAP, accounting and reporting for equity accounts, statements required, and any other categories you might think meaningful.

12–5. With regard to accounting for nongovernmental, not-for-profit health care entities, do the following:
  a. List the three net asset classes required under FASB *Statement 117*.
  b. List the four financial statements required under the AICPA *Health Care Guide*.
  c. Outline the accounting required, under FASB guidance, for a(n):
    (1) Endowment gift received in cash.
    (2) Pledge received in 2003, unrestricted as to purpose but restricted for use in 2004.
    (3) Pledge received in 2003, restricted as to purpose, other than plant, which is fulfilled in 2004.
  d. Outline the accounting required, under FASB guidance, for plant acquisition, using:
    (1) Unrestricted resources.
    (2) Temporarily restricted resources.
  e. List those items required to be reported "outside" the performance indicator in the Statement of Operations.

12–6. During 2004, the following transactions were recorded by the Baton Rouge Community Hospital, a private sector, not-for-profit institution.
  1. Gross charges for patient services, all charged to Patient Accounts Receivable, amounted to $1,100,000. Contractual adjustments with third-party payors amounted to $50,000.
  2. Charity services, not included in transaction 1, would amount to $100,000, had billings been made at gross amounts.

3. Other revenues, received in cash, were parking lot, $20,000; cafeteria, $15,000; gift shop, $5,000.
4. Cash gifts for cancer research amounted to $20,000 for the year. During the year, $15,000 was expended for cancer research (Debit Operating Expense—Research).
5. Mortgage bond payments amounted to $50,000 for principal and $30,000 for interest. Assume unrestricted resources are used.
6. During the year, the hospital received, in cash, unrestricted contributions of $40,000 and unrestricted income of $60,000 from endowment investments. (It is the hospital's practice to treat unrestricted gifts as nonoperating income.)
7. New equipment, costing $100,000, was acquired, using donor-restricted cash that was on hand at the beginning of the year. Baton Rouge's policy is to record all equipment in the unrestricted net asset class.
8. An old piece of lab equipment that originally cost $50,000 and that had an undepreciated cost of $10,000 was sold for $8,000 cash.
9. Pledges made in 2003 for use in 2004 that were unrestricted as to purpose were collected in the amount of $80,000. The $80,000 had been recorded in the Temporarily Restricted Net Asset Class. At the end of 2004, pledges received in the amount of $120,000 are intended to be paid and used for unrestricted purposes in 2005.
10. Cash contributions were received as follows: temporarily restricted for purposes other than plant, $40,000; temporarily restricted for plant acquisition, $30,000.
11. Bills totaling $1,000,000 were received for the following items:

Professional Care of Patients	$800,000
General Services	120,000
Administrative Services	80,000

12. Depreciation of plant and equipment amounted to $70,000, all charged to Professional Care of Patients.
13. Cash payments on vouchers payable amounted to $980,000. Cash collections of patient accounts receivable amounted to $1,080,000.
14. Closing entries were prepared.
    a. Record the transactions in the general journal of the Baton Rouge Community Hospital.
    b. Prepare, in good form, a Statement of Operations for the Baton Rouge Community Hospital for the year ended December 31, 2004.

12–7. Record the following transactions on the books of Hope Hospital, which follows FASB and AICPA standards. The year is 2003.
1. Hope received $120,000 in cash from pledges made in 2002 that were unrestricted as to purpose but intended to be expended in 2003.

2. Hope received $150,000 in pledges that indicated the money was to be paid in 2004 and used in that year for any purpose desired by the board.
3. Hope expended $30,000 for nursing training, using temporarily restricted resources that had been given in 2002 for that purpose.
4. Hope received $40,000, restricted by the donor for cancer research. The funds were not expended in 2003.
5. Hope received $50,000 in cash. The board decided to invest the funds for future plant expansion.

12–8. St. Joseph's Hospital follows FASB standards of accounting and reporting. On January 1, 2003, St. Joseph's received $1,000,000, restricted to the purchase of cancer diagnostic equipment. On January 1, 2004, the equipment was purchased with the cash. The equipment is expected to last four years and have a salvage value of $200,000 at the end of its useful life. Straight-line depreciation is used by St. Joseph's.
1. Record the journal entries on January 1, 2003, January 1, 2004, and December 31, 2004 (to record depreciation), assuming St. Joseph's follows the policy of recording all fixed assets as unrestricted.
2. Record the journal entries on January 1, 2003, January 1, 2004, and December 31, 2004 (to record depreciation), assuming St. Joseph's follows the policy of recording all fixed assets as temporarily restricted.
3. Compute the amount that would be included in net assets (after closing the books on December 31, 2004) for *(a)* unrestricted net assets and *(b)* temporarily restricted net assets under requirements (1) and (2). What incentives might exist for St. Joseph's to choose either (1) or (2)?

12–9. As of January 1, 2004, the trial balance for Haven Hospital was as follows:

	Debits	Credits
Cash	$ 130,000	
Patient Accounts Receivable	3,200,000	
Allowance for Uncollectible Patient Accounts Receivable		$ 650,000
Contributions Receivable	2,930,000	
Allowance for Uncollectible Contributions Receivable		353,000
Supplies	430,000	
Investments—Board Designated	1,300,000	
Investments—Other	11,500,000	
Property, Plant, and Equipment	6,500,000	
Accumulated Depreciation—Property, Plant, and Equipment		3,100,000
Accounts Payable		600,000
Long-Term Debt—Current Installment		200,000
Long-Term Debt—Noncurrent		4,600,000
Net Assets—Unrestricted—Board Designated		1,300,000
Net Assets—Unrestricted—Undesignated		2,036,000
Net Assets—Temporarily Restricted		6,144,000
Net Assets—Permanently Restricted		7,007,000
Totals	$25,990,000	$25,990,000

During the fiscal year ended December 31, 2004, the following transactions occurred:

1. Patient service revenue amounted to $21,200,000, all recorded on account. Contractual adjustments were recorded in the amount of $3,500,000. Cash was received on account in the amount of $18,100,000.
2. Other revenue (cafeteria, parking lot, etc.) amounted to $2,530,000, all received in cash.
3. Patient accounts in the amount of $430,000 were written off.
4. Unrestricted gifts and bequests were received in cash in the amount of $1,600,000. Unrestricted income on investments of endowment funds amounted to $600,000. (It is the hospital's practice to treat unrestricted gifts as nonoperating revenue.)
5. Investment income on board designated funds, which is limited by board policy to provide renewals and replacements, amounted to $120,000 and was received in cash. Do not increase board designated net assets at this stage but close out the revenue account to board designated net assets in entry 19.
6. Investment income, restricted for current restricted purposes was received in cash in the amount of $600,000. Investment income, required by donor agreement to be added to endowment balances, was received in cash in the amount of $50,000.
7. Cash contributions were received in the following amounts: $2,200,000 for current restricted purposes; $2,500,000 for future plant expansion; and $1,000,000 required by the donor to be invested permanently.
8. Pledges receivable in the amount of $2,100,000 were received in cash. These pledges were on hand at the beginning of the year (reflected in temporarily restricted net assets, for purposes of time) and were unrestricted as to purpose. In addition, pledges for endowment purposes were collected in the amount of $400,000.
9. $1,600,000 in temporarily restricted net assets were expended, as the donors stipulated, for cancer research. Debit Operating Expense—Research.
10. $2,350,000 in temporarily restricted net assets were expended for equipment, as provided for by the donor. The policy of Haven Hospital is to record all property, plant, and equipment as unrestricted.
11. A pledge drive during 2004 resulted in $2,700,000 in pledges that are intended by the donors to be used in 2005 for any purposes desired by the donor. In addition, $600,000 was received in pledges for endowment purposes. It was decided that the allowance for contributions was sufficient.
12. Supplies were purchased in the amount of $750,000, on account.

13. Additional expenses included: *(a)* professional care of patients, $18,100,000; *(b)* general services, $3,200,000; *(c)* administrative services, $2,610,000. All expenses were on account, except for $690,000 in supplies used, depreciation of $600,000, and bad debt estimates of $460,000.
14. Accounts were paid in the amount of $23,100,000.
15. Long-term debt was paid in the amount of $200,000. The portion to be paid next year is $300,000. Interest was paid in the amount of $280,000 and is reported as an operating expense.
16. Investments, carried at a basis of $4,000,000, were sold for $4,050,000. The $50,000 gain is considered to be temporarily restricted.
17. Cash in the amount of $6,530,000 was invested. Of that amount, $120,000 was from Cash—Assets Whose Use Is Limited and is designated by the board for renewals and replacements (see entry 5).
18. A reading of the financial press indicated that investments increased in market value by $1,200,000. Of that amount, $250,000 was in investments designated by the board for renewals and replacements, $800,000 is required by donors to be added to endowment balances, and the remainder is unrestricted.
19. Closing entries were prepared.

Required:

a. Prepare journal entries for each of the previous transactions.
b. Prepare a Statement of Operations for Haven Hospital for the year ended December 31, 2004.
c. Prepare a Statement of Changes in Net Assets for Haven Hospital for the year ended December 31, 2004.
d. Prepare a Statement of Financial Position for Haven Hospital as of December 31, 2004.
e. Prepare a Statement of Cash Flows for Haven Hospital for the year ended December 31, 2004, using the indirect method.
f. Using the direct method, prepare the Cash Flows from Operating Activities section of the Cash Flow Statement for Haven Hospital for the year ended December 31, 2004.

Chapter Thirteen

Governmental Auditing; The Single Audit Act; Tax-Exempt Organizations; Service Efforts and Accomplishments

Chapters 2 through 12 present accounting and financial reporting requirements for state and local government units and not-for-profit organizations. This chapter describes (1) the unique aspects of governmental auditing, (2) the Single Audit Act, (3) certain tax issues related to tax-exempt organizations, and (4) a possible future direction of the GASB—service efforts and accomplishments reporting.

GOVERNMENTAL AUDITING

Auditing of governmental and not-for-profit entities has much in common with auditing of business enterprises, including making judgments about internal controls, selectively testing transactions, assessing the fairness of financial statements, and issuing audit reports. However, governmental auditing, like governmental accounting, follows a unique set of professional guidelines established by a separate governing organization.

Governmental units and many not-for-profit organizations are subject to *Government Auditing Standards* in addition to the *Statements on Auditing Standards,* issued by the American Institute of Certified Public Accountants. *Government Auditing Standards* are issued by the U.S. General Accounting Office and apply to audits conducted to satisfy the requirements of the Single Audit Act as well as other governmental audits. In common terminology, the standards issued by the AICPA are known as GAAS (Generally Accepted Auditing Standards), and the standards issued by the GAO are known as GAGAS (Generally Accepted Government Auditing Standards).

Government Auditing Standards, commonly known as the yellow book, incorporate the AICPA standards and provide extensions that are necessary due to the unique nature of public entities. These extensions, for example, require auditor knowledge of government accounting and auditing, public availability of audit reports, written evaluations of internal controls, and distribution of the reports and availability of working papers to federal and state funding authorities. The standards also emphasize the heightened importance of government audits in a democratic society: "In an audit of a government entity or entity that receives government assistance, auditors may need to set lower materiality levels than in audits in the private sector because of the public accountability of the audited entity, the various legal and regulatory requirements, and the visibility and sensitivity of government programs, activities and functions" (paragraph 4.27).

At the time of this printing, the General Accounting Office had proposed substantial changes to *Government Auditing Standards*. The descriptions presented in the chapter reflect these proposed changes. However, it is possible that some modifications may have been rejected or other modifications accepted and the reader is encouraged to obtain a current copy of *Government Auditing Standards* before beginning a governmental audit engagement.

Additional guidance for audits of state and local governments is found in the *AICPA Audit and Accounting Guide: Audits of State and Local Governments.* Following the issuance of GASB *Statement 34, Basic Financial Statements and Management's Discussion and Analysis for State and Local Governments,* the AICPA formed a task force to revise the previous guide. The new guide was issued in 2002 and is effective for audits of fiscal periods beginning after June 15, 2003.

Types of Governmental Audits *Government Auditing Standards* identify four categories of professional engagements: financial audits, attestation engagements, performance audits, and nonaudit services. These are described in detail in Illustration 13–1. Nonaudit services are not covered by *Government Auditing Standards* and differ from the other types of engagements in that the auditors are providing information to a requesting party without providing verification or evaluation of the information. These engagements may result in a report but not an opinion on the information.

Financial audits must comply with the American Institute of Certified Public Accountants' (AICPA) generally accepted auditing standards for fieldwork and reporting as well as *Government Auditing Standards*. Governmental standards prescribe additional fieldwork and reporting requirements beyond those provided by the AICPA. For example, auditors are specifically required to test compliance with laws and regulations and internal control over financial reporting. With regard to communications, governmental auditors should communicate not only with officials of the audited organization, but with parties that have oversight responsibility for the audited organization such as legislative members or staff.

ILLUSTRATION 13–1 Types of Governmental Audits and Attestation Engagements*

1. **Financial audits** primarily concern providing reasonable assurance about whether financial statements are presented fairly in all material respects in conformity with generally accepted accounting principles or with a comprehensive basis of accounting other than GAAP.
2. **Attestation engagements** concern examining, reviewing, or performing agreed upon procedures on a subject matter or an assertion about a subject matter and reporting on the results....Attestation engagements can cover a broad range of financial or nonfinancial objectives and can be part of a financial audit or other type of engagement.
3. **Performance audits** are an objective and systematic examination of evidence to provide an independent assessment of the performance and management of a program against objective criteria or an assessment of best practices and other information. Performance audits provide information to improve program operations and facilitate decision making by parties with responsibility to oversee or initiate corrective action, and improve public accountability.
4. **Nonaudit services** consist of gathering, providing, or explaining information requested by decision makers or providing advice or assistance to management officials.

*Source: Comptroller General of the United States, Exposure Draft: *Government Auditing Standards* (Washington D.C.: U.S. General Accounting Office, 2002).

Attestation engagements encompass a wide range of activities. These include reporting on an entity's: (1) system of internal control, (2) compliance with laws and regulations, (3) prospective financial information, and (4) costs under contracts. Similar to financial audits, attestation engagements must comply with both the AICPA's attestation standards and *Government Auditing Standards.*

Performance audits encompass a variety of objectives and may be more analogous to the functions normally performed by internal auditors in the private sector, except that the results are made public. Generally they are undertaken to assess: program effectiveness and results; economy and efficiency; internal controls as they relate to program management and reporting; and compliance with legal requirements and other program matters. Effectiveness audits measure the extent to which a program is achieving its goals while economy and efficiency audits are concerned with whether an organization is acquiring, protecting, and using its resources in the most productive manner to achieve program objectives. For example, an auditor performing an economy and efficiency audit of a Head Start program might observe purchasing procedures and evaluate transportation routes, classroom sizes, and general office procedures. An auditor performing an effectiveness audit would look to the original legislation to determine explicit or implicit objectives, develop criteria to determine whether the objectives were being met, and evaluate the relative benefit of alternative approaches. The audit team will often include specialists outside of accounting who are better prepared to assess program effectiveness. Performance audits are not intended to be done on an annual basis but are expected to be performed periodically as a means of holding government accountable for carrying out its legislative mandates.

Opinion Units In response to changes brought about by GASB *Statement 34,* the 2002 *AICPA Audit and Accounting Guide: Audits of State and Local Governments* developed the concept of opinion units. In any audit engagement, the auditor must determine a level of materiality. This determination is then used to plan, perform, and evaluate the results of audit procedures. Because of the various levels of reporting by governments (government-wide, fund-type, and individual fund), it was not clear which level was most appropriate for determining materiality.

The 2002 guide requires a separate (quantitative) materiality evaluation at each opinion unit. Each of the following is considered an opinion unit:

- Governmental activities.
- Business-type activities.
- Each major fund (both governmental and enterprise).
- The aggregate of all discretely presented component units.
- The aggregate of all remaining fund information.

The first two categories relate to information contained in the government-wide financial statements and the remaining three relate to information contained in the fund basis financial statements. The final category includes nonmajor governmental and enterprise funds, internal service funds, and fiduciary funds.

One effect of reporting on opinion units is that some opinion units may receive unqualified or clean opinions while others receive modified opinions. For example, failure to report infrastructure assets could result in an adverse opinion regarding the governmental activities and an unqualified opinion for the business-type, major fund, aggregate component unit, and aggregate of all remaining fund information. Audit reports are discussed in the next section.

Audit Reports Reporting requirements are a combination of requirements of the *Government Auditing Standards* and the single audit requirements (described in the next section). A reporting package is due to a designated federal repository nine months after the end of the fiscal year. Part of the reporting is done by the auditor and part by the audited organization. The auditor is required to prepare up to five reports:
1. A report containing an opinion on the financial statements.
2. A report discussing the evaluation and testing of internal control and compliance with laws and regulations.
3. A report discussing significant deficiencies in internal controls.
4. A report describing instances of fraud, illegal acts, or other material noncompliance.
5. A report containing the views of responsible officials of the audited organization regarding any reported significant deficiencies.

Unlike private sector audits, the auditor is required to report directly to appropriate officials, such as funding agencies or legislative bodies, as well as to the organization's board or audit committee. Additionally, the auditor must report the existence of any privileged or confidential information not contained in the audit reports.

Guidelines for conducting and reporting on financial audits of state and local governments are contained in the 2002 AICPA publication, *Audits of State and*

Local Governmental Units. The AICPA has developed standard wording for auditor's reports to make clear the responsibility the auditor is accepting. If the financial statements are prepared in conformity with generally accepted accounting principles, the auditor expresses an "unqualified" or clean opinion. An example of an independent auditor's report expressing an unqualified opinion for a government subject to *Government Auditing Standards* is shown in Illustration 13–2. Note that the title of the report stresses that the auditor is independent. The report contains five paragraphs. The first paragraph, the introductory and scope paragraph, states that the financial statements were audited, that the financial statements are the responsibility of the city's management, and that the auditor's responsibility is to express an opinion on the financial statements based on the audit. The basic financial statements are the minimum that should be prepared under GAAP and contain the government-wide financial statements, fund financial statements, and notes to the financial statements.

The first paragraph also indicates (for each opinion unit) which financial statements were audited. Normally these include the financial statements of:

- The governmental activities.
- The business-type activities.
- Each major governmental and enterprise fund.
- The aggregate discretely presented component units.
- The aggregate remaining fund information (i.e., the nonmajor governmental and enterprise funds, the internal service funds, and the fiduciary funds).

The basic financial statements should be accompanied by required supplementary information (RSI), such as management's discussion and analysis and budgetary comparison schedules. Unless the auditor is engaged to render an opinion on the RSI, auditors are required to perform only limited procedures to make sure the information is not misleading. Information other than required supplemental information may be presented in a CAFR, such as the letter of transmittal, statistical section, and combining statements for nonmajor funds. Unless auditors are engaged to render an opinion on this supplemental information, professional standards require the auditor only to read this *nonrequired* supplemental information and consider whether the information or the manner of its presentation is materially inconsistent with the financial statements. If the auditor believes this information or the RSI is misleading, the auditor should include an explanatory paragraph in the auditor's report to explain the situation. Generally, if the auditor prepares the required or nonrequired supplemental information for the client, the auditor is to disclaim an opinion on this information. The reporting requirements for supplemental information are complex and are presented in flowchart form in Exhibit 14.1 of *Audits of State and Local Governments.*

The second paragraph includes these elements:

- A statement that the audit was conducted in accordance with generally accepted auditing standards (which include both GAAS and GAGAS).

ILLUSTRATION 13–2 Unqualified Opinions on Basic Financial Statements Accompanied by Required Supplementary Information and Supplementary Information

Independent Auditor's Report

We have audited the accompanying financial statements of the governmental activities, the business-type activities, the aggregate discretely presented component units, each major fund, and the aggregate remaining fund information of the City of Example, Any State, as of and for the year ended June 30, 20XI, which collectively comprise the City's basic financial statements as listed in the table of contents. These financial statements are the responsibility of the City of Example's management. Our responsibility is to express opinions on these financial statements based on our audit.

We conducted our audit in accordance with auditing standards generally accepted in the United States of America. Those standards require that we plan and perform the audit to obtain reasonable assurance about whether the financial statements are free of material misstatement. An audit includes examining, on a test basis, evidence supporting the amounts and disclosures in the financial statements. An audit also includes assessing the accounting principles used and significant estimates made by management, as well as evaluating the overall financial statement presentation. We believe that our audit provides a reasonable basis for our opinions.

In our opinion, the financial statements referred to above present fairly, in all material respects, the respective financial position of the governmental activities, the business-type activities, the aggregate discretely presented component units, each major fund, and the aggregate remaining fund information of the City of Example, Any State, as of June 30, 20XI, and the respective changes in financial position and cash flows, where applicable, thereof for the year then ended in conformity with accounting principles generally accepted in the United States of America.

The [*identify accompanying required supplementary information, such as management's discussion and analysis and budgetary comparison information*] on pages XX through XX and XX through XX are not a required part of the basic financial statements but are supplementary information required by the Governmental Accounting Standards Board. We have applied certain limited procedures, which consisted principally of inquiries of management regarding the methods of measurement and presentation of the required supplementary information. However, we did not audit the information and express no opinion on it.

Our audit was conducted for the purpose of forming opinions on the financial statements that collectively comprise the City's basic financial statements. The [*identify accompanying supplementary information, such as the introductory section, combining and individual nonmajor fund financial statements, and statistical tables*] are presented for purposes of additional analysis and are not a required part of the basic financial statements. The [*identify relevant supplementary information, such as the combining and individual nonmajor fund financial statements*] have been subjected to the auditing procedures applied in the audit of the basic financial statements and, in our opinion, are fairly stated in all material respects in relation to the basic financial statements taken as a whole. The [*identify relevant supplementary information, such as the introductory section and statistical tables*] have not been subjected to the auditing procedures applied in the audit of the basic financial statements and, accordingly, we express no opinion on them.

[Signature] [Date]

Source: American Institute of Certified Public Accountants, *Audits of State and Local Governments* (New York: AICPA, 2002), pp. 302–303.

- A statement that generally accepted auditing standards require that the auditor plan and perform the audit to obtain reasonable assurance about whether the financial statements are free of material misstatement.

- A statement that an audit includes:
  a. Examining, on a test basis, evidence supporting the amounts and disclosures in the financial statements.
  b. Assessing the accounting principles used and significant estimates made by management.
  c. Evaluating the overall financial statement presentation.
- A statement that the auditor believes that the audit provides a reasonable basis for the opinion.

The third paragraph, the opinion paragraph, presents the auditor's opinion as to whether the financial statements present fairly, in all material respects, the financial position of the government as of the balance sheet date and the changes in financial position and cash flows, in conformity with generally accepted accounting principles.

The fourth paragraph indicates the extent of the auditor's evaluation of required supplemental information. This evaluation consists primarily of inquiries of management. A fifth paragraph indicates the extent to which supplemental disclosures are subject to the audit opinion. If they are not, the paragraph indicates that no opinion is being expressed with regard to this information. Note that the paragraph is very specific as to which supplemental disclosures are subject to audit and which are not.

In addition to issuing the unqualified opinion shown in Illustration 13–2, independent auditors also issue qualified opinions and adverse opinions. In some circumstances the auditor may disclaim an opinion. The AICPA *Statement on Auditing Standards* and *Audits of State and Local Governments* provide guidance for when each opinion type is appropriate. Three conditions require a departure from an unqualified report: (1) the scope of the audit has been restricted, (2) the financial statements have not been prepared in accordance with generally accepted accounting principles, and (3) the auditor is not independent. The appropriate opinion depends on the type and severity of the condition:

- ***Qualified opinion*** A qualified opinion may result from either a limitation on the scope of the audit or failure to follow generally accepted accounting principles (conditions 1 or 2). The opinion states that, except for the effects of the matter(s) to which the qualification relates, the financial statements are fairly presented.
- ***Adverse opinion*** An adverse opinion is used when the auditor believes that the financial statements are so materially misstated or misleading that they do not present fairly the financial position and results of operations (and cash flows, if applicable) in accordance with generally accepted accounting principles (condition 2).
- ***Disclaimer of opinion*** A disclaimer of opinion is appropriate if the auditor is not satisfied that the financial statements are fairly presented because of a severe scope limitation (condition 1). A disclaimer is also appropriate if the auditor is not independent, as defined by the *Code of Professional Conduct* (condition 3). In a disclaimer, the auditor states that no opinion is being expressed.

THE SINGLE AUDIT ACT AND AMENDMENTS

History Federal financial assistance has been an important source of financing operating and capital expenditures of state and local governments and not-for-profit organizations for many years. Federal grants-in-aid and federal contracts, in the past, were subject to accounting, reporting, and auditing requirements that varied depending on which agency of the federal government administered the grant program or contract. Efforts were made during the 1960s and 1970s to standardize requirements but met with only moderate success.

The Single Audit Act of 1984 was enacted to provide statutory authority for uniform requirements for audits of state and local organizations receiving federal financial assistance. Following the legislation, the Office of Management and Budget (OMB) issued Circular A–128 to provide guidance for federal agencies in administering the Single Audit Act. A few years later, OMB issued Circular A–133 providing requirements for federal agencies in administering grants for nongovernmental, not-for-profit organizations, even though those organizations were not covered under the 1984 act. In addition, the American Institute of Certified Public Accountants issued Statements of Position (SOPs) to provide guidance for CPAs when conducting audits of federal assistance, and those SOPs are included in the appropriate audit and accounting guides.

Congress enacted the Single Audit Act Amendments of 1996 that extended the 1984 law to include federal assistance to nongovernmental, not-for-profit organizations. These groups are covered in Chapters 10, 11, and 12 of this text (state and local governments and public colleges and universities were covered under the 1984 act and continue to be covered). Whereas the 1984 act required a single audit for organizations receiving $100,000 or more in federal assistance (those receiving $25,000 to $100,000 could have a program-by-program audit or a single audit), the 1996 act raised that amount to $300,000, ($500,000 beginning in 2004).

In 1997 the Office of Management and Budget issued revised Circular A–133, *Audits of States, Local Governments, and Non-Profit Organizations.* This circular replaced the two previous circulars for state and local governments and for not-for-profit organizations. The American Institute of Certified Public Accountants issued Statement of Position 98–3, *Auditing of States, Local Governments, and Not-for-Profit Organizations Receiving Federal Awards,* providing additional guidance for CPAs auditing recipients of federal funds.

Purpose The main objective of the single audit process is to create a mechanism whereby those auditors conducting the regular financial audits of state and local governments and not-for-profit organizations can provide assurance to the federal government that federal and state funds are expended in accordance with grant agreements and with financial management and other standards promulgated by the federal government. Instead of having grant-by-grant audits supervised by each agency that provides funds, governments and not-for- profit organizations that expend $25 million ($50 million beginning in 2004) in federal awards are assigned **cognizant agencies** (normally the federal agencies that provide the most funding), and other federal funds recipients are expected to use **oversight agencies** (again, the agencies providing the most funding). Cognizant agencies are required to monitor the audit process and resolve findings and questioned costs. Oversight agencies may do the same, at their option. Audits are conducted according to the requirements of the Single Audit Act, as amended, OMB Circular A–133, and a *Compliance Supplement* issued by OMB that includes OMB-approved special requirements for many of the grants.

In the 1980s the General Accounting Office conducted several studies to determine the effectiveness of audits performed under the Single Audit Act.[1] A substantial proportion of these audits were found to not be in compliance with professional standards. Since then, the GAO has modified the standards to require firms conducting governmental audits to implement specialized continuing education programs (24 hours of government specific training every two years), internal quality control programs, and external peer reviews. In addition, the GAO provides guidance to audited organizations concerning auditor solicitation and evaluation and has recently issued a standard to limit the nature of consulting services that may be provided by an organization's auditing firm. This latter requirement is intended to assure the independence of external auditors.

AICPA Statement of Position 98–3 and OMB Circular A–133 provide guidance for the auditor in implementing the single audit requirement. First, a determination must be made as to whether a client is subject to the single audit act. Entities that expend $300,000 ($500,000 beginning in 2004) or more in federal awards in a fiscal year have either a single audit (when several grantors are involved) or a program-specific audit (usually when only one grantor is involved). This includes, in some cases, certain governments or not-for-profit organizations that act as **pass-through entities,** organizations that receive federal awards to be sent to **subrecipients.** The pass-through entities have responsibilities for reporting funding to the subrecipients, and the auditor must be aware of these arrangements.

The auditor is required to test controls to gain an understanding of internal controls for use in selecting programs for audit, in determining whether the auditee is low risk, and in reporting.

Major Programs A major program is a program selected for audit under the single audit approach. The auditor is required to express an opinion on compliance on major programs, which must add up to 50 percent of the federal funds expended by the auditee, unless the auditee is determined by the auditor to be a **low-risk auditee,** an auditee that for the past two years has met certain criteria such as unqualified opinions, no material weakness in internal controls, and no material noncompliance on major programs. Auditors may express an opinion on major programs for low-risk auditees adding up to no more than 25 percent of federal awards expenditures.

---

[1] General Accounting Office, *CPA Audit Quality: Many Governmental Audits Do Not Comply with Professional Standards.* Report to the House Committee on Government Operations. (Washington, DC.: GAO, August 1986).

Major programs are determined on a **risk-based approach.** First, the programs are classified into Type A and Type B programs. Type A programs are the larger programs and Type B programs are the smaller programs. Type A programs are considered major programs unless they are determined to be low risk. In order for this to happen, a Type A program must have been audited during the past two years as a major program and have had no major audit findings. Type B programs are included as major programs only if the auditor determines that they are high risk. Risk assessments are generally required for Type B programs that exceed $100,000 for most auditees and $300,000 for larger auditees.

For example, assume that an auditee that is not determined to be low risk has five programs, two Type A and three Type B, as follows:

Type A

Housing and Urban Development, $350,000, audited last year with no major control problems or compliance findings
Environmental Protection Agency, $400,000, not audited during the past two years

Type B

Department of Education, $200,000
Department of Energy, $150,000
Department of Agriculture, $50,000

The total amount of grant expenditures is $1,150,000, so at least $575,000 must be audited as major programs. The Environmental Protection Agency grant must be audited, as it does not meet the criteria of low risk, not having been audited in the past two years. Then the auditor must choose grants adding up to $175,000. The other Type A program could be audited, or the auditor could select Type B programs, based on a risk assessment. The auditor would choose either the Department of Education ($200,000) or the programs from the Departments of Energy and Agriculture, which also add up to $200,000. Remember that the auditor is not required to assess the Department of Agriculture program since it is below the threshold required. If the auditee were considered low risk, then only 25 percent of the grant expenditures would be required as major programs; if risk assessments showed that the Departments of Education and Energy were low risk, then the EPA grant could be the only grant audited as a major program.

Academic Research A significant amount of research has been conducted on governmental auditing. One line of inquiry examines the supply and demand for auditing, including the pricing of audit services. Single audit reports and the reviews of audit working papers by the General Accounting Office and Offices of Inspectors General have provided unique opportunities to explore the factors that influence the quality of audits. For example, Deis and Giroux (1992) examined audit quality in audits of Texas school districts and found that governmental audit experience and external peer reviews by other auditors improve audit quality.[2] In a similar study of Oregon municipalities, O'Keefe and Westort (1992) confirmed the benefits of specialized training, but also found that competition among auditors served to improve audit quality.[3] Using information obtained from the GAO, Copley and Doucet (1993) found that competition among auditing firms for governmental audit engagements serves to both increase quality and reduce fees.[4]

Summary Like governmental accounting, governmental auditing follows a unique set of professional guidelines. *Government Auditing Standards* are established by the U.S. General Accounting Office. These standards differ from those governing audits of private businesses. In particular, governmental standards require auditors to evaluate and report on the system of internal controls and compliance with laws and regulations. Governmental auditors are required to report to funding agencies or oversight bodies in addition to the management of the organization under audit. Significant changes are forthcoming in both the GAO's *Government Auditing Standards* and the AICPA's *Audits of State and Local Governments* that will affect auditor communications, auditor qualifications, the determination of audit materiality, and the wording of standard audit reports.

Frequently state and local governments and not-for-profit organizations receive funding under a variety of federal programs. Many of these organizations are subject to the requirements of the Single Audit Act and its amendments. Auditors of these organizations must be familiar with governmental auditing standards as well as specific requirements under the act for determining major programs subject to audit.

TAX-EXEMPT ORGANIZATIONS

Accountants working for, auditing, or providing consulting services to not-for-profit organizations must be aware of certain tax issues related to those organizations. Generally, not-for-profit organizations are exempt from federal income taxes. However, it is possible for them to engage in activities that result in **unrelated business income** that is taxable. In some cases, such activities are so significant that the not-for-profit organization can lose its tax-exempt status. This section of the chapter discusses the provisions in the tax code that provide exemption for certain types of not-for-profit organizations, discusses and illustrates the tax form that is used for many of these organizations (**Form 990**), and concludes by examining the unrelated business income sections of the tax code that may cause an exempt organization to pay taxes or even lose its exempt status.

---

[2] D. Deis and G. Giroux, "Determinants of Audit Quality in the Public Sector," *The Accounting Review* 67 (1992), pp. 462–79.
[3] T. O'Keefe and P. Westort, "Conformance to GAAS Reporting Standards in Municipal Audits and the Economics of Auditing: The Effects of Audit Firm Size, CPA Examination Performance, and Competition," *Research in Accounting Regulation* 6 (1992), pp. 39–77.
[4] P. Copley and M. Doucet, "The Impact of Competition on the Quality of Governmental Audits," *Auditing: A Journal of Practice and Theory* 12 (1993), pp. 88–98.

Tax Code Section 501 provides that nonprofit organizations organized for charitable purposes may be exempt from federal income taxes. These include corporations organized under an Act of Congress as a U.S. instrumentality, **501(c)(3) entities,** civic leagues, trade and professional associations, social clubs and country clubs, fraternal societies, and veterans organizations. In order to qualify as tax exempt, the entity must have a limited purpose, must not have the authority to engage in activities other than exempt purposes, and must not be engaged in political activities.

The most common form of tax-exempt organization is the 501(c)(3) organization, which will be the focus of the remainder of this section. A 501(c)(3) organization is a "corporation and any community chest, fund, or foundation organized and operated exclusively for religious, charitable, scientific, testing for public safety, literary or educational purposes, or to foster national or international amateur sports competition (so long as none of its activities involve the providing of athletic facilities or equipment) or for the prevention of cruelty to children or animals, no part of the net earnings of which inures to the benefit of any private shareholder or individual, no substantial part of the activities of which is carrying on propaganda, participate or intervene in any political campaign."[5] To apply for tax-exempt status, an organization should file IRS Form 1023, *Application for Recognition of Exemption Under Section 501(c)(3) of the Internal Revenue Code.* Certain special rules apply to churches and to private foundations, as distinguished from **public charities.**

A public charity is defined as (1) a church, school, hospital, governmental unit, or publicly supported charity; (2) an organization that receives more than one-third of its support from a combination of contributions, membership fees, and gross receipts from exempt activities and no more than one-third of its support from a combination of investment income and net unrelated business income after taxes; (3) an organization operated exclusively for the benefit of organizations already described; or (4) an organization founded and operated exclusively for public safety. The remainder of this section will concentrate on public charities.

Applying for Tax-Exempt Status

Organizations that received substantial support from outside contributors find it particularly important to have Section 501(c)(3) status. Contributions made to such organizations are deductible when computing income taxes as well as estate taxes. Because state laws govern sales taxes, 501(c)(3) status does not exempt the organization from sales taxes. The ability to deduct donations reduces the net cost of contributions to the donor but places some restrictions on the activities of the tax-exempt organization and imposes reporting requirements. For example, exempt organizations are prohibited from supporting political candidates or campaigning to influence legislation. Reporting requirements are described in the next section of this chapter.

To qualify for tax-exempt status, the organization must:
1. Have an Employer's Identification Number (IRS form SS–4).
2. Be organized as a corporation, trust, or association.

---

[5] U.S. Internal Revenue Code Section 501(c)(3).

3. Complete IRS form 1023, *Application for Recognition of Exemption.*
4. Receive notice from the IRS that the organization has been determined to be tax exempt.

Form 1023 requires the organization to provide information regarding its purpose and activities and provide up to four years of financial information or budgets.

Copies of the organizing documents (articles of incorporation or association, bylaws, or trust agreement) must accompany the application. Again state law determines what an organization must do to incorporate. Many times it is easier for the organization to prepare Articles of Association, but these articles must include specific language regarding the purpose of the organization, the distribution of any earnings, and disposition of assets in the event the organization is dissolved. Example articles of association for a Boy Scout troop appear in Illustration 13–3.

Federal Filing Requirements

Organizations exempt under 501(c)(3) of the code are required to file Form 990 or in some cases an alternate form by the 15th day of the fifth month following the taxable year of the organization. The following entities are not required to file: (1) certain religious organizations, (2) instrumentalities of the U.S. government, and (3) organizations whose gross receipts are normally less than $25,000. Public charities must also include Schedule A with Form 990, as described next.

Page one of the Form 990 and page one of Schedule A are presented as Illustrations 13–4 and 13–5. Space limitations preclude the presentation of the entire form which can be viewed and printed from www.IRS.gov. The major components of the forms are presented next to illustrate the kinds of information required. It should be noted, as indicated in Illustration 13–4 that Form 990 is open to public inspection.

Form 990 The major sections of Form 990 are:
1. As can be seen from Illustration 13–4, Part I is a schedule of revenues, expenses, and changes in net assets or fund balances. Note that the form is similar to the total column in the Statement of Activities in Chapter 10 and that expenses are categorized as Program, Management and General, Fund-Raising, and Payments to Affiliates.
2. Part II is a Statement of Functional Expenses that allocates expenses, by object classification, to Program Services, Management and General, and Fund-Raising. This part also asks about joint costs of fundraising appeals.
3. Part III asks for a statement of program service accomplishments, by program, along with the expenses incurred.
4. Part IV requires a balance sheet, a reconciliation of the revenue per audited financial statements with the tax return, and a reconciliation of the expenses per audited financial statements with expenses reported on the tax return.
5. Part V requires a list of officers, directors, trustees, and key employees, the time spent by each, and the amount paid to each.
6. Part VI asks a series of questions to help the IRS determine if the organization should continue to be tax exempt. Part VII asks for an analysis of income-producing activities, Part VIII asks for the relationship of those activities to the

ILLUSTRATION 13–3

<table>
<tr><td colspan="2" align="center">Boy Scout Troop 388
Watkinsville, Georgia
Articles of Association</td></tr>
<tr><td>First:</td><td>The name of the organization shall be Boy Scout Troop 388, herein referred to as Troop 388.</td></tr>
<tr><td>Second:</td><td>The place in this state where Boy Scout Troop 388 is to be based in the Town of Watkinsville, Oconee County, Georgia.</td></tr>
<tr><td>Third:</td><td>Said Troop 388 is organized exclusively for educational and charitable purposes. The purpose of Troop 388 is to provide an educational program for boys and young adults to build character, to train in the responsibilities of participating citizenship, and to develop personal fitness and to contribute to the community through charitable and service projects.</td></tr>
<tr><td>Fourth:</td><td>The names and addresses of the persons who are the initial trustees of the organization are as follows:</td></tr>
<tr><td>Fifth:</td><td>No part of the net earnings of Troop 388 shall inure to the benefit of, or be distributable to its members, officers or other private persons, except that Troop 388 shall be authorized and empowered to pay reasonable compensation for services rendered and to make payments and distributions in furtherance of the purposes set forth in Article Third hereof. No substantial part of the activities of Troop 388 shall be the carrying on of propaganda, or otherwise attempting to influence legislation, and Troop 388 shall not participate in, or intervene in (including the publishing or distribution of statements) any political campaign on behalf of or in opposition to any candidate for public office. Notwithstanding any other provision of these articles, Troop 388 shall not carry on or engage in any activities or exercise any powers that are not in furtherance of the purposes of Troop 388.</td></tr>
<tr><td>Sixth:</td><td>Upon the dissolution of the organization, assets shall be distributed for one or more exempt purposes within the meaning of section 501(c)(3) of the Internal Revenue Code, or corresponding section of any future federal tax code, or shall be distributed to the federal government, or to a state or local government, for a public purpose. Any such assets not disposed of shall be disposed of by the Court of Common Pleas of the county in which the principal office of the organization is then located, exclusively for such purposes or to such organization or organizations, as said Court shall determine, which are organized and operated exclusively for such purposes.</td></tr>
<tr><td colspan="2">Dated this 15th day of November 2001.
(Include signatures of three principal officers)</td></tr>
</table>

accomplishment of exempt purposes, and Part IX asks for information regarding taxable subsidiaries. The form must be signed by an officer and the preparer, if applicable.

Schedule A Most public charities are required to file a Schedule A. Illustration 13–5 reveals that this schedule requires information on the compensation of the

ILLUSTRATION 13–4

Form 990 — Return of Organization Exempt From Income Tax
Under section 501(c), 527, or 4947(a)(1) of the Internal Revenue Code (except black lung benefit trust or private foundation)
Department of the Treasury, Internal Revenue Service
▶ The organization may have to use a copy of this return to satisfy state reporting requirements.

OMB No. 1545-0047
2001
Open to Public Inspection

A For the 2001 calendar year, or tax year beginning _____, 2001, and ending _____, 20 ____

B Check if applicable:
- ☐ Address change
- ☐ Name change
- ☐ Initial return
- ☐ Final return
- ☐ Amended return
- ☐ Application pending

Please use IRS label or print or type. See Specific Instructions.

C Name of organization
Number and street (or P.O. box if mail is not delivered to street address) Room/suite
City or town, state or country, and ZIP + 4

D Employer identification number

E Telephone number ( )

F Accounting method: ☐ Cash ☐ Accrual ☐ Other (specify) ▶

• Section 501(c)(3) organizations and 4947(a)(1) nonexempt charitable trusts must attach a completed Schedule A (Form 990 or 990-EZ).

G Web site: ▶

H and **I** are not applicable to section 527 organizations.
H(a) Is this a group return for affiliates? ☐ Yes ☐ No
H(b) If "Yes," enter number of affiliates ▶ _____
H(c) Are all affiliates included? ☐ Yes ☐ No (If "No," attach a list. See instructions.)
H(d) Is this a separate return filed by an organization covered by a group ruling? ☐ Yes ☐ No
I Enter 4-digit GEN ▶

J Organization type (check only one) ▶ ☐ 501(c) ( ) ◀ (insert no.) ☐ 4947(a)(1) or ☐ 527

K Check here ▶ ☐ if the organization's gross receipts are normally not more than $25,000. The organization need not file a return with the IRS; but if the organization received a Form 990 Package in the mail, it should file a return without financial data. Some states require a complete return.

M Check ▶ ☐ if the organization is **not** required to attach Sch. B (Form 990, 990-EZ, or 990-PF).

L Gross receipts: Add lines 6b, 8b, 9b, and 10b to line 12 ▶

Part I — Revenue, Expenses, and Changes in Net Assets or Fund Balances (See Specific Instructions on page 16.)

Revenue

1. Contributions, gifts, grants, and similar amounts received:
   a. Direct public support 1a
   b. Indirect public support 1b
   c. Government contributions (grants) 1c
   d. **Total** (add lines 1a through 1c) (cash $ _____ noncash $ _____) 1d
2. Program service revenue including government fees and contracts (from Part VII, line 93) — 2
3. Membership dues and assessments — 3
4. Interest on savings and temporary cash investments — 4
5. Dividends and interest from securities — 5
6. a. Gross rents 6a
   b. Less: rental expenses 6b
   c. Net rental income or (loss) (subtract line 6b from line 6a) — 6c
7. Other investment income (describe ▶ _____) — 7
8. a. Gross amount from sales of assets other than inventory — (A) Securities 8a | (B) Other
   b. Less: cost or other basis and sales expenses — 8b
   c. Gain or (loss) (attach schedule) — 8c
   d. Net gain or (loss) (combine line 8c, columns (A) and (B)) — 8d
9. Special events and activities (attach schedule)
   a. Gross revenue (not including $ _____ of contributions reported on line 1a) 9a
   b. Less: direct expenses other than fundraising expenses — 9b
   c. Net income or (loss) from special events (subtract line 9b from line 9a) — 9c
10. a. Gross sales of inventory, less returns and allowances — 10a
    b. Less: cost of goods sold 10b
    c. Gross profit or (loss) from sales of inventory (attach schedule) (subtract line 10b from line 10a) — 10c
11. Other revenue (from Part VII, line 103) — 11
12. **Total revenue** (add lines 1d, 2, 3, 4, 5, 6c, 7, 8d, 9c, 10c, and 11) — 12

Expenses

13. Program services (from line 44, column (B)) — 13
14. Management and general (from line 44, column (C)) — 14
15. Fundraising (from line 44, column (D)) — 15
16. Payments to affiliates (attach schedule) — 16
17. **Total expenses** (add lines 16 and 44, column (A)) — 17

Net Assets

18. Excess or (deficit) for the year (subtract line 17 from line 12) — 18
19. Net assets or fund balances at beginning of year (from line 73, column (A)) — 19
20. Other changes in net assets or fund balances (attach explanation) — 20
21. Net assets or fund balances at end of year (combine lines 18, 19, and 20) — 21

For Paperwork Reduction Act Notice, see the separate instructions. Cat. No. 11282Y Form **990** (2001)

ILLUSTRATION 13–5

SCHEDULE A
(Form 990 or 990-EZ)

Department of the Treasury
Internal Revenue Service

Organization Exempt Under Section 501(c)(3)
(Except Private Foundation) and Section 501(e), 501(f), 501(k),
501(n), or Section 4947(a)(1) Nonexempt Charitable Trust
Supplementary Information—(See separate instructions.)
▶ MUST be completed by the above organizations and attached to their Form 990 or 990-EZ

OMB No. 1545-0047

2001

Name of the organization | Employer identification number

Part I Compensation of the Five Highest Paid Employees Other Than Officers, Directors, and Trustees
(See page 1 of the instructions. List each one. If there are none, enter "None.")

(a) Name and address of each employee paid more than $50,000	(b) Title and average hours per week devoted to position	(c) Compensation	(d) Contributions to employee benefit plans & deferred compensation	(e) Expense account and other allowances

Total number of other employees paid over $50,000 . . . . ▶

Part II Compensation of the Five Highest Paid Independent Contractors for Professional Services
(See page 2 of the instructions. List each one (whether individuals or firms). If there are none, enter "None.")

(a) Name and address of each independent contractor paid more than $50,000	(b) Type of service	(c) Compensation

Total number of others receiving over $50,000 for professional services . . . . ▶

For Paperwork Reduction Act Notice, see the Instructions for Form 990 and Form 990-EZ.   Cat. No. 11285F   Schedule A (Form 990 or 990-EZ) 2001 five highest-paid employees making more than $50,000 and the compensation of the five highest-paid independent contractors for professional services. Other information on Schedule A includes more questions about the activities of the public charity, reasons for status as a nonprivate foundation, more information for those entities that indicate they have related foundations (such as colleges, health care entities, and other not-for-profit organizations), a separate questionnaire for private schools, questions about lobbying activities, and information relating to transfers and transactions between the public charity and noncharitable exempt organizations.

Public Disclosures

The Taxpayer Bill of Rights 2 (1996), called for increased public disclosures of tax-exempt organizations. In 1999 the IRS issued final rules interpreting the expanded requirements. Exempt organizations are required to provide copies, upon request, of the three most recent annual information returns (Form 990) including all schedules and attachments, except those parts giving the names and addresses of contributors. Many organizations choose to satisfy the requirement to provide copies by placing their documents on their Web page or on that of another entity as part of a database of similar documents.

State Filing Requirements

In addition to having federal filing requirements, an organization has a number of state filing requirements. Many require a copy of Form 990, and others supplement this form with additional requirements. It should be noted that not-for-profit organizations are normally corporations created under the laws of individual states; as such, they are subject to state laws and regulations as well as those of the federal government.

Unrelated Business Income Tax (UBIT)

A tax-exempt organization is required to pay tax at the corporate or trust rate on income generated from any trade or business activities unrelated to the entity's tax-exempt purposes. The purpose of this requirement is to eliminate advantages that tax-exempt organizations have over profit-making organizations. For example, a college bookstore, when selling certain items to nonstudents, would be competing with private business engaged in the same activities. In 1997 taxable profits from unrelated business activities totaled $1.4 billion and tax-exempt groups paid $418.4 million in unrelated business income tax.[6]

This provision has created a great deal of controversy, as might be expected. Many activities could be judged by some to be related to the tax-exempt purposes of a not-for-profit and by others as unrelated. As a result, a body of case law has evolved, and certain specific situations have been addressed by legislation.

The existence of one or more of the following conditions will exempt income-producing activities from UBIT: (1) the business is not regularly carried on, (2) volunteers perform most of the labor, (3) the not-for-profit sells donated merchandise,

---

[6] L. Asinof, "Tax-Exempt Groups Expand their Profit-Making Ventures," *The Wall Street Journal*, September 5, 2001, p. A1.

and (4) it is operated for the convenience of employees, patients, students, and so on. Additional exceptions have been provided in legislation. These include, among others, (1) royalties, dividends, interest, and annuities (except from controlled corporations); (2) income of a college or university or hospital from research performed for a person or governmental unit; (3) income from qualified public entertainment activities in connection with a fair or exposition; (4) income from labor, agricultural, and horticultural organizations and business trade associations from qualified convention or trade show activities; and (5) income from the rental or exchange of membership lists.

Assume a sheltered workshop sold goods assembled by the clients of the workshop. It is likely that the revenue produced by those sales would be related to the tax-exempt purpose, as the clients would be engaged in a meaningful activity. On the other hand, assume the same sheltered workshop operated a business across town, selling manufactured goods that were produced by regular employees, with the sole intent of raising money for the organization. It is likely that this would be perceived as unrelated to the tax-exempt purpose and, therefore, subject to the UBIT.

When computing the unrelated business income tax, not-for-profit organizations are allowed to deduct ordinary and necessary business expenses directly connected with their trade or business (as would any other business), a $1,000 special deduction, charitable contributions, and many of the other deductions available to business organizations. The applicable tax return is Form 990T. Estimated tax payments are required, when applicable.

Academic Research Following the 1996 Taxpayer Bill of Rights, tax-exempt organizations are required to make their tax returns (Form 990s) available to the public. As a result, information is now more readily available for research on these organizations. For example, Yetman (2001) examined Form 990s filed by tax-exempt entities to determine the extent of taxes paid on unrelated business income.[7] He found that a large number of not-for-profits report losses on their taxable (business) activities. Since it is unlikely that not-for-profits would engage in unprofitable business activities, the reported losses are attributable to provisions in the tax law that permit allocations of expenses in determining taxable income. Yetman's findings call into question the effectiveness of the Unrelated Business Income Tax in either providing tax revenue to the government or eliminating tax advantages that not-for-profit organizations have over commercial enterprises.

Summary and Some Conclusions Related to Exempt Entities

A major portion of the practice of CPAs and a major concern of not-for-profit organizations is the obtaining and preservation of tax-exempt status and the avoidance or minimization of unrelated business income tax. During the initial organizing of a nonprofit, care must be taken to define and limit its purpose to tax-exempt activities. Decisions related to fund-raising activities must constantly be monitored to determine the impact of tax law. Some not-for-profit organizations create separate related

---

[7] R. Yetman, "Tax Motivated Expense Allocation by Nonprofit Organizations," *The Accounting Review* 76, no. 3 (2001), pp. 297–312.

organizations, that may not be tax exempt, to ensure that the primary organization does not lose its tax-exempt status. While the taxation of tax-exempt entities may seem to be a contradiction in terms, not-for-profit organizations must be continually vigilant and prepared to file the necessary forms and meet the regulations of the federal and state governments.

SERVICE EFFORTS AND ACCOMPLISHMENTS

The Governmental Accounting Standards Board has been engaged in a major effort related to service efforts and accomplishments. GASB Concepts Statement 2, *Service Efforts and Accomplishments Reporting,* was issued in April 1994. In addition, a series of research reports related to colleges and universities, economic development programs, elementary and secondary education, fire department programs, hospitals, mass transit, police department programs, public assistance programs, public health, road maintenance, sanitation collection and disposal, water and wastewater treatment, and other activities has been issued. A summary research report includes chapters for each of these areas.

According to the GASB, reporting on **Service Efforts and Accomplishments** (SEA) is necessary to make governmental financial reporting complete. No decisions have been made as to how the information should be reported—as a part of the Comprehensive Annual Financial Report, as a special report, or in some other form. However, according to the GASB, "The Objective of SEA reporting is to provide more complete information about a governmental entity's performance than can be provided by the operating statement, balance sheet, and budgetary comparison statements and schedules." SEA reporting will be discussed next in the context of measuring and reporting crime prevention, detection, and apprehension of criminal offenders. This activity would be one among others, such as traffic control and assistance to people in distress, carried out by a government's police force.

Service efforts are defined as "measures of costs or inputs; the financial and nonfinancial resources applied to provide services." Direct costs include salaries and benefits for police officers who are directly engaged in crime prevention, detection, and apprehension of offenders. To the extent that the costs are separately identifiable, occupancy, vehicle, and equipment costs are directly allocated. Indirect costs of the police department and general government may also be allocated. Inputs may also include nonfinancial measures such as number of personnel and hours expended.

Service accomplishments include outputs and outcomes. According to the GASB, output measures are the quantity of a service provided or the quantity of a service that meets a certain quality requirement. Examples of output measures include number of responses, number of arrests, and the hours of patrol. Output measures should be distinguished from measures of outcome. Outcomes measure the extent to which results are achieved or needs are met at least partially due to the services provided. Examples of outcome measures are the number of violent crimes committed, the value of property lost due to crime, and response time.

Relationships between service efforts and accomplishments should be illustrated. Efficiency measures relate costs and other inputs to output measures, such as the number of responses per dollar spent or per police officer. Cost-outcome measures relate inputs to outcomes, such as the value of property lost to crime per dollar spent.

No single measure should be used to evaluate or present information. A variety of measures should be presented. Those measures should be reported consistently, in a timely manner, and in a way that is easily understood. Comparisons with prior periods and with other governments are also useful. Explanatory variables, such as socioeconomic data, should be included to help readers understand that not all the results are controllable and are affected by more than government action. Ratios, such as expressing measures on a per capita basis, are helpful.

Example of SEA Reporting: School Report Cards

Many states require school systems or individual schools to publish annual "school report cards." Illustration 13–6 provides websites for school report cards by state. These reports are an example of service efforts and accomplishments reporting for an important and highly visible government service, public schools. The content of these report cards is frequently dictated by the state government and varies by state. However most of these reports contain the following types of information:

Service Inputs:	Tax revenues, state appropriations, and federal grants.
	Number of teachers, administrators, and support personnel.
	Education level (certificate levels) of teachers and administrators.
	Demographics of student population (income, race, language).
Service Outputs:	Enrollment.
	Gifted or alternative programs.
	Degrees conferred.
Service Outcomes:	Standardized test scores.
	Dropout rates.
	Competency tests and high school graduation tests.
	Accreditation results.

Summary

Some cautions are in order regarding SEA reporting. Until standards are developed and commonly reported and used, there is a risk that governments will present only that information that is favorable. Audit opinions are not associated with this information, and it is unlikely they will be for some time. Problems exist in the measurement and allocations of costs, not to mention the measurement of outputs and outcomes. Even with the problems, however, SEA reporting is essential for measuring the performance of a government or an activity of a government. The general purpose financial statements do not measure efficiency or effectiveness, especially for activities of governmental funds. The governmental funds Statement of

ILLUSTRATION 13-6 State Websites for School Performance Reports

Alabama: www.alsde.edu
Alaska: www.eed.state.ak.us/stats/
Arizona:www2.ade.state.az.us/srcs/
Arkansas: N/A
California: http://www.cde.ca.gov/psaa/
Colorado:http://www.cde.state.co.us/index_assess.htm
Connecticut: N/A
Delaware: http://issm.doe.state.de.us/profiles/
Florida: N/A
Georgia:www.doe.k12.ga.us, http://168.31.216.190/
Hawaii: N/A
Idaho: N/A
Illinois: www.isbe.state.il.us/research/reports.htm#Report%20Card
Indiana: N/A
Iowa: www.state.ia.us/educate/publications/coe.html
Kansas: http://www.ksbe.state.ks.us/reportcard.html
Kentucky: www.kde.state.ky.us/comm/commrel/school_report_card/
Louisiana: www.lcet.doe.state.la.us/doe/omf/sps9899/spsframe.asp
Maine: http://janus.state.me.us/education/lres/lres.htm
Maryland: http://www.msde.state.md.us/MSPReportCard/default.htm
Massachusetts: www.doe.mass.edu/mcas/99mcas/toc.html
Michigan: www.mde.state.mi.us/reports/msr/
Minnesota: http://cfl.state.mn.us/PUB&RES.htm
Mississippi: www.mde.k12.ms.us/account/report/mrc.htm
Missouri: www.dese.state.mo.us/reportsummary/
Montana: www.metnet.state.mt.us?Montana%20Education/OPIMeasurement&Acctability/
   Education%20Profile/HTM/index.shtml
Nebraska: N/A
Nevada: www.nsn.k12.nv.us/nvdoe/
New Hampshire: www.state.nh.us/doe/Reports%20and%20Statistics/reports.htm
New Jersey: www.state.nj.us/njded/stass/index.html or
   www.state.nj.us/njded/reportcard/index.html
New Mexico: N/A
New York: www.emsc.nysed.gov/repcrd399
North Carolina: www.dpi.state.nc.us/accountability/reporting/index.html#Report
   See also: http://www.smartschools.org/
North Dakota: www.dpi.state.nd.us/dpi/reports/publicat.htm
Ohio: www.ode.state.oh.us/rc_download.htm
Oklahoma: http://sde.state.ok.us/pro/stutest/drc.html
Oregon: www.ode.state.or.us/ReportCard/
Pennsylvania: www.paprofiles.org/
Rhode Island: N/A
South Carolina: N/A
South Dakota: www.state.sd.us/deca/DATA/99digest/
Tennessee: www.state.tn.us/education/rptcrd99/index.html
Texas: www.tea.state.tx.us/perfreport/account/

ILLUSTRATION 13–6 (concluded)

Utah: www.usoe.k12.ut.us/pr/facts.htm
Vermont: http://crs.uvm.edu/schlrpt/
Virginia: www.pen.k12.va.us/html/reportcard.shtml
Washington: www.k12.wa.us/assessment/default.asp
West Virginia: wvde.state.wv.us/data/report_cards/
Wisconsin: N/A
Wyoming: N/A

Source: M. Rubin, "A Literature Review and Accounting Research Agenda for Educational Performance Indicators," *Research in Governmental and Nonprofit Accounting* 11 (2002).

Revenues, Expenditures, and Changes in Fund Balances is an accountability document that displays categories of expenditures as well as sources of revenues and transfers, but it does not tell much about performance. SEA measures are now a part of the budget process of many governments. Standardization and public reporting would make the SEA measures more useful.

Questions and Exercises

13–1. Using the annual financial report obtained for Exercise 1–1, answer the following questions:

  a. Examine the auditor's report. Is the auditor identified as an independent CPA firm? A state audit agency? Other? Is the wording of the auditor's report the same as illustrated in this chapter? Does the scope paragraph indicate exactly what is covered by the auditor's opinion? If the auditor is expressing an opinion only on the basic financial statements, what responsibility is taken for the combining and individual fund statements? Is the opinion unqualified? If not, what are the qualifications?

  b. Does the annual financial report contain a single audit section? If not, does the report refer to the existence of a single audit report? If so, does the report include a Schedule of Federal (and State) Financial Assistance? Are all of the reports illustrated in this chapter included? Can you identify the major programs, if any?

13–2. Beside each number, write the letter corresponding with the *best* answer to each of the following questions:

  1. Which of the following promulgates *standards* for audits of federal financial assistance recipients?
     a. U.S. General Accounting Office.
     b. U.S. Office of Management and Budget.
     c. Governmental Accounting Standards Board.
     d. Financial Accounting Standards Board.

2. Which of the following is true regarding, the *Government Auditing Standards?*
   a. Performance audits are required annually.
   b. A performance audit is considered a subset of a financial audit.
   c. *Government Auditing Standards* are required in addition to, not as a replacement of, the *Auditing Standards* issued by the AICPA.
   d. None of the above are true.
3. The *Government Auditing Standards* incorporate which of the following types of audits?
   a. financial
   b. attestation
   c. performance
   d. all of the above
4. The Single Audit Act Amendments of 1996
   a. Extended the single audit act requirements to not-for-profit organizations.
   b. Raised the amount to $300,000 ($500,000 beginning in 2004) before audits of federal funds are required.
   c. Both (a) and (b) above
   d. None of the above.
5. OMB Circular A-133
   a. Applies only to state and local governmental units.
   b. Applies only to not-for-profit organizations.
   c. Applies to both state and local governments and not-for-profit organizations.
   d. Applies to neither state and local governments nor not-for-profit organizations.
6. In single audits, the federal governmental agency that deals with the auditor and the recipient entity is:
   a. The cognizant agency.
   b. The oversight agency.
   c. Either the cognizant or oversight agency, depending on the size of the recipient.
   d. Either the cognizant or oversight agency, depending on the amount of federal expenditures.
7. In the single audit approach, a "major program" is determined by:
   a. A risk-based approach.
   b. The size of the program.
   c. The amount of federal expenditures by the recipient government on the program.
   d. The government's desire to have a certain program audited.

8. The total amount of grant expenditures that must be covered in the audit of major programs is:
   a. $300,000.
   b. 50 percent of federal expenditures.
   c. 25 percent of federal expenditures.
   d. 50 percent of federal expenditures generally but only 25 percent if the government is considered to be a low-risk auditee.
9. Reporting requirements of the single audit and the *Government Auditing Standards* include:
   a. An opinion on the basic financial statements.
   b. A report discussing the testing and evaluation of internal control and compliance with laws and regulations.
   c. A report discussing instances of fraud, illegal acts, and material noncompliance.
   d. All of the above.
10. Which of the following is *not* true regarding the single audit process?
    a. Reports are to be filed with a federal repository no more than nine months after the end of the fiscal year.
    b. Required supplemental information is considered to be within the scope of the audit.
    c. The financial statements are the responsibility of the auditee.
    d. None of the above

13–3. Beside each number, write the letter corresponding with the *best* answer to each of the following questions:
   1. A 501(c)(3) entity might be:
      a. A trade association.
      b. A charitable organization.
      c. A fraternal society.
      d. All of the above; all are true.
   2. When organizing a not-for-profit organization, one needs to ensure that:
      a. The charter is limited and is for exempt purposes.
      b. The organization never engages in a trade or business that would result in taxable income.
      c. The entity does not have related organizations, as those organizations might cause loss of tax-exempt status.
      d. All of the above are adhered to.
   3. A 501(c)(3) organization:
      a. Never pays income taxes.
      b. Pays income taxes on unrelated business income at the corporate or trust rate.

c. Pays income taxes on unrelated business income at the individual rate.
d. Pays income taxes on all its income at the corporate or trust rate.

4. Which of the following is *not* true regarding a 501(c)(3) organization?
   a. An IRS Form 1023 must be filed to apply for tax-exempt status.
   b. An IRS Form 990 must be filed each year by the fifteenth day of the fourth month following its fiscal year.
   c. Public charities are required to file a Schedule A along with Form 990.
   d. None of the above; all are true.

5. Which of the following would cause a 501(c)(3) to lose its tax-exempt status?
   a. Engaging in political activities.
   b. Paying dividends to individuals.
   c. A provision in its charter allowing it to engage in business activities.
   d. All of the above.

6. Which of the following organizations is (are) *not* required to file a Form 990?
   a. A 501(c)(3) that has gross receipts less than $300,000.
   b. Certain educational institutions.
   c. Certain religious organizations.
   d. None of the above.

7. Which of the following is *not* a part of Form 990?
   a. Expenses broken down by function, including program, management and general, fund-raising, and payments to affiliates.
   b. A list of officers, directors, trustees, and key employees.
   c. Information regarding taxable subsidiaries.
   d. An auditor's report.

8. Schedule A:
   a. Is required of all 501(c)(3) organizations.
   b. Is filed in lieu of Form 990 by public charities.
   c. Requires information on the five highest-paid employees making more than $50,000.
   d. All of the above.

9. Which of the following will exempt income-producing activities from unrelated business income tax?
   a. The business is not regularly carried on.
   b. Volunteers provide most of the labor.
   c. The business is operated for the convenience of employees, patients, students, and so on.
   d. All of the above.

10. Which of the following is deductible from unrelated business income tax?
    a. A $10,000 special deduction.
    b. Dividends paid to shareholders.
    c. Charitable contributions.
    d. None of the above.

13–4. The National Center for Charitable Statistics maintains a database of Form 990 filings. Access a Form 990 for an organization in your hometown or nearby city as follows: (1) go to the website of the National Center for Charitable Statistics: http://nccs.urban.org/990/; (2) click on the option: *Check Charity Finances;* (3) enter your hometown or nearby city; and (4) select an organization and access its Form 990. Answer the following questions:
    a. What is the amount of public support and government contributions received in the year?
    b. What were the other sources of revenue?
    c. What was the amount of surplus or deficit reported for the year?
    d. Is there a Statement of Functional Expenses (Part II)? Compute the ratio of program to total expenses.
    e. Is there a Statement of Program Service Accomplishments (Part III). What programs are described?
    f. Is there a Balance Sheet (Part IV)? Are there three categories of net assets?
    g. Are there any employees making in excess of $50,000 (Schedule A)?

13–5. With regard to the Government Auditing Standards:
    a. Differentiate among the different types of professional engagements.
    b. Assume you are auditing a city that has a summer youth employment program. List some factors you might investigate in terms of (1) financial statement audits, (2) attestation engagements, and (3) performance audits.

13–6. You have been assigned the task of writing the audit report for the City of X. The scope includes the basic financial statements, although the report is attached to a complete Comprehensive Annual Financial Report.
    a. Write the opinion paragraph.
    b. Differentiate among opinions that are unqualified, qualified, adverse, and disclaimed. Give examples of situations that might cause you to (1) qualify an opinion, (2) issue an adverse opinion, and (3) disclaim an opinion.

13–7. With respect to the Single Audit Act of 1984 and amendment of 1996 relating to state and local governments and not-for-profit organizations:
    a. Distinguish between major and nonmajor programs.
    b. List the criteria used to determine whether an entity is subject to the Single Audit Act.

c. List the audit reports that should be included in a single audit report.

d. List some of the sources of information that an auditor would need to conduct an audit of a government subject to the Single Audit Act. List both GAAP and audit sources.

13-8. A local government has five federal grants. Expenditures amounted to $2,000,000 during the year, as follows:

Type A	
HUD grant, new and never audited	$600,000
HHS grant, audited last year, no major findings	500,000
Type B	
EPA grant	400,000
Summer Youth Employment grant	450,000
Dept. of Agriculture grant	50,000

Describe how you, as an auditor, would determine major programs for audit, assuming (*a*) the local government is not a low-risk auditee, and (*b*) the local government is a low-risk auditee.

13-9. With regard to tax-exempt organizations:
   a. Define a 501(c)(3) organization.
   b. Define a public charity.

13-10. With regard to filing requirements for 501(c)(3) organizations:
   a. List those entities that are not required to file.
   b. Discuss the major parts of Form 990.
   c. Discuss the major parts of Schedule A. Which organizations are required to file Schedule A?

13-11. With regard to Unrelated Business Income Tax (UBIT), answer the following questions:
   a. Which four conditions will automatically exempt entities from UBIT?
   b. What are some exceptions to UBIT provided by legislation?
   c. How is UBIT computed? What deductions are allowed?

13-12. You and a few friends have decided to establish a not-for-profit organization in your community to help provide shelter and food to the homeless and transients. Outline the steps you would take to obtain tax-exempt status, avoid paying unrelated business income tax, and so on. Consider the creation of a related entity, a foundation, as a part of your planning.

13-13. With regard to service efforts and accomplishments reporting, define the following terms:
   a. Service efforts
   b. Service accomplishments
   c. Inputs

d. Outputs
  e. Outcomes
  f. Efficiency measures
  g. Cost-outcome measures

13–14. Use the websites provided in Illustration 13–6 to access your high school, or school system school report card (or any other school report card of your choice). Answer the following questions:
  a. What measures of service inputs are presented on the report card?
  b. What measures of service outputs are presented on the report card?
  c. What measures of service outcomes are presented on the report card?
  d. What information is presented to provide comparisons between the school selected and other schools in the state?

Appendix

Governmental and Not-For-Profit Accounting Terminology

A

accounting entity   Where an entity is established for the purpose of accounting for a certain activity or activities. See *fiscal entity*.

accounts receivable   Amounts owing on open account from private persons, firms, or corporations for goods and services furnished by a governmental unit (but not including amounts due from other funds of the same governmental unit). *Note:* Although taxes and assessments receivable are covered by this term, they should each be recorded and reported separately in *Taxes Receivable* and *Special Assessments Receivable* accounts. Similarly, amounts due from other funds or from other governmental units should be reported separately.

accrual basis   Basis of accounting under which revenues are recorded when earned and expenditures (or expenses) are recorded as soon as they result in liabilities for benefits received, notwithstanding that the receipt of cash or the payment of cash may take place, in whole or in part, in another accounting period.

activity   Specific and distinguishable line of work performed by one or more organizational components of a governmental unit for the purpose of accomplishing a function for which the governmental unit is responsible. For example, "Food Inspection" is an activity performed in the discharge of the "Health" function. See also *Function*.

actuarial basis   Basis used in computing the amount of contributions to be made periodically to a fund so that the total contributions plus the compounded earnings thereon will equal the required payments to be made out of the fund. The factors taken into account in arriving at the amount of these contributions include the length of time over which each contribution is to be held and the rate of return compounded on such a contribution over its life. Commonly used to compute annual required contributions (q.v.) to pension plans.[1]

additions   GASB term for fiduciary fund financial reporting, replacing the term *revenues*. Additions are reported on the accrual basis.

ad valorem   In proportion to value. Basis for levy of taxes on property.

advance refunding   A bond refunding (q.v.) in which the proceeds are placed in an escrow account pending the call date or the maturity date of the existing debt. In this case, the debt is said to be *defeased* (q.v.) for accounting purposes.

advances, interfund   Long-term loans between funds. A long-term loan to another

---

[1] The letters *q.v.* signify *which see*.

fund would be represented in the account Advances to Other Funds. A long-term loan from another fund would be represented in the account Advances from Other Funds. Should be contrasted with Due to and Due from accounts, which represent short-term interfund loans.

adverse opinion Audit report in which the auditor states that the financial report "does not present fairly" due to major departures from generally accepted accounting principles (q.v.).

agency fund Fiduciary fund consisting of resources received and held by the governmental agent for others; for example, taxes collected and held by a municipality for a school district.

agent multiple-employer defined benefit pension plan Statewide pension plan in which separate account balances are maintained for each participating employer, expected to fund any deficits. Contrast with cost-sharing multiple-employer defined benefit pension plan.

AICPA SOP 98-3, Audits of States, Local Governments, and Not-for-Profit Organizations Receiving Federal Awards Guidance provided by the AICPA for auditors when conducting audits in accord with the Single Audit Act and OMB Circular A–133 (q.v.).

American Institute of Certified Public Accountants (AICPA) Organization of Certified Public Accountants that provides auditing guidance, including the GAAP Hierarchy (q.v.) and accounting and auditing guidance, in the case of *Audit and Accounting Guides*, when approved by the FASB (q.v.) and/or the GASB (q.v.).

annual required contributions Term used by GASB to determine the amount required by a retirement fund to be contributed, including normal cost and funding of past service cost. Used in the Schedule of Employer Contributions (q.v.).

annuity Series of equal money payments made at equal intervals during a designated period of time. In governmental accounting, the most frequent annuities are accumulations of debt service funds for term bonds and payments to retired employees or their beneficiaries under public employee retirement systems.

appropriation Authorization granted by a legislative body to incur liabilities for purposes specified in the appropriation act (q.v.).

appropriations, expenditures, and encumbrances ledger Subsidiary ledger used by governmental funds in which a budget is recorded to track the appropriations, expenditures, and encumbrances that apply to the subsidiary account. Using this ledger, a department head, for example, could determine the unencumbered balance in the department.

assessed valuation Valuation set on real estate or other property by a government as a basis of levying taxes. A state government may provide that the local governments within its jurisdiction assess property at 100 percent, 33⅓ percent, or other percentages of market value.

assessment (1) Process of making the official valuation of property for purposes of taxation. (2) Valuation placed on property as a result of this process.

assets whose use is limited Account title used by health care organizations to indicate those assets that are unrestricted but limited by board action, bond resolutions, or the like.

attestation agreements Under Government Auditing Standards (q.v.), concerns examining, reviewing, or performing agreed upon procedures on a subject matter or an assertation about a subject matter and reporting on the results.

audit Examination of documents, records, reports, systems of internal control, accounting and financial procedures, and other evidence and the issuance of a report relating to the examination.

auditor's report Report included with financial statements that expresses an opinion of the fairness of the material presented.

authority Governmental unit or public agency created to perform a single function or a restricted group of related activities. Usually such units are financed from service charges, fees, and tolls, but in some instances they also have taxing powers.

auxiliary enterprises Activities of a college or university that furnishes services to students, faculty, or staff on a user-charge basis. Charge is directly related to, but not necessarily equal to, the cost of the service. Examples are college unions, residence halls, stores, faculty clubs, and intercollegiate athletics.

available One condition that must be met before a revenue can be recognized under modified accrual accounting. The amount must be available in time to pay expenditures related to the current period.

B

balance sheet Format where assets equal liabilities plus net assets (fund balance). Required governmental funds basic statement; may be used as government-wide and proprietary fund in lieu of Statement of Net Assets.

basic financial statements The primary financial statements required by the GASB in order for state and local governments to meet GAAP. The nature of the government (general-purpose, special-purpose) and of the governmental activities (governmental-type, business-type, and fiduciary-type) determine which statements are basic.

basis of accounting Rule (or rules) used to determine the point in time when assets, liabilities, revenues, and expenses (expenditures) should be measured and recorded as such in the accounts of an entity. An organization might use the cash, modified accrual, or accrual basis of accounting.

blended presentation One method of reporting the financial data of a component unit in a manner similar to that in which the financial data of the primary government are presented. Under this method, the component unit data are combined with the appropriate fund types of the primary government and reported in the same columns as the data from the primary government. See *Discrete Presentation.*

bond discount Excess of the face value of a bond over the price for which it is acquired or sold.

bond indenture Contract between an entity issuing bonds and the trustees or other body representing prospective and actual holders of the bonds.

bond ordinance or resolution Ordinance (q.v.) or resolution (q.v.) authorizing a bond issue.

bond premium Excess of the price at which a bond is acquired or sold over its face value.

bonded debt That portion of indebtedness represented by outstanding bonds.

bonds, authorized and unissued Bonds that have been legally authorized but not issued and that can be issued and sold without further authorization. *Note.* This term must not be confused with the term *legal debt margin,* which represents the difference between the legal debt limit (q.v.) of a governmental unit and the debt outstanding against it.

budget Plan of financial operation embodying an estimate of proposed expenditures for a given period and the proposed means of financing them. Used without any modifier, usually indicates a financial plan for a single fiscal year.

budgetary accounts Accounts that reflect budgetary operations and conditions, such as Estimated Revenues, Appropriations, and Encumbrances, as distinguished from proprietary accounts (q.v.). Other examples include Estimated Other Financing Sources, Estimated Other Financing Uses, Budgetary Fund Balance, and Budgetary Fund Balance Reserved for Encumbrances. As distinguished from actual revenues, expenditures, etc.

budgetary comparison schedule Schedule, part of RSI (q.v.) where actual revenues and expenditures are compared with the original and revised budget. Required for General Fund and all special revenue funds for which an annual budget is legally adopted. A basic statement may be prepared in lieu of this schedule.

budgetary fund balance Budgetary account for state and local governmental funds that reflects the difference between estimated revenues, estimated other financing sources, and so on and appropriations, estimated other financing uses, and so on. Closed at the end of the year.

budgetary fund balance reserved for encumbrances Budgetary account for state and local governmental funds that reflects the amount offsetting Encumbrances (q.v.), or purchase orders or contracts issued during the current year. Year-end balance closed to Fund Balance Reserved for Encumbrances, an equity account.

business-type activities Business-type activities are reported separately in the government-wide statements and include activities normally accounted for in enterprise funds.

C

CAFR See *Comprehensive Annual Financial Report*.

capital and related financing activities Cash flow statement category required by GASB. Includes proceeds from bond issues, payment of debt, acquisition of fixed assets, and payment of interest on capital-related debt.

capital assets Term used by GASB to include land, improvements to land, easements, buildings, building improvements, vehicles, machinery, equipment, works of art and historical treasures, infrastructure, and all other tangible or intangible assets that are used in operations and that have initial useful lives extending beyond a single reporting period.

capital lease Lease that substantively transfers the benefits and risks of ownership of property to the lessee. Any lease that meets certain criteria specified in applicable accounting and reporting standards. See also *Operating Lease*.

capital outlays Expenditures that result in the acquisition of or addition to fixed assets. One of the Character classifications, the others being Current and Debt Service.

capital projects fund Fund created to account for all financial resources to be used for the construction or acquisition of designated fixed assets by a governmental unit except those financed by proprietary or fiduciary funds.

cash basis Basis of accounting under which revenues are recorded when received in cash and expenditures are recorded when cash is disbursed.

cash equivalent Short-term, highly liquid investments that are both readily convertible into known amounts of cash and so near their maturity (with original maturities of three months or less) that they present insignificant risk of changes in value due to changes in interest rates.

character classification Grouping of expenditures on the basis of the fiscal periods they are presumed to benefit. The three groupings are (1) current expenditures, presumed to benefit the current fiscal period; (2) debt service, presumed to benefit prior fiscal periods primarily but also present and future periods; and (3) capital outlay, presumed to benefit the current and future fiscal periods.

charitable gift annuity Split interest agreement that exists when no formal trust agreement is signed but that otherwise is similar to a charitable remainder trust (q.v.) in which a specified amount or percentage of the fair value of assets is paid to a beneficiary during the term of the agreement; at the end of the agreement, the trust assets go to the not-for-profit organization.

charitable lead trust Split interest (q.v.) agreement in which an organization receives a fixed amount (charitable lead annuity trust) or a percentage of the fair value of the trust (charitable lead unitrust) for a certain term. At the end of the term, the remainder of trust assets is paid to the donor or other beneficiary.

charitable remainder trust Split interest (q.v.) agreement in which a fixed dollar amount (charitable remainder annuity trust) or a specified percentage of the trust's fair market value (charitable remainder unitrust) is paid to a beneficiary. At the end of the term of the trust, the trust principal is paid to a not for-profit organization.

cognizant agency Under Single Audit Act and amendments, an agency that deals with the auditee, as representative of all federal agencies. Is assigned by the U.S. Office of Management and Budget (q.v.) for auditees with more than $25 million in federal awards ($50 million beginning in 2004).

collection Under both FASB and GASB standards, collections are works of art, historical treasures, etc. that are (1) held for public exhibition, education, or research in furtherance of public service, other than financial gain, (2) protected, kept unencumbered, cared for and preserved, and (3) subject to an organizational policy that requires the proceeds from sales of collection items to be used to acquire other items for collections. Collections may or may not be capitalized and depreciated.

combining financial statements CAFR section where nonmajor funds are presented. The total column of the nonmajor funds in the combining statements is equal to the nonmajor funds column in the basic financial statements.

compliance audit Audit designed to provide reasonable assurance that a governmental entity has complied with applicable laws and regulations. Required for every audit performed in conformity with *Government Auditing Standards*.

compliance supplement Supplement to OMB Circular A–133 (q.v.) that provides specific guidance to use when conducting audits of certain programs.

component unit Separate governmental unit, agency, or nonprofit corporation that, pursuant to the criteria in the GASB Codification, Section 2100, is combined with other component units and the primary government to constitute the reporting entity (q.v.).

Comprehensive Annual Financial Report (CAFR) A governmental unit's official annual report prepared and published as a matter of public record. In addition to the basic financial statements (q.v.), the CAFR should contain introductory material, schedules to demonstrate compliance, and statistical tables specified in the GASB Codification.

Comptroller General of the United States Head of the U.S. General Accounting Office. One of the Principals that reviews the recommendations of the Federal Accounting Standards Advisory Board (FASAB)(q.v.).

concepts statements Documents issued by the GASB (q.v.), FASB (q.v.), and FASAB (q.v.) to provide guidance to those boards and a conceptual framework that can be used to establish future standards.

condition Under both FASB and GASB, a condition is an event that must take place in order for a donation or grant to be recognized, such as a requirement for a matching pledge. Neither FASB nor GASB permits a pledge containing a condition to be recorded as a revenue.

construction work in progress Cost of construction work that has been started but not yet completed. Fixed asset account.

consumption method Refers to method used to recognize expenditures for governmental funds (q.v.) in which an expenditure (q.v.) is recognized when inventory is consumed.

contingencies Term used by both GASB and FASB. Something must happen (for example a matching requirement) before a revenue (expense) can be recognized. For GASB, an eligibility requirement.

contributions Amounts given to an individual or to an organization for which the donor receives no direct private benefits. Contributions may be in the form of pledges, cash, securities, materials, services, or fixed assets.

control account Account in the general ledger in which are recorded the aggregate of debit and credit postings to a number of identical or related accounts called *subsidiary accounts* (q.v.). For example, Expenditures is a control account supported by the aggregate of individual balances in individual departmental expenditure accounts.

cost-sharing multiple-employer defined benefit pension plan Statewide pension plan in which separate account balances are not maintained for each participating employer. Contrast with *agent multiple-employer defined benefit pension plan.*

current Term that, applied to budgeting and accounting, designates the operations of the present fiscal period as opposed to past or future periods. One of the Character classifications of expenditures.

current financial resources measurement focus Measurement focus used for governmental funds by GASB that measures current financial resources, not fixed assets and long-term debt. Contrast with *Economic Resources Measurement Focus* (q.v.).

current refunding A bond refunding (q.v.) in which new debt is issued, and the proceeds are used to call in the existing debt. Contrast with *advance refunding* (q.v.).

customer advances for construction Amounts required to be deposited by a customer for construction projects undertaken by the utility at the request of the customer.

D

debt limit Maximum amount of gross or net debt that is legally permitted.

debt margin Difference between the amount of the debt limit (q.v.) and the net amount of outstanding indebtedness subject to the limitation.

debt service fund Fund established to finance and account for the payment of interest and principal on all tax-supported long-term debt, including that payable from special assessments in which the government assumes some level of liability.

deductions GASB term for fiduciary fund financial reporting, replacing the term *expenses.* Deductions are reported on the accrual basis.

defeased In an advanced refunding (q.v.) where proceeds are placed in an escrow account pending the call date or maturity date of the existing debt, the old debt is considered not to exist and to be replaced by the existing debt.

deferred revenues or deferred credits In governmental or nonprofit accounting, items that may not be recognized as revenues of the period in which received and the related asset (cash or receivable) is first recognized.

deferred serial bonds Serial bonds (q.v.) in which the first installment does not fall due for two or more years from the date of issue.

deficit (1) Excess of liabilities and reserved equity of a fund over its assets. (2) Excess of expenditures and encumbrances over revenues during an accounting period; or, in the case of Enterprise and Internal Service Funds, excess of expense over revenue during an accounting period.

defined benefit retirement plans Retirement plans in which the benefit is defined, normally as a percentage multiplied by average or highest salaries multiplied by the number of years worked.

defined contribution retirement plans Retirement plans in which the amount to be paid at retirement is based on employee and employer contributions and interest income.

delinquent taxes Taxes remaining unpaid on and after the date on which a penalty for nonpayment is attached. Even though the penalty may be subsequently waived and a portion of the taxes may be abated or canceled, the unpaid balances continue to the delinquent taxes until abated, canceled, paid, or converted into tax liens.

derived tax revenues One of the four classes of nonexchange transactions established by GASB. Examples are sales taxes and income taxes.

designated (1) In nonprofit accounting, assets, or equity set aside by action of the governing board, as distinguished from assets or equity set aside in conformity with requirements of donors, grantors, or creditors, which are properly referred to as *restricted*. (2) In governmental accounting, equity that is unreserved but set aside by the governing board, as opposed to equity that is committed or otherwise tied up beyond the control of the governing board, which is *reserved*.

direct debt Debt that a governmental unit has incurred in its own name or assumed through the annexation of territory or consolidation with another governmental unit. See also *Overlapping Debt.*

direct method Method for cash flow statements in which operating cash flows are presented "directly" such as receipts from customers, payments to suppliers and employees, etc. Contrast with *indirect method* (q.v.). GASB requires the direct method, whereas FASB permits either the direct or indirect method.

disclaimer of opinion Audit report in which the auditor does not provide an opinion due to a severe scope limitation or for other reasons.

discrete presentation Method of reporting financial data of component units (q.v.) in a column or columns separate from the financial data of the primary government (q.v.).

donated services Services of volunteer workers who are unpaid or who are paid less than the market value of their services. In certain circumstances, donated services are recognized as revenues of nonprofit organizations.

E

economic resources measurement focus Term used by GASB to indicate measurement focus for government-wide, proprietary fund, and fiduciary fund statements. The economic resources measurement focus measures all economic resources, including fixed assets and long-term debt. Contrast with *Current Financial Resources Measurement Focus* (q.v.).

eligibility requirements Term used by GASB, in *Statement 33,* that describes certain conditions or events that must be met before a nonexchange revenue can be recognized. The four eligibility requirements are (1) required characteristics of recipients, (2) time requirements, (3) reimbursements, and (4) contingencies.

encumbrances The estimated amount of purchase orders, contracts, or salary commitments chargeable to an appropriation.

endowments Exist when a donor contributes an amount, never to be expended by donor restriction. The income from endowments may or may not be *restricted* (q.v.). See also term endowment.

enterprise fund Fund used in state and local government accounting. Established to finance and account for the acquisition, operation, and maintenance of governmental facilities and services that are entirely or predominantly self-supporting by user charges; or for which the governing body of the governmental unit has decided periodic determination of revenues earned, expenses incurred, and/or net income is appropriate. Government-owned utilities and hospitals are ordinarily accounted for by enterprise funds.

escheat property Private property that reverts to government ownership upon the death of the owner if there are no legal claimants or heirs.

estimated other financing sources Amounts of financial resources estimated to be received or accrued during a period by a governmental or similar type fund from interfund transfers or from the proceeds of noncurrent debt issuances. Budgetary account.

estimated other financing uses Amounts of financial resources estimated to be disbursed or accrued during a period by a governmental or similar type fund for transfer to other funds. Budgetary account.

estimated revenues Budgetary account providing an estimate of the revenues that will be recognized during an accounting period by a governmental fund, such as the General Fund.

estimated uncollectible taxes (credit) Provision out of tax revenues for that portion of taxes receivable that it is estimated will never be collected. Amount is shown on the balance sheet as a deduction from the Taxes Receivable account in order to arrive at the net taxes receivable.

exemption Statutory reduction in the assessed valuation of taxable property accorded to certain taxpayers. Typical examples are senior citizens and war veterans.

exchange transactions A transaction in which each party receives and gives up essentially equal values. FASB and GASB require that exchange transactions be recognized when the exchange takes place. See *nonexchange transactions*.

exchange-like transactions Where the values exchanged, though related, may not be quite equal or in which the direct benefits may not be exclusively for the parties to the transaction. Recognized in same manner as *exchange transactions* (q.v.).

expendable Resources, where focus is on the receipt and expenditure of resources; for example, modified accrual accounting. See *nonexpendable*.

expended Term describing outflow of resources or reduction of liabilities associated with receipt of goods or services. Especially used in budgetary accounting, e.g., when an appropriation (q.v.) is expended.

expenditures Recorded when liabilities are incurred pursuant to authority given in an appropriation (q.v.). Designates the cost of goods delivered or services rendered, whether paid or unpaid, including current items, provision for interest and debt retirement, and capital outlays. Used for governmental funds of governmental units.

F

face value As applied to securities, the amount of liability stated in the security document. Sometimes called *par value*.

fair value Amount at which an investment could be exchanged in a current transaction, other than a forced or liquidation sale, between willing parties. Certain investments are required by the FASB and GASB to be reported at fair value.

Federal Accounting Standards Advisory Board (FASAB) Standards-setting body that promulgates federal government accounting and financial reporting standards.

fiduciary activities Fiduciary activities are not included in the government-wide statements but are included, as fiduciary funds, in the fund financial statements.

fiduciary funds Any fund held by a governmental unit in a fiduciary capacity, ordinarily as agent or trustee. Also called *trust and agency funds*. Four categories exist: agency funds, pension trust funds, investment trust funds, and private-purpose trust funds.

Financial Accounting and Reporting Manual (FARM) Issued by the National Association of College and University Business Officers (NACUBO) (q.v.) as additional illustrative guidance for accounting and financial reporting for both public and private institutions of higher education.

Financial Accounting Foundation (FAF) Parent organization of the Financial Accounting Standards Board (FASB) and the Governmental Accounting Standards Board (GASB). Responsible for overall policy direction, raising funds, and selecting board members, but not for setting standards.

Financial Accounting Standards Board (FASB) Independent seven-member body designated to set accounting and financial reporting standards for commercial entities and nongovernmental not-for-profit entities.

financial audits Under Government Auditing Standards (q.v.), type of governmental audit that provides assurance about the fairness of financial statements.

financial section One of the three major parts of the Comprehensive Annual Financial Report (q.v.). Contains the auditor's opinion, the MD&A, the basic financial statements, required supplementary information, and any combining and individual fund financial statements and schedules.

financing activities Cash flow statement category required by FASB. Includes all borrowing and repayment of debt.

fiscal agent Bank or other corporate fiduciary that performs the function of paying interest and/or principal on debt when due on behalf of the governmental unit, nonprofit organization, or other organization.

fiscal entity Where assets are set aside, for example in a fund, for specific purposes. See *accounting entity*.

501(c)(3) entities Not-for-profit organizations that receive tax-exempt status through Section 501(c)(3) of the Internal Revenue Code.

forfeiture Automatic loss of cash or other property as a punishment for not complying with legal provisions and as compensation for the resulting damages or losses.

Form 990 Tax form information return filed by certain tax exempt organizations under Section 501(c)(3)(q.v.) of the Internal Revenue Code.

full faith and credit Pledge of the general taxing power for the payment of debt obligations. General obligation bonds are backed by the full faith and credit of a given governmental unit.

function Group of related activities aimed at accomplishing a major service or regulatory responsibility for which a governmental unit is responsible. For example, public health is a function. The GASB provides for functional reporting of expenditures for governmental funds, and the FASB provides for functional reporting of expenses for private-sector not-for-profit organizations.

functional classification Grouping of expenditures on the basis of the principal purposes for which they are made. Examples in government are public safety, public health, and public welfare. Examples in not-for-profit organizations are the various programs, fund-raising, management and general, and membership development.

functional expenses, statement of Statement that displays, in a matrix format, expenses reported by function (q.v.) and expenses reported by object (q.v.). Required by the FASB for voluntary health and welfare organizations and recommended for other not-for-profit organizations, either as a statement or in the notes.

fund Fiscal and accounting entity with a self-balancing set of accounts recording cash and other resources together with all related liabilities, net assets or fund balances, and changes therein that are segregated for the purpose of carrying on specific activities or attaining certain objectives in accordance with special regulations, restrictions, or limitations.

fund accounting Accounting system organized on the basis of funds, each of which is considered a separate accounting entity. The operations of each fund are accounted for with a separate set of self-balancing accounts that comprise its assets, liabilities, fund equity, revenues, and expenditures, or expenses, as appropriate.

fund balance Term used for governmental funds (q.v.) representing the difference between assets and liabilities. Fund balance may be reserved for various purposes or unreserved (q.v.).

fund balance—reserved for encumbrances Portion of fund equity of governmental and expendable trust funds that is set aside for outstanding purchase orders and contracts.

fund balance—reserved for inventories Portion of fund equity of governmental funds that is set aside for inventories reported as fund assets.

fund balance—reserved for long-term advances Portion of fund equity of governmental funds that is set aside for long-term receivables reported as fund assets.

fund balance—unreserved In governmental accounting, portion of Fund Equity (q.v.) that is available for appropriation.

fund equity Excess of fund assets and resources over fund liabilities. A portion of the equity of a governmental fund may be reserved (q.v.) or designated (q.v.).

fund financial statements Fund financial statements are required by GASB *Statement 34* as well as government-wide statements. Statements include those for governmental funds (q.v.), proprietary funds (q.v.), and fiduciary funds (q.v.).

G

GAAP hierarchy Priority listing of Generally Accepted Accounting Principles (GAAP) (q.v.) established by the American Institute of Certified Public Accountants for governmental and nongovernmental units.

General Accounting Office, U.S. Legislative Branch Agency of the federal government that prepares *Government Auditing Standards* (q.v.), responsible for audit of U.S. government executive branch.

general fixed assets Fixed assets of a governmental unit that are not accounted for by a proprietary or fiduciary fund.

general fund Fund used to account for all transactions of a governmental unit that are not accounted for in another fund.

general long-term debt Long-term debt legally payable from general revenues and backed by the full faith and credit of a governmental unit.

general obligation bonds Bonds for whose payment the full faith and credit of the issuing body is pledged. More commonly, but not necessarily, considered to be those payable from taxes and other general revenues (q.v.). In some states, called *tax-supported* bonds.

general revenues (governmental) All tax revenues and those other revenues that are not associated directly with a particular function or program. Deducted from net program costs in Statement of Activities (q.v.).

general-purpose government Includes states, counties, municipalities, and other governments that have a range of purposes. General-purpose governments are by definition primary governments. In addition, general-purpose governments are required to prepare the full range of basic financial statements, including government-wide and fund.

Generally Accepted Accounting Principles (GAAP) Body of accounting and financial reporting standards as defined by Rule 203 of the American Institute of Certified Public Accountants (AICPA). "Level A" GAAP is set by the FASB, the GASB, and the FASAB.

Generally Accepted Auditing Standards (GAAS) Standards prescribed by the American Institute of Certified Public Accountants to provide guidance for planning, conducting, and reporting audits by Certified Public Accountants.

Government Auditing Standards (GAS) Auditing standards set forth by the Comptroller General of the United States to provide guidance for federal auditors and state and local governmental auditors and public accountants who audit federal organizations, programs, activities, and functions. Also referred to as *Generally Accepted Government Auditing Standards (GAGAS).*

Government Finance Officers Association Association of government finance officials, primarily state and local. Sponsored the National Council on Governmental Accounting (NCGA), the predecessor standards-setting body to the GASB. Administers the Certificate of Achievement programs to encourage excellence in financial reporting and budgeting by state and local governments.

Governmental Accounting Standards Board (GASB) Independent agency established under the Financial Accounting Foundation in 1984 to set accounting and financial reporting standards for state and local governments and for governmentally related not-for-profit organizations.

governmental activities Governmental activities are reported separately in the government-wide statements and include activities normally accounted for in the governmental funds and internal service funds.

governmental funds Generic classification used by the GASB to refer to all funds other than proprietary and fiduciary. Includes the General Fund, special revenue funds, capital projects funds, debt service funds, and permanent funds.

government-mandated nonexchange transactions One of the four classes of nonexchange transactions established by GASB. Example would be a grant to a school district to carry out a mandated state program.

government-wide financial statements Government-wide statements included in the financial reporting requirements of GASB *Statement 34* include the Statement of Net Assets and Statement of Activities.

grant Contribution by one governmental unit to another unit. The contribution is usually made to aid in the support of a specified function (for example, education), but it is sometimes also for general purposes or for the acquisition or construction of fixed assets.

H-I

Health Care Guide The AICPA (q.v.) Auditing and Accounting Guide: Health Care Organizations, which provides guidance for all health care entities, governmental, not-for-profit and for-profit.

imposed tax revenues One of the four classes of nonexchange transactions established by GASB. Examples are property taxes and fines and forfeits.

indirect method Method for cash flow statement in which operating cash flows begin by reconciling from change in net assets to cash flows from operations. Contrast with *direct method* (q.v.). GASB prohibits the indirect method, whereas FASB permits either the direct or the indirect method.

infrastructure assets Long-term assets including roads, bridges, storm sewers, etc. Under *Statement 34,* governments are required to capitalize and depreciate infrastructure, or to use the modified approach (q.v.).

in-substance defeasance Transaction in which low-risk U.S. government securities are placed into an irrevocable trust for the benefit of debt holders and the liability for the debt is removed from the accounts of the entity even though the debt has not been repaid.

interfund loans and advances Interfund transaction where one fund provides a short-term loan or a long-term advance to another. Type of reciprocal interfund transaction (q.v.). One fund recognizes a receivable and the other a liability.

interfund reimbursements Type of interfund transaction in which one fund reimburses another for expenditures already incurred. One fund recognizes an expenditure or expense; the other reduces an expenditure or expense.

interfund services provided and used Interfund transaction in which one fund provides service to another. Type of reciprocal interfund transaction (q.v.). One fund recognizes a revenue and the other fund recognizes an expenditure or expense. Replaces the term *quasi-external* transaction.

interfund transactions GASB term to describe transactions between funds. Four types of interfund transactions exist. Reciprocal interfund transactions (q.v.) include interfund loans and advances (q.v.) and interfund services provided and used (q.v.). Nonreciprocal interfund transactions include interfund transfers (q.v.) and reimbursements (q.v.).

interfund transfers Type of interfund transaction in which one fund transfers resources to another, without an exchange transaction. One fund recognizes an Other Financing Source (q.v.) (or Transfer In) and the other fund recognizes an Other Financing Use (q.v.) (or Transfer Out).

intergovernmental revenue Revenue from other governments, a source classification of revenues in governmental accounting. Includes grants, shared revenues, and entitlements.

internal service fund Fund established to finance and account for services and commodities furnished by a designated department or agency to other departments and agencies within a single governmental unit or to other governmental units. Type of proprietary fund. Resources used by the fund are restored either from operating earnings or by transfers from other funds so that the original fund capital is kept intact.

interpretations Documents issued by the GASB (q.v.), FASB (q.v.), and FASAB (q.v.), that provide guidance regarding previously issued statements (q.v.).

introductory section One of the three major parts of the Comprehensive Annual Financial Report (CAFR)(q.v.), including the letter of transmittal, organization chart, and list of principal officials.

invested in capital assets, net of related debt Equity account, used for government-wide and fiduciary fund statement of net assets (q.v.) that represents the amount reported for capital assets (q.v.), net of accumulated depreciation, less debt issued to obtain those capital assets.

investing activities Cash flow statement category required by both FASB and GASB. FASB and GASB have differing content requirements for this category.

investment trust fund Fiduciary fund that accounts for the external portion of investment pools reported by the sponsoring government.

IRS 457 deferred compensation plans Tax deferred plans allowed by law to be offered by state and local governmental units. In some cases, reported as Pension Trust Funds.

J-L

lapse As applied to appropriations, denotes the automatic termination of an appropriation. As applied to encumbrances, denotes the termination of an encumbrance (q.v.) at the end of a fiscal year.

levy To impose taxes, special assessments, or service charges for the support of governmental activities. Total amount of taxes, special assessments, or service charges imposed by a governmental unit.

limited obligation debt Debt secured by a pledge of the collections of a certain specified tax (rather than by all general revenues).

low-risk auditee Auditee determined by an auditor who is auditing under the Single Audit Act (q.v.) to have met certain criteria.

M

major funds Major funds must be displayed in the basic statements for governmental and proprietary funds. Funds are considered major when both of the following conditions exist: (1) total assets, liabilities, revenues, or expenditures/expenses of that individual governmental or enterprise fund constitute 10 percent of the governmental or enterprise activity, and (2) total assets, liabilities, revenues, or expenditures/expenses are 5 percent of the governmental and enterprise category.

major programs Programs that must be audited under the provisions of the Single Audit Act (q.v.). Determined by a risk-based approach. Auditors must audit larger (Type A) programs unless they judge them to be low risk; auditors must audit smaller (Type B) programs if they judge them to be high risk.

Management's Discussion and Analysis (MD&A) Required part of the financial section of a CAFR that provides an opportunity for management to explain, in plain English terms, an overview of the government's financial activities. Considered Required Supplementary Information (q.v.) by the GASB.

matured bonds payable Bonds that have reached their maturity but remain unpaid.

matured interest payable Bond interest that is due but remains unpaid.

measurable One condition that must be met before a revenue can be recognized under the modified accrual basis of accounting. The amount must be measurable.

measurement focus Nature of the resources, claims against resources, and flows of resources that are measured and reported by a fund or other entity. For example, governmental funds measure and report current financial resources, whereas proprietary and fiduciary funds measure and report economic resources.

mill Tax rate (q.v.) expressed in thousands per net assessed valuation. For example, a tax rate of $2.50 per $100 net assessed valuation would be $0.25 per $1,000 net assessed valuation, or 25 mills.

modified accrual basis of accounting Basis of accounting required for use by governmental funds (q.v.) in which revenues are recognized in the period in which they become available and measurable, and expenditures are recognized at the time a liability is incurred except for principal and interest on long-term debt, which are recorded when due.

modified approach (infrastructure) When a government chooses not to depreciate infrastructure assets (q.v.). Under this approach, improvements and additions would be capitalized; expenditures that extend the life would be expenses. When using the modified approach, a government must provide certain RSI (q.v.) schedules that demonstrate that infrastructure is maintained at a certain level.

N

National Association of College and University Business Officers (NACUBO) Association of college and university financial vice presidents, controllers, budget officials, and other finance officers that produces and distributes *Financial Accounting and Reporting Manual for Higher Education* (q.v.).

National Council on Governmental Accounting (NCGA) Body that established accounting and financial reporting standards for state and local governments prior to the formation of the Governmental Accounting Standards Board.

net assets Difference between total assets and total liabilities. Used by the FASB and GASB to describe equity accounts.

net assets—invested in capital assets, net of related debt (governmental) The portion of net assets of a governmental unit representing capital assets less accumulated depreciation less debt associated with the capital assets.

net assets—permanently restricted (not for-profit) Used in accounting for not-for-profit organizations indicating the amount of net assets whose use is permanently restricted by an external donor.

net assets—restricted (governmental) That portion of net assets of a governmental unit or proprietary fund that is restricted. See *Restricted (governmental)*.

net assets—temporarily restricted (not-for-profit) Used in accounting for not-for-profit organizations indicating the amount of net assets whose use is temporarily restricted by donors or grantors. Released by program, time, plant acquisition, and term endowments.

net assets—unrestricted (governmental and not-for-profit) Used in accounting for governmental and not-for-profit organizations indicating that portion of net assets that is unrestricted.

net increase/decrease in fair value of investments Account title used by governments to report realized and unrealized gains or losses on investments.

Net Pension Obligation (NPO) In a pension plan, anticipated present value of future payments based on past service.

nominal interest rate Contractual interest rate shown on the face and in the body of a bond and representing the amount of interest to be paid, in contrast to the effective interest rate (q.v.).

nonaudit services Under Government Auditing Standards (q.v.), gathering, providing, or explaining information requested by decision makers or providing advice or assistance to management officials.

noncapital financing activities Cash flow statement category required by GASB. Includes cash flows from financing not related to capital acquisition, including borrowing and transfers to and from other funds.

nonexchange transactions Transactions that are not the result of arms-length exchange between two parties that are bargaining for the best position. Contrasted with exchange transactions, such as sales and services for user charges. Examples are taxes and contributions. GASB has established accounting rules for nonexchange transactions in *Statement 33*.

nonexpendable Resources, which are maintained, and focus is on the recognition of revenues and expenses; for example, in accrual accounting. See *expendable*.

nonmajor funds All funds other than major. Nonmajor funds are not required to be presented separately in the basic fund financial statements of governmental and enterprise funds. See *major funds*.

nonreciprocal interfund transactions Type of interfund transaction where the direction is "one-way." Includes interfund transfers and interfund reimbursements. The interfund equivalent of nonexchange transactions (q.v.).

normal cost Amount that would be required to be contributed to a retirement plan and charged as expenditure/expense, assuming the plan was currently funded; present value of future payments based on current earnings.

Not-for-Profit Guide AICPA (q.v.) *Audits of Not-for-Profit Organizations,* which provides guidance for private sector colleges and universities, voluntary health and welfare organizations, and other not-for-profit organizations, excluding health care.

not-for-profit organization An entity that possesses the following characteristics: (1) receives significant resources from donors who do not expect equivalent value in return, (2) operates for purposes other than to provide goods or services at a profit, and (3) lacks an identifiable individual or group of individuals who hold a legally enforceable residual claim. Entities that fall outside this definition include all investor owned enterprises and other organizations that provide economic benefits to the owners, members or participants.

notes to the financial statements Required part of the basic financial statements for state and local governments. Includes a summary of significant accounting policies, other required and optional disclosures.

O

object As used in expenditure classification, applies to the article purchased or the service obtained (as distinguished from the results obtained from expenditures). Examples are personal services, contractual services, materials, and supplies.

object classification Grouping of expenditures on the basis of goods or services purchased. See also *Functional Classification, Activity Classification,* and *Character Classification.*

objectives statements Issued by the FASB, FASAB, and GASB for guidance and reference when preparing standards of accounting and financial reporting.

Office of Management and Budget, U.S. (OMB) Executive agency of the federal government responsible for the preparation of the executive budget proposal and for the form and content of agency financial statements. The director is one of the Principals (q.v.) that approves the recommendations of the Financial Accounting Standards Advisory Board (FASAB) (q.v.).

OMB Circular A–133, *Audits of States, Local Governments, and Not-for-Profit Organizations Receiving Federal Awards* Replaces former OMB Circular A–128 for state and local governments and A–133 for not-for-profit organizations. Provides guidance for auditors when engaged in audits required by the Single Audit Act. See *Compliance Supplement.*

operating activities Cash flow statement category required by both FASB and GASB. Includes receipts from customers, payments to suppliers and employees, etc.

operating lease Rental-type lease in which the risks and benefits of ownership are substantively retained by the lessor and that does not meet the criteria in applicable accounting and reporting standards of a capital lease (q.v.).

opinion units Under proposed AICPA *State and Local Government Guide* (q.v.), opinion units are reporting levels where materiality is set and audit reporting is done. Opinion units are (1) governmental activities (q.v.), (2) business-type activities (q.v.), (3) each major governmental and enterprise fund (q.v.), (4) the aggregate of all discretely presented component units (q.v.), and (5) the aggregate of all remaining fund information.

other financing sources Operating statement classification in which financial inflows other than revenues are reported; for example, proceeds of general obligation bonds and transfers in.

other financing uses Operating statement classification in which financial outflows other than expenditures are reported; for example, operating transfers out.

other not-for-profit organizations Term describing category of not-for-profit organizations. Includes all but *voluntary health and welfare organizations* (q.v.), colleges and universities, and health care organizations.

other postemployment benefits Health plan payments for retirees and other payments made pursuant to agreements between employers and employees. Currently, GASB does not require accrual of these benefits.

overlapping debt Proportionate share of the debts of local governmental units located wholly or in part within the geographic borders of the government reporting entity that must be borne by property owners within each governmental unit.

oversight agency Under Single Audit Act and amendments, agency that deals with auditee, as representative of all federal agencies. Agency with the most dollars expended by the auditee assumes the role.

P

pass-through entity Entity that receives federal funds and transfers some or all of the funds to other entities, called *subrecipients* (q.v.).

pension (and other employee benefit) trust fund One of the fiduciary fund types. Accounts for pension and other employee benefit plans when the governmental unit is trustee.

performance audits Under Government Auditing Standards (q.v.), an independent assessment of the performance and management of a program against objective criteria.

performance indicator Used in *Health Care Guide* (q.v.) to describe a measure of operations. Required in the Statement of Operations (q.v.) by the *Health Care Guide*.

permanent fund Governmental fund that is legally restricted so that only earnings, not principal, may be expended, and for purposes to benefit the government and its citizenry.

permanently restricted net assets Category used by FASB in not-for-profit accounting to describe *net assets* (q.v.) as being permanently restricted by donors. Permanent *Endowments* (q.v.) represent an example.

perpetual trust held by third party Split interest (q.v.) agreement in which trust assets are held by a third party but the income is to go to a not-for-profit organization.

pooled life income fund Split-interest agreement described in AICPA *Not-for-Profit Guide* (q.v.) in which several life income agreements are pooled together. A life income fund represents a situation where all of the income is paid to a donor or beneficiary during his or her lifetime.

primary government State government or general-purpose local government. Also, special-purpose government that has a separately elected governing body, is legally separate, and is fiscally independent of other state or local governments.

principals The Director of the Office of Management and Budget (q.v.), the Secretary of the Treasury (q.v.), and the Comptroller General of the United States (q.v.). These three individuals review standards passed by the FASAB (q.v.) and, unless they object, those standards become GAAP (q.v.).

private-purpose trust fund All trust arrangements other than pension and investment trust funds under which principal and income benefit individuals, private organizations, or other governments.

proceeds of bonds (or long-term notes) Account used in governmental accounting for governmental funds to indicate the issuance of long-term debt. Considered an "other financing source." (q.v.)

program revenues (governmental) Charges for services, operating grants, and contributions, and capital grants and contributions that are related to specific programs and subtracted from those programs in the Statement of Activities (q.v.) to obtain net program costs.

program services Category of functional expenses used by many not-for-profit organizations to describe expenses related to fulfilling the mission of the organization. Contrasted with *Supporting Services*. Program expenses are listed individually with all direct and allocated costs assigned.

property taxes Taxes levied by a legislative body against agricultural, commercial, residential, or personal property pursuant to law and in proportion to the assessed valuation of said property, or other appropriate basis. See *Ad Valorem*.

proprietary funds One of the major fund classifications of governmental accounting, the others being governmental (q.v.) and fiduciary (q.v.). Sometimes referred to as *income determination* or *commercial type funds*. Includes enterprise funds and internal service funds.

public charity Churches, schools, hospitals, governmental units, and publicly supported charities and certain other entities. Distinguished from private foundations, which are subject to different tax rules.

Public Employee Retirement Systems (PERS) Organizations that collect retirement and other employee benefit contributions from government employers and employees, manage assets, and make payments to qualified retirants, beneficiaries, and disabled employees.

purchases method Refers to method used to recognize expenditures for governmental funds (q.v.) in which an expenditure (q.v.) is recognized when inventory is acquired.

Q-R

qualified opinion Audit report in which the auditor provides an "except for" opinion, due to failure to follow generally accepted accounting principles (q.v.) or due to a scope limitation.

quasi-endowment Term to describe a situation where a governing board of a not-for-profit organization takes resources that are unrestricted and sets them aside "as if" those resources were an endowment; the intent is to never expend those funds. Such funds continue to be unrestricted for financial reporting purposes.

quasi-external transaction Outdated term. See *Interfund Services Provided and Used.*

reciprocal interfund transactions Type of interfund transaction where all funds receive benefit. Includes interfund loans and advances (q.v.) and interfund services provided and used (q.v.). The interfund equivalent of exchange transactions (q.v.).

reclassification Term created by the FASB to describe the transfer of net assets from temporarily restricted to unrestricted. Done when restrictions have expired, for expiration of time restriction, for expiration of term endowments, for satisfaction of program restrictions, or for satisfaction of plant acquisition restrictions.

reconciliation As used in state and local government accounting, reconciliations are required between fund statements and government-wide statements. Specifically, a reconciliation is required between the governmental fund Balance Sheet and the government-wide Statement of Net Assets. Also, a reconciliation is required between the governmental fund Statement of Revenues, Expenditures, and Changes in Fund Balances and the government-wide Statement of Activities.

refunding bonds Bonds issued to retire bonds already outstanding. May be sold for cash and outstanding bonds redeemed in cash or may be exchanged with holders of outstanding bonds.

reimbursements An eligibility requirement imposed by GASB. A nonexchange revenue (or expense) cannot be recognized until the resources are expended, when a grant or contribution makes this requirement. Also, see *Interfund reimbursements.*

reporting entity Primary government and all related component units, if any, combined in accordance with the GASB Codification Sec. 2100 constituting the governmental reporting entity.

repurchase agreement Agreement wherein a governmental unit transfers cash to a financial institution in exchange for U.S. government securities and the financial institution agrees to repurchase the same securities at an agreed-upon price.

Required Supplementary Information (RSI) Information required by GASB to be reported along with basic financial statements. Includes MD&A (q.v.) and, when applicable, the Schedule of Funding Progress, the Schedule of Employer Contributions, Budgetary Comparison Schedules, and information about infrastructure assets required using the modified format.

reserve Account that records a portion of the fund equity that must be segregated for some future use and that is, therefore, not available for further appropriation or expenditure. Fund Equity is often reserved for encumbrances (q.v.), inventories (q.v.), and long-term advances to other firms (q.v.).

restricted (governmental) According to GASB, a restriction on resources of a state or local government is (*a*) externally imposed by creditors (such as through debt covenants), grantors, contributors, or laws or regulations of other governments, and (*b*) imposed by law through constitutional provisions or enabling legislation. See *Net Assets-Restricted.*

restricted (not-for-profit) According to FASB, in order to report resources as restricted, those resources must be restricted by a contributor or grantor. See *Permanently Restricted Assets* and *Temporarily Restricted Net Assets.*

restricted assets Assets (usually of an enterprise fund) that may not be used for normal operating purposes because of the requirements of regulatory authorities, provisions in bond indentures, or other legal agreements but that need not be accounted for in a separate fund.

revenue bonds Bonds whose principal and interest are payable exclusively from earnings of a public enterprise.

revenues Additions to fund financial resources other than from interfund transfers (q.v.) and debt issue proceeds.

revenues ledger Subsidiary ledger, used in accounting for governmental funds that record budgets to support the Revenues control account. Normally established by revenue source.

reverse repurchase agreement Agreement in which a broker-dealer or financial institution (buyer-lender) transfers cash to a governmental entity (seller-borrower); the entity transfers securities to the broker-dealer or financial institution and promises to repay the cash plus interest in exchange for the same securities or for different securities.

risk-based approach Approach to be used by auditors when conducting audits with the newly revised A–133 to determine major programs, based on perceived risk as well as size of programs.

risk management Policies adopted by a governmental or not-for-profit organization to manage risk that might result in liabilities for health care, accidents, and so on, including the purchase of insurance, self-insurance, and participation in public entity or other risk pools.

RSI See *Required Supplementary Information.*

S

schedule of employer contributions Schedule required by the GASB to be presented as Required Supplementary Information (RSI) (q.v.) for public employee retirement systems and pension trust funds. Compares the annual required contributions with the contributions actually made.

schedule of funding progress Schedule required by the GASB to be presented as Required Supplementary Information (RSI) (q.v.) for public employee retirement systems and pension trust funds. Compares the actuarial accrued liability with the actuarial value of plan assets.

schedules Explanatory or supplementary statements that accompany the balance sheet or other principal statements periodically prepared from the accounts.

segment information Note disclosures required in general-purpose financial statements to report the financial condition and operating results of individual enterprise activities.

self-insurance Decision of an entity not to purchase insurance but instead to accept the risk of claims as a part of its risk-management policy. When a government uses one fund to report that risk, it is required to use either the General Fund or an internal service fund.

serial bonds Bonds the principal of which is repaid in periodic installments over the life of the issue.

service efforts and accomplishments Conceptualization of the resources consumed (inputs), tasks performed (outputs) and goals attained (outcomes), and the relationships among these items in providing services in selected areas (e.g., police protection, solid waste garbage collection, and elementary and secondary education).

shared revenue Revenue levied by one governmental unit but shared, usually on a predetermined basis, with another unit of government or class of governments.

single audit Audit prescribed by federal law for state and local governmental units, colleges and universities, and not-for-profit organizations that receive federal financial assistance above $300,000 ($500,000 beginning in 2004).

Single Audit Act Amendments of 1996 Legislation that extended the single audit to not-for-profit organizations and provided for a risk-based approach to determine major programs.

solid waste landfill Landfill accepting waste from citizens and also waste management firms. Charges are normally levied against those depositing waste. Managed by government. Due to certain federal environmental requirements to maintain those landfills many years, the GASB (q.v.) has adopted accounting requirements that bring forward future charges to offset current revenues.

special assessment Compulsory levy made against certain properties to defray part or all of the cost of a specific improvement or service that is presumed to be a general benefit to the public and of special benefit to such properties.

special assessment bonds Bonds payable from the proceeds of special assessments (q.v.).

special district Independent unit of local government organized to perform a single governmental function or a restricted number of related functions. Examples of special districts are water districts, drainage districts, flood control districts, hospital districts, fire protection districts, transit authorities, port authorities, and electric power authorities.

special item Classification by GASB in financial statements to indicate that a revenue, expense, gain, or loss is either unusual or infrequent and within the control of management.

special-purpose government Governments that are not general-purpose (q.v.) governments and have a more limited range of purposes. Often includes townships, park districts, sanitation districts, authorities, and other special-purpose

special revenue fund Fund used to account for revenues from specific taxes or other earmarked revenue sources that by law are designated to finance particular functions or activities of government. An example is a motor fuel tax fund used to finance highway and road construction.

split-interest agreement Agreement between a donor and a not-for-profit organization in which the donor (or beneficiary) and the organization "split" the income and/or principal of the gift. Examples are charitable lead trusts (q.v.) and charitable remainder trusts (q.v.).

State and Local Government Guide AICPA (q.v.) *Audits of State and Local Governmental Units,* which provides guidance for state and local governmental units.

statement of activities (not-for-profit accounting) One of the three statements required for not-for-profit organizations by FASB *Statement 117*. Requirements are to show revenues, expenses, gains, losses, and reclassifications (q.v.) and to show the change in net assets by net asset class (unrestricted, temporarily restricted, permanently restricted).

statement of activities (governmental accounting) Required basic government-wide financial statement in which program revenues are subtracted from expenses to get net program costs. General revenues are then deducted, to get the change in net assets.

statement of cash flows Required basic statement for proprietary funds for governmental units and for public colleges and universities. Also required statement for nongovernmental not-for-profit organizations.

statement of changes in fiduciary net assets Required basic statement for fiduciary funds. Reported by fund type.

Statement of Federal Financial Accounting Concepts (SFFACs) Concepts statements passed by the FASAB that provide objectives of accounting and financial reporting for the federal government. Do not have the authoritative status of statements.

statement of fiduciary net assets Required basic statement for fiduciary funds where assets less liabilities equals net assets. Reported by fund type.

statement of financial accounting concepts Concepts statements passed by the FASB that provide objectives of accounting and financial reporting for nongovernmental entities. Do not have the authoritative status of statements.

statement of functional expenses Statement required by FASB *Statement 117* for voluntary health and welfare organizations (q.v.). Shows a matrix of expenses by function (q.v.) and by object classification (q.v.).

statement of net assets Balance sheet format where assets less liabilities equal net assets. Encouraged for government-wide statements and may be used for proprietary and fiduciary fund statements.

statement of operations Required by the *Health Care Guide* (q.v.) to be prepared by all health care organizations. Includes a performance indicator (q.v.).

statement of revenues, expenditures, and changes in fund balances Basic operating statement for governmental funds, included in the CAFR.

statement of revenues, expenses, and changes in fund net assets Basic statement used for proprietary funds to reflect operations and changes in net assets.

statements Issues by the GASB (q.v.), FASB (q.v.), and FASAB (q.v.) outlining accounting principles for those entities under each board's jurisdiction. Constitutes GAAP (q.v.). Also principal financial presentations of governments and not-for-profit organizations.

statistical section One of the three major parts of the Comprehensive Annual Financial Report (CAFR) (q.v.), listing schedules that assist users in evaluating the financial condition of a government and its community.

subrecipient Entity that receives federal funds through another government or not-for-profit entity. For example, a state may pass through funding to certain local governments. See *Pass-Through Entities*.

subsidiary account One of a group of related accounts that support in detail the debit and credit summaries recorded in a control account. An example is the individual property taxpayers' accounts for taxes receivable in the general ledger.

subsidiary ledger Group of subsidiary accounts (q.v.) the sum of the balances of which is equal to the balance of the related control accounts. This text illustrates the Revenues Ledger (q.v.) and the Appropriations, Expenditures, and Encumbrances Ledger (q.v.).

supporting services Functional expense category recommended, but not required, by the FASB for not-for-profit organizations. Includes fund-raising, management and general, and membership development expenses.

T

tax agency fund Agency fund, usually maintained by a county official, to handle the collection of all property taxes within the county or other jurisdiction and the distribution of proceeds to all governments within the borders of that county or other jurisdiction.

tax increment debt Debt issued by a governmental unit to finance improvements in a Tax Increment Financing (TIF) District; the incremental taxes from those improvements are dedicated to the repayment of the debt.

tax rate Amount of tax stated in terms of a unit of the tax base; for example, $2.50 per $100 of net assessed valuation, or 25 mills (q.v.).

tax supported bonds Bonds supported by the full faith and credit of the governmental unit, by specific taxes.

technical bulletins Issues by the staffs of the standards-setting bodies and approved by the boards, providing additional information regarding questions and answers that might be addressed by those bodies.

temporarily restricted net assets Category used by FASB to describe *net assets* (q.v.) as being restricted by donors, but are not *permanently restricted net assets* (q.v.). Temporarily restricted net assets may be restricted for purpose, time, plant acquisition, or *term endowments* (q.v.).

term bonds Bonds for which the principal is paid at the end of the term. Contrast with *serial bonds* (q.v.).

term endowments Exist when a donor contributes an amount, which is not to be expended for a certain period of time. Term endowments are classified as *temporarily restricted net assets* (q.v.) by FASB.

time requirements An eligibility requirement imposed by GASB. A nonexchange revenue (or expense) cannot be recognized until the time specified by the donor or grantor or contributor for expenditure.

transfers As used in state and local government accounting, the shifting of resources from one category to another. In fund reporting, the transfer of resources from one fund to another. In government-wide reporting, the transfer of resources from one type of activity to another, such as from governmental activities to business-type activities. Transfers may be regularly recurring and routine (formerly called "operating transfers") or non-routine (formerly called "equity transfers").

Treasury, U.S. Department of Federal executive branch agency; prepares Consolidated Financial Statements of the Federal Government. One of the "principals" that approves FASAB standards of financial reporting for the Federal Government.

trust fund Fund consisting of resources received and held by the governmental unit as trustee, to be expended or invested in accordance with the conditions of the trust. In governmental accounting, includes investment (q.v.), private-purpose (q.v.), and pension trust (q.v.).

U-Z

unfunded actuarial liability In a pension plan, difference between the net pension obligation (NPO) (q.v.) and the net assets available for benefits. Included in the Schedule of Funding Progress.

unqualified opinion Audit report in which the auditor states that the financial statements are "fairly presented."

Unrelated Business Income Tax (UBIT) Tax that applies to business income of otherwise tax-exempt not-for-profit entities. Determined by relationship to exempt purpose and other criteria.

unrestricted net assets Portion of the excess of total assets over total liabilities that may be utilized at the discretion of the governing board of a not-for-profit entity. Separate classification provided in FASB *Statement 117* and in GASB *Statement 34*.

voluntary health and welfare organizations Not-for-profit organizations formed for the purpose of performing voluntary services for various segments of society. They are tax exempt, supported by the public, and operate on a not-for-profit basis.

voluntary nonexchange transactions One of the four classes of nonexchange transactions established by GASB. Examples are contributions and grants for restricted purposes but which purposes are not mandated independent of the grant.

Index

A

Accounting, 3, 6
  budgetary. *See* Budgetary accounting
  capital projects funds, 10, 127–132, 143–145
  full accrual. *See* Accrual basis accounting
  long-term debt, 14, 244–248
  modified accrual. *See* Modified accrual accounting
  nonexchange transactions, 9, 90–93, 277
  public colleges and universities, 271–288
  special revenue funds, 10, 64, 108–112
  See also Debt service funds; General fund
Accounting entity, 10
Accrual basis accounting, 8–9, 200
  for assets, 225–227
  for debt, 227–228
  for governmental health care entities, 374
  for proprietary funds, 158
  recording of expenses, 229
  required for not-for-profit organizations, 306, 322
  revenue recognition, 228
Activities, classification by, 79
Additions, 192
Ad valorum taxes, 77–79
Advance refunding, 140
Advances, 159
Adverse opinion, 392
Agency funds, 11, 192, 193–196
Agency pension plan, 201
American Institute of Certified Public Accountants (AICPA), 2, 15
  audit guides for state and local governments, 387, 388–392, 393, 394, 396
  Audits of Voluntary Health and Welfare Guide, 54
  Government Auditing Standards, 386–387
  Health Care Organizations guide, 301, 361–363, 374–375
  on not-for-profit organizations, 301–302, 321
  Not-for-Profit Organizations guide, 301–302, 333, 335, 336, 344, 349
  Statement on Auditing Standards, 392
Annual required contributions (ARC), 202, 206, 207
Annuity serial bonds, 136
Appropriations, 68–69, 73, 74, 79
Appropriations budget, 65
Appropriations control account, 67, 68
Appropriations process, 65
ARC (annual required contributions), 202, 206, 207
Attestation engagements, 388
Auditing
  financial audits, 387, 388
  governmental auditing, 386–392
  major programs, 394–395
  performance audits, 388
  Single Audit Act, 386, 393–396
Audit reports, 389–392
Audits of Voluntary Health and Welfare Guide (AICPA), 54
Auxiliary enterprises, 334
Available revenue, 94

B

Balance Sheet
  balance sheet accounts, 65–66
  governmental funds, 31, 34–36, 142, 143
  private not-for-profit hospitals, 370, 371–372
  proprietary funds, 36, 42–43
  for special-purpose government, 267, 268
  year-end financial statements, 107–108
Basic governmental services, 266
Blending, 24–25
Bonds
  bond refundings, 140
  debt service accounting for, 136
  deferred, 136, 139
  general obligation bonds, 164–165, 262
  limited obligation bonds, 262
  premiums and discounts, 129–130
  regular, 136–139, 143–145
  revenue bonds, 164, 262, 265, 280–281
  term bonds, 139
Budget amendments, 102
Budgetary accounting, 12, 64–79
  ad valorum taxes, 77–79
  appropriations and expenditures, 79
  balance sheet and operating statement accounts, 65–66
  budgetary comparison schedule, 75, 76
  budget revisions, 75

435

Budgetary accounting—*Cont.*
  budgets and budgetary accounts, 66–68
  budgets as legal documents, 65
  classification of revenues and estimated revenues, 75–77
  encumbrances and expenditures, 70–74
  recording budget, 68–69, 75
  revenues, 69–70
Budgetary accounts, 66–68
Budgetary comparison schedules, 41, 45, 50–51, 75, 76
Budgetary Fund Balance, 67, 68
Budgetary Fund Balance Reserved for Encumbrances, 67, 68, 71
Budgetary integrity, 3
Budgets
  budgetary accounts and, 66–68
  for internal service funds, 159
  as legal documents, 65
  recording, 68–69, 97
  revisions of, 75
Business-type activities, 49, 54, 270, 272–273

C

CAFR. *See* Comprehensive annual financial report
Capital and related financing activities, 176
Capital asset accounting, 12–13
Capital assets, 225–227, 242
Capital leases, 132, 139–140
Capital projects funds, 10, 127–132, 143–145
Cash flows, 176
Cash revenue, 100
Certificate of Achievement for Excellence in Financial Reporting, 26
Change in net assets, 320
Character, classification by, 79
Charitable gift annuity, 347
Charitable lead trust, 345–346
Charitable remainder trust, 346–347
Cognizant agencies, 393–394
Collections, 12–13, 244, 305
Colleges and universities
  private. *See* Private colleges and universities
  public. *See* Public colleges and universities
Combining financial statements, 45, 53
Commercial health-care entities, 360, 374–375
Community colleges, 272
Component units, 24–25
Comprehensive annual financial report (CAFR), 7, 8, 23
  auditor's report, 26–27
  combining financial statements, 45, 53

Comprehensive annual financial report (CAFR)—*Cont.*
  financial section of, 26–45
  fund financial statements, 31, 34–37
  government-wide financial statements, 27–31
  introductory section of, 26
  MD&A, 27
  note disclosures to financial statements, 37, 40–41
  outline of, 25–26
  pension trust funds in, 201–206
  ratio analysis of, 261–266
  required supplementary information, 41, 45
  state and local government reporting, 7, 8
Computation of Legal Debt Margin, 245, 247
Construction-type special assessments, 133–134
Consumption method of accounting for inventories, 111
Contingencies, recognizing, 91
Contracts, 71
Contributed services, 305–306
Contributions, 304, 305–306
Conversion to government-wide financial statements, 224–233
  capital assets, capital outlays and depreciation, 225–227
  debt, accrual accounting of, 227–228
  expenses, adjusting, 229
  fiduciary funds, 232
  interfund activities, 231–232
  internal service funds, 229
  revenue recognition, 228
  sale of fixed assets, 229
  worksheet illustration of, 232–235
  See also Government-wide financial statements
Costs, 66
Cost-sharing pension plan, 201
Current costs, 171
Current refunding, 140

D

Debt limit, 245
Debt margin, 245
Debt-rating services, 262, 263
Debt service funds, 10, 134–142
  accounting for serial bonds. *See* Bonds
  for capital lease payments, 139–140
  illustrative case, 136–139, 143–145
  modified accrual accounting for, 135
  permanent funds, 140–142
  uses of, 135–136

Debt service to total expenditures, 264
Deductions, 192
Defeasance of debt, 140
Deferred serial bonds, 136, 139
Defined benefit pension plans, 201–206, 207
Defined contribution pension plan, 201
Delinquent taxes, 99, 104–105
Department, classification by, 79
Depreciation, 162, 242, 243, 279–280
Depreciation expense adjustments, 226–227
Derived tax revenues, 92, 93
Disclaimer of opinion, 392
Discrete presentation, 25
Dues or memberships, 306

E

Economic resources measurement focus, 8–9, 200
Effectiveness audits, 388
Eligibility requirements, 91
Encumbrance procedure, 72–73
Encumbrances, 65, 67, 70–74, 97, 98, 100–101
Endowments, 196, 334
Enterprise funds, 11, 164–171
    illustrative case, 165–171, 173–175
    solid waste landfills, 171
Entity differences, 67
Error correction, 102
Escheat property, 199–200
Estimated Other Financing Sources, 67, 68, 77
Estimated Other Financing Uses, 67, 69
Estimated revenues, classification of, 75–77
Estimated Revenues budget, 65
Estimated Revenues control account, 67–68, 69, 70, 77
Exchange-like transactions, 9
Exchange transactions, 9, 306
Expendability, 9
Expenditures, 65, 66
    in budgetary accounting, 79
    for capital outlay, eliminating, 226
    of capital projects funds, 127–128
    encumbrances and, 70–74
    recognizing, 94–95, 100–101
    from special funds, 110
    subsidiary ledger for, 73, 74
    time requirements for, 91
Expenses, 66
    classification of, 363
    depreciation expense adjustments, 226–227
    health care organizations, 366
    of not-for-profit organizations, 304

Expenses—*Cont.*
    recording, 229
    restricted and unrestricted, 279
    revenue reduction contrasted, 335
External investment pools, 200

F

FAF (Financial Accounting Foundation), 2
Fair value, 196–197, 198
FASAB (Federal Accounting Standards Advisory Board), 1, 3, 300
FASB (Financial Accounting Standards Board), 2
Federal Accounting Standards Advisory Board (FASAB), 1, 3, 300
Fiduciary funds, 11, 192–211
    accounting and reporting, 211
    agency funds, 193–196
    eliminating, 232
    interfund transactions, 208–211
    investment trust funds, 200
    pension trust funds, 201–208
    private-purpose trust funds, 196–200
    Statement of Changes in Fiduciary Net Assets, 37, 48, 193, 205, 206
    Statement of Fiduciary Net Assets, 37, 48, 193, 196, 197, 205
Fiduciary-type activities, 270–271
Financial Accounting Foundation (FAF), 2
Financial Accounting Standards Board (FASB), 2
Financial audits, governmental, 387, 388
Financial reporting
    by federal government, 3
    by not-for-profit entities, 6, 303
    objectives of, 3, 6
    Service Efforts and Accomplishments, 404–405
    by state and local governments, 6, 7–15
Financial reporting entity, 24
Financial section of CAFR, 26–45
Financial statements
    in CAFR. *See* Comprehensive annual financial report
    fund. *See* Fund financial statements
    government-wide. *See* Government-wide financial statements
    health care organizations, 362, 370–373
    note disclosures to, 37, 40–41, 208, 242–244
    private colleges and universities, 335, 344–348
    of state and local governments, 261–266, 288

438 Index

Financial statements—*Cont.*
   year-end, 107–108, 111, 112
   See also specific financial statements
Fiscal entity, 10
Fiscal period, 72, 77, 92–93, 336
501(c)(3) entities, 397–402
Fixed assets, 13, 225–226, 229, 240–244
   of not-for-profit organizations, 305, 317–318, 320
   of public colleges and universities, 273–274, 283–284
Flow of current financial resources, 9–10
Form 990, 396, 398–399, 400, 402
Foundations, 273
Free-riding, 300
Full accrual accounting. *See* Accrual basis accounting
Full faith and credit, 244
Function, classification by, 79
Fund, classification by, 76–77, 79
Fund accounting, 10–11, 273
Fund Balance, 65–66
Fund Balance—Unreserved, 66, 107
Fund financial statements, 31, 34–37
   Balance Sheet—governmental funds, 31, 34–36
   conversion to government-wide statements, 224–233
   Statement of Cash Flows—proprietary funds, 37, 46–47
   Statement of Changes in Fiduciary Net Assets, 37, 48, 193, 205, 206
   Statement of Fiduciary Net Assets, 37, 48, 193, 196, 197, 205
   Statement of Net Assets, or Balance Sheet—proprietary funds, 36, 42–43
   Statement of Revenues, Expenditures, and Changes in Fund Balances—governmental funds, 36, 38–40, 142, 144–145
   Statement of Revenues, Expenses, and Changes in Fund Net Assets—proprietary funds, 36–37, 44

G

GAAP (generally accepted accounting principles), 2, 4–5, 23
GAAS (Generally Accepted Auditing Standards), 387
GAGAS (Generally Accepted Government Auditing Standards), 387
GAO (General Accounting Office), 387, 396
GARS (Governmental Accounting Research System), 14
GASB (Governmental Accounting Standards Board), 1–2, 6
General Accounting Office (GAO), 387, 396
General Fixed Asset Account Group, 241–242
General fixed assets, 225–226, 240–244
General fund, 10, 11
   account structure, 96
   budgetary accounting for, 64
   illustrative case, 96–108
   modified accrual accounting and, 94–95
   nonexchange transactions, 90–93
   recognition of inventories in, 111–112
   reimbursements from special revenue funds, 110
General long-term debt, 244, 245
Generally accepted accounting principles (GAAP), 2, 4–5, 23
Generally Accepted Auditing Standards (GAAS), 387
Generally Accepted Government Auditing Standards (GAGAS), 387
General obligation bonds, 164–165, 262
General obligation debt, 244
General-purpose governments, 266
GFOA (Government Finance Officers Association), 15, 26, 262
Government, defined, 2–3, 24
Governmental Accounting Research System (GARS), 14
Governmental Accounting Standards Board (GASB), 1–2, 6
Governmental activities
   of governmental not-for-profits, 54
   interfund activities within, 231–232
   internal service funds, 229–231
   of special-purpose governments, 49, 267–270
Governmental auditing, 386–392
Governmental funds, 10–11, 66
   accounting and reporting, 211
   Balance Sheet, 31, 34–36, 142, 143
   budgetary accounting for. *See* Budgetary accounting
   capital projects funds, 127–132
   debt service funds, 134–142
   financial reporting for, 142–145
   lease agreements, 132–133
   other fund types, 126–145
   special assessment debt, 133–134
   Statement of Revenues, Expenditures, and Changes in Fund Balances, 36, 38–40, 142, 144–145
Governmental health-care entities, 360, 374

Index **439**

Governmental not-for-profit organizations, 54
Governmental (financial) reporting entity, 24–25
Governmental revenues per capita ratio, 265
Government Auditing Standards (AICPA), 386–387, 396
Government Finance Officers Association (GFOA), 15, 26, 262
Government-mandated nonexchange transactions, 92, 93
Government-wide financial statements, 14, 27–31, 211, 233–240
  required reconciliation to, 237, 240, 241
  Statement of Activities, 30–33, 230–231, 236–239
  Statement of Net Assets, 28–30, 233, 236
  See also Conversion to government-wide financial statements
Grants, 110–111, 282–283

H

Health care organizations, 360–375
  academic research on, 375
  accounting and reporting summary, 375
  commercial entities, 374–375
  financial statements, 362, 370–373
  governmental entities, 374
  Health Care Guide requirements, 361–363
  nonprofit hospitals, 361, 363–373
  overview, 360–361
Health Care Organizations (AICPA guide), 301, 361–363, 374–375
Health plans, postemployment, 208
Hospitals, private not-for-profit, 361
  beginning trial balance, 363–364
  financial statements for nonprofit hospitals, 370–373
  illustrative transactions, 364–370

I

Imposed nonexchange transactions, 92, 93
Infrastructure assets, 13, 41, 45, 52, 242–244
Intentions to give, 306–307
Interest, 226, 227–228
Interest and penalties, 99, 105
Interest coverage—revenue bonds, 265
Interfund activities, 231–232
  nonreciprocal, 95, 209, 210–211
  reciprocal, 95–96, 208–210
Interfund loans, 95
Interfund transactions, 95–96, 102–104, 208–211, 231–232

Interfund transactions—*Cont.*
  reimbursements, 95–96, 104, 210
  services provided and used, 95, 102–103, 209–210
  transfers, 95, 103–104, 210
Internal service funds, 11, 229–231
  establishment and operation of, 159–160
  illustrative case, 160–163, 173–175
Interpretations, 2, 95
Inventories, 111–112, 161
Investing activities
  cash flows from, 176
  of health care organizations, 368
  of not-for-profit organizations, 305, 311–312
  of private-purpose trust funds, 196–198
  public colleges and universities, 278
Investment trust funds, 11, 192, 200
Invoices, liability for, 72
Irregular serial bonds, 136
IRS 457 Deferred Compensation Plans, 208

L

Lapse, 65
Law, compliance with, 12
Lease agreements, 132–133, 135–136, 139–140
Liabilities, 14, 98
Life (pooled) income fund, 347–349
Limited obligation bonds, 262
Liquidity measures, 265
Long-term debt, 14, 244–248
Low-risk auditee, 394

M

Major programs, auditing, 394–395
Management's discussion and analysis (MD&A), 3, 23, 27, 49
Materiality evaluations, 389
MD&A (management's discussion and analysis), 3, 23, 27, 49
Measurable revenue, 94
Memorandum records, 242
Modified accrual accounting, 9–10, 13, 135
  expenditure recognition, 94–95
  revenue recognition, 94

N

National Association of College and University Business Officers (NACUBO), 333, 335, 336, 349–350

National Federation of Municipal
    Analysts, 262
Net assets
    classification of, 302–303, 322, 334–335
    permanently restricted, 302, 334, 369–370
    restricted, 165–166, 172, 233, 236
    temporarily restricted or unrestricted, 303, 304, 334, 369
Net assets to expenses ratio, 264
Net debt per capita ratio, 263
Net debt to assets ratio, 264
Net debt to fair value of property ratio, 263
Net pension obligation (NPO), 206–207
Nonaudit services, governmental, 388
Noncapital financing activities, 176
Nonexchange transactions, 9, 90–93
    classes of, 90, 92, 93
    eligibility requirements, 91
    recognition requirements, 92, 277
    timing of recognition, 92–93
Nonreciprocal interfund activity, 95, 209, 210–211
Note disclosures to financial statements
    on collections, 244
    for defined benefit pension plans, 208
    in financial section of CAFR, 37, 40–41
    on infrastructure assets, 243
    not-for-profit organizations, 303–304
    regarding capital assets, 242
Not-for-profit organizations, 6, 54, 300–322
    accounting, 304–305
    classes of net assets, 302–303, 322
    contributed services, 305–306
    exchange transactions, 306
    financial reporting, 303
    financial statements, 315–319, 321–322
    fixed asset recording, 317–318, 320
    illustrative example, 307–320
    intentions to give, 306
    kinds of, 302
    note disclosures, 303–304
    performance evaluation, 319, 320–321
    transfers of assets, 307
Not-for-Profit Organizations (AICPA guide), 301–302, 333, 335, 336, 344, 349
NPO (net pension obligation), 206–207

O

Object, classification by, 79
Objectives of financial reporting, 6
Office of Management and Budget (OMB), 393, 394

Operating activities, 176
Operating leases, 132–133
Operating performance, 3
Operating ratio—enterprise funds, 265–266
Operating statement accounts, 65–66
Opinion units, 26–27, 388–389
Other Financing Sources, 66
Other Financing Uses, 66
Oversight agencies, 394

P

Pass-through entities, 394
Payrolls and payroll taxes, 73, 101
Pension trust funds, 11, 49, 192, 201–208
    defined benefit plans, 201–206, 207
    employer reporting for, 206–208
    IRS 457 plans, 208
    other postemployment benefits, 208
    as special-purpose governments, 270–271
Performance audits, governmental, 388
Performance evaluation, 319, 320–321
Permanent funds, 11, 140–145
Permanently restricted net assets, 302, 334, 369–370
Perpetual inventory system, 161
Perpetual trust held by third party, 346
PERS (Public Employee Retirement Systems). *See* Pension trust funds
Perspective differences, 67
Pooled (life) income fund, 347–349
Postemployment health plans, 208
Preclosing trial balance, 106–107
Present value, 133
Primary government, 24, 25
Private colleges and universities, 333–350
    academic research on, 349
    accounting and reporting requirements, 349–350
    FASB requirements, 336–337
    financial statements, 335, 344–348
    fiscal year issues, 336
    illustrative transactions, 337–343
    net asset classification, 334–335
    revenue reduction v. expenses, 335
    split-interest agreements, 344–349
Private (commercial) health-care entities, 360, 374–375
Private-purpose trust funds, 11, 140, 192, 196–200
    accounting for investments, 196–198
    escheat property and, 199–200
    illustrative case, 198–199, 205, 206

Proceeds of debt issues, 127
Program, classification by, 79
Program service expenses to total expenses ratio, 320–321
Promises to give, 304
Property assessment, 77
Property taxes
    accounting for tax agency funds, 194–196
    available revenue and, 94
    current tax collection, 99–100
    deferral of revenue, 106
    delinquent taxes, 99, 104–105
    reclassification of current taxes, 105
    recording as revenues, 97–98
    taxable property, 78–79
    tax anticipation notes, 98, 100
    tax levy, 78–79, 98–99
    uncollectible, 78
Proprietary funds, 11, 14, 158–176
    accounting and reporting, 211
    enterprise funds, 164–171
    financial statements for, 158–159, 172–176
    internal service funds, 159–163
    risk management activities, 164
    Statement of Cash Flows for, 37, 46–47, 158, 175, 176
    Statement of Net Assets (Balance Sheet), 36, 42–43, 158, 172, 173
    Statement of Revenues, Expenses, and Changes in Fund Net Assets, 36–37, 44, 158, 172–175
Public charities, 397
Public colleges and universities, 271–288
    accounting and financial reporting, 272–274
    beginning trial balance, 274–275
    closing entries for, 281–284
    environment of, 271–272
    financial statements for, 284–288
    illustrative case, 274–288
    journal entries for, 275–281
    reporting model for, 49
Public Employee Retirement Systems (PERS). *See* Pension trust funds
Public finance market, 262
Purchase orders, 71, 72–73, 98
Purchases method of accounting for inventories, 111, 161

Q

Qualified opinion, 392
Quasi-endowments, 335, 342

R

Recipients, characteristics of, 91
Reciprocal interfund activity, 95–96, 208–210
Reconciliation to government-wide statements, 237, 240, 241
Regular serial bonds, 136–139, 143–145
Reimbursement grants, 110–111
Reimbursements, 91, 95–96, 104, 110, 210
Required supplementary information (RSI), 7, 12, 23
    budgetary comparison schedules, 45, 50–51, 64, 66
    in fiduciary fund reporting, 193
    in financial section of CAFR, 41, 45
    for governmental audits, 390–392
    infrastructure asset reporting, 45, 52
    for pension trust funds, 202
    special purpose governments, 49
Reserve accounts, 65–66
Restricted net assets, 165–166, 172, 233, 236
Retention, 130
Revenue bonds, 164, 262, 265, 280–281
Revenue recognition, 94, 100, 228
Revenue reduction, expenses contrasted, 335
Revenues, 66, 94
    in budgetary accounting, 69–70
    classification of, 75–77
    health care organizations, 362, 364–366
    for public colleges and universities, 272
    sources of, 64, 77–78
    See also Property taxes; Special revenue funds; Taxation
Revenues Control account, 69
Risk-based approach, 395
Risk management activities, 164
RSI. *See* Required supplementary information

S

Schedule A, 399, 401, 402
Schedule of Changes in Long-Term Debt, 245, 246
Schedule of Direct and Overlapping Debt, 245, 248
Schedule of Employer Contributions, 41, 193, 202, 206, 207
Schedule of Funding Progress, 41, 193, 202, 205, 207
Schedule of Principal and Interest Due in Future Years, 245, 246–247
Self-insurance, 164

Service Efforts and Accomplishments (SEA) reporting, 404–407
Service-type special assessments, 133–134
SFFACs (Statements of Federal Financial Accounting Concepts), 3, 6, 7
Single Audit Act (1984), 386, 393–396
Single Audit Act Amendments (1996), 393
Solid waste landfills, 171
Special assessment debt, 133–134
Special items, in general fund, 106
Special-purpose governments, 266, 288
  business-type activities of, 49, 270
  fiduciary-type activities of, 270–271
  governmental activities of, 49, 267–270
  reporting requirements, 45, 49, 266–271
Special revenue funds, 10, 64
  illustrative case, 108–111
  year-end financial statements, 111, 112
Split-interest agreements, 344–349
Standard-setting organizations, 1–2
State and local government reporting, 7–15, 23–54
  budgetary accounting, 12
  CAFR, 7, 8
  capital asset accounting, 12–13
  financial statements, 261–266, 288
  fund structure for, 10–11
  governmental not-for-profit organizations, 54
  long-term debt and liabilities, 14
  measurement focus of, 7–10
  number of funds required, 11
  objectives of, 6
  special purpose governments, 45, 49
Statement of Activities, 344
  in CAFR, 30–33
  in government-wide financial statements, 30–33, 230–231, 236–239
  not-for-profit organizations, 303, 315, 316
  private colleges and universities, 335
  for special-purpose government, 267, 269–270
Statement of Cash Flows, 344, 348
  governmental health care entities, 374
  not-for-profit organizations, 303, 315–316, 318, 319
  private colleges and universities, 335
  private not-for-profit hospitals, 370, 373
  for proprietary funds, 37, 46–47, 158, 175, 176
  for public colleges and universities, 274, 286–288
Statement of Changes in Fiduciary Net Assets, 37, 48, 193, 205, 206

Statement of Changes in Net Assets, 344, 346, 370, 371
Statement of Changes in Plan Net Assets—pension trust funds, 202
Statement of Fiduciary Net Assets—fiduciary funds, 37, 48, 193, 196, 197, 205
Statement of Financial Position, 344, 347
  not-for-profit organizations, 303, 315, 317
  private colleges and universities, 335
  private not-for-profit hospitals, 370, 371–372
Statement of Functional Expenses, 303, 316, 319
Statement of Governmental Fund Revenues Expenditures, and Changes in Fund Balances, 267, 269–270
Statement of Net Assets, 14
  in CAFR, 28–30
  governmental health care entities, 374
  government-wide financial statements, 28–30, 233, 236
  internal service funds, 230
  proprietary funds, 36, 42–43, 158, 172, 173
  public colleges and universities, 284, 285
  for special-purpose government, 267, 268
Statement of Operations, 370, 371
Statement of Plan Net Assets—pension trust funds, 202
Statement of Revenues, Expenditures, and Changes in Fund Balances—governmental funds, 36, 38–40, 142, 144–145
Statement of Revenues, Expenditures, and Changes in Fund Net Assets, 108
Statement of Revenues, Expenses, and Changes in Fund Net Assets—proprietary fund, 36–37, 44, 158, 172–175
Statement of Revenues, Expenses, and Changes in Net Assets
  governmental health care entities, 374
  public colleges and universities, 284, 286
Statement of Unrestricted Revenues, Expenses, and Other Changes in Unrestricted Net Assets, 344, 345
Statements, 2
Statements of Federal Financial Accounting Concepts (SFFACs), 3, 6, 7
Statements of Financial Accounting Standards (SFAS), 132
Stewardship, 3
Straight-line depreciation, 242
Subrecipients, 394

Subsidiary ledgers, 73, 74
Supplies fund, 160–163, 173–175
Systems and controls, 3

T

Taxable property, 78–79
Tax agency funds, 194–196
Tax anticipation notes, 98, 100
Taxation
   ad valorum taxes, 77–79
   derived tax revenues, 92, 93
   motor fuel tax revenues, 109, 110
   property taxes. *See* Property taxes
   special assessments, 133–134
Tax-exempt organizations, 396–404
   academic research on, 403
   applying for tax-exempt status, 397–398, 399
   conclusions regarding, 403–404
   federal filing requirements, 398–402
   Form 990, 396, 398–399, 400, 402
   public disclosures of, 402
   Schedule A, 399, 401, 402
   state filing requirements, 402
   unrelated business income tax, 402–403
Tax levy, 78–79, 98–99
Taxpayer Bill of Rights 2 (1996), 402, 403
Technical bulletins, 2
Temporarily restricted net assets, 303, 304, 334, 369
Term bonds, 139
Term endowments, 334–335
Time requirements for expenditures, 91
Timing differences, 67
Transfer accounts, 66

Transfers, 159, 307
Trust and agency funds, 11
Trust funds. *See* Fiduciary funds; *specific kinds of trust funds*

U

UBIT (Unrelated Business Income Tax), 402–403
Uncollectible taxes, 78
Unfunded actuarial liability, 206
Unlapsed encumbrances, 65
Unqualified opinion, 390–392
Unrelated business income, 396
Unrelated Business Income Tax (UBIT), 402–403
Unreserved fund balance to revenues ratio—General Fund, 265
Unrestricted net assets, 303, 304, 334, 369
Unrestricted net assets to expenses ratio, 264–265
Utility fund, 165–171, 173–175

V

Variance column, 67
Voluntary health and welfare organizations, 302, 361
Voluntary nonexchange transactions, 92, 93
Vouchers, 101

Y

Year-end financial statements, 107–108, 111, 112